Made in the USA
Columbia, SC
18 February 2020

INFORMATION RETRIEVAL

Computational and Theoretical Aspects

LIBRARY AND INFORMATION SCIENCE

CONSULTING EDITOR: *Harold Borko*
GRADUATE SCHOOL OF LIBRARY SCIENCE
UNIVERSITY OF CALIFORNIA, LOS ANGELES

Thomas H. Mott, Jr., Susan Artandi, and Leny Struminger.
Introduction to PL/I Programming for Library and Information Science.

Karen Sparck Jones and Martin Kay.
Linguistics and Information Science.

Manfred Kochen (Ed.).
Information for Action: From Knowledge to Wisdom.

Harold Borko and Charles L. Bernier.
Abstracting Concepts and Methods.

G. Edward Evans.
Management Techniques for Librarians.

James Cabeceiras.
The Multimedia Library: Materials Selection and Use.

F. W. Lancaster.
Toward Paperless Information Systems.

H. S. Heaps.
Information Retrieval: Computational and Theoretical Aspects.

Harold Borko and Charles L. Bernier.
Indexing Concepts and Methods.

INFORMATION RETRIEVAL,

Computational and Theoretical Aspects .

H. S. HEAPS
Department of Computer Science
Concordia University
Montreal, Quebec
Canada

ACADEMIC PRESS   New York   San Francisco   London   1978
A Subsidiary of Harcourt Brace Jovanovich, Publishers

Z
699
H38

ACADEMIC PRESS, INC.
111 Fifth Avenue, New York, New York 10003

United Kingdom Edition published by
ACADEMIC PRESS, INC. (LONDON) LTD.
24/28 Oval Road, London NW1   7DX

Library of Congress Cataloging in Publication Data

Heaps, H   S
    Information retrieval, computational and theoretical
aspects.

    (Library and information science)
    Includes bibliographical references.
    1. Information storage and retrieval systems.
I. Title. II. Series.
Z699.H38   029.7   78–3338
ISBN 0–12–335750–0

PRINTED IN THE UNITED STATES OF AMERICA

Contents

3

Document Data Bases for Computer Search   **39**

4

Question Logic and Format   **81**

5

Data Structures for Storage and Retrieval   **105**

6

Structure of Search Programs   **159**

7

Vocabulary Characteristics of
Document Data Bases   **183**

8

Information Theory Considerations **209**

9

Coding and Compression of Data Bases **229**

10

Example of Design of a Document Retrieval System **247**

11

Document Indexing and Term Associations **263**

12

Automatic Question Modification 293

13

Automatic Document Classification 309

14

Concluding Remarks 333

Preface

The purpose of the present book is twofold. On the one hand, an attempt is made to introduce the student of computer science to some of the basic concepts of information retrieval and to describe the techniques required to develop suitable computer programs. On the other hand, an attempt is made to describe the general structure of the relevant computer programs so that basic design considerations may be understood by those not well versed in the details of computer science, such as librarians and information officers.

The material is organized with a view to create a textbook-like presentation rather than a comprehensive account of the state of the art. At the end of the chapters are problems intended to test the reader's understanding of the material and to lead the reader to consider further development of the basic principles.

The material in Chapters 1–4 and Chapters 6, 7, 10, and 11 has been found to be suitable for a one-term course for undergraduate computer science students who previously have covered the material in Chapter 5. Selected portions of Chapters 1–10 have been covered in a two-term course for students with a more general background. The material in Chapters 7–13 has also formed the basis of a course for graduate students.

It is believed desirable that the text should be reasonably self-sufficient so as to provide the non-computer-science student with a certain amount of background material that is likely to be well known to the reader who has some previous education in computer science. This background material is contained at the beginning of Chapter 3 and in Chapter 5. Chapter 3 also serves to provide the student of computer science with illustrations chosen from the area of information retrieval.

Some mathematical maturity is required for a full understanding of Chapters 13 and 14. However, it is believed that a student not well-versed in mathematics should be able to appreciate the value of the techniques, and the significance of the results, without understanding the details of the analysis.

In Chapter 1 the reader is given a brief account of the motivation for development of the discipline of information retrieval from bibliographic data bases. A number of elementary general concepts are introduced in Chapter 2, and illustrations of the type of data base encountered in information retrieval are provided in Chapter 3. The portion of an information retrieval service that provides an interface between the user and the computer search is emphasized in Chapter 4 which deals with possible forms of question formulation. Thus Chapters 1–4 deal with aspects of information retrieval that are not directly concerned with the computational details and organization of the structure of the computer programs.

The structure of computer search programs for information retrieval is discussed in Chapter 6. This chapter refers to the data structures described in Chapter 5.

Chapters 7–10 are concerned with the vocabulary characteristics of document data bases and the manner by which a knowledge of vocabulary statistics may be used to advantage in the design of retrieval systems. Thus some general properties of bibliographic data bases are described in Chapter 7; the implications with respect to storage and transmission of information are discussed in a theoretical manner in Chapter 8. Some practical means of coding bibliographic data in order to economize in storage space are outlined in Chapter 9. Illustration of the application of the techniques to the design of a practical information retrieval system is given in Chapter 10.

The effectiveness of information retrieval from bibliographic data bases is dependent not only on the efficiency of the search programs but also on the extent to which the terms used to index the documents are good indicators of subject matter. This is discussed in Chapter 11. In Chapters 12 and 13 consideration is given to the problem of automatic selection of index terms and the related problems of automatic question modification and automatic document classification.

1
Introduction

1.1 Growth of Recorded Knowledge

Information retrieval is a new discipline in the sense that many of its modern applications depend on concepts that have been formulated only during the past few decades. Nevertheless the subject has roots that extend back through many centuries.

The traditional library, as a collection of documents, led to the development of standard procedures for manual cataloguing, use of card indexes, bibliographies, and the circulation and ordering of books, journals, and reports. However, the traditional library was oriented more to the provision of documents than to the supply of information. This orientation is efficient provided that library users are interested primarily in well-defined subjects covered by a small number of books and journals. Yet at the present time there are many fields of study whose investigation requires information from a number of different disciplines, and for which requests for relevant information cannot be met by reference to a small, easily specified set of documents.

As remarked by C. P. Snow,[1] during all of human history until the present century the rate of social change has been sufficiently slow as to

[1] C. P. Snow, *The Two Cultures and the Scientific Revolution* (Cambridge: Cambridge University Press, 1959), p. 45.

1

pass unnoticed in one person's lifetime. This is no longer so. People are generally aware that social and technological changes are taking place very rapidly and are the result of discoveries that are understood by only a few specialists. Yet the consequences of many new discoveries affect the lives of entire populations to a degree that has never been the case previously. Thus more and more people are vitally interested in having fast access to more and more information.

The ability to maintain the rapid growth of technological and social changes requires that vast amounts of information be instantly available when required. The problem involved in meeting such a requirement may be emphasized by noting that it has been estimated that the number of scientific journals that existed in the year 1800, 1850, 1900, and 1966 was approximately 100, 1000, 10,000, and 100,000, respectively.[2] Holt and Schrank[3] have indicated that between 1920 and 1960 the periodical literature in economics increased from 5000 to 40,000 articles per year. Likewise, the periodical literature in psychology increased from 30,000 to 90,000 articles per year. The annual number of papers published in mathematics during the period from 1868 to 1966 increased from about 800 to 13,000.[4,5]

For a number of different disciplines the increases in the number of articles published in periodicals over the period between 1960 and 1970 have been estimated by Carter as shown in Table 1.1.[6] Presumably the disagreement with Holt and Schrank's estimate for psychology is caused by a different definition of what constitutes a periodical article in psychology. The particular values of the individual figures are, however, less important than the implied growth rates of values estimated according to the same criteria.

The manner in which a new discovery may lead to an increase in the number of publications may be illustrated by noting the growth caused by the proposal of the laser structure in 1958.[6] In 1960 there were approximately 20 papers on the subject of the ruby laser; in 1961 there were approximately 100 on the helium–neon laser; in 1962 there were 325 on the solid-state laser; in 1963 there were 700 papers on the GaAs laser,

[2] Proceedings of the Royal Institute of Great Britain, vol. 41, Part I, 1966.

[3] C. C. Holt and W. E. Schrank, "Growth of the professional literature in economics and other fields, and some implications," *American Documentation* 19(1968):18–26.

[4] K. O. May, "Quantitative Growth of the mathematical literature," *Science* 154 (1966):1672–1673.

[5] K. O. May, "Growth and quality in the mathematical literature," ISIS 59(1968):363–371.

[6] A. Neelameghan, "Theoretical Foundation for UDC: Its need and formulation," *Proceedings of the International Symposium,* Herceg Novi, Yugoslavia, June 28–July 1, 1971.

Table 1.1
Number of Articles Published in Periodicals During 1960 and 1970.

Subject	1960	1970
Mathematics	15,000	30,000
Physics	75,000	155,000
Civil engineering	15,000	15,000
Mechanical engineering	10,000	20,000
Electrical and electronic engineering	80,000	150,000
Aerospace engineering	35,000	75,000
Industrial engineering	15,000	15,000
Chemistry	150,000	260,000
Metallurgy	35,000	50,000
Biology	150,000	290,000
Geosciences	91,000	158,000
Agriculture	150,000	260,000
Medicine	220,000	390,000
Psychology	15,000	30,000
Other subjects	929,000	1,882,000
Totals	1,985,000	3,780,000

pulsed laser, and Q switching; in 1964 there were 1000 on the ion laser; and in 1965 there were 1200 papers on the N_2-CO_2 high efficiency laser.

The term *information explosion* has been accepted very readily by workers in scientific fields who tend to be extremely conscious of the possibility of being unaware of work done previously, or being undertaken concurrently, by other scientists. There has even been a tendency, perhaps, to exaggerate the consequences of overlooking the work of others.[7]

The information needs of physicists and chemists engaged in research, administration, and teaching have been discussed in the literature.[8] The roles of abstracting services in physics and summary papers in chemistry have been discussed respectively by Urquart[9] and Bernal.[10] A general discussion of the sources of information available to chemists and physi-

[7] A. G. Oettinger, "An essay in information retrieval or the birth of a myth," *Information and Control* 8 (1965):64–79.

[8] Survey of information needs of physicists and chemists. The report of a survey undertaken in 1963–4, in association with Professor B. H. Flowers, on behalf of the Advisory Council on Scientific Policy. Journal of Documentation, vol. 21, pp. 83–112, 1965.

[9] D. J. Urquart, "Physics abstracting use and users," *Journal of Documentation* 21(1965):113–121.

[10] J. D. Bernal, "Summary papers and summary journals in chemistry," *Journal of Documentation* 21(1965):122–127.

cists was given by Bottle.[11] The need for ready access to literature in the social sciences has been discussed by Guttsman.[12]

1.2 The Discipline of Information Retrieval

Although recorded information usually is retrieved by means of stored data that represents documents, it is the emphasis on information relevant to a request, rather than direct specification of a document, that characterizes the modern subject of information retrieval. In addition to being concerned with the practical aspects of the design of operational computerized retrieval systems the subject of information retrieval includes aspects of the theory of measurement and definition, and of information content and relevance.

Some aspects of information retrieval may be compared to statistical communication theory as applied by electrical engineers and applied mathematicians during the past 30 years. The problem of locating relevant information from a body of widely dispersed knowledge is analogous to detection of the presence of a signal pulse in the presence of a noise background. Concepts such as the Wiener root-mean-square criterion, matched filters, feedback, and correlation detectors have their counterparts in the theory of information retrieval. It is perhaps rather curious that Norbert Wiener, who displayed great insight in the application of linear prediction techniques to problems in control theory and cybernetics, was very sceptical of the value of studies in information retrieval as he claimed that any information that he might require for study of his own subject could be obtained most easily by writing to any of the half dozen world experts in the field.

Wiener's point of view is interesting in that it serves to emphasize the difference between the environments of today's scholars and those of previous generations. Just as the number of people presently alive is a surprisingly large proportion of all people who have ever been born, so the amount of information in recorded form is many times larger than at any previous time. Moreover, not only is scientific, technological, and sociological information required by experts in these fields but also by nonspecialists who are unlikely to know the names of the leading authorities.

The rate of increase of available information has many philosophical

---

[11] R. T. Bottle, "A user's assessment of current awareness services," *Journal of Documentation* 21(1965):177–189.

[12] W. L. Guttsman, "The literature of the social sciences and provision for research in them," *Journal of Documentation* 22(1966):186–194.

implications. The concept of man as a solitary traveller through time with some interaction from other human beings, and later the concept of man surrounded by a mechanistic universe, may now be replaced by the idea of man as an information receiver. Since information does not necessarily relate to physical quantities or to precisely measurable terms, it might be speculated that techniques developed for information retrieval and information evaluation eventually should be developed in a direction leading to further understanding of the process by which human beings associate ideas and gain understanding of scientific and humanistic concepts.

Spoken communication between humans is by sound waves that travel a distance of about 1000 feet in 1 sec. Communication between computers, or between computers and peripheral devices, is by electrical impulses that travel approximately 1000 feet in 1 μsec. For a simple introduction to the principles of data transmission between computers, or through communication networks, the reader may refer to a paper of Kallenbach.[13]

Relays and switching devices within modern computers have response times of a few nanoseconds (1 nsec = 10^{-9} sec). Consequently, large amounts of information may be processed and transmitted by computers in a short time interval. Scientifically, well-informed, imaginative speculation on the possible consequences of utilizing such high transmission rates, and the ability of computers to absorb information at such speed, has led to many science-fiction writings such as, for example, those of the astronomer Hoyle.[14-16] The degree to which instant communication has already affected contemporary society has been particularly emphasized from a popular viewpoint by McLuhan.[17]

Computerized information retrieval systems must be economical as well as feasible. In the same manner that economic considerations have led to more critical and hence more mathematically sophisticated design of engineering structures and chemical engineering processes, it is the economic considerations that are leading to a requirement for more precise mathematical formulation of the principles of information retrieval in order to ensure that the computers and computer accessible storage devices are used in an economic manner. Concurrently with the develop-

[13] P. A. Kallenbach, "Introduction to data transmission for information retrieval," *Information Processing and Management* 11(1975):137–145.

[14] F. Hoyle and G. Hoyle, *A for Andromeda* (Greenwich, Connecticut: Fawcett Publications Inc.).

[15] F. Hoyle, *The Black Cloud* (London: Heinemann, 1957).

[16] F. Hoyle, *October the First Is Too Late* (London: Heinemann, 1966).

[17] M. McLuhan, *Understanding Media: The Extensions of Man* (New York: McGraw-Hill, 1964).

ment of new theory it is also important to study the behavior of operational retrieval systems in order to gain insight into the problems that arise from the point of view of the users of the system.

To some extent, the efficiency of a computerized information retrieval system is dependent on the computer hardware. Since computer hardware is continually being improved, and since computers become obsolete with the advent of more powerful and more economical ones, it is likely that operational retrieval systems will continue to be subject to constant revision and expansion. This fact presents less difficulty than might first be thought since it is the hardware and computer programs that change; the vast quantities of stored information may remain unchanged or be converted within the computer.

In analysis of complex or vaguely defined problems, the importance of good notation cannot be overemphasized. An efficient notation allows concepts to be stated clearly and allows data to be visualized as a whole, instead of as a number of isolated items. It also enables problems to be formulated in a precise manner with a true appreciation of any assumptions involved.

For formulation of information retrieval problems the concept of matrix transformation often allows statements to be made in a very compact form. The structure of written text, including the extent to which it is predictable, may be analyzed by probability theory.

Information theory, as developed in mathematical terms by Shannon,[18] is concerned with information content in terms of the amount of information required for identification of symbols or words rather than in terms of the knowledge communicated by them. Randomness, or uncertainty or lack of knowledge, is measured in terms of entropy. The power and limitations of the theory have been discussed by a number of authors.[19] Extension of Shannon's theory and computer analysis of written text to analyze information content, subject matter, and style, offers a number of problems to the student of information science. It also suggests the possibility of further cooperation between computer scientists and workers in other disciplines.

A study of information retrieval is necessarily concerned with optimization since it is desired to retrieve relevant items in the shortest possible time, or with minimum expense, or with maximum efficiency in regard to some estimate of relevance. The measure of relevance may be formulated

---

[18] C. E. Shannon, "A mathematical theory of communication," *Bell System Technical Journal* 27(1948):379–423, 623–656.

[19] P. L. Garvin (ed.), *Natural Language and the Computer* (New York: McGraw-Hill, 1963).

in mathematical terms and leads to considerations based on the mathematical theory of pattern recognition.

The subject of information retrieval is thus developing through application of matrix notation, probability theory, optimization techniques, pattern recognition, and systems analysis through which operations are represented by mathematical models that may be programmed on a computer.

The practical problems of information retrieval involve sufficient quantities of data that the introduction of any reasonable attempt to be systematic and independent of human intuition involves the handling of a large amount of data. The greater the degree of sophistication required, the greater the task of dealing with the information, and the greater the need for computer use since modern computers can store large quantities of data on computer accessible files and can examine the data very rapidly.

The systems analyst who designs a computer program for information retrieval or for some aspect of library automation first represents the entire operation by a mathematical model. The subsequent computer programming then proceeds in relation to this assumed model, which is described to the computer by means of a program written in some computer language. The resulting situation is that when the computerized system is in use, the librarians who use it tend to describe and evaluate it in terms of traditional library concepts while the computer analysts and programmers describe it using a different language and tend to think about the mathematical model rather than the operational system. It is clearly necessary for the two groups of people, those with traditional library backgrounds and those with computer science backgrounds, to have sufficient knowledge of each others' problems and the means of describing them. Otherwise, no effective communication may occur between the two groups. Ability to treat the problems from a wider viewpoint than generally acquired in the course of either a library science or computer science education is one of the skills expected of the information scientist.

The purpose of the present text is twofold. On the one hand an attempt is made to introduce the computer science student to some of the basic problems of information retrieval and to describe the techniques required to develop suitable computer programs. On the other hand an attempt is made to describe the general structure of the relevant computer programs so that basic design considerations may be understood by information officers and librarians not well versed in the details of computer science.

The ability of computers to perform complex arithmetic operations is more important for scientific computations than for information retrieval. The problems that arise in information retrieval are more concerned with identification, storage, rearrangement, and sorting of alphabetic data. It is the ability of computers to be used for these tasks that makes them of use in information retrieval.

Efficiency of a retrieval system is sometimes defined solely in terms of user satisfaction with the items retrieved. If efficiency is also related to economics then the search procedure should produce the desired results through utilization of minimum computer time and with compact storage of the information in computer memory or in computer accessible files. It is most important that all who are concerned with the system design should appreciate the fact that user convenience and economic efficiency are not always compatible. Both the computer scientist and the non-computer-oriented information specialist should be aware of the price that may have to be paid for an increased emphasis on either factor.

1.3 Computer Learning and Adaptive Systems

One measure of the efficiency of an information retrieval system, whether manual or computerized, is in terms of the user's estimate of the relevance of the documents retrieved and the nonrelevance of the documents not retrieved by the system. If the retrieval procedure is dependent on parameters that may be varied within the system, then in response to certain requests the parameters may be varied until a maximum efficiency is believed to result. The same values of the parameters then may be assigned automatically whenever similar requests are encountered. The resulting system then may be said to have a learning capacity since in response to a given situation it behaves in a manner that was found to be efficient in dealing with similar situations in the past.

Retrieval of information by human beings is often dependent on the human ability to infer associations between different concepts and to generalize specific requests in order to cover broader fields of interests. Attempts have been made to formulate means by which computers may infer associations between different concepts. Such formulations usually are based on the premise that if one concept is often associated with a second one, and also is often associated with a third one, then there is a strong probability of some connection between the second and third concept even in the absence of the first. Clearly such a premise is not always true but is, nevertheless, true in many instances. Associations of such nature may be studied by means of term connection matrices as introduced in Chapter 10.

Since a computer has memory and is able to recognize and compare words, it may be programmed to recognize that certain words are equivalent in meaning, that certain words are broader or narrower in meaning than others, and that certain words have special meanings when used in association with other words. Thus a considerable amount of information based on human judgment and experience may be incorporated into a purely mechanistic system. Various aspects of this are discussed further in Chapters 11 and 12.

The basic problem in the design of systems with learning capacity is not one of computer programming, but rather is the formulation of what is meant by most efficient, by relevance, and by other terms of judgment. The problem is similar to computer recognition of patterns and is discussed in reference to automatic classification of documents in Chapter 13. Examination of the problems in more generality would lead to a study of topics in the branch of computer science known as *artificial intelligence*. This subject is concerned with the study of the use of machines to undertake tasks which, if performed by humans, would be said to indicate the exercise of intelligence.

1.4 Computer Identification of Meaning

Although we may readily appreciate that a computer may be programmed to compare, recognize, and identify words, it might be contended that a computer lacks human intuition and therefore cannot be expected to discover the meaning that a passage of text is able to convey to a human reader. However, the human being is conditioned by years of education, through learning by success and failure, by association of ideas, and by experience in evaluation of the consequences of assumptions.

When a body of text is read by a human it may cause the reader to respond by expressing an opinion, proving a theorem, ordering a book, or writing a literary criticism of the material read. Suppose the same text read into a computer memory causes the computer to print a statement, write an order for a book, write a literary criticism, or write a poem. This is clearly possible if the action may be made to depend on identification of textual words rather than on an understanding of them. Some aspects of information theory, based on identification rather than semantic meaning of text, are introduced in Chapter 8.

Identification of the subject matter of text is a problem that is suitable for present-day computers. It is of importance in computer preparation of abstracts, in computer selection of indexing terms, and in the use of computers to recognize the authorship of manuscripts of disputed origin.

Because computers may process large amounts of information in a short time, they may be used systematically to examine language for structural qualities not easily deduced by intuitive means. Although a computer has no understanding of the meaning of language it may be used to deduce structural relations of value in linguistics and in studies of relationships between different languages. It may be remarked, however, that the problem of machine translation of one language into another is a very difficult one and is significantly more complex than many of the problems that arise in information retrieval.

It appears that the languages of related disciplines form a system of intersecting vocabularies, each with its own characteristic structure. Each major discipline has its own basic vocabulary. For each subdiscipline there is a special vocabulary of the names of the things or concepts studied, and there is also a further well-defined vocabulary of the specialized terms that form the so-called jargon of the subdiscipline. The jargon words are not necessarily unique to the subdiscipline but have their special meanings only when used with the special vocabulary of the subdiscipline. Determination of these special vocabularies and their structures requires use of a large computer and is of considerable importance for future application of computers to analyze the meaning of printed text.

1.5 Document Retrieval, Library Automation, and Privacy of Files

Methods for search of computer accessible data bases that contain document references are discussed in Chapter 6. As the files grow in size, the problem of their storage in an economic manner becomes very important. It becomes necessary to consider various methods of compression so that storage costs may be reduced. Various means have been proposed and some are described in Chapter 9.

Computers may be used to automate many aspects of library operation, including circulation, cataloguing, ordering, and searching for books by specified authors or on particular topics. For library applications the computer is particularly useful if it may be accessed through remote terminals situated in the different departments of the library. All records may then be on magnetic tape or disk files at a central location, but may be searched or updated through remote terminals. If the computer has time-sharing capabilities it may work on other processing while at the same time appearing to be always available for library use. Library automation is not considered separately in the present text but constitutes an important practical application for many of the techniques discussed. It is particularly suitable for application of the compression techniques discussed in Chapter 9.

With increased use of computer-accessible files there arises the question of how to protect such files against access by unauthorized persons. File privacy is clearly of great concern to all involved with file maintenance, and many of the sociological and legal implications are still unknown. File privacy is not discussed in the present text since it is regarded as more important in the design of management and personnel information systems than in the design of systems for information retrieval relating to documents.

2
General Concepts

2.1 Document Data Bases and Selected Dissemination of Data

A number of organizations issue magnetic tapes that contain information about reports, books, and journal articles that relate to particular disciplines. Such tapes form computer-accessible document data bases that may be computer searched for information of interest.

The information about each document usually includes the names of the authors, sometimes their professional affiliations, the title of the article, and a reference to the journal name, the volume and year, and the page numbers of the article. Sometimes an abstract of the article is included, and sometimes there is included a list of references to which the article refers.

With each document description there also may be included a set of descriptors consisting of *keywords,* or phrases, to provide additional indication of the subject matter. This is particularly useful if the title is not very informative or is not inclusive of all the topics discussed. For similar reasons a set of subject headings or subject category numbers may be included.

Unless the published article contains a list of *descriptors* or subject headings, their inclusion significantly increases the cost of preparation of the searchable data base since the article must first be read by a reviewer familiar with both the subject matter of the article and the scheme of selection of the descriptors or subject headings.

In a typical computer search of a document data base the user of the search service requests a list of all the articles that contain certain combinations of title words, author names, subject headings, and so forth. The user's specified set of terms and logical connections between them is said to form an interest profile. The computer search program is designed to examine each item of the data base and to print a list of the items that satisfy the user's request.

An example of a user's interest profile follows.

```
SEARCH FOR:
    EITHER  [title words (breeze OR wind) AND (sea OR ocean OR waves) ]
            [BUT author NOT (Jones, A. C)                              ]
       OR   [keywords (marine AND atmosphere) ].
```

In response to the preceding profile a computer search of a suitable data base might produce the following output of items or "hits."

```
SMITH, P, EFFECT OF WIND ON OCEAN WAVES.
  J. MARINE PHYSICS, VOL. 6, 1969, PP. 11-32.
  KEYWORDS: METEOROLOGY, OCEANOGRAPHY.

JONES, S. AND WILSON, A, RELATION BETWEEN WAVES AND WIND.
  PROC. SOCIETY FOR APPLIED PHYS, VOL. 14, 1970, PP. 58-60.
  KEYWORDS: PHYSICS, THEORY, MARINE, HISTORICAL.

DAWSON, L. P, STUDIES OF SEA AND AIR.
  J. ATMOSPHERIC RESEARCH, VOL. 3, 1969, PP. 104-112.
  KEYWORDS: MARINE, PHYSICS, ATMOSPHERE.
```

A number of document data bases are created in the form of regular issues of magnetic tapes that contain references to the most recent articles published within some set of journals.[1] Some examples of the form of such tapes are given in Chapter 3. For instance, each issue of a tape created at biweekly or monthly intervals might contain about 5000 references to articles that have appeared in some 800 journals. Some users of a search service might have standing interest profiles to be searched on each issue of the tape as it is-received by the organizers of the search service. Services to provide such regular searches with respect to standing profiles may be said to provide selective dissemination of information (SDI) for current awareness. In contrast, a search on all back issues of a document data base is called a *retrospective search.*

---

[1] J. H. Schneider, M. Gechman, and S. E. Furth, eds., Survey of Commercially Available Computer-Readable Bibliographic Data Bases, 1973. American Society for Information Science, 1140 Connecticut Ave., N.W., Washington, D.C.

As will be apparent from the discussion in subsequent chapters, particularly Chapters 6 and 9, the basic search techniques used in computer programs for current awareness searches tend to be different from those used in computer programs suitable for retrospective searches. This is because a retrospective search is likely to be on a large data base, and also because a current awareness search may often be performed with respect to a batch of questions.

2.2 Coden Abbreviations

In data bases whose items refer to articles published in scientific journals, the journal name is sometimes replaced by a five-character *coden* chosen according to the abbreviation convention of the American Society for Testing Materials (ASTM).[2] Examples of such codens are JCEDA for *Journal of Chemical Education* and CHRGB for the journal, *Chromatographia*. The ASTM convention is not the only one used for codens, but it is one of the most frequently used at the present time.

The advantage of use of codens in specification of interest profiles is that otherwise the user must be careful to ensure that any journal names in the profile are expressed in a manner consistent with their form in the data base. The user must therefore be consistent in the use of abbreviations such as J. or Journ. for Journal, and Math. or Maths. for Mathematics.[3,4] If codens are used the user need check only the coden list in order to verify the correct representation. Moreover, use of codens tends to eliminate similar inconsistencies that are likely to arise during manual preparation of the searchable data base.

If codens are used to represent journal names, the search program may refer to a computer-accessible table of codens and journal names so that, if desired, the printed output may contain the full, or abbreviated, journal names instead of the codens.

The ASTM codens are based on a proposal of Bishop.[5] The 1966 issue of the ASTM coden list contained 38,993 codens for periodicals and other publications such as proceedings of symposia. The August 1968 supplement contained a further 24,877 codens of which 22,778 correspond to

[2] L. E. Kuentzel, *Coden for Periodical Titles* vols. 1 and 2. ASTM Data Series DS23A, 2nd ed. 1966. American Society for Testing and Materials.

[3] Documentation-International Code for the Abbreviation of Titles of Periodicals. International Organization for Standardization, ISO 4-1972(E), 4 pages, 1972.

[4] Documentation-International List of Periodic Title Word Abbreviations, ISO 833-1973(E), 42 pages, 1973.

[5] C. Bishop, *American Documentation* 4(1953):54.

periodicals. The ASTM definition of a periodical is a publication that has appeared at least twice under the same title. For periodicals all five coden characters are chosen from the letters A to Z, whereas for nonperiodicals the codens consist of two numerical digits followed by three alphabetic characters. The codens and corresponding periodical names are also available on magnetic tape issued by the ASTM.

In a data base issued by the Chemical Abstracts Service each coden consists of six characters; the first five are according to the ASTM code, and the sixth character is a check character. The method of choosing the check character is explained here.

Each of the five characters of the ASTM coden is assigned a number n equal to

$$1, 2, 3, ..., 25, 26, 27, 28, ..., 35, 36$$

according as the character is equal to

$$A, B, C, ..., Y, Z, 1, 2, ..., 9, 0.$$

To each coden there then corresponds a set of five numbers n_1, n_2, n_3, n_4, n_5. Two numbers x and y are then determined to satisfy the relation

$$\frac{11n_1 + 7n_2 + 5n_3 + 3n_4 + n_5}{34} = x + \frac{y}{34}$$

where $0 \leq y \leq 33$. The check character is then chosen as

$$A, B, C, ..., Y, Z, 2, 3, ..., 8, 9$$

according as the value of y is

$$0, 1, 2, ..., 24, 25, 26, 27, ..., 32, 33.$$

For example, the ASTM coden JAPIA for the *Journal of Applied Physics* gives $y = 21$ and hence receives a check character of U to become the six-character coden JAPIAU.

Whenever a coden with a check character is used it may be checked by a program stored in computer memory. If the check finds an inconsistency a message may be printed to indicate that a keypunching error has occurred.

A list of some of the codens used by the Chemical Abstracts Service in 1971 is shown in Table 2.1. Updated lists are contained in the biweekly issues of *Chemical Titles* published by the Chemical Abstracts Service.[6]

---

[6] Editorial Office: The Ohio State University, Columbus, Ohio, 43210.

Table 2.1
Examples of Codens Used by Chemical Abstracts Service in 1971.

Coden	Abbreviated journal name
ACHEAT	Advan. Chem. Eng.
AJBOAA	Amer. J. Bot.
ANBCA2	Anal. Biochem.
ANCHAM	Anal. Chem.
ANPYA2	Ann. Phys. (Leipzig)
BJCAAI	Brit. J. Cancer
BCSJA8	Bull. Chem. Soc. Jap.
CJBIAE	Can. J. Biochem.
CMERA9	Chem. Eng. (London)
CRYOAX	Cryogenics
EPSLA2	Earth Planet. Sci. Lett.
FOTEAO	Food Technol. (Chicago)
IEZQA7	IEEE J. Quantum Electron.
IJHMAK	Int. J. Heat Mass Transfer
JACSAT	J. Amer. Chem. Soc.
JDSCAE	J. Dairy Sci.
JISIAX	J. Iron Steel Inst., London
KRISAJ	Kristallografiya
MPYSB6	Metal Phys.
MIKBA5	Mikrobiologiya
NATUAS	Nature (London)
NUIMAL	Nucl. Instrum. Methods
NIMSA9	Nucl. Instrum. Methods, Suppl.
PCHEAO	Petro/Chem. Eng.
PNASA6	Proc. Nat. Acad. Sci. U.S.
PSEBAA	Proc. Soc. Exp. Biol. Med.
RMPHAT	Rev. Mod. Phys.
RPCJAP	Rev. Phys. Chem. Jap.
SUSCAS	Surface Sci.
TBCSAA	Trans. Brit. Ceram. Soc.
WWEIAY	Water Wastes Eng., Ind.
ZPCLAH	Z. Phys. Chem. (Leipzig)

2.3 Library Data Bases

Before the advent of computers the standard means of summarizing the details of a library collection was through use of a standard card catalogue. A typical entry on one card is shown in Figure 2.1.

A card catalogue entry contains an author name, sometimes the author dates, a title, and supplementary information such as other authors, publisher, date of publication, volume or series number if applicable, and

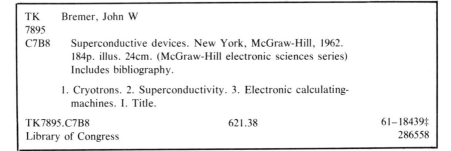

TK   Bremer, John W
7895
C7B8   Superconductive devices. New York, McGraw-Hill, 1962.
          184p. illus. 24cm. (McGraw-Hill electronic sciences series)
          Includes bibliography.

          1. Cryotrons. 2. Superconductivity. 3. Electronic calculating-
          machines. I. Title.

TK7895.C7B8   621.38   61–18439‡
Library of Congress   286558

Figure 2.1.   Example of a catalog card issued by the U.S. Library of Congress.

place of publication. The size of the book, the number of pages, and the number of copies in the library often are included. In addition scope notes such as "Includes bibliography" may be included. The subject headings such as "Cryotrons" provide an indication of the subject matter of the book or monograph.

An important part of each card catalogue entry is the class, or call, number that is related to the subject matter and is also usually a guide to where the monograph may be found on the library shelves. The three most widely used schemes of call numbers are those of the U.S. Library of Congress (LC), the Universal Decimal Classification (UDC), and the Dewey Decimal system. The catalogue card shown in Figure 2.1 contains both an LC number TK7895.C7B8, a Dewey Decimal number 621.38, and an LC catalogue card number 61–18439‡ which does not indicate subject matter but may be quoted if further copies of the card are required.

Each catalogue card may contain an accession number, such as 286558, which is assigned when the book is processed by the particular library. It is useful for purposes of bookkeeping rather than as an aid to information retrieval. The presence of the portion "I. Title" in Figure 2.1 indicates that there is a similar card filed under the heading "Superconductive devices" in addition to the card filed under the author heading "Bremer, John W."

A more detailed discussion and further examples of catalogue cards are given by Ball *et al.*[7]

The card catalogue has become such a well-established part of library

[7] K. L. Ball, M. E. Cockshutt, G. S. Pannu, K. H. Packer, and N. J. Williamson, *Sample Catalogue Cards Exemplifying the Anglo-American Cataloguing Rules* 3rd. ed. (Toronto: University of Toronto Press, 1968).

systems that a computer-accessible library data base is likely to be arranged so that librarians may readily relate it to the conventional card catalogue. For example, the form of the MARC library tapes, as described in Section 3.10, has been greatly influenced by the arrangement of the standard catalogue card.

It may be noted that many books contain an assigned International Standard Book Number, such as ISBN 0–408–70717–8, and that many periodicals contain an International Standard Serial Number such as ISSN: 0318–0166. These numbers usually are not of interest for searching purposes, but may be useful for ordering the documents believed to be relevant to a request.

A computer-accessible library data base also should contain files of user names, books outstanding, and books on order. The various files should be arranged so that information may be transferred between them with the minimum amount of manual bookkeeping. The result is an integrated library automation system rather than a set of independent, and possibly incompatible, files.

2.4 Numerical Data Bases

In contrast to document and library data bases whose data is expressed primarily in textual form, numerical data bases are stores of numerical values that might be obtained from observation or experiment. Quite frequently the stored values are arranged in sets that are not themselves searched but are associated with a searchable key or descriptor expressed in either alphabetic or numeric form.

For example, a data base might contain tables of meterological data, each table being associated with a particular city and date. It might be necessary to search for particular cities and dates and then print the associated numerical tables. Alternatively, it might be necessary to print names of all cities whose maximum temperature exceeded a given value on a particular date. In such an instance the city names, dates, maximum temperatures, and minimum temperatures might be regarded as searchable data, whereas the tables of hourly temperatures might be regarded as nonsearchable but associated with particular values of the searchable data. This is similar to a document data base in which title words and author names constitute searchable data, whereas page numbers are included in the printed output but are not of interest in formulation of the search question.

2.5 Management Information Systems

Data bases for management information systems (MIS) contain data of a form required by management of industrial or commercial enterprises. Such information is required primarily to make policy decisions, and hence includes information such as personnel details, pay roll information, office correspondence, sales statistics and projections, product specifications, inventory figures, and economic data.

In comparison to document data bases the information stored for management information systems is more varied in nature, but it may be more easily structured for search purposes since its form of preparation may be related directly to the purposes for which it is required. The data often may be stored in a form that is more explicit than a document title or abstract.

As data bases for management information systems grow in size, their economic storage in computer-accessible files presents the same problems as does storage of large document or library data bases. The problem of ensuring file privacy is more important than it is for document or library data bases.

2.6 Keyword in Context and Keyword Out of Context Indexes

For purposes of information retrieval it is sometimes convenient to have computer produced lists of textual items, such as titles of documents or sentences of abstracts, arranged so that all the items that contain any particular word may be determined rapidly by a manual scan through the list. A convenient arrangement of items for this purpose is in the form of a keyword in context (KWIC) index. The form of a KWIC index is explained here.

Consider the following set of titles in which the numbers at the left are for purposes of identification.

```
1876   ELECTRONIC COMPUTERS AND THE LAW
3048   SOME LEGAL ASPECTS OF COMPUTERS
1498   COMPUTER PROCESSING OF STATUTE LAW
6577   THE PATENT LAWS RELATING TO COMPUTER USE
4885   COMPUTER PROGRAMS AND THE LAW OF PATENTS
```

In the following list, which is in the form of a KWIC index, each title is repeated several times with appropriate displacements and truncations so that the beginning of each significant title word may be found by scanning down a certain column located in an approximately central position on the

page. The separate items are arranged in alphabetic order of the centrally placed word.

```
1498                                COMPUTER PROCESSING OF STATUTE LAW
6577    PATENT LAWS RELATING TO     COMPUTER USE
4885                                COMPUTER PROGRAMS AND THE LAW OF PAT
1876                    ELECTRONIC  COMPUTERS AND THE LAW
3048      SOME LEGAL ASPECTS OF     COMPUTERS
1876                                ELECTRONIC COMPUTERS AND THE LAW
1876    TRONIC COMPUTERS AND THE    LAW
1498    ER PROCESSING OF STATUTE    LAW
4885    OMPUTER PROGRAMS AND THE    LAW OF PATENTS
6577    THE PATENT                  LAWS RELATING TO COMPUTER USE
3048                        SOME    LEGAL ASPECTS OF COMPUTERS
6577                         THE    PATENT LAWS RELATING TO COMPUTER USE
4885    PROGRAMS AND THE LAW OF     PATENTS
4885                    COMPUTER    PROGRAMS AND THE LAW OF PATENTS
1498                    COMPUTER    PROCESSING OF STATUTE LAW
1498    COMPUTER PROCESSING OF      STATUTE LAW
6577    AWS RELATING TO COMPUTER    USE
```

The portion of the KWIC index that contains the centrally placed word is said to constitute a gutter. The words in the gutter are usually preceded by two or more blanks or are double printed or underlined on order to make them easily locatable.

In the preceding KWIC index the following words have not been guttered and are said to form a stop list:

AND, ASPECTS, OF, RELATING, SOME, THE, TO.

It is usual to specify a stop list so that the KWIC index does not become unnecessarily long through guttering of unimportant words. It is sometimes convenient to specify that the stop list include all words of three, or fewer, characters except for some particular words that are specified in an include list.

There are many variations of the simple form of the KWIC index just described. For example, in the following index whenever a title word, such as COMPUTER or LAW, appears in three or more titles a subindex is included in the form of a KWIC index guttered on the remaining words.

```
                          COMPUTER
1498    ER PROCESSING OF STATUTE    LAW
4885    OMPUTER PROGRAMS AND THE    LAW OF PATENTS
4885    PROGRAMS AND THE LAW OF     PATENTS
1498                    COMPUTER    PROCESSING OF STATUTE LAW
4885                    COMPUTER    PROGRAMS AND THE LAW OF PATENTS
1498    COMPUTER PROCESSING OF      STATUTE LAW
6577    AWS RELATING TO COMPUTER    USE
1876                    ELECTRONIC  COMPUTERS AND THE LAW
3048      SOME LEGAL ASPECTS OF     COMPUTERS
1876                                ELECTRONIC COMPUTERS AND THE LAW
```

```
                                        LAW
1498                            COMPUTER PROCESSING OF STATUTE LAW
4885                            COMPUTER PROGRAMS AND THE LAW OF PAT
1876              ELECTRONIC    COMPUTERS AND THE LAW
1876                            ELECTRONIC COMPUTERS AND THE LAW
4855  PROGRAMS AND THE LAW OF   PATENTS
1498              COMPUTER      PROCESSING OF STATUTE LAW
1498  COMPUTER PROCESSING OF    STATUTE LAW
6577           THE PATENT       LAWS RELATING TO COMPUTER USE
3048                 SOME       LEGAL ASPECTS OF COMPUTERS
6577                  THE       PATENT LAWS RELATING TO COMPUTER USE
4885  PROGRAMS AND THE LAW OF   PATENTS
4885              COMPUTER      PROGRAMS AND THE LAW OF PATENTS
1498              COMPUTER      PROCESSING OF STATUTE LAW
1498  COMPUTER PROCESSING OF    STATUTE LAW
6577  AWS RELATING TO COMPUTER  USE
```

A KWIC index may prove to be a very uneconomical means of representation of textual items, since if each item contains an average of N significant terms the storage in the form of a KWIC index involves an expansion factor equal to N. However, a printed KWIC index may be scanned manually very rapidly and is therefore a useful aid to locate items within a relatively small collection. A further advantage is that once a KWIC index has been printed it is available to users without the need for further computer use.

It may be remarked that a computer printout is often on paper that allows about 60 lines per page of which 100 pages form a stack of approximately ⅜ inches. Thus if each item contains an average of six significant words then a KWIC index of 10,000 titles will occupy a stack of paper of height approximately 4 inches.

The keyword out of context (KWOC) index is similar to the KWIC index, but the guttered words are placed to one side of the text so that no displacements are required. Thus the following is a KWOC index that corresponds to the KWIC index previously shown.

```
1498  COMPUTER     COMPUTER PROCESSING OF STATUTE LAW
6577  COMPUTER     THE PATENT LAWS RELATING TO COMPUTER USE
4885  COMPUTER     COMPUTER PROGRAMS AND THE LAW OF PATENTS
1876  COMPUTERS    ELECTRONIC COMPUTERS AND THE LAW
3048  COMPUTERS    SOME LEGAL ASPECTS OF COMPUTERS
1876  ELECTRONIC   ELECTRONIC COMPUTERS AND THE LAW
1876  LAW          ELECTRONIC COMPUTERS AND THE LAW
1498  LAW          COMPUTER PROCESSING OF STATUTE LAW
4885  LAW          COMPUTER PROGRAMS AND THE LAW OF PATENTS
6577  LAWS         THE PATENT LAWS RELATING TO COMPUTER USE
3048  LEGAL        SOME LEGAL ASPECTS OF COMPUTERS
6577  PATENT       THE PATENT LAWS RELATING TO COMPUTER USE
4885  PATENTS      COMPUTER PROGRAMS AND THE LAW OF PATENTS
4885  PROGRAMS     COMPUTER PROGRAMS AND THE LAW OF PATENTS
```

```
1498  PROCESSING  COMPUTER PROCESSING OF STATUTE LAW
1498  STATUTE     COMPUTER PROCESSING OF STATUTE LAW
6577  USE         THE PATENT LAWS RELATING TO COMPUTER USE
```

A particular example of a KWOC index is that issued periodically by the Defence Scientific Information Service (DSIS) of Canada. The index refers to unclassified documents acquired by DSIS. The gutter contains no word of less than four characters unless it is one contained in an antistop list. In July, 1973 the antistop list contained 53 words and the stop list contained about 700 words or word prefixes such as ANALY/.[8] A disadvantage in the use of such a large stop list is that the user must consult it frequently in order to avoid a search for words that are not guttered.

2.7 Boolean Search

A Boolean search of a data base is one in which items are examined to determine whether their terms satisfy a question expressed in terms of the Boolean logic operations AND, OR, NOT, and NOR. The operation NOR is generally treated as being synonymous with OR, so that a search for

```
      (diffraction OR reflection)
AND   (light)
NOT   (experimental OR measurement)
```

is equivalent to a search for

```
      (diffraction OR reflection)
AND   (light)
NOT   (experimental NOR measurement).
```

In either instance it is required to search for all items that contain either diffraction or reflection, as well as the word light, but only if they do not contain either experimental or measurement.

It may be noted that a search for items that contain

```
AT LEAST 2 OF (traffic, automobile, travel)
```

is of Boolean type since it may be expressed as a search for

```
      (traffic AND automobile)
OR    (traffic AND travel)
OR    (automobile AND travel).
```

[8] DSIS Standard for the Cataloguing of Scientific and Technical Reports, vol. 2. Defense Scientific Information Service Report No. DSIS R4, July 1973. Defense Research Board, Ottawa, Canada.

However, a search for items that contain

```
process IMMEDIATELY PRECEDING control
```

is not Boolean unless process control may be searched for as a single item.

The Boolean type of search as defined previously examines items of a data base for the occurrence of terms without regard to their relative positions in the text. It is modified frequently so that searches may be made with some regard given to the context in which the terms are used. Also, it is often appropriate to regard the occurrence of some terms as more important than others. Such modifications are discussed in Chapter 4.

2.8 Inverted Index and Double Dictionary

A set of textual items, such as

```
1. CONTROL OF POLLUTION IN RIVERS
2. REDUCTION OF ATMOSPHERIC POLLUTION
3. POLLUTION AND ITS EFFECT ON RIVERS
4. EFFECT OF SMOKE POLLUTION
5. ATMOSPHERIC SMOKE CONTENT
6. POLLUTION CONTROL OF RIVERS
```

associated with sequence numbers 1–6, may be stored in sequence to form entries in a linear file, which may also be termed a sequential file.

Thus if the semicolon is used as a delimiter, the linear file of the preceding items consists of:

```
CONTROL OF POLLUTION IN RIVERS;   REDUCTION OF ATMOSPHERIC
POLLUTION;   POLLUTION AND ITS EFFECT ON RIVERS;   EFFECT OF
SMOKE POLLUTION;   ATMOSPHERIC SMOKE CONTENT;   POLLUTION
CONTROL OF RIVERS
```

In order to determine which entries of a linear file contain any given word it is necessary to examine each file item in sequence. This is a serious disadvantage of the linear file organization of data.

The occurrence of words within items also may be represented by a table of the following form, which indicates the sequence numbers of the items that contain each word:

```
AND: 3
ATMOSPHERIC: 2, 5
CONTENT: 5
CONTROL: 1, 6
EFFECT: 3, 4
```

```
IN:  1
ITS:  3
OF:  1, 2, 4, 6
ON:  3
POLLUTION:  1, 2, 3, 4, 6
REDUCTION:  2
RIVERS:  1, 3, 6
SMOKE:  4, 5
```

Such a table is said to form an inverted index to the occurrence of words in the items. It may be stored to form an inverted file.

If the words AND, IN, ITS, OF, and ON are regarded as insignificant and are omitted from the preceding inverted index, it takes the form

```
ATMOSPHERIC:  2, 5
CONTENT:  5
CONTROL:  1, 6
EFFECT:  3, 4
POLLUTION:  1, 2, 3, 4, 6
REDUCTION:  2
RIVERS:  1, 3, 6
SMOKE:  4, 5
```

Although the corresponding inverted file could consist of eight separate sets of alphabetic and numeric data a more convenient arrangement for computer storage is to use two files, one for the alphabetic data in the form

```
ATMOSPHERIC;  CONTENT;  CONTROL;  EFFECT;  POLLUTION;
REDUCTION;  RIVERS;  SMOKE
```

and one for the corresponding sets of numeric data in the form

```
2, 5;  5;  1, 6;  3, 4;  1, 2, 3, 4, 6;  2;  1, 3, 6;  4, 5
```

An inverted index may be regarded as equivalent to a document term matrix of rows and columns in which the rows correspond to document items and the columns correspond to terms. Thus the preceding inverted index is equivalent to the following document term matrix of six rows and eight columns in which the element in the ith row and jth column is set to 1, or 0, according as the ith document contains, or does not contain, the jth term.

It should be noted that, regardless of whether insignificant words are included, the inverted index does not provide all the information stored in the linear file since it does not indicate the relative positions of words in the items. A modified form of inverted index may be derived by setting the element in the ith row and jth column equal to the position of the jth word within the ith item. Such a form of matrix allows each item of text to be reconstructed from a row of the inverted index. However, if a word

	ATMOSPHERIC	CONTENT	CONTROL	EFFECT	POLLUTION	REDUCTION	RIVERS	SMOKE
1.	0	0	1	0	1	0	1	0
2.	1	0	0	0	1	1	0	0
3.	0	0	0	1	1	0	1	0
4.	0	0	0	1	1	0	0	1
5.	1	1	0	0	0	0	0	1
6.	0	0	1	0	1	0	1	0

appears several times within one item of text then either several columns must be included in the inverted index in order to represent the separate occurrences or else the matrix must be augmented by inclusion of a table of duplicates. Such a table could be arranged in a similar manner to the duplicate stack that is described in Section 6.3.

A Boolean search on a document data base stored in the form of an inverted file may be made through application of the appropriate logic operations to the columns of the associated document term matrix. The rules of application of such logic operations to a pair of columns of elements u_i and v_i to produce a column of elements w_i are as listed here.

1. For AND operation:

$$w_i = \begin{cases} 1 & \text{if } u_i = v_i = 1 \\ 0 & \text{otherwise} \end{cases}$$

2. For OR or NOR operation:

$$w_i = \begin{cases} 0 & \text{if } u_i = v_i = 0 \\ 1 & \text{otherwise} \end{cases}$$

3. For NOT operation applied to elements u_i:

$$w_i = \begin{cases} 1 & \text{if } u_i = 0 \\ 0 & \text{if } u_i = 1. \end{cases}$$

Thus for the items that correspond to the document term matrix just listed, the ones that contain POLLUTION AND RIVERS may be determined by noting that

$$
\begin{bmatrix} 1 \\ 1 \\ 1 \\ 1 \\ 0 \\ 1 \end{bmatrix} \quad \text{AND} \quad \begin{bmatrix} 1 \\ 0 \\ 1 \\ 0 \\ 0 \\ 1 \end{bmatrix} = \begin{bmatrix} 1 \\ 0 \\ 1 \\ 0 \\ 0 \\ 1 \end{bmatrix}
$$

and hence the relevant document items are the first, third, and sixth.

A search expressed in terms of a single AND operation may be performed manually by use of a double dictionary, the form of which is shown in Figure 2.2. It consists of a pair of printed inverted indexes with separate pages arranged so that the pages of either index fold along a common axis. To search for the sequence numbers of the items that contain both AIR AND POLLUTION, the separate indexes are opened so that a page that contains AIR may be viewed at the side of a page that contains POLLUTION. The common document numbers, such as 18, 43, and 51, may then be read.

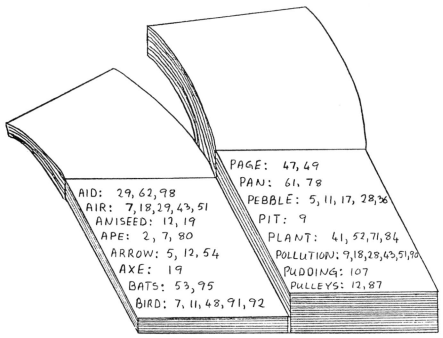

Figure 2.2. A double dictionary.

Although a double dictionary may be applied only to very simple Boolean searches, it has proven to be a useful aid to manual searching of small data bases.[9]

2.9 Precision and Recall

The user of a retrieval service, whether it is automated or manual, attempts to describe interest in it by means of a question that initiates a search of the data base. Ideally, the list of data base items that the user receives should include none that are not of interest and should omit none that are relevant. The extent to which both criteria may be met depends on the extent to which the user's question adequately represents his or her interest, and also on the extent to which the terms used in the user's question are also terms used to describe, or index, items in the data base.

Suppose the user of a retrieval service receives a list of M items in response to a search, and suppose that after examination of the items the person decides that P of them are relevant. The search is then said to have a precision, or relevance, equal to P/M. The precision is thus equal to unity only if every output item is relevant to the interest of the user.

Suppose that, after receipt of a list of M items of which P are relevant, the user examines manually the entire data base and finds that it contains a total of R relevant items. The search that produced the M items is then said to have a recall equal to P/R. It follows that the recall is equal to unity only if the search located all the relevant items contained in the data base.

The two requirements that a search have a precision of unity and a recall of unity are somewhat conflicting since, if a question is formulated in a sufficiently general manner to ensure that no relevant items are missed, it will usually lead to retrieval of some nonrelevant items. Conversely, if a question is formulated in a very specific manner to retrieve only relevant items, it is likely to miss some items that are also relevant.

The manner in which precision and recall tend to change as a question is made more specific, or more general, is shown in Figure 2.3. Point A corresponds to a question that is formulated so that all retrieved items are relevant but many relevant items are not retrieved; thus P/M is equal to 1 and P/R is small. As the question is progressively generalized, the precision and recall vary as represented by the points $B, C, D, E,$ and F. Point F corresponds to a question that is designed to find all the relevant items at the expense of finding many that are not relevant; thus P/R is equal to 1 and P/M is small.

[9] J. W. Cherry, "Computer-produced indexes in a double dictionary format," *Special Libraries* 57 (1966):107–110.

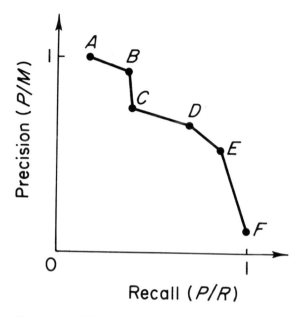

Figure 2.3. Change in precision and recall as a question is made more specific or more general.

The variation of precision with recall shown in Figure 2.4 represents an idealized search service in which point C corresponds to a perfect question for which both the precision and recall are equal to 1. If the question is made narrower, that is more specific, then a smaller value of recall results as represented by points B and A for which the precision remains equal to 1. If the question is made broader, then a smaller value of precision results as represented by points D, E, and F for which the recall remains equal to 1. The ideal situation represented by Figure 2.4 is not likely to occur in practice, and Figure 2.3 represents the more typical form of variation of precision with recall.

It is important to note that, while precision may be determined by examination of only the items output by the search service, determination of recall requires a manual examination of all items of the data base in order to determine which are relevant to the interest of the user. It is seldom practical to make such an examination. Thus, except in the instance of a very small data base, values of recall usually are based on approximate estimates such as might be obtained from manual examination of only a portion of the data base or of a list of items output in response to a more general question that is believed to be so general as to ensure a recall value close to 1.

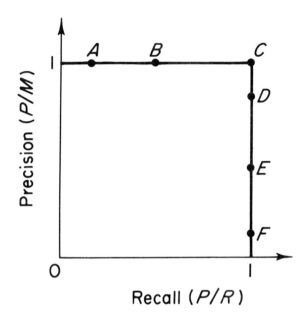

Figure 2.4. Change in precision and recall as a perfect question, represented by point C, is broadened or narrowed.

An early use of precision and recall to measure the effectiveness of an information retrieval service was made by Cleverdon.[10,11] Detailed consideration of the two concepts has been made by Salton,[12] who has used them extensively in discussion of results obtained with the SMART system. Measures of retrieval effectiveness based on precision and recall, or on similar quantities, have been discussed by Keen,[13] Swets,[14] Königová,[15] and Robertson.[16]

[10] C. W. Cleverdon, "The testing of index language devices," *Aslib Proceedings* 15 (1963):106–130.

[11] C. W. Cleverdon, "Identification of criteria for evaluation of operational information retrieval systems," Cranfield College of Aeronautics, England, November, 1964.

[12] G. Salton, *Automatic Information Organization and Retrieval* (New York: McGraw-Hill, 1968).

[13] E. M. Keen, "Evaluation parameters," in *The SMART Retrieval System*, G. Salton, ed. (Englewood Cliffs, N.J.: Prentice-Hall, 1971), Chapter 5.

[14] J. A. Swets, "Effectiveness of information retrieval methods," *American Documentation* 20 (1969):72–89.

[15] M. Königová, "Mathematical and statistical methods of noise evaluation in a retrieval system," *Information Storage and Retrieval* 6 (1971):437–444.

[16] S. E. Robertson, "The parametric description of retrieval tests," *Journal of Documentation* 1 (1969):1–27.

2.10 Thesauri

The term thesaurus, as used in information retrieval, is employed to denote a list of terms together with some information about their use and mutual relations. Most thesauri are special purpose in the sense that their terms are chosen from the vocabulary of a particular discipline or data base. For each listed term some relations may be included to indicate other terms that have identical meaning and are called synonyms, terms that are narrower or broader in meaning, terms that are related in meaning, and so forth. Bracketed or footnoted scope notes may be included for further explanation, and are often used to indicate homonyms, which are words that may be used with several different meanings. A thesaurus does not usually contain definitions of terms. When used with a particular data base the purpose of a thesaurus is to acquaint the user with the relevant vocabulary and with any rules that have governed the choice of descriptor vocabulary within the data base.

Glossaries, or specialized dictionaries, contain definitions of terms and may include specification of synonyms and homonyms.

Processing of data for compilation of thesauri and glossaries is greatly facilitated by use of computers since the programming involved for sorting, determining cross references, and so forth is of a fairly simple nature.

Discussion of the problems involved in production of glossaries and thesauri have been given by a number of authors.[17] The desired properties of a thesaurus relevant to engineering have been discussed by Wall.[18] A summary of the work of the Engineers Joint Council in development of thesauri and information systems has been given by Speight and Cottrell.[19] Some of the problems that led to the development of interest in engineering thesauri and indexing were outlined in a symposium.[20] The *Engineers Joint Council Thesaurus* is an example of a technical thesaurus that lists synonyms, generic, and related terms.[21]

An example of a small specialized glossary would be one to classify radio communications equipment. It appears that about 500 descriptors are sufficient for this task.[22]

[17] I. H. Gould, and G. C. Toothill, "The terminology work of IFIP and ICC," *The Computer Journal* 7 (1964-1965):264–270.

[18] E. Wall, *Information Retrieval Thesauri*. Engineers Joint Council, 345 East 47th Street, New York 17, November, 1962.

[19] F. Y. Speight, and N. E. Cottrell, The EJC Engineering Information Program—1966–1967. Engineers Joint Council, 345 East 47th Street, New York 17, February, 1967.

[20] Proceedings of the Engineering Information Symposium. Engineers Joint Council, 345 East 47th Street, New York 17, January, 1962.

[21] *Thesaurus of Engineering Terms*. Engineers Joint Council, 347 East 47th Street, New York 17, 1964.

[22] Third Annual Report. EDCPF Report No. 23, Bell Aerosystems Company, May, 1965.

Two particular and widely used thesauri are described here. One is issued by the U.S. Bureau of Ships and the other by the Engineers Joint Council.

A thesaurus issued by the U.S. Bureau of Ships in 1965 relates to a collection of 170,000 reports that were indexed by some 4600 terms.[23] It lists the terms in alphabetic order with an indication of broader terms, narrower terms, related terms, synonymous (INCLUDES) terms, and preferred (USE) terms. A portion of the thesaurus is as follows:

```
COAXIAL CABLES
 BROADER TERMS:
  ELECTRICAL CABLES
 NARROWER TERMS:
  LIQUID FILLED COAXIAL CABLES
 RELATED TERMS:
  PULSE CABLES
  RADIOFREQUENCY CABLES
COAXIAL FILTERS
 BROADER TERMS:
  ELECTRIC FILTERS
  FILTERS (ELECTROMAGNETIC WAVE)
 RELATED TERMS:
  RADIOFREQUENCY FILTERS
COBALT
 BROADER TERMS:
  GROUP VIII ELEMENTS
  METALS
  TRANSITION ELEMENTS
COBALT ALLOYS
 BROADER TERMS:
  ALLOYS
COBALT COMPOUNDS
COBALT ISOTOPES (RADIOACTIVE)
 USE:
  COBALT
  RADIOACTIVE ISOTOPES
```

A *Thesaurus of Engineering and Scientific Terms* (TEST) is issued by the Engineers Joint Council.[24] The 1967 issue contained 23,364 main entries associated with broader terms (BT), narrower terms (NT), related terms (RT), synonymous or used-for terms (UF), and preferred terms (USE). A sample of the listing is as follows:

---

[23] Bureau of Ships Thesaurus of Descriptive Terms and Code Book, 2nd. edition, March, 1965. Bureau of Ships, Navy Department, Washington, D.C. 20360.

[24] *Thesaurus of Engineering and Scientific Terms,* 1967. Engineers Joint Council, 347 East 47th Street, New York 17.

```
Coaxial cables  0901
 UF Coaxial lines
     Liquid filled coaxial cables
 BT Transmission lines
 RT-Power lines
     Submarine cables
     Telegraph cables
     Telephone cables
Coaxial filters  0901
 BT Electric filters
 RT Microwave filters
     Radiofrequency filters
Coaxial lines
 USE Coaxial cables
Cobalt  0702
 BT Metals
     Transition metals
 RT-Cobalt isotopes
Cobalt  60  1802
 BT Cobalt isotopes
     Isotopes
     Nuclides
     Radioactive isotopes
```

In the engineering thesaurus the prefix - is used to indicate when an NT or RT term is also associated with a further set of narrower terms. Thus "Cobalt isotopes" also appears as a main term in the form

```
Cobalt isotopes    1802
 BT Isotopes
    Nuclides
 NT Cobalt  60
 RT Cobalt
```

The numbers that follow the main terms refer to a particular set of subject categories. For example, 0901 denotes the subject "Electronics and electrical engineering: components," whereas 1802 denotes the subject "Nuclear science and technology: isotopes."

2.11 Terms and Vocabularies Associated with Attributes

A document, library, or similar data base may be envisaged as a set of records in which each record contains information about a single document. Each record may be divided into fields, and each field associated with a particular attribute such as "authors," "abstract," "subject headings," "journal name," "publication date," and so forth. The value of the attribute is stored within the field and consists of a subset of terms, or descriptors, chosen from a set that forms the vocabulary associated with the particular attribute. The subset of descriptors may or may not be an ordered set.

Thus the value of a title field might be the ordered set

AN ANALYSIS OF FACTORING METHODS

of five descriptors that are words chosen from the vocabulary of all the title words present in the data base. The value of a subject heading field might be the unordered set

NUMERICAL ANALYSIS, PHYSICS, COMPUTING SCIENCE

of three descriptors chosen from the subject heading field vocabulary of subject phrases.

The descriptors that form the vocabularies associated with the different attributes may consist of words, as in title fields; names and initials, as in author fields; groups of words, as in subject heading fields; numbers, as in date fields; and so forth. Even if the vocabularies of two different attributes, such as "title" and "abstract," contain the same descriptors the statistical distribution of the occurrences of the descriptors may be different within the different fields, and it may be desirable to regard the two vocabularies as distinct. It should be noted that throughout the present text a descriptor is used to denote the basic elements of a vocabulary. Whether these are words, phrases, author names, or other elements, depends on the particular application.

A search question is an expression of logical operators that act on pairs that consist of an attribute descriptor and a term. The following is an example of a question that might be used to request a search for all records that contain the term SMITH PG in the author field, and also either the terms SIMULATION or LEARNING in the title field or else the term ARTIFICIAL INTELLIGENCE in the subject headings field.

```
        SMITH PG (author)
    AND SIMULATION  (title word)
        OR LEARNING  (title word)
        OR ARTIFICIAL INTELLIGENCE (subject heading).
```

As items are added to a data base the vocabularies associated with each attribute tend to grow in size although, because of descriptor repetitions, the rate of growth may decrease with increasing size of the data base. In order to formulate search questions that are effective, it is clearly desirable to be aware of the composition and statistical structure of each of the vocabularies associated with the searchable attributes. As will become apparent from the subsequent chapters, associated lists of vocabularies, descriptor associations, and thesauri are all useful as aids to proper formulation of search questions.

2.12 Components of a Mechanized Information Retrieval System

The user of an information retrieval service wishes to obtain a list of documents that relate to a particular interest. This interest may not be well defined, and an inexperienced user may have difficulty in formulating a question that is sufficiently well expressed for use in a computer search of a data base.

The first step in the retrieval process is therefore the formulation of a question that is both simple enough for initiation of a computer search and yet sufficiently comprehensive to describe adequately the interest of the user. The question formulation stage also includes the decision as to which particular data bases should be searched. Following the initial question formulation it may be advisable to consult a thesaurus in order to expand the question by inclusion of some related terms. Also, after a search has been performed it may be decided to broaden, or narrow, the question in a manner determined by further examination of a suitable thesaurus.

The complete retrieval process may be summarized as shown in Figure 2.5. Search of the data base produces a list of document items that satisfy the question logic. The user may then decide whether they are also relevant. The user's decision may be made by examination of only the output items or by reference to the complete documents that they represent. If a sufficient number of the output items are not relevant to the user's interest, or if the user believes that many relevant items have not been found, then the question formulation and expansion is at fault, an inappropriate data base has been searched, or the data base items do not properly represent the complete documents. This latter situation could occur, for example, through badly chosen titles or poor choice of keywords.

The provision of question logic to represent properly the interest of a variety of users is discussed in Chapter 4. Chapters 5 and 6 are concerned with the search phase of the retrieval process. Automatic methods of question expansion and modification are discussed in Chapter 11. Some examples of the representation of documents within searchable data bases are given in Chapter 3.

2.13 Alphabetizing Conventions

When descriptors such as words, phrases, or call numbers are to be arranged in alphabetic order as in creation of a thesaurus or KWIC index, there arises the question of how to assign alphabetic rank to punctuation,

36

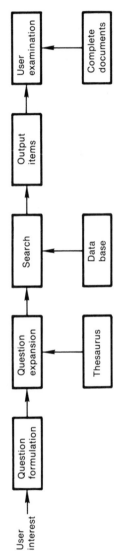

Figure 2.5. Components of a mechanized information retrieval system.

numerical digits, and other special symbols such as /, (, \$, -, and Greek letters. There are a number of generally accepted conventions to deal with various situations in which productions of ordered lists are required.

One simple convention is to assign increasing rank to symbols in the following order

```
(blank) ABCDEFGHIJKLMNOPQRSTUVWXYZ0123456789
```

and to ignore other symbols such as punctuation.

With this convention the descriptors RIGHT—HAND and IBM/360 are treated as respectively equivalent to RIGHTHAND (not RIGHT HAND) and IBM360. The terms CAT'S and CATS and CATS' are treated as equivalent. Because a blank is ranked lower than a letter the term LEFT LEG is ranked lower than LEFT—HAND. The descriptors CATS, AND DOGS and CATS AND DOGS are treated as equivalent. The convention is generally satisfactory for the ordering of single, or hyphenated, words but may be open to criticism for its ordering of some phrases.

Data stored in computer-accessible files are often coded in either the EBCDIC or ASCII character codes as described in Section 3.2. A more convenient order of alphabetic rank is then as follows

```
(blank) (Special symbols ordered according to EBCDIC or ASCII)
        ABCDEFGHIJKLMNOPQRSTUVWXYZ0123456789
```

If the latter convention is adopted the descriptor RIGHT HAND ranks lower than either RIGHT—HAND or RIGHT—ARM both of which rank lower than RIGHTHAND. The term CAT ranks lower than CAT'S, which ranks lower than CATS. Because a blank ranks lower than a comma, the descriptor CATS AND DOGS will be ranked lower than CATS, AND BIRDS.

With most computers there is a particular alphabetizing convention that corresponds to the manner in which stored characters may be identified with integer numbers as stored by that computer. Although this particular convention makes for ease of programming, it varies for different machines and hence should be well defined if it is to be understood by a general user.

2.14 Problems

1. State the advantages of using codens in a data base designed for retrieval of periodical articles. State why codens constitute a better form of abbreviation than do the first five letters in the name of the periodical. Would you suggest the use of check characters in specification of author names or keywords?

2. Examine six articles published in a scientific or technical journal and comment on the extent to which their content is well described by their titles, abstracts, subject headings within the printed article, and descriptors such as keywords or phrases.

3. Examine a collection of newspaper headlines in order to propose a stop list that would be suitable if the headlines were listed in a KWIC index.

4. Describe some of the limitations of use of precision and recall as measures of retrieval effectiveness.

5. It is desired to print an alphabetically ordered list of proper names, some of which are in the form of a surname followed by initials, and some of which are in the form of a surname followed by given names. Describe an alphabetizing convention that would rank the name SMITH A, G equally with the name SMITH ANDREW, GEORGE.

3

Document Data Bases for Computer Search

3.1 Magnetic Tape and Disk Storage

Prior to storage in computer-accessible files, data are often prepared on punched cards, the most common form of which measure approximately $7\frac{3}{8}$ by $3\frac{1}{4}$ inches and contain 80 columns. Each column contains 12 positions in which holes may be punched to represent alphabetic characters, numerical digits, or other symbols. A stack of 140 cards is approximately 1 inch in height.

Card readers, which read data from cards into computer memory, read cards at rates varying from about 250 to 1000 cards per minute. Card punches, which punch data from internal memory to cards, transfer data at rates of from about 50 to 200 characters per sec.

Magnetic tape offers a more compact means of storing data. The tape is made of plastic material coated with a magnetic layer that is regarded as divided into tracks that run longitudinally along the tape. One track is used to store a check bit. The remaining tracks are used to store characters of data according to the coding convention of the particular computer. Thus seven-track tape is used with computers whose characters are coded in six-bit code, whereas nine-track tape is used with computers whose characters are expressed in eight-bit code.

The number of characters that may be stored on a 1-inch length of magnetic tape is called the tape density and is measured in units of bits per inch (BPI) that may be stored on each track. Many computers use tape of 800 BPI or 1600 BPI stored on reels of length up to 2400 feet. Such a reel of tape with characters stored at 800 BPI may be used to store up to 23 million characters. The same amount of data stored on cards would require a stack of height 170 feet.

The speed at which characters may be read or written on magnetic tape depends on the type of tape drive; a rate of 90,000 characters per sec. is quite common. Because of inertia of the tape reels it is not possible to halt the tape between successive characters, but only within record gaps that separate blocks of data and are often approximately .6 inches in length. Thus in transfer of data between computer memory and magnetic tape storage, it is entire blocks that are transferred.

Magnetic tape provides sequential storage in the sense that if a particular tape record has been read, and it is desired to read a record at another position on the tape, then all the intervening records must first be moved past the read–write head.

Magnetic tape offers low-cost storage of data in a form that is convenient for input to computers. Goodman[1] has remarked that, apart from considerations of space, the cost of storing data on magnetic tape is less than that for storage on cards, magnetic disks, drums, and core memory by factors of 6, 20–60, 30,000, and 150,000–600,000, respectively. However, in comparison with magnetic disks, drums, and core storage the saving in cost is at the expense of greater time to access the data.

For storage on magnetic tape the data often are punched first on cards, read card by card into core memory, and then output to tape through magnetic tape drives. An alternative is to type the data through a data recorder, which places it directly on magnetic tape without intermediate use of cards. The data recorder may also be used for some editing and error correction of the data. The economies and convenience of the data recorder have been described by Price.[2]

Magnetic disk storage, also called random-access or direct-access storage, involves storage of characters on magnetically coated rotating circular disks. Each disk face is divided into tracks on which data may be written or read through read–write heads that may be positioned over any track. The time required to position each read–write head is called the access time and may be of the order of 100 msec. Thus the time to access data stored on disk is much less than the time required to position tape

---

[1] J. V. Goodman, "Auditing magnetic-tape systems," *Computer Journal* 7(1964–1965): 4–7.

[2] D. G. Price, "Whither keypunch?" *Datamation* 13(1967): 32–34.

records within a tape drive. Once a read–write head is set to the appropriate track, any data on that rotating track will periodically pass the read–write head. The time that elapses between positioning of a read–write head and the subsequent aligning of the required data is called the rotational delay. It is frequently of the order of .30 msec.

The IBM 2314 disk pack for use with the IBM 360 computer contains eight disk drives, each of which contains 20 disk surfaces of 200 tracks each. Each track may store up to 7294 characters, and hence each disk drive has a storage capacity of approximately 30 million characters. The read–write rate is 312,000 characters per sec, the average access time is 75 msec, and the average rotational delay is 12.5 msec.

Apart from the smaller access times and larger read–write rates of magnetic disks in comparison to magnetic tapes, an advantage of disk storage is that characters are written in set positions on the tracks. These positions are determined by precise synchronization, so that when characters are written they do not affect neighboring characters. It is this important feature of magnetic disk storage that has led to its designation as direct-access or random-access storage. In contrast, magnetic tapes are said to provide sequential storage of data.

A serious limitation in the use of magnetic tape storage is the following. When a record is rewritten on magnetic tape, the mechanical imperfections of the tape drive cause the end of the record to be incorrectly aligned with the beginning of the next record gap and, it is generally impossible to read the next and indeed all subsequent records. Thus to rewrite or correct a record on magnetic tape it is usual to read first all previous records and store them on a second tape, then read but do not store the record to be changed, then write the new record on the second tape, and finally read all subsequent records from the first tape and write them on the second one. If desired, all records on the second tape may then be copied back to the first tape. This is not a disadvantage in storage of permanent records, but it is a serious disadvantage in storage of records that require frequent updating.

Magnetic drum storage is similar to disk storage in that if offers random access, but the data are stored in circular tracks on the surface of a rotating drum. Very high read–write rates, and low-access times, are possible. For example, the IBM 2301 magnetic drum used with the IBM 360 computer allows a read–write rate of 1.25 million characters per sec with an access time of 0–17.5 msec. The storage capacity is in excess of 4 million characters. Unfortunately the cost of drum storage is much higher than that of disk storage, and so drum storage usually is not feasible for files used in information retrieval.

3.2 Bit Codes for Data Storage

Textual data stored on computer-accessible files, or in internal memory, is usually coded character by character although alternative methods of coding text are described in Chapter 9. Three examples of character codes are shown in Tables 3.1–3.3. The first is the six-bit binary coded decimal (BCD) code used with the CDC 6000 series type of computer. The second is the eight-bit extended binary coded decimal interchange code (EBCDIC), and the third example is the eight-bit American standards code for information interchange (ASCII). The six-bit and eight-bit codes are for use with seven- and nine-track tapes, respectively.

The expanded eight-bit ASCII code, shown in Table 3.4, is used for data representation on the MARC library tapes, which are discussed in Section 3.11. The code allows representation of many special characters

Table 3.1
Six-bit BCD Character Code.

Character	Code	Character	Code
A	000001	0	011011
B	000010	1	011100
C	000011	2	011101
D	000100	3	011110
E	000101	4	011111
F	000110	5	100000
G	000111	6	100001
H	001000	7	100010
I	001001	8	100011
J	001010	9	100100
K	001011	+	100101
L	001100	−	100110
M	001101	*	100111
N	001110	/	101000
O	001111	(	101001
P	010000	)	101010
Q	010001	$	101011
R	010010	=	101100
S	010011	[space]	101101
T	010100	'	101110
U	010101	.	101111
V	010110	#	110100
W	010111		
X	011000		
Y	011001		
Z	011010		

Table 3.2
EBCDIC Character Code.

Character	Code	Character	Code[a]	Character	Code
(Blank)	01000000	A	11000001	0	11110000
¢	01001010	B	11000010	1	11110001
.	01001011	C	11000011	2	11110010
<	01001100	D	11000100	3	11110011
(	01001101	E	11000101	4	11110100
+	01001110	F	11000110	5	11110101
|	01001111	G	11000111	6	11110110
&	01010000	H	11001000	7	11110111
!	01011010	I	11001001	8	11111000
$	01011011	J	11010001	9	11111001
*	01011100	K	11010010		
)	01011101	L	11010011		
;	01011110	M	11010100		
¬	01011111	N	11010101		
−	01100000	O	11010110		
/	01100001	P	11010111		
,	01101011	Q	11011000		
%	01101100	R	11011001		
_	01101101	S	11100010		
>	01101110	T	11100011		
?	01101111	U	11100100		
:	01111010	V	11100101		
#	01111011	W	11100110		
@	01111100	X	11100111		
'	01111101	Y	11101000		
=	01111110	Z	11101001		
''	01111111				

[a] The code listed is for characters in uppercase. Lowercase alphabetic characters are coded with the two left-hand bits 10 instead of 11.

and also provides for control functions such as carriage return of a printer and end of file marks on magnetic tape.

Numerical data also may be stored in files in character form, and will be in such form if written by a program statement that refers to a format specification. Thus if numbers 217328, 18, and 2784.138 are stored in internal memory under the names M, N, and C, the FORTRAN statements

```
        WRITE(1,4)M,  N,  C
    4 FORMAT(I6, I4, F12.3)
```

cause the following sequence of characters to be written in a record of the file identified with device No. 1:

Table 3.3
ASCII Character Code.

Character	Code	Character	Code[a]	Character	Code
(Blank)	01000000	A	10100001	0	01010000
!	01000001	B	10100010	1	01010001
"	01000010	C	10100011	2	01010010
#	01000011	D	10100100	3	01010011
$	01000100	E	10100101	4	01010100
%	01000101	F	10100110	5	01010101
&	01000110	G	10100111	6	01010110
'	01000111	H	10101000	7	01010111
(	01001000	I	10101001	8	01011000
)	01001001	J	10101010	9	01011001
*	01001010	K	10101011		
+	01001011	L	10101100		
,	01001100	M	10101101		
−	01001101	N	10101110		
.	01001110	O	10101111		
/	01001111	P	10110000		
:	01011010	Q	10110001		
;	01011011	R	10110010		
<	01011100	S	10110011		
=	01011101	T	10110100		
>	01011110	U	10110101		
?	01011111	V	10110110		
@	10100000	W	10110111		
[	10111011	X	10111000		
	10111100	Y	10111001		
]	10111101	Z	10111010		
∧ ⌐	10111110				
_	10111111				
`	11100000				
{	11111011				
|	11111100				
}	11111101				
~	11111110				

[a] The code listed is for characters in uppercase. Lowercase alphabetic characters are coded with the two left-hand bits 11 instead of 10.

$$217328\text{bb}18\text{bbbb}2784.138$$

in which b denotes a single blank.

In order to be read by a FORTRAN statement of the form

```
READ(1,5)N, (B(I), I=1, N)
```

the values of N and the B(I) must have been written on the record through reference to a format specification. The READ operation converts the data into binary or floating point form for storage in internal memory.

Table 3.4
Expanded ASCII Code Used on the MARC II Tapes.

Character, or function	Code	Character, or function	Code
Null	00000000	0	00110000
Start of heading	00000001	1	00110001
Start of text	00000010	2	00110010
End of text	00000011	3	00110011
End of transmission	00000100	4	00110100
Enquiry	00000101	5	00110101
Acknowledge	00000110	6	00110110
Bell	00000111	7	00110111
Backspace	00001000	8	00111000
Horizontal Tabulation	00001001	9	00111001
Line feed	00001010	:	00111010
Vertical Tabulation	00001011	;	00111011
Form Feed	00001100	<	00111100
Carriage return	00001101	=	00111101
Shift out	00001110	>	00111110
Shift in	00001111	?	00111111
Data link escape	00010000	@	01000000
Device control 1	00010001	A	01000001
Device control 2	00010010	B	01000010
Device control 3	00010011	C	01000011
Device control 4	00010100	D	01000100
Negative acknowledge	00010101	E	01000101
Synchronous idle	00010110	F	01000110
End of trans. block	00010111	G	01000111
Cancel	00011000	H	01001000
End of medium	00011001	I	01001001
Substitute	00011010	J	01001010
Escape	00011011	K	01001011
End of file	00011100	L	01001100
End of record	00011101	M	01001101
Field terminator	00011110	N	01001110
‡	00011111	O	01001111
(Blank)	00100000	P	01010000
!	00100001	Q	01010001
"	00100010	R	01010010
#	00100011	S	01010011
$	00100100	T	01010100
%	00100101	U	01010101
&	00100110	V	01010110
`	00100111	W	01010111
(	00101000	X	01011000
)	00101001	Y	01011001
*	00101010	Z	01011010
+	00101011	[	01011011
,	00101100	\	01011100
−	00101101	]	01011101
/	00101110		

Table 3.4 *(Continued)*

Character, or function	Code	Character, or function	Code
a	01100001	″ (Tvërdyĭ Znak)	10110111
b	01100010	ı (Turkish i)	10111000
c	01100011	£	10111001
d	01100100	ð (Eth)	10111010
e	01100101	σ	10111100
f	01100110	ν	10111101
g	01100111	ʔ (Pseudo Question)	11100000
h	01101000	` (Grave)	11100001
i	01101001	´ (Acute)	11100010
j	01101010	ˆ (Circumflex)	11100011
k	01101011	˜ (Tilde)	11100100
l	01101100	¯ (Macron)	11100101
m	01101101	˘ (Breve)	11100110
n	01101110	˙ (Superior dot)	11100111
o	01101111	¨ (Umlaut)	11101000
p	01110000	ˇ (Haček)	11101001
q	01110001	° (Angstrom)	11101010
r	01110010	⁀ (Ligature)	11101011
s	01110011	‿ (Ligature)	11101100
t	01110100	ʼ (High comma)	11101101
u	01110101	˝ (Double acute)	11101110
v	01110110	◡ (Candrabindu)	11101111
w	01110111	¸ (Cedilla)	11110000
x	01111000	ϲ (Right hook)	11110001
y	01111001	˳ (Underlying dot)	11110010
z	01111010	.. (Underlying dots)	11110011
Delete	01111111	ₒ (Underlying circle)	11110100
Ł (Polish L)	10100001	₌ (Double underscore)	11110101
Ø (Scandinavian O)	10100010	＿ (Underscore)	11110110
Đ	10100011	Ͻ (Left hook)	11110111
Þ (Icelandic thorn)	10100100	ₔ (Right cedilla)	11111000
Æ	10100101	― (Upadhmanīya)	11111001
Œ	10100110	⁀ (Double tilde)	11111010
´ (Mıagkiĭ Znak)	10100111	‿ (Double tilde)	11111011
· (Central dot)	10101000	ʼ (High, centered)	11111110
b (Musical flat)	10101001		
®	10101010		
±	10101011		
σ	10101100		
ν	10101101		
ʼ (Alif)	10101110		
ʻ (ʻAyn)	10110000		
ł (Polish l)	10110001		
ø	10110010		
đ	10110011		
Þ (Icelandic thorn)	10110100		
æ	10110101		
œ	10110110		

Numerical data may be represented alternatively in binary or floating point form in which case it is not coded character by character. Instead, each entire number is coded to occupy a fixed amount of storage space such as the size of a computer word, or double word, depending on the particular specified scheme of coding. This form of storage is the most convenient if arithmetic operations are to be performed on the stored numbers. Also, numbers stored on files in purely binary or floating point code may be read rapidly since no conversion of format is required. For example, the FORTRAN statement

```
READ(1)N, (B(I), I=1, N)
```

might be used to transfer a sequence of bits from a magnetic tape of disk record to internal memory without any conversion of the form in which the data are represented.

If the numerical data form only a small proportion of the entire data, it may be desirable to represent it in character form so that printing of records may be performed very simply without any knowledge of the position of the numbers within the data. In contrast, if numerical data forms a significant proportion of the record and is to be used in arithmetic computations, it may be more desirable to store it in a purely numerical code such as pure binary or floating point code.

3.3 Blocks, Records, and Fields

The data stored within computer-accessible files are grouped within blocks, which also may be termed physical records. When stored on magnetic tape the blocks are separated by record gaps. When files are read into computer memory only complete blocks are transferred, and if only part of a block is required it must be selected from the complete block within internal memory.

Associated with the input of each block of data from a file, there is an access time required to position the read–write mechanism to the beginning of the block. Whenever data are to be transferred from a file to internal memory, it is advisable to have the data contained in few blocks in order to reduce the total access times. Of course, large blocks require use of large amounts of internal memory for their storage. Although a large block takes longer to read than a short one, the additional time is often small in comparison to the access time.

It is usually convenient to regard the blocks as divided into records. The records, sometimes termed logical records to distinguish them from physical records, may be chosen to form a convenient grouping of data with respect to the information it contains. In contrast, the blocks or physical records are chosen to allow compact storage and fast access. For example, in a file that represents journal articles each record might contain the author names, title, and journal reference to a single article; whereas each block might contain a set of 10 records. To examine the information about the 953rd article it would be necessary to read the 96th block and the extract its 3rd record.

Within each record the data may be regarded as further divided into fields. Thus a record that describes a single journal article might consist of an author field, a title field, an abstract field, a keyword field, and so forth. It is sometimes convenient to regard some of the fields as further divided into subfields that may themselves be divided into subsubfields and so forth. Thus a keyword field might be subdivided into a set of fields each of which contains a single keyword.

It should be emphasized that files are read block by block, and that extraction of required records from any block is done through a program that operates on the content of a block that has first been transferred from an external file to a block of space, or buffer, contained in internal memory.

The program for extraction of records from blocks may be formulated to fit the particular file structure, or it may form part of the software of a particular operating system. In the latter event the file structure must conform to that supported by the operating system.

For example, the IBM operating system OS/360 and its successors contain the software for extraction of records from certain very simple file structures. In the OS/360 terminology a file may be designated as consisting of fixed length blocked (FB) records or variable length blocked (VB) records. The space required for storage of each eight-bit character is said to constitute one byte of storage. In FB records each block consists of the same number of fixed length records, and hence its length is a multiple of the record length. A file described as FB, LRECL=135, BLKSIZE = 1080 would have fixed length blocks of length 1080 bytes, each divided into eight records 135 bytes in length.

In VB records for OS/360 each block is of a length not exceeding a specified amount, and consists of as many variable length records as may be fitted into it without subdivision of records between successive blocks. The first 4 bytes of each record contain a number in binary form to indicate the length in bytes of the entire record including the first 4 bytes. The first 4 bytes of each block also contain a binary number that indicates the length in bytes of the entire block. A file described as VB, LRECL=40, BLKSIZE = 204 would have variable length blocks of length not exceeding 204 bytes; each block would contain a whole number of records each of a length not greater than 40 bytes. One block might be 204 bytes long and contain five records of length 40 bytes. Another block might be of length 194 bytes and contain six records of lengths 29, 40, 36, 40, 23, and 22 bytes, respectively. A further record of more than 10 bytes could not be contained in this block but could form the first record of the following block.

In the VB block just described, and containing records of length 29, 40, 36, 40, 23, and 22 bytes, there are 166 bytes used for the data and 28 used for the length indicators. Thus in order to be stored in this particular form of file the data in the six records is expanded by a factor of 194/166 = 1.17. In contrast, if each separate record were expanded into one of 36 bytes for storage within FB blocks of six records the expansion factor would be 1.30.

Under OS/360 a program to process blocked records may be written as if each record is a single block, and in VB records the first 4 bytes of each record are automatically skipped to locate the data. Thus the FORTRAN statements

```
      WRITE(1,5)(L(I), I=1, 6), (K(I), I=1, 10)
    5 FORMAT(6A3,/,10A4)
```

might be used to write two records in a block of a file declared to be VB, LRECL=44, BLKSIZE=884. The records will have the record lengths 22 and 44 bytes placed in their respective first 4 bytes. They may be read by a corresponding READ(1,5) statement provided the file to be read is declared to be VB, LRECL=44, BLKSIZE=884. If the same file were declared to be undefined (U) for input the same data could be retrieved from it by the FORTRAN statements

```
      READ(1, 5)(L(I), I=1, 6), (K(I), I=1, 10)
    5 FORMAT (8X, 6A3, 4X, 10A4)
```

that cause selection of the appropriate portions of the two records while ignoring both the block and the record length indicators.

In general, the file structuring of records within blocks supported by a particular operating system is not necessarily the most suitable for storage of files for information retrieval. It may be preferable to arrange the files so that each block may be treated as a complete entity, and the records, or fields within records, extracted by a program that operates on the whole block rather than on the component records. Choice of fixed length blocks avoids the necessity to include a block length indicator, but it usually means that either most blocks end with an empty portion or else provision must be made for inclusion of an indicator to specify when the final record of a block is to be continued at the beginning of the subsequent block. This is further illustrated in the following section.

3.4 Fixed and Variable Length Fields, Tags, and Directories

If records are divided into fields it may prove convenient for some fields to have the same length in all records. For example, if a six-character coden abbreviation is used for names of journals it may be placed as a six-character field at the beginning of each record that contains a reference to the particular journal.

Page numbers also may be placed in fixed length fields, but sufficient space must be allowed for pages such as 1124A. If volume numbers and dates are placed in fixed length fields then the fields must be of sufficient length to allow for the largest that may occur, or else provision should be made for inclusion of an exceptional data code to indicate that the relevant data exceed the field length and are located in a supplementary data field within another portion of the record.

In general, regardless of the care that is taken to estimate the maximum length of particular data fields, there will occur some pieces of data that exceed the estimated length. Hence, it is advisable to choose the fixed length fields of size sufficient for most, rather than all, of the data and to use supplementary fields for all data that exceed the chosen length.

An alternative to the introduction of supplementary fields is to add a further field of the same length whenever the data are too long to be contained in the single field. In this instance the first field must contain some indication that its data are continued in a subsequent field.

An alternative to the use of fixed length fields is to use variable length fields whose lengths vary from record to record and are specified through inclusion of length indicators. Addition of length indicators increases the field length, and this disadvantage should be weighed against that of having to choose the fixed length fields large enough to avoid the necessity for frequent inclusion of supplementary fields.

It may be desirable to place tags within certain fields in order to indicate the field type. For example, fields that contain author names, titles, keywords, and abstracts might begin with the three-character tag AUT, TIT, KEY, and ABS, respectively.

An alternative to the use of field-type tags and length indicators within fields is the inclusion of a directory within each record. The directory may indicate the position within the record at which various types of field begin. A missing field may be treated as one of zero length. Thus a directory that contains the numbers 20, 34, 107, 107, and 152 might signify that an author field begins at position 20, a title field begins at position 34, there is no abstract field, and the journal reference field begins at position 107 and ends at position 152.

```
7008  110463      000DC010665DS010665                           0690011001#END#
DATE                       S01/06/65
7008  110463      001DC010665DS010665                    1A     TUNGSTEN-T
ITANIUM-BORON METASTABLE PHASE DIAGRAM AT 1B      ROOM TEMPERATURE 2A
    ARIEL E 2B        BARTA J 2C        NIEDZWIEDZ S 3A      J LESS-COMMON MET
ALS, MAR. 1970, 20, --3--, 3B        199-206.
7008  110463      099DC010665DS010665                          6ATUNGSTEN, 6AT
ERNARY SYSTEMS 6BTITANIUM, 6BTERNARY SYSTEMS 6CBORON, 6CTERNARY SYSTEM
S 6DTERNARY SYSTEMS, 6DPHASES #STATE OF MATTER# 6EPHASE DIAGRAMS 6FSOL
ID SOLUBILITY
7008  110464      000DC010665DS010665                           0690011001#END#
DATE                       S01/06/65
7008  110464      001DC010665DS010665                    1A     SOLID SOLU
BILITY OF COSI2 IN BETA-FESI2 2A        HESSE J 2B        BUCKSCH R 3A       J
MAT SCI, MAR. 1970, 5, --3--, 272-273.
7008  110464      099DC010665DS010665                          6ACOBALT COMPOU
NDS, 6ASOLUBILITY 6BIRON COMPOUNDS, 6BSOLUBILITY 6CSILICIDES, 6CSOLUBI
LITY 6DSOLID SOLUBILITY 6ETHERMAL CONDUCTIVITY
7008  110465      000DC010665DS010665                           0690011001#END#
DATE                       S01/06/65
7008  110465      001DC010665DS010665                    1A     EFFECT OF
ORDERING ON THE SOLUBILITY OF HYDROGEN IN 1B        NICKEL-IRON ALLOYS 2A
    GOLTSOV V A 2B        GELD P V 2C        SIMAKOV YU P 2D        SHTEINBERG
M M 2E        VYKHODETS V B 3A        AKAD NAUK UKRAIN SSR METALLOFIZIKA, 1
968, --17--, 3B      92-94. RUSSIAN
7008  110465      099DC010665DS010665                          6ANICKEL BASE A
LLOYS, 6ASOLUBILITY 6BHYDROGEN, 6BSOLUBILITY 6CNICKEL, 6CSOLUBILITY 6D
ORDER DISORDER 6ESTOICHIOMETRY 6FSOLUBILITY
7008  110466      000DC010665DS010665                           0690011001#END#
DATE                       S01/06/65
7008  110466      001DC010665DS010665                    1A     MECHANISM
AND KINETICS OF THE FORMATION AND GROWTH 1B        OF INTERMETALLIC INTER
LAYERS IN WELDED JOINTS 1C        BETWEEN METALS OF DIFFERENT KINDS 2A
    LARIKOV L N 3A        AKAD NAUK UKRAIN SSR METALLOFIZIKA, 1969, --28--,
 3B      5-49. RUSSIAN
7008  110466      099DC010665DS010665                          6ACOPPER, 6APHA
SES #STATE OF MATTER# 6BALUMINUM, 6BPHASES #STATE OF MATTER# 6CIRON, 6
CPHASES #STATE OF MATTER# 6DSTAINLESS STEELS, 6DPHASES #STATE OF MATTE
R# 6EWELDMENTS, 6EPHASES #STATE OF MATTER# 6FINTERMETALLIC PHASES, 6FW
ELDING EFFECTS 6GKINETICS 6HDISSIMILAR METALS, 6HWELDING
7008  110467      000DC010665DS010665                          0 690011001#END#
DATE                       S01/06/65
7008  110467      001DC010665DS010665                    1A     NEW PHASES
IN THE SC-TI-O SYSTEM 2A        POKROVSKY B I 2B        MIKHAILOR YU YA 2C
    KOMISSAROVA L N 3A        DOKLADY AKAD NAUK SSSR, 11 FEB. 1970, 190,
 3B      --5--, 1117-1120. RUSSIAN
7008  110467      099DC010665DS010665                          6ASCANDIUM, 6AT
ERNARY SYSTEMS 6BTITANIUM, 6BTERNARY SYSTEMS 6COXYGEN, 6CTERNARY SYSTE
MS 6DTERNARY SYSTEMS, 6DPHASES #STATE OF MATTER# 6EPHASE DIAGRAMS
7008  110468      000DC010665DS010665                           0690011001#END#
DATE                       S01/06/65
7008  110468      001DC010665DS010665                    1A     STABILITY
OF INTERSTITIAL SOLID SOLUTIONS IN 1B        MOLYBDENUM 2A        AGEEV N V
2B        EGOSHINA S G 2C        MODEL M S 3A        DOKLADY AKAD NAUK SSSR, 11
 FEB. 1970, 190, --5--, 3B      1155-1158. RUSSIAN
7008  110468      099DC010665DS010665                          6AMOLYBDENUM BA
SE ALLOYS, 6ASOLUBILITY 6BINTERSTITIAL SOLUTIONS 6CTITANIUM, 6CALLOYIN
G ELEMENTS 6DCARBON, 6DALLOYING ELEMENTS 6EPHASE DECOMPOSITION, 6EALLO
YING EFFECTS 6FPHASE STABILITY 6GBRITTLENESS 6HCASTING DEFECTS
```

Figure 3.2.   Eighteen segments of the METADEX tape.

Table 3.5
Section Numbers, and Relevant Branches of Metallurgy, Used on the METADEX Tapes.

1.1	Constitution
1.2	Crystal properties
1.3	Lattice defects
1.4	Structural hardening
1.5	Physics of metals
1.6	Irradiation effects
2.1	Metallography
2.2	Testing and control
2.3	Analysis
3.1	Mechanical properties
3.2	Physical properties
3.3	Electrical and magnetic phenomena
3.4	Chemical and electromechanical properties
3.5	Corrosion
4.1	Ores and raw materials
4.2	Extraction and smelting
4.3	Refining and purification
4.4	Physical chemistry of extraction and refining
4.5	Ferrous alloy production
4.6	Nonferrous alloy production
5.1	Foundry
5.2	Working (forming)
5.3	Machining
5.4	Powder technology
5.5	Joining
5.6	Thermal treatment
5.7	Finishing
5.8	Metallic coating
6.1	Engineering components and structures
6.2	Composites
6.3	Electronic devices
7.1	General and nonclassified
7.2	Special publications

An example of a possible set of index main terms and subordinate terms is the following, which is in the last segment shown in Figure 3.2.

```
6A  MOLYBDENUM BASE ALLOYS, 6A SOLUBILITY
6B  INTERSTITIAL SOLUTIONS
6C  TITANIUM, 6C ALLOYING ELEMENTS
6D  CARBON, 6D ALLOYING ELEMENTS
6E  PHASE DECOMPOSITION, 6E ALLOYING EFFECTS
6F  PHASE STABILITY
6G  BRITTLENESS
6H  CASTING DEFECTS
```

3.6 Example of Fixed Length Tagged Fields—COMPENDEX Tape

The COMPENDEX (COMPuterized ENgineering inDEX) tapes are issued by Engineering Index, Inc.,[4] and contain information about published items whose abstracts are included in the publication *Engineering Index Monthly.*

Information on the tape relates to articles published in professional and trade journals, publications of engineering organizations, conference and symposium papers, books, and other types of articles that relate to engineering. About 6000 new items are included in each monthly issue of the tapes. The details include author names, titles, abstracts, subject headings, subheadings, and access words, chosen from the publication *Subject Headings for Engineering,* and citations to the appropriate journals or other sources. A set of CARD-A-LERT codes is included to refer to index cards issued by Engineering Index Inc.

The nine-track tape is divided into variable length blocks, which may contain up to 8016 bytes. Each block contains a 24-byte field followed by a set of fields of length 72 bytes. Within the 72-byte fields all data is in EBCDIC and may include both upper and lower case characters.

Each 24-byte field contains data as listed here:

Bytes 1, 2:	Block length in binary form.
3, 4:	Zero in binary form.
5, 6:	Block length—4 in binary form.
7, 8:	Zero in binary form.
9–20:	In character form: EIX, followed by two-digit year such as 71, followed by X, followed by two-digit month such as 09, followed by four-digit sequence number. e.g., EIX71X090006.
21:	Blank in EBCDIC.
22:	*Y,* or *N,* in EBCDIC to indicate that the abstract is, or is not, available on microfilm.
23–24:	The sequence number in binary form.

Each 72-byte field consists of a 3-byte tag followed by 69 bytes of data. The tags are chosen as shown in Table 3.6.

If any character within a 72-byte field is intended to represent a superscript it is preceded by two asterisks. Similarly, any character that is intended to represent a subscript is preceded by two slashes. Thus A^{27} is represented as $\underline{A}**2**7$ and C_6^3 is represented as $\underline{c}//6**3$.

[4] Engineering Index, Inc., 345 East 47th Street, New York, N.Y. 10017.

Table 3.6
Tags and Fields of the COMPENDEX Tape.

Tag	Field content
00ƀ	First title field.
ƀƀƀ	Subsequent title fields.
09ƀ	Subject heading, possibly followed by subheading. An Engineering Index number is in bytes 67–72.
10ƀ	Identification number repeated from bytes 9–20 of the 24-byte field.
15ƀ	Appears only on 1969 tapes, to include a CITE number.
201–299	Author fields. Each field contains one author name.
3ƀƀ	The Engineering Index number.
4ƀZ	First field of citation.
ƀƀƀ	Subsequent fields of citation.
4ƀ4	ASTM coden.
401	Affiliation of first author.
50ƀ	First abstract field
ƀƀƀ	Subsequent abstract fields. The last abstract field includes the Engineering Index number.
60ƀ	Subject heading, and subheading, as in field 09ƀ
610	CARD-A-LERT Code.
650–699	Access words.
750	First field of additional free language terms.
ƀƀƀ	Subsequent fields of free language terms.

3.7 Example of Fields with Noncharacter Tags—ERIC (AIM/ARM) Tape

The ERIC (Educational Resources Information Center) tapes, available from Leasco Systems and Research Corporation,[5] contain information about reports and journal articles relating to educational research. At the end of 1969 the tapes included 31,623 reports and 11,702 journal articles selected from over 500 journals. The number of new reports and journal articles added each month was approximately 900 and 1500, respectively.

The information on the ERIC tapes includes an identification number, the publication date, the title of the article, the author names, a set of descriptors each of one or more words, the number of pages, an abstract, and the name of the publisher. There also may be an address of the issuing body, and there is a statement of whether a microfilm or hard copy is available from ERIC. Some of the descriptors are preceded by an asterisk to indicate that they form major descriptors.

[5] Leasco Systems and Research Corporation, 4833 Rugby Avenue, Bethesda, Maryland 20014.

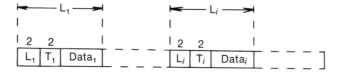

Figure 3.3 Arrangement of data in each record of the ERIC AIM/ARM tape.

The descriptors are chosen from the *Thesaurus of ERIC Descriptors,* which is available in printed form or on tape. This thesaurus contains main, use, broader, narrower, and related terms. At the end of 1969 it contained 6878 terms and was growing at the rate of about 30 terms each month.

The ERIC tape also contains additional subject terms, not in the ERIC thesaurus. Such subject terms are called identifiers.

The nine-track tape is divided into variable length blocks of up to 7000 bytes, whose records may contain up to 6996 bytes. The abstract contains EBCDIC data in both uppercase and lowercase. The remaining data consist of sequences of EBCDIC uppercase characters preceded by binary tags and field length indicators.

The AIM (Abstracts of Instructional Materials) and ARM (Abstracts of Research and Related Materials) tapes relate only to vocational and technical education, and are available from the ERIC Clearing House Center for Vocational and Technical Education.[6] Each record describes a single article, and is arranged in variable length fields as shown in Figure 3.3. The first two bytes of each field contain a binary number L_1 equal to the field length in bytes. The next two bytes of each field contain a binary number that constitutes a tag T_1 to identify the type of data stored in the remaining portion of the field. The relation between the tag and the field content is shown in Table 3.7. A printout of four records of the ERIC tape is shown in Figure 3.4.

3.8 Example of Tagged Fields and Subfields—SPIN Tape

The SPIN, initially SPIN/O, tapes issued by the American institute of Physics, contain information about articles published in various physics journals. The information includes keyword phrases, title, author names, location of authors, bibliography, abstract, and journal details.

[6] ERIC Clearing House Center for Vocational and Technical Education, Ohio State University, 1900 Kenney Road, Columbus, Ohio 4320.

```
□□□VT000282□A TRAINI
NG PROGRAM FOR VOCATIONAL AGRICU
LTURE IN WILDLIFE AND RECREATION
.□BURNS, VAN H., AND OTHERS□
□*CURRICULUM GUIDES; *VOCATIONA
L AGRICULTURE; *OFF FARM AGRICUL
TURAL OCCUPATIONS; *WILDLIFE MAN
AGEMENT; *RECREATION; GRADE 11;
GRADE 12; AGRICULTURAL PRODUCTIO
N; AGRICULTURAL ENGINEERING□M
F AVAILABLE IN VT-ERIC SET.□1
46P.□AIM FALL1970□Prepared
 in a 6-week curriculum workshop
 to develop training programs fo
r off-farm agricultural occupati
ons, this curriculum guide is fo
r use in planning and implementi
ng 11th-and 12th-grade training
programs in wildlife and recreat
ion. The 520-hour course is divi
ded into three general subject a
reas: applied agricultural mecha
nics, applied production agricul
ture, and applied business princ
iples and procedures basic to wi
ldlife and recreation. Some repr
esentative titles included in th
e 19 units under these three gen
eral headings are: (1) Small Eng
ines and Equipment, (2) Maintena
nce and Operation of Tractors an
d Allied Equipment, (3) Tool Sel
ection and Maintenance, (4) Irri
gation Systems, (5) Insect, Dise
ase, and Pest Control, (6) Game
and Fish Management, (7) Care of
 Plants and Soils, (8) Ornamenta
l Horticulture, (9) Wildlife and
 Recreation Communication, and (
10) Human Relations. Each unit p
rovides content, objective, comp
etencies to be developed, studen
t motivation, teaching outline a
```

```
nd suggestions, student activiti
es, references and teaching aids
, and evaluation. (AW)|□LOUIS
IANA STATE DEPT. OF EDUCATION, B
ATON ROUGE. VOCATIONAL EDUCATION
 DIV.;.LOUISIANA STATE UNIV., BA
TON ROU□□VT000378□
66□A SPECIALIZED COURSE OUTLI
NE FOR ADVANCED VOCATIONAL AGRIC
ULTURE STUDENTS IN FOREST PRODUC
TS PRODUCTION SALES AND SERVICE
.□RAWLS, BYRON F.□*CURRICU
LUM GUIDES; *VOCATIONAL AGRICULT
URE; *FORESTRY; *FORESTRY OCCUPA
TIONS; SALES OCCUPATIONS; SERVIC
E OCCUPATIONS□ALABAMA□MF A
VAILABLE IN VT-ERIC SET.□14P.
□AIM FALL1970□Prepared by
a subject matter specialist, thi
s course outline is designed to
prepare advanced vocational agri
culture students for employment
in a forestry occupation. Teachi
ng units, providing content, lab
oratory experiences, and referen
ces, are given for: (1) Orientat
ion to Forest Occupations, (2) S
upervised Practice Program, (3)
Forestry in Alabama, (4) Forest
Trees, (5) Protecting the Forest
, (6) Measurements in Forestry,
(7) Cuttings, (8) Reforestation,
 (9) Marketing Forest Products,
(10) Multiple Use of Forests, (1
1) Agricultural Mechanics, and (
12) Leadership. A list of sugges
ted references is included. (AW)
|□ALABAMA STATE DEPT. OF EDUC
ATION, MONTGOMERY. AGRICULTURAL
EDUCATION SERVICE□□VT00037
9□ MAR66□FORESTRY PRODUCT
ION SALES AND SERVICES (A STUDEN
T STUDY GUIDE. AGRIBUSINESS EDUC
```

Figure 3.4. Four records of the ERIC tape.

The nine-track tape file is divided into variable length blocks whose lengths do not exceed 3520 characters. All data are stored in EBCDIC character form to include representation of both uppercase and lowercase. The first eight characters in each block are not used for storage of data. Some of the blocks constitute issue records that are used to describe a particular issue of a particular journal. Each issue block is followed by one or more blocks that are designated as article records. Each article record contains data relevant to one of the articles published in the journal issue described in the previous issue record.

ATION SERIES.⬛RAWLS, BYRON F.
⬛*STUDY GUIDES; *VOCATIONAL A
GRICULTURE; *FORESTRY; *FORESTRY
OCCUPATIONS; *SALES OCCUPATIONS
; SERVICE OCCUPATIONS; AGRICULTU
RAL PRODUCTION⬛MF AVAILABLE~I
N VT-ERIC SET.⬛16P.⬛AIM FA
LL1970⬛Prepared by a subject
matter specialist, this study gu
Ide Is for use by students not e
nrolled In specialized courses o
f Instruction In forestry. Conte
nts Include study questions, lea
rning activities, and suggested
references for the following top
Ics: (1) Forestry In Alabama, (2
) Forest Trees, (3) Protecting t
he Forest, (4) Measurements In F
orestry, (5) Cutting, (6) Refore
station, (7) Marketing Forest Pr
oducts, and (8) Multiple Use of
Forests. (AW)I⬛ALABAMA STATE
DEPT. OF EDUCATION, MONTGOMERY.
AGRICULTURAL EDUCATION SERVICE⬛
⬛JVT000380⬛ 66⬛JA S
PECIALIZED COURSE OUTLINE FOR AD
VANCED VOCATIONAL AGRICULTURE ST
UDENTS IN AGRICULTURAL SUPPLY, S
ALES AND SERVICES.⬛GREEN, H.W
.⬛*CURRICULUM GUIDES; *VOCATI
ONAL AGRICULTURE; *AGRICULTURAL
SUPPLIES; *AGRICULTURAL SUPPLY O
CCUPATIONS; *SALES OCCUPATIONS;
SERVICE OCCUPATIONS; SECONDARY G
RADES⬛MF AVAILABLE IN VT-ERIC
SET.⬛17P.⬛AIM FALL1970⬛
⬛Prepared by a district supervis
or of vocational agriculture, th
Is curriculum guide Is for use I
n conducting a specialized cours
e In agricultural supplies, sale
s and services for advanced voca

tional agriculture students. Obj
ectives of the course are to tra
In students for future employmen
t In the field, to aid students
In developing the personality tr
aits and abilities needed In agr
Icultural sales and services, an
d to assist students In developi
ng a sense of responsibility thr
ough leadership activities In Th
e Future Farmers of America (FFA
). Some of the topics covered, i
n outline form, are: (1) career
opportunities, (2) leadership tr
aining (FFA), (3) operation and
maintenance of small power tools
and equipment, (4) shop skills
needed for sales and service per
sonnel, (5) home and farm electr
Ification, (6) agricultural sale
smanship, (7) agricultural busin
ess procedures, (8) livestock fe
eds, fertilizers, and crop, lawn
, and garden seeds sales and ser
vice, and (9) agricultural chemi
cals sales and services. Lists o
f Instructional materials and su
pplies are also provided. (AW)I⬛
⬛ALABAMA STATE DEPT. OF EDUCAT
ION, MONTGOMERY. AGRICULTURAL ED
UCATION SERVICE⬛ JVT00 0581⬛
⬛ MAR66⬛AGRICULTURAL SUPPLI
ES, SALES AND SERVICES (A STUDEN
T STUDY GUIDE). AGRIBUSINESS EDU
CATION SERIES.⬛GREEN, H.W.⬛
⬛*STUDY GUIDES; *VOCATIONAL AGRI
CULTURE; *AGRICULTURAL SUPPLY OC
CUPATIONS; *SALES OCCUPATIONS; *
SERVICE OCCUPATIONS; AGRICULTURA
L SUPPLIES; EQUIPMENT; MARKETING
; MERCHANDISING⬛MF AVAILABLE
IN VT-ERIC SET.⬛21P.⬛AIM F

Figure 3.4. (*Continued*)

Table 3.7

Relation between Binary Tag and Field Content of the ERIC AIM/ARM Tape.

Binary tag (in hexadecimal)	Field content
11	VT (vocational and technical) identification number.
17	Publication date.
1A	Title.
1B	Author(s).
23	Descriptors.
24	Identifier.
25	Microfilm, or hard copy, availability from ERIC.
26	Number of pages.
2B	AIM date.
2C	Abstract.
31	Address of issuing body.
80	Publisher.

For example, a set of eight consecutive blocks might have the form

IB1,   A1,   A2,   B1,   C1,   C2,   C3,   IB2

in which IB1 denotes a one-block issue record that specifies Issue No. 2 of
Volume 44 of the *Journal of Chemical Physics*. The first article in this
issue is described by the article record A1, A2, which uses two
blocks. The second article is described in the article record B1, which
uses one block; and the third article is described in the article record
C1, C2, C3, which consists of three blocks. The issue block IB2
specifies a further journal issue whose articles are described in the subsequent article records.

Each issue record begins with the four-character tag !ISS and each
article record begins with the four-character tag !ART. These and all
other tags are followed by a single blank. The second, third, and subsequent blocks of each issue record begin with five blank characters.

Each issue record is divided into a set of fields, each of whose first four
characters contains a tag chosen from among the *tags listed in Table 3.8.
The fields tagged by *JOU, *STR, *VOL, and *DAT are further subdivided into subfields that are tagged by # tags as listed in Table 3.8. Some
fields and subfields may be absent from some records.

Table 3.8
Fields and Subfields within Issue Records of the SPIN/O Tapes.

*Tag	#Tag	Field content
*ISR		Nine-character month, day, year, hyphen, accession number within that date. (mmddyy-nn)
*RSR		The six characters OOOOON.
*JOU		Journal details arranged with #tagged subfields.
	#COD	Five-character ASTM coden.
	#STN	Standard name.
	#CAB	Canonical abbreviation.
	#SES	Serial series.
	#SEP	Parallel series.
*STR		Structure details arranged within #tagged subfields.
	#SUP	Supplement.
	#PAR	Part.
	#SCT	Section.
*VOL		Volume details arranged within #tagged subfields.
	#VNO	Volume number.
	#NUM	Issue number.
*DAT		Issue date arranged within #tagged subfields.
	#MOD	Four-character month and day. (mmdd)
	#YEA	Last two digits of year.

The article records are divided into fields that contain *tags and that are further divided into subfields with #tags, subfields with ¢tags, and subfields with %tags. The tagging scheme is shown in Table 3.9.

If any characters within a field are intended to represent superscripts they are preceded by the symbol < and are followed by either $ or a blank. Thus <12$C is used to represent ^{12}C. Similarly, subscripts are preceded by the symbol > and are followed by either $ or a blank.

Greek letters, the 10 special symbols ! *#¢%@><$?, and other characters not representable during preparation of the tape, are spelled in full between two pairs of the double characters =(and)=. Thus the symbol β is represented on the tape as =(beta)=, and $\geq$ is represented by =(greater-or-equal-to)=. Consequently, if either of the pairs of characters =(or)= are to be used other than to contain a spelled term they must themselves be spelled and placed within =(and)=.

A listing of three consecutive records of the SPIN/O tape is shown in Figure 3.5. The first is an issue record tagged by !ISS and the other two are article records tagged by !ART.

A brief discussion of the value of the data stored on the SPIN tapes has been given by Jerome[7] who made a comparison with the CA Condensates tapes issued by the Chemical Abstracts Service. The two tapes contain references to many of the same articles but the stored fields are very different in form and content.

3.9 Example of a Directory—CAIN Tape

The CAIN tapes are issued by the United States National Agricultural Library (NAL) and contain information about books and periodical articles relating to agriculture. The information includes author names, title, a subject classification code, and journal or publisher details. It may also include subject terms, an abstract, patent information, author biographic data, and other details. For each document there is an indication of whether it appears in the printed NAL New Book Shelf List, the *Bibliography of Agriculture* (BAL), the *Pesticides Documentation Bulletin Publication* (PIC), or the *Agricultural Economics* publication (AGEC).

The nine-track tape file contains blocks of variable length up to 3998 bytes. All data are stored in uppercase EBCDIC characters, and an asterisk is sometimes used to precede a letter whose capitalization is to be emphasized, as in MC*LAUGHLIN or *N. *S. *W. or *KANSAS.

[7] S. Jerome, ''Comparative study of the coverage of physics journals by two computerized data bases—SPIN (Searchable and Physics Information Notes) and CAC (Chemical Abstracts Condensates),'' *Information Storage and Retrieval* 9(1973): 449–455.

Table 3.9
Fields and Subfields within Article Records of the SPIN/O Tapes.

*Tag	#Tag	¢Tag	%Tag	Field content
*ISR				*tags and #tags as in Table 3.1 except that
.				the *RSR field contains a six-character:
.				article number, zero, physical record number, Y or
.				N. (aaaOpY)
				Y, or N, indicates that the article record does,
*DAT				or does not, extend to further blocks.
*PAG				Page subfields.
	#PNO			Page number.
	#SNO			Sequence number on page.
*CLS				Classification subfields.
	#CLA			AIP classification number (optional).
	#DAN			Document analysis number subfields.
		¢DTP		Document type.
				E for experimental.
				T for theoretical.
				R for review.
				E/T for experimental and theoretical.
				T/E for theoretical and experimental.
		¢DKD		Document kind.
				L for letter.
				C for communication.
				N for note.
		¢DNO		Document number group subfields.
			%DNI	Individual document numbers.
	#JXN			Journal index number subfields.
		¢JTP		Journal index type.
		¢JKD		Journal index kind.
		¢JNO		Journal index number group subfields.
			%JNI	Individual journal index numbers.
*KWP				Keyword phrases subfields.
	#KWI			Keyword phrase.
*TIT				Title.
*AUT				Author subfields.
	#AGR			Author group subfields.
		¢AUI		Author (individual) subfields.
			%AUF	First and/or middle name or initial string.
			%AUS	Surname.
			%AUP	Post-particle string.
		¢AUC		Corporate author.
*LOC				Location of authors subfields.
	#LGR			Location group for particular author group subfields.
		¢LOI		Location (individual).
*CIN				Total number of citations.
*BIB				Bibliography subfields.

Table 3.9 (*Continued*)

*Tag	#Tag	¢Tag	%Tag	Field content
	#FON			Footnote number (as it appears).
	#CIN			Citation number (sequence number).
	#BAU			Bibliography authors subfields.
		¢BAI		Bibliography author (individual) subfields.
			%BUF	First and/or middle name or initial string.
			%BUS	Surname.
			%BUP	Post-particle string.
		¢BAC		Corporate author.
	#JOU			Journal (bibliography) subfields.
		¢COD		Coden.
		¢SES		Serial series (bibliography).
		¢SEP		Parallel series (bibliography).
	#STR			Structure (bibliography) subfields.
		¢SUP		Supplement.
		¢PAR		Part (bibliography).
		¢SCT		Section (bibliography).
	#VOL			Volume (bibliography) subfields.
		¢VNO		Volume number (bibliography).
		¢NUM		Issue number (bibliography).
	#PAG			Page number (bibliography).
	#DAT			Date (bibliography).
	#TIT			Title (bibliography).
	#PUN			Publisher's name.
	#PUL			Publisher's location.
	#PUP			Publisher's page number.
	#PUD			Publisher's date.
*ABS				Abstract subfields.
	#ABP			Abstract paragraph.

Each block describes a single document item, and consists of a set of fixed fields of total length 68 bytes, followed by a directory of length 85 bytes, followed by a set of fixed length codes of total length 20 bytes, followed by a variable number of fixed length fields designated as segments and each of length 65 bytes.

The first 68 bytes in each record contain fixed fields arranged as in Figure 3.6 in which the meaning of the abbreviations is as listed here:

Cre.Date: Year record was created.
ID: For monographs: 9, followed by NAL accession number. For serials: Arbitrary.
Class Code: Six-digit subject classification code.
LANG: 0 (or 1) if text in (not in) English, followed by 1 (or 0) if translation available (not available), followed by a three-character abbreviation of the language if other than English.

!ISS *ISR 010570-10 *RSR 00000N *JOU #COD SPHJA #STN Soviet Physics-Jo
urnal of Experimental and Theoretical Physic s #CAB Sov. Phys.JETP *VO
L #VNO 29 #NUM 3 *DAT #MOD 0900 #YEA 69

!ART *ISR 010570-10 *RSR 00100N *JOU #COD SPHJA #STN Soviet Physics-Jo
urnal of Experimental and Theoretical Physic s #CAB Sov. Phys.JETP *VO
L #VNO 29 #NUM 3 *DAT #MOD 0900 #YEA 69 *PAG #PNO 391 #SEQ 1 *TIT Elec
tron Heating in a Plasma at the Cyclotron Frequency in an Inhomogeneou
s Magnetic Field *AUT #AGR ¢AUI %AUF D. K. %AUS Akulina ¢AUI %AUF A. P
. %AUS Bykov ¢AUI %AUF S. E. %AUS Grebenshchikov ¢AUI %AUF A. V. %AUS
Ivanov ¢AUI %AUF Yu. I. %AUS Nechaev ¢AUI %AUF I. S. %AUS Shitnikova ¢
AUI %AUF I. S. %AUS Shpigel' *LOC #LGR ¢LOI P. N. Lebedev Physics Inst
itute, USSR Academy of Sciences *CIN 10 *BIB #FON 1 #CIN 0010 #BAU ¢BA
I %BUF M. C. %BUS Becker ¢BAI %BUF R. A. %BUS Dandl ¢BAI %BUF H. O. %B
US Eason ¢BAI %BUF A. C. %BUS Englund ¢BAI %BUF R. J. %BUS Kerr ¢BAI %
BUF W. B. %BUS Ard #JOU ¢COD NUFSA #VOL ¢VNO NONE ¢NUM 1 #PAG 345 #DAT
1962 *BIB #FON 2 #CIN 0020 #BAU ¢BAI %BUF V. E. %BUS Golant ¢BAI %BUF
B. V. %BUS D'yachenko ¢BAI %BUF K. M. %BUS Novak ¢BAI %BUF K. A. %BUS
Podushnikova #JOU ¢COD SPTPA #VOL ¢VNO 11 #PAG 756 #DAT 1966 *BIB #FO
N 3 #CIN 0030 #BAU ¢BAI %BUF V. V. %BUS Alikaev ¢BAI %BUF V. M. %BUS G
lagolev ¢BAI %BUF S. A. %BUS Morozov #TIT 2-nd International Conferenc
e on Plasma Physics and Controlled Nuclear Fusion Research #PUL Culham
#PUP Paper 21/140 #PUD 1965 *BIB #FON 4 #CIN 0040 #BAU ¢BAI %BUF M. S
. %BUS Berezhetskii ¢BAI %BUF S. E. %BUS Grebenshchikov ¢BAI %BUF N. M
. %BUS Zverev ¢BAI %BUF I. S. %BUS Shpigel #JOU ¢COD Proc. Phys. Inst.
Acad. Sci #VOL ¢VNO 32 #PAG 20 #DAT 1966 *BIB #FON 5 #CIN 0050 #BAU ¢
BAI %BUF D. K. %BUS Akulina ¢BAI %BUF G. M. %BUS Batanov ¢BAI %BUF M.
S. %BUS Berezhetskii ¢BAI %BUF S. E. %BUS Grebenshchikov ¢BAI %BUF M.
S. %BUS Rabinovich ¢BAI %BUF I. S. %BUS Shitnikova ¢BAI %BUF I. S. *BU
S Shpigel' #TIT 2-nd International Conference on Plasma Physics and Co
ntrolled Nuclear Fusion Research #PUL Culham #PUP Paper 21/244 #PUD 19
65 *BIB #FON 6 #CIN 0060 #BAU ¢BAI %BUF D. K. %BUS Akulina #JOU ¢COD S
PTPA #VOL ¢VNO 11 #PAG 482 #DAT 1966 *BIB #FON 7 #CIN 0070 #BAU ¢BAI %
BUF V. N. %BUS Budnikov ¢BAI %BUF N. I. %BUS Vinogradov ¢BAI %BUF V. E
. %BUS Golant ¢BAI %BUF A. A. %BUS Obukhov #JOU ¢COD SPTPA #VOL ¢VNO 1
2 #PAG 610 #DAT 1966 *BIB #FON 8 #CIN 0080 #BAU ¢BAI %BUF L. S. %BUS B
ogdankevich ¢BAI *BUF A. A. %BUS Rukhadze #TIT Phys. Inst. Acad. Sci.
Preprint No. 72 *PUD 1968 *BIB #FON 9 #CIN 0090 #BAU ¢BAI %BUF A. P. %
BUS Popryadukhin *JOU ¢COD AENGA #VOL ¢VNO 18 #PAG 96 #DAT 1965 *BIB #
FON 10 #CIN 0100 #BAU ¢BAI %BUF R. A. %BUS Ellis ¢BAI %BUF L. P. %BUS
Goldberg ¢BAI %BUF J. G. %BUS Gorman #JOU ¢COD PFLDA #VOL ¢VNO 3 #PAG
468 #DAT 1960 *ABS #ABP Results on experiments concerned with electron
cyclotron heating of a plasma in the L-1 stellarator are reported. Th
e absorption conditions, the decay length for the microwave energy, an
d the plasma lifetime have been investigated as functions of the magne
tic field and the applied microwave energy.It is shown that the plasma
lifetime is inversely proportional to the absorbed microwave energy.

!ART *ISR 010570-10 *RSR 00200N *JOU #COD SPHJA #STN Soviet Physics-Jo
urnal of Experimental and Theoretical Physic s #CAB Sov. Phys.JETP *VO
L #VNO 29 #NUM 3 *DAT #MOD 0900 #YEA 69 *PAG #PNO 396 #SEQ 1 *CLS #DAN
¢DTP T/E ¢DNO %DNI SRMJAW %DNI SRMGAN %DNI SRLPAB *KWP #KWI (Ba>0.2$S
r>0.8$)>3$Zn>2$Fe>24$O>41 #KWI Magnetization curves #KWI anisotropy co
nstants *TIT Critical Fields in a Hexagonal Strontium Ferrite *AUT #AG
R ¢AUI %AUF D. G. %AUS Sannikov ¢AUI %AUF T. M. %AUS Perekalina *LOC #
LGR ¢LOI Institute of Crystallography, Academy of Sciences, U.S.S.R *C
IN 2 *BIB #FON 1 #CIN 0010 #BAU ¢BAI %BUF J. %BUS Smit ¢BAI %BUF H. P.
J. %BUS Wijn #TIT Ferrites #PUN Wiley #PUL New York #PUD 1959 *BIB #F
ON 2 #CIN 0020 #BAU ¢BAI %BUF L. %BUS Neel #JOU ¢COD BUPSA #VOL ¢VNO 2
1 #PAG 889 #DAT 1957 *ABS #ABP The magnetic properties possessed by si
ngle crystals of the hexagonal ferrite (Ba>0.2$Sr>0.8$)>3$Zn>2$Fe>24$O
>41 are investigated. Magnetization curves which exhibit the existence
of critical fields are measured at different temperatures. The temper
ature dependences of the anisotropy constants are measured. Magnetizat
ion curves are calculated using the model of two magnetic sublattices
with a weak exchange interaction, and are found to be in good agreemen
t with experiment.

Figure 3.5. Three records of the SPIN/O tape.

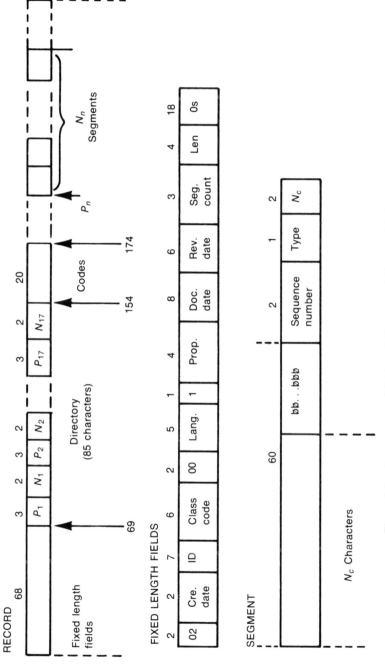

Figure 3.6. Arrangement of fields and directory within each block of the CAIN tape.

67

Prop:	0000. May be used later for a proprietory restriction code.
Doc.Date:	Date of document publication (YYYYMMDD).
Rev.Date:	Date record was created or last revised (YYMMDD).
Seg.Count:	Number of fixed length segments in the record.
Len:	Length of record in bytes = 173 + 65(Seg.Count).

The fixed fields are followed by a directory of 17 entries each of which contains a three-byte number followed by a two-byte number; they specify, respectively, the number of the first segment, and the total number of segments, used to contain the associated data. Thus a directory of 00203 signifies that the associated data is contained in the second, third, and fourth segments. A directory of 00000 signifies the absence of any associated data. The type of data associated with the Nth directory entry is as shown here where N ranges from 1 to 17:

$N =$ 1: New book shelf descriptive information.

2: Document title.

3: Personal author names and descriptive data, each author name beginning in a new segment (e.g., INGRAM, W R)

4: Corporate authors.

5: Author biographic data.

6: Abbreviated journal title or imprint data. (e.g., J EXP BIOL)

7: Volume, issue, and page numbers. (e.g., 34(4):464–467 or 35(1):15–26. @MAP.)

8: Date of document publication. (e.g., SEPT 1969 or JUNE 23, 1968)

9: Bytes   1–20: NAL call number. (e.g., 99.0 F7652S)

            21–28: Book catalogue citation number.

            29–36: B of A citation number (e.g., 70031052)

            37–44: PDB citation number.

            45–52: AGEC citation number.

10: Subject terms or phrases, each beginning in a new segment. The subject terms may be of four types designated by the letters P, S, T, or G.

12: Information relating to patents, support grants, analyses, contracts, or reports, and designated respectively be the letters P, S, A, C, or R.

13: Series statement.

14: Abstract or extract.

15: Tracings.

16: 00000. Reserved for future use.

17: Nonvocabulary cross references.

Following the directory there is a 20-byte field that contains a sequence of codes chosen as indicated in Table 3.10.

Table 3.10

Codes in the 20-byte Field of the CAIN Records.

Position	Code
Bytes 1,2:	00 if NAL main entry code is personal author.
	20 if NAL main entry code is title.
	30 if NAL main entry code is corporate author.
	85 if NAL main entry code is tracings.
Byte 3:	0 (or 1) according as title is (or is not) a tracing.
Byte 4:	0,1,2 according as document is a journal article, monograph, or serial.
Bytes 5–7:	Three-character abbreviation for NAL filing location of the document.
Byte 8:	Cataloguing users code:
	0 if record does not require a card.
	2 (or 1) if catalogue card required with (or without) subject terms.
	9 if record not to be printed in NAL catalogue or publication.
Byte 9:	NBS users code:
	1, 2, or 3, to indicate section of entry in NAL New Book Shelf List.
	0 if not to be entered.
Byte 10:	B of A users code:
	2 (or 1) indicates an entry in B of A with (or without) subject terms.
	0 if not an entry in B of A.
Byte 11:	PIC users code:
	0, 1, or 2, as in byte 10 but referring to the PIC.
Byte 12:	0, 1, or 2, as in byte 10 but referring to the AGEC.
Bytes 13–19:	0000000
Byte 20:	Code to indicate the source of the document used to provide the stored information.

Each fixed length segment of length 65 bytes contains data left-justified within its first 60 bytes. Bytes 61, 62 contain a sequence number. For example, if there are three authors the corresponding three segments contain sequence numbers 01, 02, and 03. Sequence numbers in segments that are used for titles, alternate titles, and translated titles, have sequence numbers in the respective ranges 01–15, 21–35, and 41–55. Secondary corporate author segments have sequence numbers in the range 11–14. Each subject term may use up to three segments; continued segments repeat the previous segment number.

For subject term, or patent (etc.), segments the 63rd byte contains one of the type description characters P, S, T, G, A, C, or R.

The last two bytes in each segment, except NAL call numbers segments, contain a count of the number of bytes used to store the data exclusive of right-hand blanks. Thus a sequence of two title segments might contain

```
OBSERVATIONS ON THE NODULATION STATUS OF RAINFOREST LEGUMI- 01059
```

and

```
NOUS SPECIES IN *AMAZONIA AND *GUYANA.                    02038
```

In NAL call number segments the count that appears in the last two bytes is the length of the NAL call number.

A listing of seven records of the CAIN tapes is shown in Figure 3.7. Details of preparation of the data, editing, and updating are described by Van Dyke.[8]

3.10 Example of a Tapped Directory—MARC Tape

The MARC (MAchine Readable Catalogue) tapes, issued by the U.S. Library of Congress, contain cataloguing data for monographs catalogued by the U.S. Library of Congress. The tapes are available to libraries that wish to use the data for their own cataloguing and other purposes. Provision is made for inclusion of many different attributes of which only a few are assigned values for any particular monograph.

The MARC tapes are available on either seven- or nine-track tape. The nine-track tapes are written in the expanded ASCII code as listed in Table 3.4. This code allows both uppercase and lowercase characters as well as many special symbols. The file is divided into variable length blocks whose lengths do not exceed 2048 bytes. The blocks are grouped in sets of one or more to form what are designated as logical records. Each logical record contains a monograph description relevant to a single monograph.

The discussion in the present section is directed toward an explanation of the directory structure and general organization of the file. Complete details are given in the MARC Manuals.[9]

To the beginning of the first logical record of the file there is attached an 80-character volume header label (VHL), followed by an 80-character file header label (FHL), followed by a one-byte tape mark (TM) that is set to be 00010011. To the last logical record of the file there is appended a similar tape mark, followed by an 80-character end of file label (EFL),

[8] V. J. Van Dyke, and N. L. Ayer, "Multipurpose cataloging and indexing system (CAIN) at the National Agricultural Library," *Journal of Library Automation* 5(1972): 21–29.

[9] MARC Manuals Used by the Library of Congress. Prepared by the Information Systems Office, Library of Congress, 2nd. edition. Information Science and Automation Division, American Library Association, Chicago, 1970.

[____]027090000018500000000   10000196903007003130060563000000000000
000000000000010100201000000000000301004010050100601000000000000000000000
0000000000000000000000000   00100000000000IRRIGATION IN THE *HUNTER *VA
LLEY, *N.*S.*W.   01044MC*MAHON, T T
                         01013AUSTRALIAN INST AGR SCI J
                    0102535(1):15-26. @MAP.
               01018MAR 1969
          0100823 AU74   70007960
     01007[____]027090000024500000010JAP10000196800007003200070628000000
000000000000000000010200301000000000000040100501006010070100000000000000
0000000000000000000000000000001   0010000000000JIH-PEN LIN YEH HSI PA
O KAO.   01028REPORT OF INVESTIGATION AND
  PRACTICE OF FORESTRY IN *JAPAN 41058K'ANG, T J
                    01010TAIPEI, JAPAN
               0101332 @P.
          010061968
     0100499.9 F7652S   70031052
     01011[____]027090000037000000000   10000196909007003130070628000
00000000000000000000010100202000000000000040100501006010070100000000000
0000000000000000000000000000000000000   0010000000000ORCHID GENERA, ILLUS
TRATED. *X.   01031SHEEHAN, T
                    01010SHEEHAN, M
                    02010AMER ORCHID SOC BULL
               0102038(9):784-785.
          01014SEPT 1969
     0100980 AM329   70006826
     01008[____]027090000040500000000   10000196800007007150060563 0
000000000000000000000001010000000201000000301004010050100601000000000
00000000000000000000000000000000000001   0010000000000ANNUAL REPORT FOR
THE YEAR 1967--68   01035QUEENSLAND. DEPT. @OF A
GRICULTURE   01033BRISBANE
               0100835 @P.
          010061968
     0100499.9 0312   70034873
     01009[____]027090000052000000000   100001969070070031300
050498000000000000000000000000000000010100000000000000000201003010040100
5010000000000000000000000000000000000000000   0010000000000SELECTING T
HE 1968 ANIMAL HOSPITAL OF THE YEAR.   01047VET ECON
               0100810(7):25.
          01009JULY 1969
          0100941.8 V6458   700
02578   01010[____]027090000062000000000   10000196
9080070031300605630000000000000000000000000000000010100201000000000003010040
10050100601000000000000000000000000000000000000000   001000000000
0MASTITIS LOSSES.   01016DOBB
INS, C N   01012MOD VET P
RACT   0101350(9):38-41.
               01012AUG 1969
          0100841.8 N812
     70001533   01009[____]027090000072000000000   1
0000196908007003130070628000000000000000000000000000001020030100000000000
40100501006010070100000000000000000000000000000000000000000   00100
00000000ANIMAL HOSPITAL GROUP COMMUNICATION: AN INTEGRAL PART OF THE01
060DIAGNOSTIC PROCESS.   02019AN
TELYES, J   01011MOD VET
PRACT   0101350(9):42-46.
               01012AUG 1969
          0100841.8 N812
     70001197   01009[____]

Figure 3.7. A block of seven records of a copy of the CAIN tape arranged in VB format. The rectangles contain the record and block lengths in binary, and are not printed.

followed by two tape marks. Thus the arrangement of the file in logical records is as follows where Mon denotes a monograph description

(VHL, FHL, TM, Mon) (Mon) (Mon) . . . (Mon) (Mon, TM, EFL, TM, TM).

Each monograph description contains a 24-character leader, followed by a record directory, followed by a one-byte field terminator (FT) that is set to be 00011110, followed by a set of "control fields," followed by a set of variable length fields, as shown in Figure 3.8. The difference between the control fields and the variable fields is that the latter contain internal tags to indicate the position of subfields. Each control field, and each variable field, contains a field terminator as its last byte, except that in the last variable field the field terminator is replaced by a record terminator (RT) set equal to 00011101.

The first 5 bytes of the leader are used to store the record length, and the 13–17th bytes are used to store a base address (B) that indicates the position in the record at which the set of control fields begins.

Each entry in the record directory contains a three-byte tag T_i to indicate the corresponding attribute, a four-byte length L_i to indicate the length of the corresponding field, and a five-byte pointer P_i to indicate the position of the beginning of the field with respect to the base address B.

A directory tag of 001 identifies a control field that contains a "control number" that usually is set equal to the LC card number. A directory tag of 008 identifies a control field of length 40 characters that are set as follows:

Character positions	Content
0–5	Date entered on file.
6	Type of publication date code.
7–10	Date 1.
11–14	Date 2.
15–17	Country of publication code.
18–21	Illustration codes.
22	Intellectual level code.
23	Form of reproduction code.
24–27	Form of content codes.
28	Government publication indicator.
29	Conference or meeting indicator.
30	Festschrift indicator.
31	Index indicator.
32	Main entry in body of entry indicator.
33	Fiction indicator.
34	Biography code.
35–37	Language code.
38	Modified record indicator.
39	Cataloging source code.

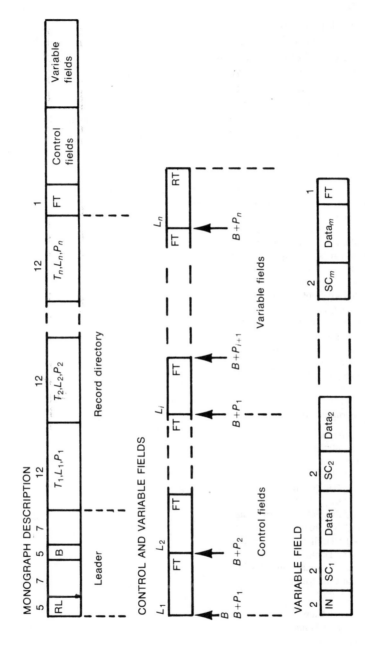

Figure 3.8. Arrangement of fields within records of the MARC tapes.

   Directory tags whose values are in the range 010 to 999 identify variable
fields as listed in Table 3.11. Each variable field begins with a pair of
one-character indicators that may be used to classify the field content.
Within the variable fields there are subfields each of which begins with a
two-byte tag, or subfield code, that consists of 00011111 followed by a
lowercase alphabetic character. The allowed values, and meanings, of the
subfield codes depend on the field attribute. Throughout the present
section the value 00011111 will be denoted by $.

Table 3.11
Directory Tags in the Range 010–840 as used on the MARC Tape.

Control Numbers
*0 1 0 LC Card Number
*0 1 1 Linking LC Card Number
 0 1 5 National Bibliography Number
*0 1 6 Linking NBN
*0 1 7 U.S. Copyright Number
 0 2 0 Standard Book Number
*0 2 1 Linking SBN
 0 2 5 Overseas Acquisitions Number
*0 2 6 Linking OAN Number
*0 3 5 Local System Number
*0 3 6 Linking Local Number
 0 4 0 Cataloguing Source
 0 4 1 Languages
*0 4 2 Search Code
*0 4 3 Geographic Area Code

Knowledge Numbers
 0 5 0 LC Call Number
 0 5 1 Copy Statement
 0 6 0 NLM Call Number
 0 7 0 NAL Call Number
*0 7 1 NAL Copy Statement
*0 7 2 NAL Subject Category Number
*0 8 0 UDC Number
*0 8 1 BNB Classification Number
 0 8 2 Dewey Decimal Classification No.
*0 8 6 Supt. of Documents Classification
*0 9 0 Local Call Number

Main Entry
1 0 0 Personal Name
1 1 0 Corporate Name
1 1 1 Conference or Meeting
1 3 0 Uniform Title Heading

Supplied Titles
2 4 0 Uniform Title
2 4 1 Romanized Title
*2 4 2 Translated Title

Title Paragraph
2 4 5 Title
2 5 0 Edition Statement
2 6 0 Imprint

Collation
3 0 0 Collation
3 5 0 Bibliographic Price
*3 6 0 Converted Price

Series Notes
4 0 0 Personal Name-Title (Traced Same)
4 1 0 Corporate Name-Title (Traced Same)
4 1 1 Conference-Title (Traced Same)
4 4 0 Title (Traced Same)
4 9 0 Series Untraced or Traced Differently

Bibliographic Notes
5 0 0 General Notes
5 0 1 "Bound With" Note
5 0 2 Dissertation Note
*5 0 3 Bibliographic History Note
5 0 4 Bibliography Note
5 0 5 Contents Note (Formatted)
*5 0 6 "Limited Use" Note
5 2 0 Abstract or Annotation

Subject Added Entries
6 0 0 Personal Name
6 1 0 Corporate Name (excluding
            political jurisdiction alone)
6 1 1 Conference or Meeting
6 3 0 Uniform Title Heading

LC Subject Headings
6 5 0 Topical
6 5 1 Geographic Names

Other Subject Headings
*6 6 0 NLM Subject Headings (MESH)
*6 7 0 NAL Subject Headings
*6 9 0 Local Subject Heading Systems

Other Added Entries
7 0 0 Personal Name
7 1 0 Corporate Name
7 1 1 Conference or Meeting
7 3 0 Uniform Title Heading
7 4 0 Title Traced Differently

Series Added Entries
8 0 0 Personal Name—Title
8 1 0 Corporate Name—Title
8 1 1 Conference or Meeting—Title
8 4 0 Title

---

* The Library of Congress will not supply data for these fields at present (1970).

An example of a variable field is the personal name field for which the corresponding directory tag is 100. In this field the first indicator is set as 0, 1, 2, or 3, according as the name is a forename (given name), single surname, multiple surname, or family name. The second indicator is set as 1 or 0, according as the personal name is or is not also the subject of the work. The subfield codes and the corresponding subfields may be any of the following:

Subfield code	Subfield content
$a	Surnames and forenames.
$b	Roman numerals following a forename.
$c	Personal titles such as Lord or poet.
$d	Dates.
$e	Relator such as ed (for editor) or tr (for translator).
$k	Form subheading such as legend or liturgy.
$t	A title used in conjunction with a name heading.

Thus any of the following might appear as the content of a personal name field followed by a field terminator:

```
00$aAlexander$bI,$cEmperor of Russia,$d1777-1825
00$aFrancesco d'Assisi,$cSaint.$kLegend.
10$aSmith, John,$d1906-1941,$eed.
10$aKames, Henry Home,$cLord,$d1696-1782
20$aDay-Lewis, Cecil,$d1904-
20$aSanta Cruz, Alonso de,$dd. 1567.
31$aMedici, House of,$kSpurious and doubtful works.
```

Within any field a set of characters intended to represent subscripts is preceded by a two-byte tag set to be $\underline{e}b$ where $\underline{e}$ denotes the "escape character" 00011011. Similarly, sets of characters to represent superscripts or Greek letters are preceded by $\underline{e}p$ or $\underline{e}g$, respectively. Return to the standard character representation is signified by the escape character $\underline{e}s$. A diacritical mark such as an accent is placed immediately preceding the letter that it modifies.

A listing of five logical records of the MARC tapes is shown in Figure 3.9. For this listing all characters have been converted to upper case, and the symbol | has been substituted for the field terminator.

3.11 Preparation of Document Data Bases

Although retrieval of document information is often from data bases that are purchased from a supplier, it is sometimes desired to add addi-

```
00662NAM  2200169        001001300000008004100013050001300054082001200 0
671000026000079245016100105260000550026630000270032150400300034865000410
037870000380041970000360045 7|    64023532  |690320C19681964CTUA      B
 00110 ENG0 |0 $AH62$B.W2|   $A372.8./3|10$AWAGNER, GUY W.$D1902-|1 $ASO
CIAL STUDIES, GAMES, AND ACTIVITIES;$BSTRENGTHENING SOCIAL STUDIES SKI
LLS WITH INSTRUCTIONAL AIDS$C(BY) GUY WAGNER, EDNA CHRISTOPHEL (AND) L
AURA GILLOLEY.|0 $ADARIEN, CONN.,$BTEACHERS PUB. CORP.$C(1968, C1964)|
   $A114 P.$BILLUS.$C23 CM.|  $ABIBLIOGRAPHY: P. 109-111.|00$ASOCIAL SC
IENCES$XSTUDY AND TEACHING.|10$ACHRISTOPHEL, EDNA,$EJOINT AUTHOR.|10$A
GILLOLEY, LAURA,$EJOINT AUTHOR.|
```
```
00720NAM  2200169        001001300000008004100013050001500054082001400 0
691100039000083245022600122260000280034830000430037635000090041950000330
042865000510046165000390051 2|    64066336  |690320C19661965NYUA
 00000 ENG0 |0 $AT73$B.A797|   $A620/.0076|20$AARCO PUBLISHING COMPANY,
NEW YORK.|1 $AOPERATIONS AND MAINTENANCE TRAINEE:$BMAINTENANCE MAN TR
AINEE, TRAFFIC DEVICE MAINTAINER TRAINEE, SEWAGE TREATMENT WORKER TRAI
NEE; COMPLETE STUDY GUIDE TO PASS HIGH ON YOUR CIVIL SERVICE TEST,$CBY
THE ARCO EDITORIAL BOARD.|1 $ANEW YORK$C(1966, C1965)|   $A1 V. (VARIO
US PAGINGS)$BILLUS.$C26 CM.|   $A4.00|   $A"ARCO CATALOG NUMBER: 1241."|
00$AINDUSTRIAL ARTS$XEXAMINATIONS, QUESTIONS, ETC.|00$ACIVIL SERVICE$Z
U.S.$XEXAMINATIONS.|
```
```
00562NAM  2200121        001001300000008004100013050002200054110006900 0
762450205001452600048003503000022003986000021004201|   65061226  |690326
S1968     DCU        00000 ENG0 |0 $AHC106.5$B.A5 1965|10$AU.S.$BCON
GRESS.$BSENATE.$BCOMMITTEE ON LABOR AND PUBLIC WELFARE.|0 $ANOMINATION
.$BHEARING, EIGHTY-NINTH CONGRESS, FIRST SESSION, ON DR. GARTH L. MANG
UM TO BE EXECUTIVE SECRETARY OF THE NATIONAL COMMISSION ON TECHNOLOGY,
AUTOMATION, AND ECONOMIC PROGRESS. MARCH 5, 1965.|0 $AWASHINGTON,$BU.
S. GOVT. PRINT. OFF.,$C1965.|   $AIII, 4 P.$C24 CM.|10$AMANGUM, GARTH L
.|
```
```
00658NAM  2200133        001001300000008004100013050001600054082001300 0
701100121000083245021400020426000480018300003000046650002900496|     6506
2359  |690324S1965     DCUA        00010 ENG0 |0 $ATJ685$B.A28|   $A658
.5/62|10$AU.S.$BCONGRESS.$BHOUSE.$BCOMMITTEE ON GOVERNMENT OPERATIONS.
$BEXECUTIVE AND LEGISLATIVE REORGANIZATION SUBCOMMITTEE.|1 $AREORGANIZ
ATION PLAN NO. 3 OF 1965: LOCOMOTIVE INSPECTION.$BHEARING BEFORE A SUB
COMMITTEE OF THE COMMITTEE ON GOVERNMENT OPERATIONS, HOUSE OF REPRESEN
TATIVES, EIGHTY-NINTH CONGRESS, FIRST SESSION. JULY 7, 1965.|0 $AWASHI
NGTON,$BU.S. GOVT. PRINT. OFF.,$C1965.|   $AIV, 72 P.$BILLUS.$C24 CM.|0
0$ALOCOMOTIVES$XINSPECTION.|
```
```
00821NAM  2200181        001001300000008004100013050001600054082000800 0
702450163000782600051002413000001900029235000010003115000125003215040041 0
044665000210048770000300050871001020053 8|   66024150  |690325S1968      C
TU     B     00000 ENG0 |0 $ARA418$B.D56|   $A362|0 $ADISEASE, THE INDI
VIDUAL, AND SOCIETY; SOCIAL-PSYCHOLOGICAL ASPECTS OF DISEASE;$BA SUMMA
RY AND ANALYSIS OF A DECADE OF RESEARCH,$CBY GERALD GORDON (AND OTHERS
)|0 $ANEW HAVEN,$BCOLLEGE & UNIVERSITY PRESS$C(1968)|   $A680 P.$C23 CM
.|   $A17.50|   $ASUMMARIZES 248 RESEARCH PROJECTS LISTED IN THE 1953-60
ISSUES OF AN INVENTORY OF SOCIAL AND ECONOMIC RESEARCH IN HEALTH.|  $
AINCLUDES BIBLIOGRAPHICAL REFERENCES.|00$ASOCIAL MEDICINE.|10$AGORDON,
GERALD A.,$D1939-|21$AHEALTH INFORMATION FOUNDATION, NEW YORK.$T?N IN
VENTORY OF SOCIAL AND ECONOMIC RESEARCH IN HEALTH.|
```

Figure 3.9. A listing of five logical records of the MARC tapes. The symbol | denotes the field terminator.

tional material such as information relating to internal reports. Similarly, it may be desired to merge several data bases that are created in different formats. In fact even if all retrieval is performed on a single data base it may be desired to discard some information or to rearrange the format in order to save space or to reduce search times. Furthermore, when merging different issues of a data base in order to perform retrospective searches it may be found that certain fields have been represented differently during different intervals of time.

If document data are prepared on punched cards the keypunching instructions must be easily understood and unambiguous so that the keypuncher does not have to make decisions on how to cope with any exceptional forms of data. Each new field, such as author or title, may begin on a new card, and the first column of each card may be tagged to indicate the field attribute. In general it is better to use more cards than to economize by adoption of a scheme that uses all card columns but requires a complicated arrangement of tags and end-of-field indicators.

When keypunching textual data it should be borne in mind that some subsequent corrections may be necessary, and may involve addition or removal of characters. Correction of the second of 10 cards of an abstract should not require a retyping of the subsequent 8 cards. It may be decided to assign a special symbol, such as +, to indicate a card column that is to be ignored as the card is copied to a computer accessible file.

For example, suppose that four cards are punched as follows in which the 2 in the first column indicates that the data is to be placed in an abstract field.

```
2VERY HIGH WAVES WERE OBSERVED WITH LARGE OVERHAING CRESTS. MUCH OF THE RESULTIN
2G FOAM WAS BLOWN IN DENSE WHITE STREAKS ALONG THE DIRECTION OF THE WIND. THE SU
2RFACE HAD A WHITE APPEARRANCE. EVERYWHERE THE EDGES OF THE WAVE CRESTS WERE BLO
2WN INTO FROTH.
```

The errors in the spelling of OVERHANGING and APPEARANCE could be corrected by replacing the first card by two new ones, and by copying the third card with one of the Rs replaced by +. The corrected data would then be

```
2VERY HIGH WAVES WERE OBSERVED WITH LARGE OVERHANGING CRESTS. MUCH OF THE RESULT
2IN ++++++++++++++++++++++++++++++++++++++++++++++++++++++++++++++++++++++++++++++
2G FOAM WAS BLOWN IN DENSE WHITE STREAKS ALONG DIRECTION OF THE WIND. THE SU
2RFACE HAD A WHITE APPEAR+ANCE. EVERYWHERE THE EDGES OF THE WAVE CRESTS WERE BLO
2WN INTO FROTH.
```

It may be noted that when keypunching data as in the preceding example whenever a word ends in the 80th column of a card its delimiting blank must be placed in the first column of the subsequent card. An alternative scheme is to allow no words to overlap to the next card and to allow the keypuncher to place any number of blanks between words as in the following.

```
2VERY HIGH WAVES WERE OBSERVED WITH LARGE OVERHANGING CRESTS.
2MUCH OF THE RESULTING FOAM WAS BLOWN IN DENSE STREAKS
2ALONG THE DIRECTION OF THE WIND.
2THE SUACE HAD A WHITE APPEARANCE.
2EVERYWHERE THE EDGES OF THE WAVE CRESTS WERE BLOWN INTO FROTH.
```

Such a scheme allows very simple correction of errors and greatly simplifies proofreading. The computer program that reads the cards may be designed to store the data so that only one blank follows each word.

Proofreading for correction of spelling errors is time consuming and therefore costly. One method of spelling correction is through examination of a computer produced list of all the words arranged in alphabetic order or of all words that appear only once in the entire data base.

Whenever a new data base is keypunched, or merged from several existing data bases, it should be examined by a computer program designed to check its consistency with respect to tags, directories, missing or exceptional data, and so forth.

Details of data preparation for the TRIAL retrieval system designed for retrieval of literature abstracts have been described by Welsh.[10] The TRIAL system was intended to use data prepared by a number of different users who were prepared to make their keypunched data available to each other.

3.12 Problems

1. State the advantages and disadvantages of use of field tags versus directories. State the advantages and disadvantages of arrangement of data in fixed length fields. Under what circumstances is it desirable to allow for addition of supplementary fields?
2. If some variable length fields are searchable and some are not, should the directory entries be arranged in any particular order?
3. With the expansion factor of a record defined as the ratio

Total length of record
───────────────────────────────────────
Total length of record fields that contain values of attributes after removal of padding blanks, tags, directories, and data not relevant to the content of the original document.

   examine the records of Figure 3.2 and estimate the average expansion factor for records of the METADEX tape.
4. Show the arrangement of pointers and fields that results from specializing Figure 3.1 to apply to the METADEX data. Can you suggest a better way of arranging the data in order to economize on storage and to provide for ease of access?
5. Repeat Problems 3 and 4 for records of the SPIN/O tape.

[10] W. A. Welsh, "The TRIAL system: Information retrieval in political science," *American Behavioral Scientist* 10(1967): 11–24.

6. Repeat Problems 3 and 4 for records of the MARC tape.
7. Compare the information stored on the CAIN, SPIN, and MARC tapes from the point of view of supplying useful information to the user, and also with regard to cost of preparation of the data base. (Keypunching forms only a portion of the total cost).
8. Some of the tape files described in the present chapter represent characters in both uppercase and lowercase. State how this affects the search program, whether it affects the question formulation, and whether you would advise rewriting the tape in upper case before applying the search program to it.

4

Question Logic and Format

4.1 General Considerations

As mentioned in Section 2.11, a question for a computer search program may be expressed in the form of logic operations applied to pairs that consist of a term followed by an attribute descriptor that specifies the field within which the term is to be searched. The description of the user's interest in a form suitable for input to a search program is said to constitute an interest profile. Each profile may consist of one or more separate questions. The rules for formulation of interest profiles should be sufficiently simple to be easily understood by the user, but they also should be sufficiently comprehensive to allow a proper representation of the user's search interest.

Throughout the present chapter the word term will be used to designate the elements that form the vocabulary associated with any attribute. In the instances of titles and abstracts the terms are individual words followed in the text by either a blank or punctuation mark. In the instance of subject heading fields a term may consist of a complete subject heading in which case it may be necessary to introduce a delimiting character, such as a comma or semicolon, in order to separate the individual terms in the text. In general, each field of the data base contains terms separated by delimiting characters, and each term consists of a string of characters other than those used as delimiters.

Thus in title fields the characters . , : ; ! ?– and the blank might be chosen as delimiters, in which case a pair of words connected by a hyphen is treated as two separate terms. In author fields a pair of consecutive blanks might be chosen as the delimiter so that a field of content

```
JONES, ALAN G.  SMITH, B. CLAUDE  STOSKY, J.
```

would be regarded as containing three separate terms. Similarly, in subject heading fields the delimiter might be chosen as a semicolon so that a field of content

```
PHYSICAL CHEMISTRY; GEOLOGY, HISTORICAL; METEOROLOGY;
ART; MODERN;
```

would be regarded as formed from four separate terms.

Delimiting characters are not required in fields whose terms are of fixed length or in fields whose individual term positions are indicated by a directory.

In this chapter the illustrations are with reference to title fields, author fields, subject fields, and abstract fields. For illustration it is supposed that in title fields the terms consist of character strings formed from the characters A–Z and 0–9, all other characters serving as delimiters. It is supposed that each term in an author field consists of a surname followed by one blank followed by one or more initials; thus examples of author terms are WILLIAMS AG and JOHNSON P and MILLER KSV. Each term of a subject field is assumed to consist of a sequence of words with or without punctuation. An abstract field is envisaged as containing sets of terms grouped into sentences separated by periods; the individual terms within abstract fields have the same structure as the terms within title fields.

Since some computer search programs are designed to deal with a batch of questions placed in sequence, it is desirable that each question contain an expression to mark its own end. The logic of each question then may be examined separately, and any logic errors in the statement of a question may be prevented from affecting the subsequent questions. It will be supposed that the expression used to mark the end of each question consists of the character string END. However, an accidental omission of END would cause a question to appear as part of the next one; it is therefore advisable to require that a further character string, such as QUE, be used to indicate the beginning of each question.

It will be seen in Section 6.1 that it may prove convenient to group questions into sets designated as profiles. The beginning of each profile may be indicated by the character string PRO. Hence, with use of QUE and END as described, each profile has the following form.

```
PRO
QUE

Question No. 1
END
QUE

Question No. 2
END
.

.

.

QUE

Last question
END
```

Omission of either QUE or END may be regarded as an incorrect formulation of the question, but it need not invalidate any preceding or following question that contains QUE and END.

The question logic and format used in the illustrations of the present chapter is similar to that implemented in a search program developed by Thiel.[1] It is not the only possible or most widely used format, but it is convenient for purposes of illustration. A formal definition of the question syntax is contained in Section 4.9.

The question logic allowed by the majority of existing search services is significantly more restrictive than that described in the present chapter. In practice it may be necessary to compromise between provision of desirable logic specifications and reduction of required computer search time. Questions concerning the implementation of search programs to deal with the different logic operations are discussed in Chapter 6.

4.2 Truncation Specifications

To each term present in a question profile there may be attached a mode specification to indicate whether the question term is to be searched for as a complete term in the data base, or is to be searched for its appearance as a fragment of a larger term. Three particular forms of mode specification are untruncation, unlimited truncation, and limited truncation, as described here.

---

[1] L. H. Thiel, and H. S. Heaps, "Program design for retrospective searches on large data bases," *Information Storage and Retrieval* 8(1972): 1–20.

A question term, when specified in untruncated mode, consists of a sequence of nondelimiting characters that is to be searched for as a complete term within a specified field of the data base. Thus a search for the terms

                    SALT   JONES   CARBON14   29A176B

will not locate the terms SALTS or JONES G or CARBON 14 or 29A176B7.

A question term, when specified in unlimited truncation mode, consists of a stem or string of characters, preceded and/or followed by an asterisk to indicate that there is no restriction on whether the stem is preceded and/or followed by other characters. Thus a search for ACID* as a title term may find ACID or ACIDS or ACIDIC and so forth. A search for *MAGNETIC may find the terms MAGNETIC or PARAMAGNETIC but not MAGNETICS. A search for *RELATION* may find the terms RELATION or RELATIONS or INTERRELATION or INTERRELATIONSHIP.

Within subject heading fields a search for COMPUTER PROGRAM* might be used to find the terms COMPUTER PROGRAMS or COMPUTER PROGRAM LISTINGS but not DIGITAL COMPUTER PROGRAMS. Within author fields a search for STEVENS A* might be used to locate the terms STEVENS A or STEVENS AG but not STEVENS GA.

A question term specified in limited truncation mode consists of a stem preceded and/or followed by an indication of up to how many characters of the term may precede and/or follow the stem. It will be supposed that the character $ is used to indicate the possible occurrence of any non-delimiting character. Then a search for ACID$$ as a title term may find ACID or ACIDS or ACIDIC but not ACIDICITY. A search for $$CLEAN D in an author field may find the terms MACLEAN D or MCLEAN D or CLEAN D.

The limited truncation mode is particularly useful when it may be used to indicate that a search is for both the singular and plural forms of a term. Thus the question term PARK$ may be used to search for PARK or PARKS, whereas the question term PARK* would also include PARKING.

4.3 Comparison and Termination Modes

In search of a data base it is sometimes convenient to request only items published between specified dates, or associated with patent numbers in a given range, or whose classification keys are within a given range. To meet these and similar requirements it is desirable to allow terms to be specified in comparison mode by use of the symbols =, <, and >. The comparison modes may be defined in various ways, but the definition given here is suitable for many applications.

A search for a question term of N characters preceded by $<$, or $=$, or $>$ will find all terms of at least N characters whose set of N first characters have lower, equal, or greater rank than the specified n characters. Pairs of characters such as $<=$, or $>=$, may be used to indicate $<$ OR $=$, or $>$ OR $=$, respectively.

Thus with the ranking convention of Section 2.13, a search for <1961 will locate the terms 1960 or 1960A or 19603 in addition to 1959 or 1958, etc. In an author field a search for $>$SMITH will locate SMYTHE G and THOMAS V and WEST AB but not SMITHSON G or SMITH A. A search for $<=1958$ will find the term 1958 or 1958A or 1957 or 19517 or 0476 or B476 but not 476, which has fewer than four characters.

The termination mode is designed to allow a search to be made for a term located at a specified position in a field. Thus if the symbol / is reserved to designate the termination mode, a search for /JONES AK in an author field signifies a search for JONES AK as the first term in the field. Similarly, a search for TORONTO/ in a publisher address field signifies a search for TORONTO as the final term in the field.

Truncation and termination modes may be combined as in use of /*COMPUT* to locate any subject heading which appears as the first one in a subject heading field and which contains the character string COMPUT.

It may be desirable to extend the notion of termination mode to allow specification of more general term position within a field. Thus ///ANALY–SIS might be used to speficy a search for ANALYSIS as the third term in a field.

4.4 Boolean Operators AND, OR, NOt, WITh

Throughout the present chapter a pair consisting of a question term and attribute specification is written in the form TERM ( ) in which the parentheses contain an attribute specification such as TIT for title, AUT for author, SUB for subject heading, or ABS for abstract. Furthermore, each term and attribute is preceded by the expression CON to indicate that it constitutes a ''term concept'' and not a logic operator. Logic levels are indicated by indentations of five spaces.

One of the simplest forms of question is one expressed through a list of term concepts connected by the logic operations AND and NOt as in the following

```
QUE
    AND
        CON  BINGHAM  Z  (AUT)
        CON  ORGANIC  CHEMISTRY  (SUB)
        NOCON  SYNTHE*(TIT)
        NOCON  REDUCTION(TIT)
          CON  KEYTONE$(TIT)
    END
```

that requests a search for all items that contain each of BINGHAM Z(AUT) and ORGANIC CHEMISTRY(SUB) and KETONE$(TIT), but not SYNTHE*(TIT) and not REDUCTION(TIT).

A question may also be expressed solely in terms of OR logic as in

```
QUE
    OR
        CON  LAKE$  (TIT)
        CON  RIVER$  (TIT)
        CON  WATER RESOURCES  (SUB)
    END
```

that specifies a search for items that contain at least one of LAKE$ (TIT) or RIVER$ (TIT) or WATER RESOURCES (SUB). If the (SUB) term were replaced by

```
CON  WATER*  (SUB)
```

then the search would find items classed under the subject headings WATER RESOURCES or WATER TREATMENT or WATERFALLS and so forth.

It is desirable to allow any term concept to be replaced by a compound concept that consists of a logical combination of term concepts. If the term concept

```
CON  RIVER$  (TIT)
```

in the preceding question is replaced by the compound concept

```
AND
    CON  RIVER$  (TIT)
    CON  TIDAL  (TIT)
```

there results the following question

```
QUE
    OR
        CON  LAKE$  (TIT)
        AND
            CON  RIVER$  (TIT)
            CON  TIDAL  (TIT)
        CON  WATER RESOURCES  (SUB)
    END
```

This is a request for items that contain either LAKE$ (TIT), or both of RIVER$ (TIT) and TIDAL (TIT), or else WATER RESOURCES (SUB). It may be noted that the second and third CON are indented to indicate that they are components of a single compound concept and linked by the preceding AND. The (SUB) term is not part of this compound concept, and therefore is not indented the same amount.

An example of a question that contains three levels of logic is shown here:

```
QUE
    OR
        CON  ROAD BUILDING (SUB)
        AND
                CON  CONSTRUCTION (TIT)
             NOCON  MAINTENANCE (TIT)
             OR
                CON  ROAD$ (TIT)
                CON  HIGHWAY$ (TIT)
        CON  KELLEY PC (AUT)
    END
```

The preceding question requests a search for all items that contain

```
        ROAD BUILDING (SUB)
    or  [CONSTRUCTION (TIT) and not MAINTENANCE (TIT)
        and also at least one of ROAD$ (TIT) or HIGHWAY$ (TIT)]
    or  KELLEY PC (AUT)
```

The logic operator WIT, to denote WITh, has the same meaning as AND except that the terms must occur in the same sentence. If the field content is a single sentence, that is it contains no periods, the WIT operator is equivalent to the operator AND.

Thus a search in response to the question

```
QUE
    WIT
        CON  POLLUTION (ABS)
        CON  SULFUR* (ABS)
    END
```

would locate an item whose abstract contains the sentence INVESTIGA-TION OF POLLUTION CAUSED BY SULFURS. It would not locate an item whose abstract field consists of the two separate sentences REDUCTION OF SULFUR. A SURVEY OF TYPES OF POLLUTION.

4.5 The Ignore Specification

If truncation modes are allowed it is desirable to allow a specification of terms that are to be ignored. This is because the relevant terms may have been truncated to stems that also occur in nonrelevant terms.

For example, a search in response to the question

```
QUE
    AND
        CON  NUCLEAR (TIT)
        CON  EXPLO* (TIT)
    END
```

will find the terms EXPLODE, EXPLOSION, EXPLORATION, EXPLOIT, and so forth. If the question is about explosions it would be advisable to reformulate it with inclusion of an ignore specification as follows

```
QUE
    AND
        CON    NUCLEAR (TIT)
        CON    EXPLO* (TIT)
        IGCON  EXPLOR* (TIT)
        IGCON  EXPLOI* (TIT)
    END
```

that causes the search to ignore the presence of any title terms that begin with the stems EXPLOR or EXPLOI.

It should be realized that the IGCON specification has a different effect from NOCON since a search in response to the preceding question would locate an item whose title field contains EXPLORATION OF NUCLEAR EXPLOSION SITES, whereas a search in response to the following question would not.

```
QUE
    AND
        CON    NUCLEAR (TIT)
        CON    EXPLO* (TIT)
        NOCON  EXPLOR* (TIT)
        NOCON  EXPLOI* (TIT)
    END
```

It is convenient to allow one or more IGCON terms to be included after any term concept in order to indicate terms to be ignored. Of course the specification is meaningful only if the specified attribute of an IGCON term is the same as that of the associated term concept.

4.6 Adjacency and Precedence

The logical operator AND is used to specify a search for items that contain associations of terms. The terms do not necessarily have the same attributes. The logical operator WIT is used to specify required associations of terms within sentences, and hence of terms that have the same attribute. Sometimes it is useful to specify that particular terms be adjacent, or relatively close, within the same sentence.

Required adjacencies of terms may be specified by use of the logic operator ADJ. Thus the question

```
QUE
    OR
      CON  WELLS* (AUT)
      ADJ
          CON  WESTERN (TIT)
          CON  POLITIC* (TIT)
          CON  THEOR* (TIT)
    END
```

specifies a search for either WELLS* (AUT), or WESTERN (TIT) adjacent to POLITIC* (TIT) adjacent to THEOR* (TIT) within the same sentence of a title field. The search logic would be satisfied by either of the titles WESTERN POLITICAL THEORY and INTERACTION BETWEEN SOCIAL THEORIES, POLITICS, WESTERN PHILOSOPHY, AND EASTERN RELIGIONS.

In contrast, the question

```
QUE
    OR
      CON  WELLS* (AUT)
      PRE
          CON  WESTERN (TIT)
          CON  POLITIC* (TIT)
          CON  THEOR* (TIT)
    END
```

specifies that WESTERN (TIT) must immediately precede POLITIC* (TIT) which must immediately precede THEOR* (TIT).

It is obvious that in order for the ADJ and PRE specifications to be meaningful, the associated terms must be specified to have the same attribute.

For some purposes the specification of immediate adjacency or immediate precedence is too stringent, and it may be more useful to state a requirement for adjacency or precedence within a certain limit. This may be done by inclusion of a numerical value after the ADJ, or PRE, in order to state the length of a term sequence within which terms are regarded as adjacent or preceding.

Thus the question statement

```
QUE
    PRE04
            CON  CORRO*  (ABS)
            CON  METAL$$$ (ABS)
            CON  ELECTRODE$ (ABS)
    END
```

might be used to specify that CORRO* must precede METAL$$$, which must precede ELECTRODE$ within a sequence of not more than four terms within the same sentence. Such a sequence might be CORROSION OF METAL ELECTRODES or CORRODING METALLIC ELECTRODES. In order to include the sequences METALLIC ELECTRODE CORROSION or METAL ELECTRODES AND CORROSION the logic operator PRE04 could be replaced by ADJ04 to indicate that the order of the terms is not significant.

The following is an example of a question in which OR logic is used within the ADJ level. The request is for an item whose title field contains a sequence of up to five consecutive terms that include either CORRO* or DETERIORAT*, also either METAL$$$ or CARBON, and also ELEC-TRODE$.

```
QUE
    ADJ05
            OR
                CON  CORRO*  (TIT)
                CON  DETERIORAT* (TIT)
            OR
                CON  METAL$$$ (TIT)
                CON  CARBON (TIT)
                CON  ELECTRODE$ (TIT)
    END
```

The question shown here requests a search for a sequence of up to eight terms in which a sequence of not more than four (containing OIL and POLLUTION) precedes a sequence of not more than three (containing RIVER$ and CANAD*).

```
QUE
    PRE08
        ADJ04
                CON  OIL (ABS)
                CON  POLLUTION (ABS)
        ADJ03
                CON  RIVER$ (ABS)
                CON  CANAD* (ABS)
    END
```

For a compound concept that begins with the immediate precedence operator and contains no further compound concepts of IGCON or

NOCON terms, it is very convenient to allow omission of PRE and to write the compound concept as a sequence of consecutive terms preceded by a single CON and followed by a single attribute specification. Thus the compound concept

```
PRE
    CON  WESTERN (TIT)
    CON  POLITIC* (TIT)
    CON  THEOR* (TIT)
```

might be written in the form

```
CON  WESTERN POLITIC* THEOR* (TIT)
```

so that a question expressed in the form

```
QUE
   OR
      CON  WELLS* (AUT)
      CON  WESTERN POLITIC* THEOR* (TIT)
   END
```

is understood to be equivalent to the question

```
QUE
   OR
      CON  WELLS* (AUT)
      PRE
         CON  WESTERN (TIT)
         CON  POLITIC* (TIT)
         CON  THEOR* (TIT)
   END
```

4.7 Weighted Concepts

Each concept that appears in a question may be given a numerical weight so that if the concept is present in an item, its weight is accumulated for comparison with a threshold value. A document item is regarded as relevant only if both the question logic is satisfied and also the accumulated weight exceeds the threshold value.

In the discussion that follows the weights have the form of two-digit numbers that precede the CON or logic operators. Threshold values are also two-digit numbers placed after the logic operator. In the absence of inclusion of a weight or value specification a default value of 01 is assumed.

The following question contains concept weights of 1, and a threshold weight of 2, to request a search for any two of the three terms.

```
QUE
    OR02
        01CON  SAFETY (TIT)
        01CON  TRAFFIC (TIT)
        01CON  ROAD$ (TIT)
END
```

The following question requests a search for MIDDLETON VK (AUT) combined with any of the terms DIFFRACTION (TIT), SOUND (TIT), WAVE$ (TIT); or else all three of the terms DIFFRACTION (TIT), SOUND (TIT), and WAVE$ (TIT).

```
QUE
    OR03
        CON  DIFFRACTION (TIT)
      02CON  MIDDLETON VK (AUT)
        CON  SOUND (TIT)
        CON  WAVE$ (TIT)
END
```

The following question specifies a search for both the terms TRAFFIC and SAFETY, together with one of the terms LAW* and REGULATION$.

```
QUE
    OR03
        CON  LAW*  (TIT)
        CON  REGULATION$ (TIT)
      02AND
            CON  TRAFFIC (TIT)
            CON  SAFETY (TIT)
END
```

Further nesting of logic levels is illustrated by the following question statement

```
QUE
    OR02
        CON  INSURANCE (TIT)
        CON  MARINE (SUB)
        OR 02
            CON  SHIP*  (ABS)
            CON  VESSEL$ (ABS)
            CON  BOAT*  (ABS)
END
```

It requests a search for any two of

```
        INSURANCE (TIT)
    or  MARINE (SUB)
    or  any 2 of SHIP*  (ABS)  or VESSEL$  (ABS) or BOAT*  (ABS)
```

It may be desired to have the weight of a concept computed as the sum of the weights of any of its component concepts that are present in the item. In this instance the logic operation may be preceded by SM. Such is done in the following question that requests a search for at least one of POLITICAL or CULTURAL, together with at least two of FRANCE or BRITAIN or CANADA; but there must also be a total of at least four terms found.

```
QUE
   AND 04
        SMOR
              CON  POLITICAL (TIT)
              CON  CULTURAL (TIT)
        SMOR 02
              CON  FRANCE (TIT)
              CON  BRITAIN (TIT)
              CON  CANADA (TIT)
   END
```

Weights, threshold values, and SM may be used with any of the logic operators, but should not be attached to the expressions NOCON or IGCON. However, the most obvious application of the use of weights is in combination with OR logic.

It may be noted that throughout the present chapter the satisfaction of logic at any level within a question does not depend on the logic that surrounds that level. Interpretation of weights and threshold values is also consistent with the desirable property that the satisfaction of logic at any level may depend on the logic contained at levels within it but should be independent of the form of any outer levels of logic.

4.8 Defined Terms

The designation CON has been used with question terms. It is also convenient to use it with defined terms which denote compound concepts.

Thus consider the question

```
QUE
   AND
       OR
          CON  RUSSIAN (TIT)
          CON  AMERICAN (TIT)
          PRE
              CON  UNITED (TIT)
              CON  STATES (TIT)
       OR
          CON  OWNERSHIP (TIT)
          CON  CONTROL (TIT)
          CON  EXPLOIT* (TIT)
   END
```

It could also be expressed in the form

```
DEF FOREIGN
     OR
        CON  RUSSIAN (TIT)
        CON  AMERICAN (TIT)
        PRE
             CON  UNITED (TIT)
             CON  STATES (TIT)
END

DEF CONTROL
     OR
        CON  OWNERSHIP (TIT)
        CON  CONTROL (TIT)
        CON  EXPLOIT* (TIT)
END

QUE
    AND
        CON  FOREIGN (DEF)
        CON  CONTROL (DEF)
END
```

in which the compound concepts FOREIGN and CONTROL are defined and then quoted in the statement of the question.

It should be noted that the above question does not cause a search for the term FOREIGN but only for the terms that are listed in the definition of the concept named FOREIGN.

If defined concepts are allowed it is generally desirable to have them apply to all the questions in a single profile rather than only to single questions. The advantage of such may be seen by examination of the following profile in which the defined terms are common to three questions.

```
DEF FOREIGN

       As above

END

DEF OWNERSHIP

       As above

END

QUE
    AND
        CON  FOREIGN
        CON  OWNERSHIP
        PRE
             CON  NATURAL (TIT)
             CON  RESOURCE* (TIT)
END
```

```
QUE
    AND
        CON  FOREIGN
        CON  CANADIAN (TIT)
        CON  TRADE (TIT)
    END

QUE
    ADJO5
            CON  OWNERSHIP
            CON  LAND (TIT)
            CON  CANADA (TIT)
    END
```

4.9 Formal Description of the Question Syntax

In order to verify the logical consistency of the question formulation described in the previous sections, and in order to transform the question statements into a form convenient for computer processing, a formal description of the question syntax will be given. It will be described in terms of the Backus Naur or Backus Normal Form (BNF).

For the BNF description the symbol | will be used to denote the exclusive "or" operation. It signifies "or, but not both." The symbols ⟨ ⟩ : : = will be used to indicate that the name contained within ⟨ ⟩ denotes the expression placed after the : : =. Thus the statement

$$\langle operator \rangle ::= AND|WIT|ADJ|PRE|OR\rlap{/}b$$

defines the name "operator" to denote any of the expressions AND, WIT, ADJ, PRE, or OR$\rlap{/}b$ where $\rlap{/}b$ denotes a single blank.

The following statements define some of the names used in the language definition:

⟨question term⟩::= a character string that may be preceded and/or followed by mode specification characters
⟨defined term⟩::= a character string
⟨attribute specification⟩::= a character string of three characters within parentheses
⟨term⟩::= ⟨question term⟩ ⟨attribute specification⟩ | ⟨defined term⟩
⟨weight⟩::= a two-digit number | $\rlap{/}b\rlap{/}b$
⟨value⟩::= a two-digit number | $\rlap{/}b\rlap{/}b$ | SM
⟨logic⟩::= ⟨value⟩ ⟨operator⟩ ⟨weight⟩

Thus ⟨logic⟩ could be any of the following expressions

```
040R 02   15PRE04   ADJ06   AND   SMOR
```

A term concept and a compound concept may then be defined by the two statements

$$\langle\text{term concept}\rangle:: = \langle\text{weight}\rangle \text{ CON } \langle\text{term}\rangle$$
$$| \text{ NOCON } \langle\text{term}\rangle$$
$$| \text{ IGCON } \langle\text{term}\rangle$$
$$\langle\text{compound concept}\rangle:: = \langle\text{logic}\rangle_R \langle\text{concept sequence}\rangle_L$$

where

$$\langle\text{concept sequence}\rangle:: = \langle\text{term concept}\rangle \langle\text{term concept}\rangle$$
$$| \langle\text{concept sequence}\rangle \langle\text{term concept}\rangle$$
$$| \langle\text{concept sequence}\rangle \langle\text{logic}\rangle_R$$
$$\langle\text{concept sequence}\rangle_L$$

in which $_R$ signifies a right indentation to a lower logic level, and $_L$ signifies the end of the indentation and a return to the next higher level of logic. Examples of concept sequences are

```
02CON  HOUSE  (TIT)
01CON  HOME*  (ABS)
```

and

```
03CON  FOREIGN
```

and

```
01CON  DOG  (ABS)
02CON  CAT  (ABS)
02AND
       CON  FOOD   (ABS)
       CON  ANIMAL* (TIT)
       CON  BIRD$  (TIT)
03CON  FISH*  (ABS)
```

The following statements then lead to definition of a profile sequence suitable for input to a computer search program:

$$\langle\text{concept}\rangle:: = \langle\text{term concept}\rangle | \langle\text{compound concept}\rangle$$
$$\langle\text{question}\rangle:: = \text{QUE}_R \langle\text{concept}\rangle_L \text{ END}$$
$$\langle\text{definition}\rangle:: = \text{DEF}\langle\text{defined term}\rangle_R \langle\text{concept}\rangle_L\text{END}$$
$$\langle\text{question sequence}\rangle:: = \langle\text{question}\rangle$$
$$| \langle\text{question sequence}\rangle \langle\text{question}\rangle$$
$$\langle\text{definition sequence}\rangle:: = \langle\text{definition}\rangle$$
$$| \langle\text{definition sequence}\rangle \langle\text{definition}\rangle$$
$$\langle\text{profile}\rangle:: = \text{PRO}\langle\text{question sequence}\rangle$$
$$| \text{ PRO}\langle\text{definition sequence}\rangle \langle\text{question sequence}\rangle$$
$$\langle\text{profile sequence}\rangle:: = \langle\text{profile}\rangle$$
$$| \langle\text{profile sequence}\rangle \langle\text{profile}\rangle$$

4.10 Free Format for Question Formulation

In each of the question statements shown in Sections 4.4–4.8, separate lines were used for each logic expression, term concept, QUE, DEF, END, and PRO. Also, each concept sequence was given a further level of indentation.

A less structured format may be preferable in many instances, and a suitable one may be derived by adoption of the conventions listed here:

1. Each concept sequence preceded by a logic operation is preceded by [and followed by].
2. Any logic expressions, term concepts, QUE, DEF, END, and PRO that do not immediately follow [are preceded by either a shift to a new line or by the underscore __.
3. ᵇᵇ may be omitted from weight and value specifications.
4. Indentations and blanks may be used where convenient for clarity, but they have no syntactical significance except that each term is followed by at least one blank and, unless preceded by [is preceded by at least one blank.

With the preceding conventions the last question statement in Section 4.7 may be written in the form

```
QUE[OR O2
[CON  INSURANCE  (TIT)
 CON  MARINE (SUB)
 ORO2[CON  SHIP* *ABS) _CON  VESSEL$ *ABS)_CON  BOAT* *ABS)]]]END
```

or in the equivalent form

```
QUE[ORO2[CON  INSURANCE (TIT) CON  MARINE (SUB)_ORO2
[CON  SHIP* *ABS)_CON  VESSEL$ *ABS)_CON  BOAT)* (ABS)]]]
END
```

or in the form

```
QUE[ORO2[CON  INSURANCE (TIT)
         CON  MARINE (SUB)
         ORO2[CON  SHIP*  (ABS)
              CON  VESSEL$  (ABS)
              CON  BOAT*  (ABS)]]]END
```

It may prove convenient to allow adoption of a further pair of conventions as follows:

5. Each CON may be omitted.
6. Any logic operation that precedes a concept sequence may be removed provided it is placed, with preceding and following blanks,

between the component concepts of the concept sequence. The underscore is then not used between the component concepts.

With the adoption of these two conventions, the preceding question may then be expressed in the form

```
QUE[O2[INSURANCE (TIT) OR MARINE (SUB)
    OR O2[SHIP* (ABS) OR VESSEL$ (ABS) OR BOAT* (ABS)] ]]END
```

For formulation of short questions the free format tends to be more convenient than the fixed one used in the previous sections. In contrast, for formulation of highly structured questions the fixed format may be better in that it clearly indicates the nesting of the various logic levels. The previous rules for indentation may, of course, be used with the free format provided the square brackets are also included. If questions are submitted through a keyboard terminal, rather than as a deck of punched cards, it will almost invariably be preferably to allow a free format for question statements.

Defined concepts may be used to advantage when questions are submitted through keyboard terminals, since they allow each typed line to be short and hence easily corrected or modified if necessary. For example, the last but one question statement in Section 4.7 could be expressed in three free format lines as follows

```
DEF INSMARINE[INSURANCE (TIT) OR MARINE (SUB)]

DEF SHIP[SHIP* (ABS) OR VESSEL$ (ABS) OR BOAT* (ABS)]

QUE[O2[INSMARINE OR SHIP]]END
```

4.11 User Specification of Output Format

In addition to allowing the user of a retrieval service to specify the structure of the question, it may be desirable to offer the option of specifying the desired arrangement of the printed output that describes the documents retrieved. Such specification might include a list of the fields to be printed. Thus it might be desired to print only titles and not abstracts; alternatively it might be desired to print author names, titles, and journal names without inclusion of subject headings or category numbers.

Specification also might be made to indicate which printed fields are to begin on new lines, and which fields might be grouped together to occupy a single line with suitable spacing between fields. The order in which the fields are printed also might be specified.

Further instructions available to the user of a retrieval system may include ones to allow the user to specify the order of the printed document items. Such order, for example, might be chronological by date of publication, or alphabetic by first author. It also might be useful to allow specification that the output be in the form of a KWIC or KWOC index based on titles only.[2] This latter form of output is very useful for a question of rather general form whose purpose is to retrieve an extensive bibliography rather than a few document items that relate to a very specific question.

It should be realized that use of a sophisticated set of logic relations and detailed specification of the output format requires a relatively high degree of sophistication from the user. The casual user of a mechanized search service will probably be content to use very simple logic and to accept any form of printed output. However, as a user acquires more experience in submission of questions, he or she is likely to become aware of the shortcomings of the simpler logic and will welcome the availability of additional logic. Likewise, the user will become aware of the desirability of having the printed output in the form that is most convenient for his or her particular needs.

Comparison of the forms of the printed output of three widely used retrieval services has been made by Larson et al.[3] The particular search services discussed are the BioSciences Information Service of Biological Abstracts (BIOSIS), the Chemical Abstracts Service (CAS), and the Engineering Index Incorporated. Discussion of user control of the form of printed output in two programs, MEDLINE (MEDLARS On-Line) and STAIRS-AQUARIUS (STorage And Information Retrieval System—A QUery And Retrieval Interactive Utility System), used to search the MEDLARS tapes that contain information relating to medicine has been given by Humphrey.[4]

4.12 Specification of Character Significance and Special Use

A general scheme for representation of a data base by use of fixed and variable length fields was shown in Figure 3.1. In the discussion of Section

[2] A. K. Kent, "The Chemical Society Research Unit in information retrieval," *Svensk kemisk tidskrift* 80(1968): 39–46.

[3] J. R. Larson, G. A. Bernhard, and M. E. Padin, "Comparison of printed bibliographic descriptions distributed by BIOSIS, CAS, and Ei," *Journal of American Society for Information Science,* 27(1976): 46–52.

[4] S. M. Humphrey, "Searching the MEDLARS citation file on-line using ELHILL 2 and STAIRS: A comparison," *Information Storage and Retrieval* 10(1974): 321–329.

3.4 reference was made to the need for exceptional data codes to indicate
when a fixed length field is of insufficient length so the data are placed in a
supplementary field. An exceptional data code and supplementary field
also might be used whenever the data are represented in a manner different from the form generally used for that field. For each fixed field there
also should be a missing data code that forms the field content whenever
the value of the data is unknown.

Since the exceptional data codes and missing data codes may be chosen
differently for different data bases, it is desirable that the particular ones
in use be recorded in a record at the beginning of the data base. They may
be stored in the first block, together with the directory to the fixed length
fields.

Throughout Sections 4.1–4.11 in each question statement a three-
character attribute descriptor was placed in parentheses after each question term. Since different data bases contain different attributes, it is
advisable to have the list of allowable attribute descriptors stored at the
beginning of the data base.

There arises the question as to what characters are to be regarded as
significant characters within terms and what characters are to act as
delimiters of terms. Query terms are specified as strings of significant
characters, and the convention used to define a significant character
within query terms must be consistent with that used to define a significant character in the data base. It is clear that commas and periods are
not generally regarded as significant characters within title words, and a
search for COMPUTER is required to locate the term COMPUTER
followed by either a blank, a comma, a period, or any other punctuation
character that might arise in the occurrence of COMPUTER'S or
COMPUTER-ACCESSIBLE. On the other hand the manner in which a
search for U.S.A. must be formulated depends on whether the search
program treats it as three separate terms separated by the insignificant
period or as a single term in which the period is significant. In the letter
instance, if U.S.A. appears in the data base at the end of a sentence then
the period that follows it is an insignificant character even although the
periods contained in U.S.A. are significant.

The significance, or insignificance, of a character may depend on the
position of the character within the term. Thus within an abstract the
hyphen, or minus sign, might be regarded as nonsignificant when it occurs
between significant letters, as in WATER-COLOR, or before another
nonsignificant character as in APPLICATIONS-ƀ. However, it might be
regarded as significant if preceded by a nonsignificant character and
followed by a significant character as in ƀ-275. It might be noted that a
character string APPLICATIONS:– might be regarded as consisting of a
term followed by two nonsignificant characters. In order to know how the

search program will respond to a given query, it is necessary to know precisely the rules that govern the treatment of each separate character with regard to its being significant or nonsignificant.

The significance of a character also may depend on the attribute of the field in which it occurs. Thus an apostrophe might be regarded as significant in the term O'RILEY within an author field, but nonsignificant in the character string COUNTRY'S within a title field.

In some data bases special characters are used to mark changes of character type. For instance, in the CAIN tapes an asterisk is used to precede a letter that appears in the middle of a term and whose capitalization is to be emphasized. It is also used to indicate capitalization of a beginning letter when such is not obvious to a reader. Thus within an author field the term MacDonald is represented by MAC*DONALD whereas Macdonald is represented by MACDONALD, initialization of the first letter, M, being regarded as obvious. Within a title field Hunter Valley is represented by *HUNTER *VALLEY whereas "hunters in valleys" is represented by HUNTERS IN VALLEYS. Similarly on the SPIN tapes ^{12}C is represented by <12$C and α is represented by =(alpha)=.

In specification of question terms it is necessary to distinguish between use of characters such as * and < as type specifications that are part of the term in the data base, and their use as mode specification symbols. A method of distinguishing between the two uses is to introduce a further mode descriptor, such as an exclamation mark, to indicate that the character immediately following is to be regarded as a literal character within the term and not a truncation character. Thus question terms might be specified in the form ! 12!$C or MAC!*DONALD. In a question term specified as *C!*DONALD the first asterisk denotes truncation whereas the second is part of the term to be searched for.

To the form of the data base shown in Figure 3.1 there should therefore be added a description of the allowed mode specification characters, and also specification of the significance or nonsignificance of each character with respect to its occurrence before, after, or between significant characters of a term. The description may be different for different attributes, although some attributes may make identical use of characters with respect to mode and significance.

In view of the various considerations just described the first block of the data base shown in Figure 3.1 might be replaced by one or more blocks to contain the data arranged consecutively as shown in Figure 4.1. An initial 65-byte field may be used to contain a short description of the data base, such as METALS TAPE NO. 7 DUPLICATE, followed by the date of creation of the tape. The next 65 bytes might be left blank in order to be available for future use. The number of fixed and variable length fields are denoted by m and n respectively. If m and n are stored in character form

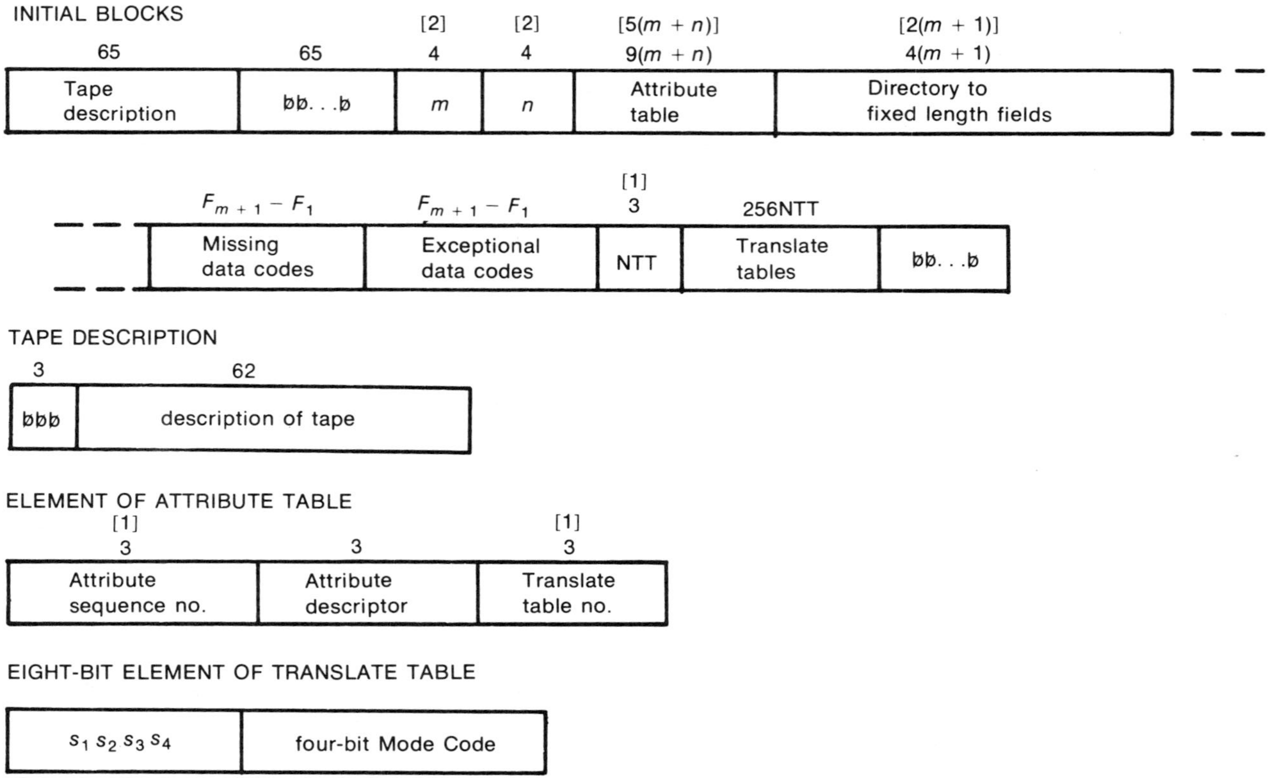

Figure 4.1. Arrangement of character specification details at beginning of data base. Numbers above the fields indicate the storage requirements in bytes for character [or binary] representation.

they may be allotted 4 bytes of storage. If stored in binary form they may each be allotted 2 bytes.

The attribute table contains an entry for each attribute. Each entry, as shown in Figure 4.1, contains an attribute sequence number that is a sequence number chosen to describe the order in which the $m + n$ fields are arranged on the tape. It also contains a translate table number that refers to a table that contains the allowed mode descriptors and character significance data. Since a translate table may apply to several different attributes there may be fewer translate tables than attributes. The number of translate tables is stored as NTT.

For data stored through use of an eight-bit character code each translate table should be of length 256 bytes. The nth byte contains mode and character significance information for the character whose eight-bit representation is equal to the binary representation of n. For example, with an EBCDIC character representation, since the asterisk has representation as 01011100 (=binary representation of 92), the mode and character significance information for * is contained in byte number 92 of the translate table.

Each byte within a translate table has its first three bits s_1, s_2, s_3 chosen as shown in Table 4.1 in order to indicate the conditions under which the character is to be regarded as significant. The last four bits constitute a mode code that indicates the manner in which the character may be used to indicate the mode of a question term. For the mode characters as used in the present chapter the mode codes may be chosen as in Table 4.2.

The fourth bit s_4 within a byte of the translate table may be set equal to 1 if the character is a sentence delimiter with respect to the logic operators WITh, PREcedence, or ADJacency.

It is clear that a proper specification of character significance requires a careful investigation of the conventions used in preparation of the data base. It is also necessary that the conventions be followed meticulously during the data base preparation. As query languages are developed to include more features and as generalized programs are developed to

Table 4.1

Type of Character Significance Expressed through s_1, s_2, and s_3.

Code	Character significant
$s_1 = 1$	Not if preceded by a nonsignificant character.
$s_3 = 1$	Not if followed by a nonsignificant character.
$s_2 = 1$	Not if both preceded and followed by a significant character.
$s_1 = s_2 = s_3 = 0$	Always significant.
$s_1 = s_2 = s_3 = 1$	Never significant.

Table 4.2
Mode Descriptors and Corresponding Mode Codes and Their Position in a Translate Table.

Mode descriptor	Mode code	Byte no. in translate table
Not a mode descriptor	0000	Other than listed below.
♭	0001	64
—	0010	109
*	0011	92
$	0100	91
/	0101	97
⌐	0110	95
<	0111	76
>	1000	110
=	1001	126
!	1010	90
:	1011	122

search a variety of data bases, the question of character significance will assume greater importance and common standards may be adopted.

4.13 Problems

1. Examine an article in a scientific publication, and then formulate a question that could be used to search for more articles on the same subject. Determine whether the question would find the papers listed as references. State whether you believe right truncation to be an essential feature for use in question statements.

2. Discuss, with examples, the relative usefulness of right truncation, left truncation, NOt logic, the IGnore specification, and PREcedence or ADJacency logic. List these six features in order of your estimate of decreasing importance.

3. Examine several articles that contain both titles and abstracts, and formulate questions that would be suitable for a search for related articles. State whether it appears preferable to search on titles only, abstracts only, or both titles and abstracts. How would the choice of searchable fields affect the form of the question?

4. Give examples of search questions to indicate how the use of weights may simplify the required question logic. Could there be advantages in using negative weights instead of NOt logic?

5. List the values you would assign to s_1, s_2, and s_3 in the translate table (Figure 4.1) for each of the following special characters within titles and abstracts:

$$. \quad , \quad / \quad - \quad + \quad (\quad)$$

5
Data Structures for Storage and Retrieval

5.1 General Considerations

In Chapter 3 consideration was given to file storage of document items that consist of sets of fields associated with certain attributes. In the present chapter the discussion is concerned with considerations that relate to the processing of data that are stored in internal memory or are to be input from files for processing in internal memory. The prime consideration is that the data be arranged in such manner as to reduce the requirements for memory space and processing time.

A sequential search of a data base to determine the document items that satisfy particular questions may be structured as in Figure 5.1. Each question is represented in computer memory by a table of question terms and a table that describes the question logic. As the data base is read sequentially each descriptor is searched for in the question term table. If it is present in the table an appropriate entry is made in the question logic table. After the reading of each complete document item the question logic table is processed to determine whether the required logic has been satisfied. If it has, then the document item is copied to a file of relevant items.

Important considerations in the design of a sequential search program are the arrangement of the question term table to allow for rapid search,

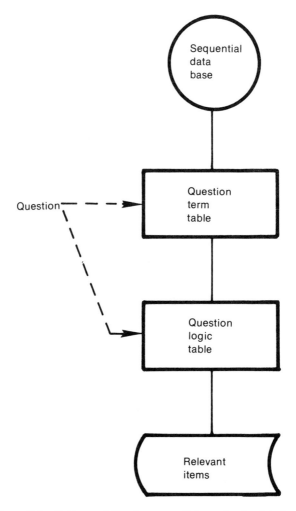

Figure 5.1. Tables and files for sequential search of a data base.

and the structuring of the question logic table to permit rapid determination of whether a document satisfies the question logic.

    Search of a data base by use of an inverted file is represented by Figure 5.2. Each question term is searched for in a dictionary that contains all the searchable descriptors of the data base. Usually each dictionary is too large to be stored in main memory. Pointers in the dictionary give the locations of document lists in the inverted file, which is likely to be stored on disk. As the question logic operations are applied to these lists it may be necessary to create temporary lists stored either in main memory or on disk. After determination of the final list of relevant document numbers,

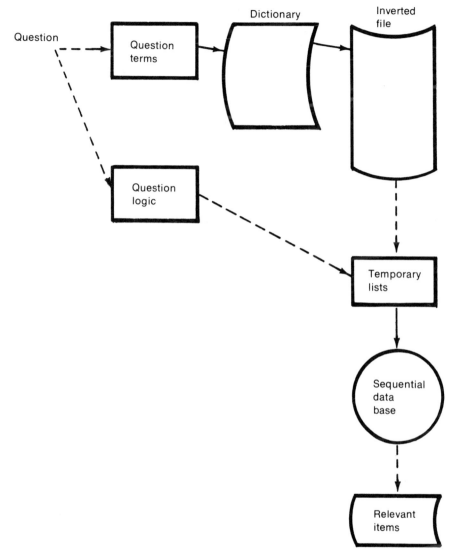

Figure 5.2. Tables and files for search of a data base by use of an inverted file.

the sequential data base is accessed and the appropriate items are transferred to a file of relevant items.

Files contain blocks of data, and each block may contain several fields. The data are not necessarily that contained in the searchable data base. For example, some fields might contain sets of question terms; others might contain the names of users authorized to have access to a certain data base. Alternatively, a file might contain a dictionary of synonyms or a thesaurus to be referred to during search of the data base.

In order to access information stored in any block the entire block must be transferred to a buffer in memory, and each transfer of a block must be executed after the elapse of a certain access time. It may be supposed that a single access to a block is sufficient to allow a read of all the fields within the block, and that whenever one field of a block is read into a buffer the entire block also is placed in the buffer.

In the subsequent sections the data generally are represented as being initially in the form of a list. The list may have been created as an array stored in internal memory, or it may be on an external file of which portions are read into main memory as required. The relative efficiencies of different methods of processing and sorting lists often depend on whether the list may be contained entirely within core, whether it is stored on a direct access device, or whether it must be read sequentially as on magnetic tape. Different processing procedures have been developed for use in different circumstances.

Information retrieval programs may include steps in which the descriptors in a data base are compared to a list or dictionary of question terms as in the sequential search of Figure 5.1. There also may be steps in which question terms are compared with entries in a dictionary of descriptors known to be present in the data base as in Figure 5.2. Such dictionaries may be structured to facilitate the problem of searching for specified terms. A simple form of structuring is through arrangement in alphabetic order. In addition to simple structuring through rearrangement of terms it may be desirable to use tables of pointers. This is illustrated by the following remarks.

Suppose a list of N terms is stored in alphabetic order, and suppose $T(N)$ denotes the maximum time required to determine whether a specified term is present in the list. The position of any term in the list may be called its address or location. Such an address might be the sequence number of the term within the list, a memory location at which the beginning of the term is stored in memory, or a block number, record number, and sequence number that indicates the position of the term within a file. Suppose a pointer table is created to contain the address of the first term that begins with the character A, the first term that begins with the character B, and so forth. Access to the pointer table allows a search through the list for a term beginning with any given letter L to be made in time $T(N_L)$, where N_L denotes the number of listed terms that begin with the particular letter L. Use of the pointer table clearly should reduce the time to search through the list since $T(N_L)$ is likely to be significantly less than $T(N)$. It may be noted that, although the pointer table requires some storage, it allows some space to be saved in storage of the terms since it is no longer necessary to store each initial character.

An alternative structure could result by grouping the terms according to term length rather than by alphabetic rank, and by storing a table of pointers to the beginning of each group. Such a structure may offer some advantage over alphabetic ranking if used to search with respect to left-truncated terms since the search need be made only on the groups whose term lengths exceed the length of the truncated term to be searched for.

Different ways of structuring data in order to facilitate efficient search procedures are described in the following sections. Although the pointers are indicated as positions of terms in a table they may, in fact, have many possible forms. In particular, they may be relative addresses or increments to be added to the location at which they are contained. Thus a pointer stored at memory location 17,834 to point to location 17,851 may be stored as the value 17 to be incremented by its storage address of 17,834. The advantage of using relative addresses is that fewer bits may be required for their storage.

5.2 Sort Tree Structure

Suppose that a set of N terms, some of which may be repetitions of previous terms, are to be arranged in alphabetic rank without repetitions. Two methods, which may be readily programmed on a computer, are summarized in Figure 5.3.

In the first method all N terms are sorted into alphabetic order. The time required for this task depends on the extent to which the original list is close to being correctly ordered. Let $T_S(N)$ denote the maximum computer time that would be required to sort the list if it initially contained the worst possible ordering. Similarly, let $T_E(N)$ denote the maximum time required to examine the sorted list and to form a new list that contains no repetitions. The total time to execute the steps of Method 1 is thus

$$T_S(N) + T_E(N). \qquad (5.1)$$

In the second method let $T_R(N)$ denote the maximum time needed to examine the N terms and to store them without repetitions. The total time required to execute the steps of Method 2 is thus

$$T_R(N) + T_S(D). \qquad (5.2)$$

As shown in Section 5.5, if the number D of different terms is significantly less than the total number of terms then $T_S(D)$ is significantly less than $T_S(N)$. Thus if the process of removal of repetitions may be made to

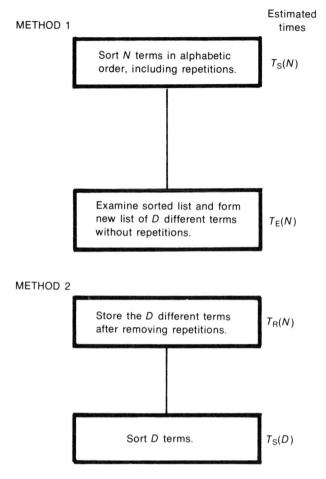

Figure 5.3. Two methods of arranging a list of N words in alphabetic rank without repetitions.

occupy sufficiently little time $T_R(N)$, then Method 2 will prove to be the more efficient. It is therefore appropriate to describe the tree sort procedure, which permits relatively fast execution of the first step of Method 2 of Figure 5.3

The sort tree procedure may be illustrated by considering the sequence of 20 terms

```
ICE,  DOG,  GAS,  JAM,  DOG,  ELK,  FAT,  APE,  HOT,  GAS,
NEW,  KEG,  LIP,  CAT,  NEW,  MAT,  OLD,  BAT,  KID,  FIT.
```

As the terms are examined in sequence they may be stored in a table of terms and three sets of pointers as shown in Table 5.1 and explained here.

Table 5.1
Terms and Pointers to Represent the Sort Tree of Figure 5.4.

TERM(N)	L(N)	R(N)	B(N)
ICE	2	4	
DOG	7	3	1
GAS	5	8	2
JAM		9	1
ELK		6	3
FAT		17	5
APE		12	2
HOT			3
NEW	10	14	4
KEG		11	9
LIP	16	13	10
CAT	15		7
MAT			11
OLD			9
BAT			12
KID			11
FIT			6

The structure of the table is indicated by the tree diagram of Figure 5.4. The tree is called a *binary tree* since not more than two downward pointers, one to the left and one to the right, lead away from each node.

The first term ICE is the first entry in the table and is identified as the label of the highest node of the tree. The next term DOG is compared with ICE and, since it is not a repetition, is placed in the table to occupy the second position. Since it ranks alphabetically less than ICE it is regarded as the label of a node at the end of a left pointer from the node labelled ICE. In the table a pointer L(1) is set to point to the position of the term DOG.

The next term GAS is compared to the first entry ICE. Since GAS ranks alphabetically less than ICE the left pointer L(1) (=2) is used to locate the term DOG. Since GAS ranks higher than DOG a right pointer R(2) is placed in the table with a value of 3 in order to point to the term GAS, which is added as the third term of the table.

The next term JAM is compared to the first entry ICE. Since it has higher rank a right pointer R(1) = 4 is placed in the table to point to the term JAM, which is added as the fourth term.

The next term DOG is compared to ICE. Since it ranks less it is then compared to the L(1)=2nd term and found to be a repetition. It is therefore not added to the table.

The next term ELK is compared to ICE, then to the L(1)=2nd term DOG,

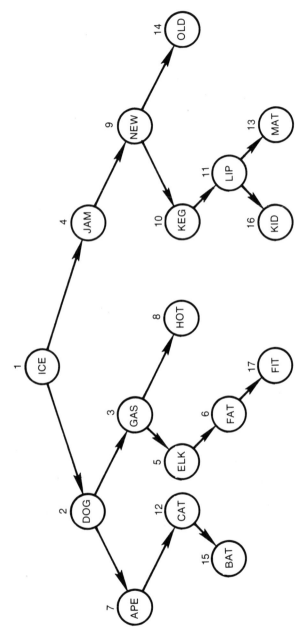

Figure 5.4. Sort tree corresponding to Table 5.1. Backward pointers are not shown. The numbers show the initial order of the terms.

then to the R(2)=3rd term GAS, and since GAS has no left pointer a pointer L(3)=5 is added to point to the term ELK, which is added to the table.

Whenever a new term is added to the table a backward pointer B(N) is added in order to indicate the location of the term whose left or right pointer is directed to the location of the new term. After examination of the entire sequence of terms the table and associated tree are as shown.

The order of the terms in Table 5.1 is identical to their original order except that all repetitions are deleted. In order to search the dictionary of terms for the presence of a given term the appropriate chain of pointers is followed through the sort tree of Figure 5.4. It may be noted that in Figure 5.4 there are some chains of pointers that have five links. A different initial ordering of the terms could lead to a tree in which some terminal nodes are at the end of pointer chains with many links, while other terminal nodes are at the end of very short chains of pointers. The number of term comparisons required to determine the presence or absence of a specified term depends on the structure of the particular tree, but the following remarks provide some indication of how the number depends on the number D of nodes.

A binary tree contains a single root node, which may be regarded as at level zero. It may contain up to two nodes at level 1, up to 4 at level 2, and so forth so that level n may have up to 2^n nodes. A binary tree that contains exactly 2^n nodes at each level n except possibly the last is said to be a balanced tree. An example of such is shown in Figure 5.5, which is the sort tree that results from the sequence of 20 terms

```
ICE,  LIP,  KEG,  FAT,  DOG,  NEW,  DOG,  KID,  NEW,  GAS,
BAT,  ELK,  APE,  GAS,  JAM,  CAT,  MAT,  FIT,  OLD,  HOT.
```

In Figure 5.5 the numbers attached to the nodes are not related to the initial order of the terms but are included for reasons explained later.

Let D denote the number of nodes in a balanced tree and let

$$\text{ceil}(\log_2 D) \tag{5.3}$$

denote the least integer greater than or equal to $\log_2 D$. The expression ceil may be called a *ceiling operator*. The longest chains of pointers from the root node to terminal nodes contain ceil$[\log_2 (D + 1)]$ nodes, and to search the tree structure for the presence or absence of a specified term requires not more than ceil$[\log_2 (D + 1)]$ comparisons of the specified term with terms represented by the nodes. Such comparisons are for lower rank, greater rank, or equal rank, and hence are equivalent to the two simple comparisons contained in the statement sequence

```
If (TERM less than NODE TERM) go to . . .
If (TERM greater than NODE TERM) go to . . .
Go to . . .
```

114

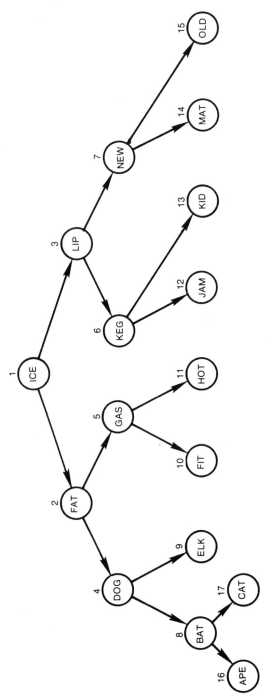

Figure 5.5. Example of a balanced tree of 17 nodes.

Creation of a sort tree of D nodes from a given list of N terms thus requires not more than

$$2N \text{ ceil}[\log_2(D + 1)] \tag{5.4}$$

simple comparisons in the special instance that the resulting binary tree is balanced. If the resulting tree is approximately balanced then $2N$ ceil[$\log_2(D + 1)$] provides an approximation for the number of simple comparisons of terms during creation of the sort tree.

In the extreme instance that the sort tree is so far from balanced that all D nodes lie on a single chain of pointers of length $D - 1$, then search of the structure for the presence or absence of a specified term could require up to $2D$ simple comparisons. The expression analogous to Eq. (5.4) is then

$$2ND. \tag{5.5}$$

In the general case the number of required comparisons during creation sort tree will lie between the values of Eqs. (5.4) and (5.5), with Eq. (5.5) being the better estimate unless the terms are initially close to being in order of their rank.

When a dictionary is stored as a sort tree as in Table 5.1 some overhead storage is required for the pointers that are associated with the terms. This overhead may be eliminated by rearranging the stored terms so that their ordering indicates the relative ranking of terms. Two useful arrangements are described here. The first is to give alphabetic order, and the second is to correspond to a certain labelling of a balanced binary tree.

Terms stored in a sort tree structure as represented by Figure 5.4 may be examined and recorded in alphabetic order by the algorithm shown in Figure 5.6. It may be noted that for a sort tree of D nodes there will be a total of approximately $2D$ tests of pointers. Thus is a list of N terms is first examined to construct a sort tree of D terms, which are then placed in alphabetic order, an estimate of the maximum number of simple comparisons required is given by the value of

$$2N \text{ ceil}(\log_2 D) + 2D. \tag{5.6}$$

If terms are stored in alphabetic order it is not necessary to store associated pointers since the presence or absence of a specified term may be determined by application of the binary, or logarithmic, search algorithm of Figure 5.7. The number of required comparisons of terms will not exceed

$$\text{ceil}(\log_2 D). \tag{5.7}$$

More detailed discussion of the number of comparisons required for a

116

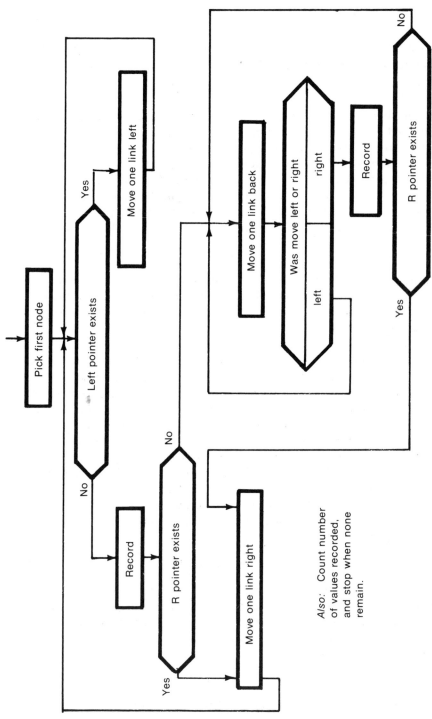

Figure 5.6. Algorithm to process the sort tree in order to record the terms in alphabetic order.

The flowchart contains the following elements:

- Pick first node
- Left pointer exists
  - Yes: Move one link left
  - No: Record
- R pointer exists
  - Yes: Move one link right
  - No: (continues)
- Move one link back
- Was move left or right
  - left
  - right
- Record
- R pointer exists
  - Yes
  - No

Also: Count number of values recorded, and stop when none remain.

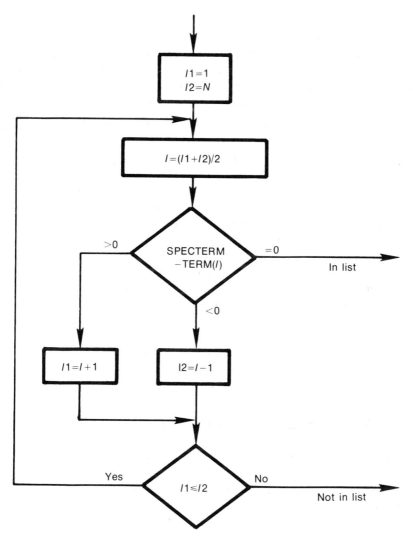

Figure 5.7. Binary search algorithm to search an alphabetically ordered list of terms TERM(I) for the presence of a specified SPECTERM.

binary search and the problems that arise if data is added or deleted are given by Lowe and Roberts.[1]

It may be noted that if the dictionary of terms is stored on magnetic tape then a binary search is likely to involve backspacing for certain term

[1] T. C. Lowe and D. C. Roberts, "Analysis of directory searching," *Journal of the American Society for Information Science* 23 (1972):143–149.

comparisons. This is clearly undesirable since it increases the time and cost of the search.

An alternative to an alphabetic ordering of terms is an ordering in which the term sequence is according to the numbers attached to the nodes of a balanced binary tree according to the scheme illustrated in Figure 5.5. The sequence in which the terms are stored in thus

```
ICE,  FAT,  LIP,  DOG,  GAS,  KEG,  NEW,  BAT,  ELK,  FIT,
HOT,  JAM,  KID,  MAT,  OLD,  APE,  CAT.
```

It is not necessary to store pointers since the left pointer associated with the ith term is to the $2i$th term of the sequence, and the right pointer associated with the ith term is to the $2i + 1$th term of the sequence. Similarly, the back pointer associated with the ith term is to the term at position floor $(i/2)$, where the floor function is defined so that floor $(i/2)$ is the greatest integer less than or equal to $i/2$.

The preceding ordering according to label numbering of the binary tree has the advantage that a binary search proceeds from comparison of an ith term to either the $2i$th or $2i + 1$th. Thus as i increases from an initial value of 1, the successive comparisons are always with terms that are stored further along the list. If the terms are stored on magnetic tape the search may proceed without the need for rewinds.

Creation of the ordered list may be effected by the algorithm of Figure 5.6 provided that, as the terms are selected from the sort tree structure, they are placed in the appropriate positions in the new list.

5.3 Dictionary Storage Using Character Tree

Instead of structuring a dictionary to correspond to a sort tree of the form represented by Figure 5.4 and Table 5.1, it may prove convenient to use a binary tree whose nodes correspond to individual characters. For example, the terms

```
CATS, CONE, CAB, CABS, COST, CABLE, COAT
```

may be stored as in Table 5.2, whose structure corresponds to the binary tree of Figure 5.8 in which each term is represented by a sequence of nodes at descending levels. It may be noted that from each node there is not more than one downward pointer $D(N)$ and one horizontal pointer $H(N)$, and that the use of horizontal pointers avoids the need for more than a single downward pointer from any node. The column ET is included in Table 5.2 in order to indicate the characters that occur at the end of terms. These are not always terminal nodes, and the corresponding characters are underlined in Figure 5.8. Since ET may be represented by a

Table 5.2
Table of Characters and Pointers to Represent the Binary Tree of Figure 5.8.

CHAR(N)	D(N)	H(N)	ET
C	2		
A	3	5	
T	4	8	
S			1
O	6		
N	7	10	
E			1
B	9		1
S		12	1
S	11	14	
T			1
L	13		
E			1
A	15		
T			1

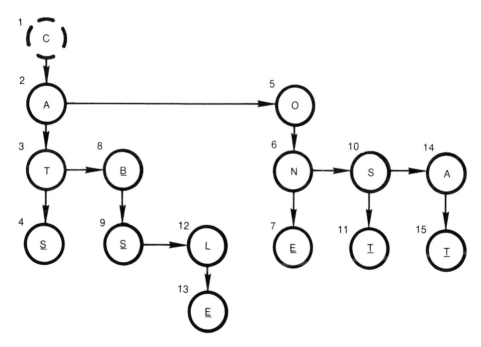

Figure 5.8. Binary tree corresponding to Table 5.2. The numbers indicate the addresses in Table 5.2.

single bit it may be convenient to code it as a sign bit absorbed within the $D(N)$ or $H(N)$ fields.

The space required for storage of the characters in Table 5.2 is clearly less than that required for storage of all the individual terms. However, during search for a term the number of nodes examined is likely to be greater than required for a sort tree of the form shown in Figure 5.4 because of the presence of horizontal pointers.

In Figure 5.8 the root node and its pointer are represented in broken form because, if it is known that the tree represents only terms that begin with the character C, there is no necessity to store this character in the table.

For a large dictionary of terms it is likely that at the highest level of the sort tree there will be close to 26 nodes. At lower levels the various chains of horizontal pointers are likely to contain significantly fewer than 26 nodes. This suggests a form of dictionary storage as shown in Figure 5.9. The first two characters of a term are used to address a table of pointers, each of whose elements indicates the beginning of a character tree whose nodes correspond to the remaining characters of terms that begin with the particular pair of characters. A one-bit column FLG is included in the index table in order to indicate any single characters or character pairs, such as AS or IT, that are themselves complete terms. Single characters are also allowed to index the FLG column in order to allow inclusion of terms of single characters, such as A or I.

It may be noted that for a large dictionary the space saved by not storing the first two characters of each term may be significantly greater than the space required to store the index table.

5.4 Table Structure to Allow Truncation Specification

With the table organization shown in Figure 5.1, during the search phase of the program each descriptor within a searchable field of the data base is searched for in the question term table. If no truncation specifications are allowed then an alphabetic ordering of the terms may prove convenient since it allows use of a binary search.

However, if truncation is allowed in the specification of question terms then a binary search of an alphabetically ordered list of terms is generally not convenient. Consider, for example, a term list that contains entries that correspond to the following terms and nodes

```
COMPARISON
COMPUT*
COMPUTATIONAL
COMPUTERS
```

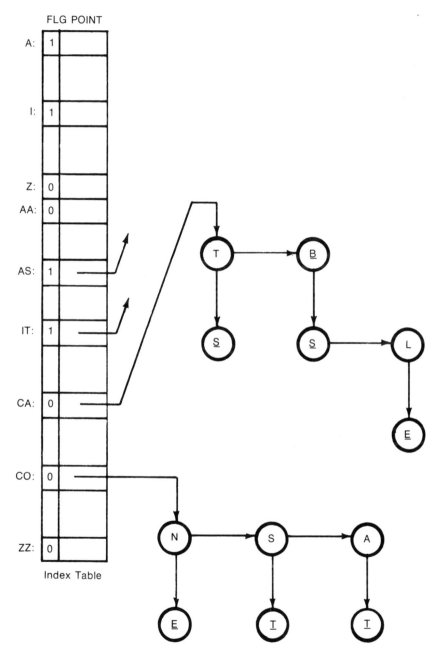

Figure 5.9. Dictionary in form of index table and character tree to store the characters that follow the first two in each term.

A binary search for COMPUTER must be modified to search, not only for COMPUTER but also for terms, such as COMPUT*, near to where COM-PUTER would be stored between COMPUTATIONAL and COMPUTERS if it had been a question term. In fact the search might be required to range through many terms that begin with C since there might be question terms such as COMP* or COM*.

The preceding discussion suggests the use of an index table addressable by the characters A to Z, 0 to 9, and any other characters present within searchable terms. Each pointer within the index table may indicate the beginning of a character tree as in Figure 5.9.

If left truncation, but not double truncation, is also allowed then the left-truncated question terms may be stored in reverse order and each data base descriptor searched for in both direct and reverse form. Thus the data base term RECLASSIFICATION would be searched for as RE-CLASSIFICATION to match with RECLASSIF*, etc., and would also be searched for as NOITACIFISSALCER to match with *CLASSIFICATION (stored as NOITACIFISSALC*), etc. Treated in this manner the allowance for left truncation increases the length of the question term list and therefore the search times. However, the method cannot be used if the question term table contains doubly truncated terms such as *CLASSIF*.

A very efficient method for structuring the question term table in a manner to allow any form of truncation has been described by Aho and Corasick.[2] It may be explained as follows.

Suppose the question terms are specified in the form

SHE*, *HE, *ER*, *HI, *HE*

that is equivalent to specifying that the relevant textual field must be searched for the character strings

ƀSHE, HEƀ, ER, HIƀ, HE.

The four characters of the first term ƀSHE may be associated with pointers that link a root node of label O to a chain of four other nodes of labels 1, 2, 3, 4 as shown in the tree of Figure 5.10. The three characters of the next term HEƀ may be associated with pointers that link the root node to a chain of three other nodes of labels 5, 6, 7. Similarly, the characters of the term ER may be associated with pointers to nodes of labels 8 and 9. The characters of the term HIƀ are associated with the existing pointer to the node of label 5 and with two further pointers to new nodes of labels 10 and 11. The characters of the remaining term HE are already associated with two pointers that form a chain from the root node.

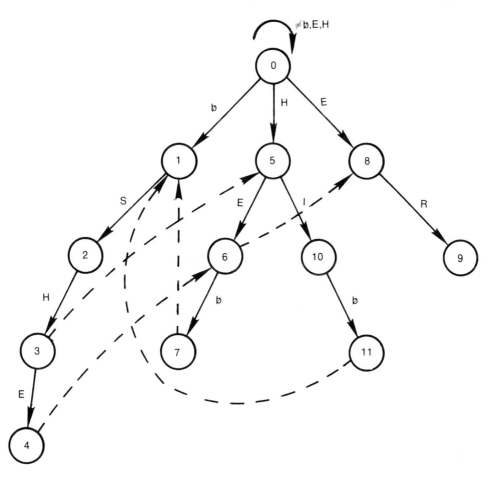

Figure 5.10. Representation of question terms by a tree of pointers according to the function $g(s, x)$, and with backward pointers according to $f(s)$.

A further pointer is added to lead from the root node to the root node. It is associated with all characters different from ƀ, E, or H.

A variable s is set initially to zero and is allowed to range over the values of the node labels. Let x denote any character that may be present in the data base. The pointers of Figure 5.10 may be represented by a "goto" function $g(s, x)$ whose value is defined such that if there is a pointer from the node of label s to the node of label n, and this pointer is associated with the character x, then

$$g(s, x) = n. \tag{5.7}$$

If there is no such pointer then $g(s, x)$ is not defined. The values of $g(s, x)$ defined by the tree of Figure 5.10 are thus:

$$g(0, x) = 0 \quad \text{if} \quad x \neq \flat, \text{E}, \text{H},$$
$$g(0, \flat) = 1, \quad g(0, \text{E}) = 8, \quad g(0, \text{H}) = 5,$$
$$g(1, \text{S}) = 2,$$
$$g(2, \text{H}) = 3,$$
$$g(3, \text{E}) = 4,$$
$$g(5, \text{E}) = 6, \quad g(5, \text{I}) = 10,$$
$$g(6, \flat) = 7,$$
$$g(8, \text{R}) = 9,$$
$$g(10, \flat) = 11.$$

Each chain of pointers from the root node to a terminal node represents one of the question terms. However, some of the question terms may contain a sequence of characters that form the beginning of other terms. For example, the term $\flat$SHE ends with two characters that form the beginning of the term HE$\flat$. Similarly, $\flat$SHE contains the character H, which forms the beginnings of terms HE$\flat$, HI$\flat$, and HE. Such overlaps are indicated by the broken pointers in Figure 5.10. These backward pointers may be represented by a function $f(s)$ so that for Figure 5.10 the nonzero values of $f(s)$ are:

$$f(3) = 5,$$
$$f(4) = 6,$$
$$f(6) = 8,$$
$$f(7) = 1,$$
$$f(11) = 1.$$

An output procedure OUTPUT(s) is defined to perform tasks as follows:

If $s = 4$ record that SHE* and *HE* are present in data base.
If $s = 6$ record that *HE* present.
If $s = 7$ record that *HE present.
If $s = 9$ record that *ER* present.
If $s = 11$ record that *HI present.

For other values of s perform no task.

Having stored the values of $g(s,x)$ and $f(s)$ the program represented by the flowchart of Figure 5.11a may be used to step through the appropriate fields of each document item character by character to determine which question terms are present. It may be noted that for each character in the data base there is one resetting of s through the relation $s = g(s, x)$. Each such resetting of s may be preceded by several resettings in the form $s = f(s)$. However, since $s = g(s,x)$ corresponds to downward movement

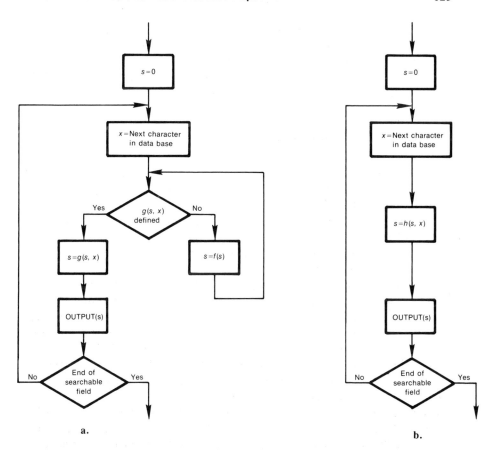

Figure 5.11. Flowcharts of programs to search data base for presence of terms that may be truncated.

between a pair of nodes and $s = f(s)$ corresponds to an upward movement, the number of transfers $s = f(s)$ cannot exceed the number of transfers $s = g(s,x)$. Thus the total number of resettings of s cannot exceed $2N$ where N is the number of data base characters present in the entirety of the data base examined.

A particularly attractive feature of the procedure is that its time of execution is independent of the number of question terms except insofar as they affect the number of executions of OUTPUT(s). It may be noted that no terms or characters need to be stored; the only stored values are in the tables of values of $f(s)$ and $g(s,x)$.

It may also be noted that, prior to beginning the search, the steps of the program that involve $g(s,x)$ and $f(s)$ could be run for all combinations of s and x in order to determine the values of a new function $h(s,x)$, which could then be stored and used in the very simple program shown in Figure 5.11b. This program, when used instead of that shown in Figure 5.11a, allows very rapid stepping through the data base character by character.

5.5 Some Sorting Algorithms

In Section 5.2 a sort tree structure was used to store a sequence of terms so that repetitions could be omitted. However, storage is required for pointers, and if the number of repeated terms is small it may be preferable to sort them by means of a procedure that does not require storage of pointers.

One such procedure is the exchange, or bubble, sort. It may be explained as follows in reference to a list of N terms.

The first term of the list is compared to the second term and is interchanged with it, if necessary, in order to place the two terms in the required order. The second term is then compared to the third and is exchanged with it if necessary. Similar comparisons of pairs of terms are made until the comparison, and possible exchange, of the N-1th and Nth terms. The result is to ensure that the Nth term of the list is properly ranked with respect to all the other terms. A total of N-1 comparisons, and possibly interchanges, will have been made.

The first and second, second and third, and etc. to the N-2th and N-1th terms are then compared and interchanged if necessary. These N-2 comparisons will ensure that the N-1th term in the list is properly ranked.

The preceding sequences of comparisons and interchanges are continued for the first N-2 terms, then the first N-3 terms, and so forth until all terms are correctly ranked. The required number of comparisons does not exceed

$$(N - 1) + (N - 2) + . . . + 2 + 1 = N(N - 1)/2. \qquad (5.8)$$

In fact, if the initial list of terms is close to being correctly ranked the number of comparisons may be significantly less. Clearly the sorting is complete whenever a sequence of comparisons results in no interchanges of terms.

In comparison to use of the sort tree structure, use of the exchange sort is very simple and does not require additional storage for pointers. However, more comparisons are required and, if the lists of terms are stored on magnetic tape, then up to N-2 rewinds may be required. Thus the exchange sort is convenient only for use with a relatively small in-core list of terms. There are many variations of the exchange sort including a procedure that has been designated as Quicksort.[3,4]

A more sophisticated sorting procedure is provided by the tree sort, not to be confused with the sort tree, algorithm that may be explained as follows.

Suppose a list of N terms, possibly with some repetitions, is stored sequentially and envisaged as associated with nodes of a balanced tree numbered as in Figure 5.5. The first term of the list is associated with node No. 1, the second with node No. 2, and so forth. Thus initially the node numbers bear no relation to the relative ranking of terms.

Let T_I denote the subtree whose root node has number I. Thus T_7 is the subtree whose nodes are numbered 7, 14, 15, and T_2 is the subtree whose nodes are numbered 2, 4, 5, 8, 9, 10, 11, 16, 17. Let ALG(I) denote the algorithm shown in Figure 5.12. If this algorithm is applied to a subtree T_I whose terms all satisfy the inequality

$$\text{TERM(J)} \leqslant \text{Both TERM(2J) and TERM(2J+1)} \qquad (5.9)$$

except when TERM(J) is the root TERM(I) of T_I, then the algorithm rearranges the terms so that the inequality becomes valid for all terms in the subtree including TERM(I). The rearrangement is performed by replacing TERM(I) at the root node by the smaller of TERM(2I) and TERM(2I+1), if necessary, in order to make it the smallest element of T_I. The value originally stored at the root node is then displaced down the tree to the appropriate position to ensure that relation (5.9) remains satisfied for all nodes including the Ith. Since the number of nodes in the subtree T_I cannot exceed N, the number of executions of the cycle ABCD in Figure 5.12 cannot exceed

$$\text{floor}(\log_2 N). \qquad (5.10)$$

By use of the algorithm ALG(*I*) the set of N unsorted terms may be arranged in ascending order by the following tree sort procedure.

(*i*)   Set I = floor ($N/2$) and execute in succession
        ALG(I), ALG(I − 1), ALG(I − 2), . . . , ALG(2)
(*ii*) Set $m = N$.
(*iii*) Do N-1 times:

    (*i*)   Execute algorithm A(1) so that the root node contains the term of
         lowest rank.

[3] C. A. R. Hoare, "Quicksort," *The Computer Journal* 5 (1962–1963):10–15.

[4] J. S. Gatehouse, "Electronic data processing for the international vocabulary of terms used in information processing," *The Computer Journal* 7 (1964–1965):271–274.

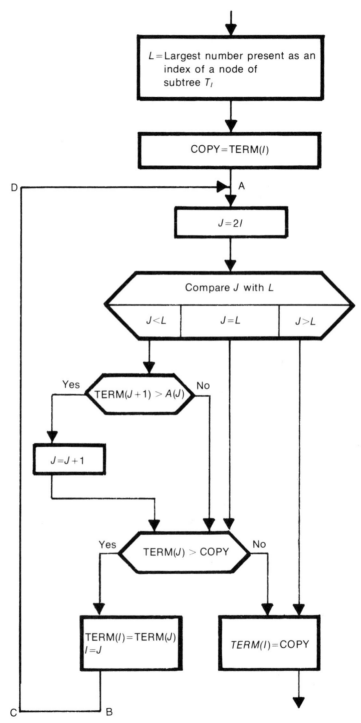

Figure 5.12. Algorithm ALG(I) for use in tree sort.

(ii)   Interchange the terms of node 1 and node *m*.

(iii) Remove node *m* from the tree and store its term.

On completion of the preceding procedure the terms will have been stored in ascending alphabetic rank. They may be stored in the area that becomes vacant as the sort tree is successively reduced by removal of nodes.

It may be noted that during execution of the preceding tree sort procedure the algorithm ALG is performed $N - 1 + \text{floor}(N/2)$ times, which is certainly not greater than $3N/2$. Thus the number of executions of the cycle ABCD in Figure 5.12 cannot exceed

$$(3/2)N \ \text{floor}(\log_2 N). \tag{5.10}$$

In contrast to use of the sort tree structure as described in Section 5.2, the tree sort procedure requires no additional space for storage of pointers. The maximum time required for execution is approximately proportional to $N \log_2 N$, which is the same expression that results for use of the sort tree method when there are no repeated terms. For large values of N the execution time is significantly less than that required by the exchange sort. If the terms are stored on magnetic tape then a rewind is required before execution of each ALG(I), and hence up to $3N/2$ rewinds may be required. Thus in common with the exchange sort and sort tree method, the tree sort is designed primarily to process lists that may be stored in internal memory.

Lists that are too large for storage in internal memory may be sorted by the merge–sort procedure that is illustrated by reference to Table 5.3, which represents an initial list on magnetic tape together with lists on four further tapes. Values in the initial list of terms are read and written on Tape 1 until a value is found that is not of higher alphabetic rank. Thus the first few terms placed on Tape 1 form an ordered sublist. Further terms are read from the initial list and placed on Tape 2 until there is found a value that is not of higher alphabetic rank; thus Tape 2 also begins with an ordered sublist. For the example chosen in Figure 5.3 the two sublists are ICE and DOG, GAS, JAM. Further terms are read from the initial list and are placed on Tape 1 to form a further ordered sublist such as ELK, FIT. The process of writing ordered sublists alternately on Tape 1 and Tape 2 is continued until all terms have been copied from the initial list.

Tape 1 and Tape 2 are then read sequentially. Terms of each first sublist are compared and written in appropriate order to form a merged ordered sublist DOG, GAS, ICE, JAM on Tape 3. Terms of the second sublists are then read and merged to form an ordered sublists APE, ELK, FIT, HOT, NEW at the beginning of Tape 4. Reading and merging of further sublists then continues as shown.

Table 5.3
Successive Merges of Ordered Sublists According to the Merge–Sort Procedure.

Initial	Tape 1,Tape 2		Tape 3,Tape 4		Tape 1,Tape 2		Tape3,Tape 4
ICE	ICE	DOG	DOG	APE	APE	BAT	APE
DOG	ELK	GAS	GAS	ELK	DOG	CAT	BAT
GAS	FIT	JAM	ICE	FIT	ELK	KID	CAT
JAM	KID	APE	JAM	HOT	FIT	LID	DOG
ELK	LIP	HOT	CAT	NEW	GAS	MAT	ELK
FIT	BAT	NEW	KID	BAT	HOT	PAT	FIT
APE	PAT	CAT	LID	PAT	ICE	TAP	GAS
HOT	USE	MAT	MAT	TAP	JAM	USE	HOT
NEW	VAT	TAP		USE	NEW	VAT	ICE
KID		WIT		VAT		WIT	JAM
LIP				WIT			KID
CAT							LID
MAT							MAT
BAT							NEW
PAT							PAT
USE							TAP
VAT							USE
TAP							VAT
WIT							WIT

The sublists on Tape 3 and Tape 4 are then merged in pairs to form new ordered sublists that are written on Tape 1 and Tape 2. The process of merging lists from Tape 1 and Tape 2, or from Tape 3 and Tape 4, is continued until one tape contains the entire ordered list.

Since the sublists are combined in pairs it follows than an initial list of N terms may be sorted by use of not more than $\text{ceil}(\log_2 N)$ transfers between pairs of tapes. During each transfer each comparison of terms determines the next term to be placed on the new tape; hence transfer to a pair of tapes involves N comparisons of terms. The total number of term comparisons required to sort the list is therefore not greater than

$$N \ \text{ceil}(\log_2 N). \tag{5.11}$$

The operation of transferring between pairs of tapes is repeated not more than $\text{ceil}(\log_2 N) - 1$ times, and hence the total number of pairs of rewinds is not more than

$$\text{ceil}(\log_2 N) - 2. \tag{5.12}$$

It may be noted that the merge–sort requires approximately half as many comparisons as the tree sort and significantly fewer rewinds. Thus for sorting of lists that are too large for storage in main memory the merge–sort offers significantly advantage over the methods discussed previously.

The merge–sort procedure may be generalized to transfer data between two sets each of q tapes where $q \geq 2$. The maximum number of required comparisons is then

$$(q-1)N \text{ ceil}(\log_q N) \tag{5.13}$$

which for $q > 2$ is larger than the value for $q = 2$. However, the number of times that the tapes must be rewound is not more than

$$\text{ceil}(\log_q N) - 2 \tag{5.14}$$

which for $q > 2$ is significantly less than for $q = 2$.

An evaluation of various sorting methods is given by Brooks and Iverson.[5] It may be remarked that for most computer operating systems there are standard sort programs that may be used to sort either numeric or alphabetic data. However, there may be some instances in which the data base does not conform to the requirements of the standard sort package, and it is then necessary to write a sort program for the particular problem.

5.6 Inverted File Structure

A sequential search on a large data base may be very expensive in computer execution time, and it is therefore better to perform the search through logic operations applied to lists of an inverted file as introduced in Section 2.8. Each list of the inverted file contains a set of entries to indicate all the documents that contain a given term.

Since the lists of the inverted file contain different numbers of entries, it is convenient to store the entries in a sequence of linear lists rather than as matrix elements. A directory may then be used to indicate the beginning of the entries associated with each searchable term.

For example, if four terms a, b, c, and d are contained in three documents according to the arrangement

$$\begin{array}{ll} \text{Doc. 1:} & a,b \\ \text{Doc. 2:} & c,a,d,b \\ \text{Doc. 3:} & d,b \end{array}$$

then the inverted file and its associated dictionary are as shown in Figure 5.13. Any term may be searched for in the dictionary, and the correspond-

---

[5] F. B. Brooks, and K. E. Iverson, *Automatic Data Processing* (New York: Wiley, 1963), Chapter 7.

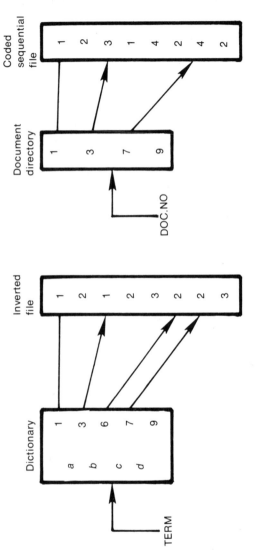

Figure 5.13. Inverted file and sequential file with associated dictionary and document directory.

ing pointer may be used to locate the associated list of document numbers in the sequential file.

If the question logic is applied to the appropriate lists of an inverted file there results a set of numbers of relevant documents, and the corresponding document records may then be read from storage. In order to avoid the need for a sequential read of the stored document records, it may prove desirable to use a document directory as included in Figure 5.13. The document directory indicates the beginning of each document item in the sequential file. The sequential file may store either the document terms or else codes for them, such as the positions at which they appear in the dictionary. The latter form of storage is the one used in Figure 5.13; thus the second document corresponds to the second pointer in the document directory, and the directory indicates that the second document contains terms whose positions in the dictionary are 3, 1, 4, and 2.

The advantage of storing codes rather than terms, and hence of creating a coded sequential file, is that codes usually may be stored in less space and in fixed length fields. It may be noted that 16-bit fields are sufficient for storage of pointers of value up to 65,535, whereas alphabetically spelled terms usually require significantly more than 16 bits. The price paid for the reduction in storage is that, as each code is read from the sequential file, the dictionary must be accessed in order to determine the alphabetic representation of the term.

The amount of space required for storage of the four files of Figure 5.13 may be estimated as follows. Suppose the original sequential data base consists of R document records that contain a total of N terms of which only D are different. The required inverted file then contains N numbers, each of whose value is at most R, and hence may be stored in ceil($\log_2 R$) bits. The space required for storage of the inverted file is thus

$$N \text{ ceil}(\log_2 R) \qquad (5.15)$$

bits. The pointers in the dictionary have values not greater than N, and so the space required for storage of the dictionary is

$$D[L + \text{ceil}(\log_2 N)] \qquad (5.16)$$

bits where L is the average term length in bits. Similarly, the space required for storage of the sequential records and the document directory is

$$N\text{ceil}(\log_2 D) + R \text{ ceil}(\log_2 N). \qquad (5.17)$$

The total space required to store the four files of Figure 5.13 is therefore

$$N[\text{ceil}(\log_2 D) + \text{ceil}(\log_2 R)] + DL + (R + D)\text{ceil}(\log_2 N). \qquad (5.18)$$

In contrast, if the data base of N terms is stored in sequential records instead of through an inverted file structure the required storage is for

$$NL \tag{5.19}$$

bits exclusive of any space required to store tags or delimiters, such as blanks, between terms.

It may be remarked that for a data base of 10,000 document records that contain an average of eight terms then $N = 80,000$. If the average term length is 48 bits, and there are 10,000 different terms, the values of the quantities (5.15)–(5.19) are, respectively

   1,120,000   230,000,   1,290,000,   2,640,000,   3,840,000.

Thus representation of such a data base through the inverted file structure of Figure 5.13 requires only 2640/3840 = 70% of the space required for sequential storage in uncoded form.

For a set of document records that contain searchable terms associated with a single attribute the four tables shown in Figure 5.13 may be created on files by the steps outlined here and illustrated in Figure 5.14.

Step 1. For each document record, and term within the record, place in File 1 a record consisting of three fields that contain respectively the document number DOC, the term TERM, and the sequence position POS of the term within the record.

Step 2. Sort the elements of File 1 to be ordered within respect to terms and to form File 2.

Step 3. Transfer the document numbers from File 2 to another file to form the inverted file.

Step 4. Transfer the terms of File 2 without repetitions, together with their addresses in File 2, to form the dictionary.

Step 5. To each record of File 2 add a number CODE that indicates the ranking order of the terms. (Terms a, b, c, d are ranked as 1, 2, 3, 4 respectively.)

Step 6. Sort the elements of File 2 into File 3 so that they occur in ascending order of document number and, for each document number, are ordered with respect to increasing order of PCS.

Step 7. Transfer the numbers CODE from File 3 to form the sequential file.

Step 8. Examine the records of File 3, and whenever there is a changed value of the document number DOC transfer the CODE to another file to form the document dictionary.

It is clear that creation of an inverted file and its associated directory and dictionary involves very simple programming, particularly if the sorts

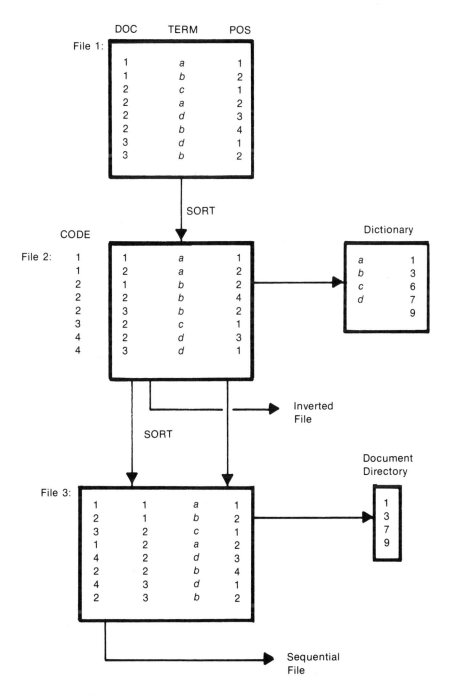

Figure 5.14. Creation of inverted file, etc., from a set of sequential document records.

135

are performed by use of standard packages. The resulting search times are so short in comparison to those required for a sequential search that the cost of creating the inverted file structure may well be negligible in comparison to the cost of performing the searches on a sequential file. A possible exception to this is when it is known that a data base will be searched only once. Such a situation might arise in an SDI service in which separate issues of a data base are searched only once with respect to a batch of standing questions.

For a set of document records that contain searchable terms arranged in two fields to correspond to two different attributes, there may be formed two sets of the four files shown in Figure 5.13. The sequential files SEQ1 and SEQ2, and also the two document directory files DIR1 and DIR2, may then be merged as described here.

Let the entries in DIR1 be $m_1, m_2, \ldots$, and let the entries in DIR2 be $n_1, n_2, \ldots$. The $m_{i+1} - m_i$ elements of the ith record in file SEQ1 and the $n_{i+1} - n_i$ elements of the ith record in file SEQ2 may be merged into a record of $m_{i+1} - m_i + n_{i+1} - n_i$ elements preceded by two pointers P_i and Q_i that form a directory to the two fields. The merged record has the form

$$P_i, \quad Q_i, \quad \text{elements from SEQ1}, \quad \text{elements from SEQ2},$$

where

$$P_i = m_{i+1} - m_i + 1, \tag{5.20}$$

$$Q_i = P_i + n_{i+1} - n_i. \tag{5.21}$$

Thus P_i, Q_i form a directory to indicate the field position immediately after the fields of elements from SEQ1 and SEQ2 respectively, regarding the first of the merged elements to be at field position 1. With respect to the merged sequential file SEQ the document directory entries are N_1, $N_2, \ldots$, where $N_1 = 1$ and

$$N_i = N_{i-1} + Q_{i-1} + 1. \tag{5.22}$$

To illustrate the preceding procedure, suppose terms a, b, c, d are associated with the first attribute, terms x, y, z are associated with the second attribute, and the occurrence of terms within three documents is according to the arrangement

Doc 1: a,b,y
Doc 2: c,a,d,b,z,x
Doc 3: d,b,x,y.

It may readily be verified that the two pairs of sequential files and document directories are

SEQ1: a,b,c,a,d,b,d,b
DIR1: 1,3,7,9

$$\text{SEQ2:} \quad y,z,x,x,y$$
$$\text{DIR2:} \quad 1,2,4,6.$$

The merged sequential file and document directory are

$$\text{SEQ:} \quad 3,4,a,b,y,5,7,c,a,d,b,z,x,3,5,d,b,x,y$$
$$\text{DIR:} \quad 6,14,20.$$

For a set of document records that contain searchable terms that correspond to several attributes the sequential files and document directories may be merged in a similar manner. In many instances it may prove desirable to merge some of the dictionaries in order to avoid duplication of terms that occur in several different fields.

5.7 Scatter Storage

Scatter, or hash, storage is used to describe storage techniques in which each item of data are stored in a table called a scatter storage table at a location whose address is computed as a function of a key formed from all, or part of, the data value. Thus alphabetic data such as TERM might be stored at position.

$$H = h(\text{TERM}) \tag{5.23}$$

where H is said to be the hash address derived from application of the scatter, or hash, function h to a key that consists of the sequence of bits that represents the data TERM. The advantage of such a scheme of storage is that a search for an item of specified value may require access only to the calculated location at which the value would be stored. Such is certainly true if the function h always transforms different terms into different hash addresses, but in practice it is rarely possible to choose a function h that has this property for all choice of data. Thus the storage scheme is usually modified so that the storage address depends on the hash address but is not always identical to it.

Most scatter storage methods proceed as follows. The scatter storage function h is applied to a key derived from the data, TERM, and a hash address H is computed. If the scatter storage table does not contain an entry at position H then TERM is stored at that position. If the scatter table already contains an entry at position H then a collision is said to have occurred at address H; a function $r(H)$ or $r(\text{TERM})$ is then used to compute a sequence of addresses $R_1, R_2, R_3, \ldots$ until there results an address at which the scatter table contains no entry. The value TERM is then stored at this address. An alternative is to use a collision table for storage of all terms for which a collision occurs.

The function $r(H)$ or $r(\text{TERM})$ is chosen so that the sequence

$$R_1, R_2, R_3, \ldots$$

contains no repetitions of values and yet ranges through all addresses of the storage area. It should supply different sequences for different hash addresses H, or values of TERM, in order to minimize the likelihood of repeated collisions. There are many well-known pseudorandom functions $r(H)$ that may be chosen with these properties, and so further details will not be given here.

The scatter storage technique may be illustrated by consideration of the following set of 20 terms

```
CAT,  TIN,  COW,  MAN,  JAM,  RAT,  DEN,  GIN,  TON,  FEE,
VAT,  USE,  TOE,  TAP,  BIN,  BOW,  DOG,  TOP,  DOE,  BUN.
```

Suppose these terms, each of three characters, are coded by the six-bit character codes of Table 3.1. There are many possible choices of hash function h. One such choice is to define $h(\text{TERM})$ to have a value equal to the remainder that results when 25 is divided into the sum of the three six-bit binary numbers that represent the character codes of the characters that form the term. Thus, for example,

$$\begin{aligned} h(\text{TIN}) &= \text{Remainder}[(010100 + 001001 + 001110)/25] \\ &= \text{Remainder } (43/25) \\ &= 18. \end{aligned}$$

Such a choice of h leads to hash addresses within the range 0 to 24 and hence is based on the assumption that a block of 25 locations is available for storage of the different values of TERM.

The various hash addresses are shown in Table 5.4. The terms CAT, TIN, COW, and MAN are stored at the addresses 24, 18, 16, and 3 respectively. The term JAM also has a hash address of 24 and hence gives rise to a collision. Suppose the function $r(24)$ is found to give the value 15; then the term JAM is stored at address 15. Terms RAT, DEN, and GIN are then stored at their hash addresses. The term TON has a hash address of 24 that also causes a collision, as does the first value (15) of $r(24)$; suppose the next value in the sequence from $r(24)$ is 7 so that TON is stored at this address. The hash address of the next term FEE also leads to a collision but the first term of the sequence $r(16)$ is 19, which may be used as the storage address for FEE. The next term VAT has a hash address of 16 and hence a collision; it is found necessary to compute three terms of the sequence $r(16)$ before finding a collision-free address. Storage of the remaining terms continues as indicated in Table 5.4. After storage of all 20 terms, their order in the 25 storage positions is as shown in Table 5.5 in which a collision bit of 1 or 0 is stored with each term to indicate whether or not a collision has occurred at the corresponding address. For

Table 5.4
Storage Addresses Derived from Hash Addresses H and Sequences $r(H)$.

TERM	Hash Address (H)	$r(H)$	Storage Address
CAT	24		24
TIN	18		18
COW	16		16
MAN	3		3
JAM	24	15	15
RAT	14		14
DEN	23		23
GIN	5		5
TON	24	15,7	7
FEE	16	19	19
VAT	16	19,3,6	6
USE	20		20
TOE	15	7,21	21
TAP	22		22
BIN	0		0
BOW	15	7,21,2	2
DOG	1		1
TOP	1	17	17
DOE	24	15,7,21,2,11	11
BUN	12		12

example, the collision bit stored with the term BOW is set to 1 because storage of the term DOE involved a value of $r(H) = 2$.

Use of a scatter table for storage of terms offers a number of advantages over storage in a tree structure or in an alphabetically ordered list. The most obvious advantage is that for many terms a search in the table requires only a single access. Also, the problem of updating is particularly simple since at the most it involves displacing a sequence of terms of the same hash address into fixed locations. It should be noted, however, that if a term such as JAM is deleted from Table 5.5, then its collision bit should remain equal to 1 so that when a search for TON examines the storage address 15 it will be clear that the sequence $r(H)$ should be continued.

If a scatter table of N possible addressses contains M entries it is said to have a load factor of $\alpha = M/N$. A small value of α is likely to lead to few collisions but is wasteful in utilization of storage space. If α is chosen to have a value close to 1, there is little waste of storage space, but there is a high likelihood that storage of a new term will involve several collisions. In practice it is usually found desirable to choose a table size so that α

Table 5.5
Hash Storage of the 20 Terms of Table 5.4 with Associated Collision Bits.

	Term	Collision Bit
0:	BIN	0
1:	DOG	1
2:	BOW	1
3:	MAN	0
4:		0
5:	GIN	0
6:	VAT	0
7:	TON	1
8:		0
9:		0
10:		0
11:	DOE	0
12:	BUN	0
13:		0
14:	RAT	0
15:	JAM	1
16:	COW	1
17:	TOP	0
18:	TIN	0
19:	FEE	1
20:	USE	0
21:	TOE	1
22:	TAP	0
23:	DEN	0
24:	CAT	1

does not exceed ⅔. Thus as the number of stored values increases, it may be necessary to increase the space allocation and to extend the hash function so that the computed addresses are extended over the entire storage area. A method of doing this has been discussed by Bays.[6]

In order to search a hash table for the presence of a given TERM, it is necessary to compare TERM with the value stored at location $h(\text{TERM})$ and, if necessary, with the values stored at R_1, R_2, R_3, etc. For the 20 terms listed in Table 5.4 there are a total of 18 collisions, and so the average number of comparisons needed to find a term stored in the table is $(20 + 18)/20 = 1.9$. In contrast, if the terms are stored in alphabetic order the average number of comparisons required to locate a stored term by use of a binary search is 3.7. Moreover, while the number of comparisons

[6] C. Bays, "The reallocation of hash-coded tables," *Communications of the Association for Computing Machinery* 16 (1973):11–14.

required to binary search an alphabetically ordered list of N terms increases proportionally to $\log_2 N$, the number of comparisons required to locate a term within a hash table depends only on the load factor and does not increase with N.

It may be noted that a simple choice of the function $r(H)$ is to produce the ascending sequence of addresses

$$h(\text{TERM})+1, h(\text{TERM})+2, \ldots, h(\text{TERM})-1 \qquad (5.24)$$

in which the last address in the table is followed by the first address, the second, and so fourth until finally reaching the address $h(\text{TERM})-1$. A further simple choice of collision addresses is through a similar sequence of successive locations beginning at address

$$h(\text{TERM}) + h_1(\text{TERM})$$

where $h_1(\text{TERM})$ is a second hash function. A possible choice of $h_1(\text{TERM})$ is the binary number represented by the character code of the first letter of TERM so that, for example,

$$h_1(\text{TOE}) = \text{Value of } (010100)$$
$$= 20.$$

In addition to allowing a search to involve relatively few comparisons, a hash storage scheme may allow a search to take place with access to relatively few file records. Consider a table of 5000 items stored as a file of 50 records each of 100 terms. A binary search would require access to many records. With hash storage, if terms that cause collisions are stored by use of the sequence (5.24), then many will be stored in the same, or the immediately following, record; and so for the majority of searches it will be necessary to retrieve only 1 or 2 records from the file.

More detailed discussions of scatter storage schemes, and proposals for choice of the hash functions and methods of handling collisions, have been made by many authors.[7-26] A large bibliography is included in the paper of Knott.[27]

[7] V. Batagelj, "The quadratic hash method when the table size is not a prime number," *Communications of the Association for Computing Machinery* 18 (1975):216–217.

[8] J. R. Bell, "The quadratic quotient method: a hash code eliminating secondary clustering," *Communications of the Association for Computing Machinery* 13 (1970):107–109.

[9] R. P. Brent, "Reducing the retrieval time of scatter storage techniques," *Communications of the Association for Computing Machinery* 16 (1973):105–109.

[10] W. Buchholz, "File organization and addressing," *IBM Systems Journal* 2 (1963):86–116.

[11] E. G. Coffman, and J. Eve, "Files structures using hashing functions," *Communications of the Association for Computing Machinery* 13 (1970):427–432.

5.8 Stack Structures

Processing of questions and searches through document data bases often require sets of terms or logic operators to be placed in temporary lists to which further terms are added or removed as the processing proceeds. Sometimes it is convenient to store the elements of the list sequentially in an array in which acess to each element is through specification of one or more index, or sequence, numbers. In other instances it may be sufficient to have access only to the last element placed in the list.

A list that is structured so that only its last element may be added or deleted is said to constitute a pushdown store or last in first out (LIFO)

---

[12] C. A. Day, "Full table quadratic searching for scatter storage," *Communications of the Association for Computing Machinery* 13 (1970):481–482.

[13] J. J. Dimsdale, and H. S. Heaps, "File structure for an on-line catalog of one million titles," *Journal of Library Automation* 6 (1973):37–55.

[14] J. A. Feldman, and J. R. Low, "Comments on Brent's scatter storage algorithm," *Communications of the Association for Computing Machinery* 16 (1973):703.

[15] F. R. A. Hopgood, and J. Davenport, "The quadratic hash method when the table size is a power of 2," *The Computer Journal* 15 (1972):314–315.

[16] P. L. Long, K. B. L. Rastogi, J. E. Rush, and J. A. Wyckoff, "Large on-line files of bibliographic data: An efficient design and a mathematical predictor of retrieval behavior," *Information Processing* 71 (1972):473–478.

[17] V. Y. Lum, "General performance analysis of key-to-address transformation methods using an abstract file concept," *Communications of the Association for Computing Machinery,* 16 (1973):603–612.

[18] V. Y. Lum, and P. S. T. Yuen, "Additional results on key-to-address transform techniques: A fundamental performance study on large existing formatted files," *Communications of the Association for Computing Machinery* 15 (1972):996–997.

[19] V. Y. Lum, P. S. T. Yuen, and M. Dodd, "Key-to-address transformation techniques: A fundamental performance study on large existing formatted files," *Communications of the Association for Computing Machinery* 14 (1971):228–239.

[20] W. D. Maurer, "An improved hash code for scatter storage," *Communications of the Association for Computing Machinery* 11 (1968):35–38.

[21] W. D. Maurer, and T. G. Lewis, "Hash table methods," *Computing Surveys* 7 (1975):5–19.

[22] R. Morris, "Scatter storage techniques," *Communications of the Association for Computing Machinery* 11 (1968):38–44.

[23] D. M. Murray, "Scatter storage for dictionary lookups," *Journal of Library Automation* 3 (1970):173–201.

[24] D. G. Severance, "Identifier search mechanisms: A survey and generalized model," *Computing Surveys* 6 (1974):175–194.

[25] R. Shneiderman, "Polynomial search," *Software–Practice and Experience* 3(1973):5–8.

[26] J. G. Williams, "Storage utilization in a memory hierarchy when storage assignment is performed by a hashing algorithm," *Communications of the Association for Computing Machinery* 14 (1971):172–175.

[27] G. D. Knott, "Hashing functions," *The Computer Journal* 18 (1975):265–278.

stack. Similarly, a list in which elements may be added only to its end, and removed only from its beginning, is said to form a *first in first out* (FIFO) store or queue.

In order to write computer programs that process elements stored in stacks, it is convenient to have a subroutine STACK(X), or PUSH(X), that places a specified element of name X at the top of the stack. Similarly, it is useful to have a subroutine FETCH(X), or POP(X), that removes the topmost element from the stack and stores it elsewhere in memory under the name X. The following could form the appropriate FORTRAN subroutines:

```
SUBROUTINE STACK(X)
COMMON VSTACK(100),NSTACK
NSTACK=NSTACK+1
IF(NSTACK.GT.100) Print message and stop.
VSTACK(NSTACK)=X
RETURN
END

SUBROUTINE FETCH(X)
COMMON VSTACK(100),NSTACK
IF(NSTACK.EQ.0) Print message and stop.
X=VSTACK(NSTACK)
NSTACK=NSTACK-1
RETURN
END
```

In the main program the stack should be emptied initially by setting NSTACK=0.

The convenience of using a stack may be illustrated by reference to Figure 5.15. It describes an algorithm that processes the elements of a sort tree of form as in Table 5.1, and records the terms in alphabetic order. A stack is used as a temporary store for terms that should not be recorded until further terms have been read. The main difference between the algorithms of Figures 5.6 and 5.15 is that use of a stack makes it unnecessary to use back pointers and to backspace through elements of TERM(N). This would be a significant advantage if the terms are stored on magnetic tape or other sequential storage.

In the subroutines STACK(X) and FETCH(X) as just described, the stack is formed within an array VSTACK of 100 elements. In some problems it is difficult to know how much space to allocate for storage of the stack. If too little space is allocated then overflow occurs. On the other hand, allocation of an unnecessarily large amount of storage is clearly undesirable.

The problem of storage allocation may be resolved by reserving a relatively small amount of core storage for a working stack, and creating a

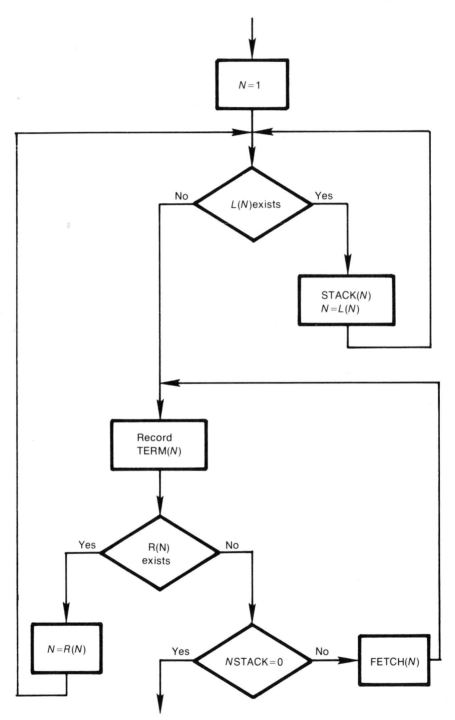

Figure 5.15. Use of a stack to process Table 5.1 to record the terms TERM(N) in alphabetic order.

backup stack that is stored on magnetic tape or disk. The programmer should be allowed to use the subroutines STACK(X) and FETCH(X) without being aware of how the stack is partitioned between core storage and the backup stack. Thus transfer of elements to, and from, the backup stack should be handled within the subroutines.

It is undesirable to transfer the entire working stack to the backup file whenever it is full, since there is some danger that during execution of a program the order of the FETCH and STACK calls will cause the stack size to oscillate about its maximum in-core capacity, and hence cause frequent transfers to and from the backup store. An alternative scheme is shown in Figure 5.16.

The scheme represented in Figure 5.16 first allows the elements of the stack to be stored in positions P1=1 to P4=200 as in Stack 1. The middle of the stack contains positions P2=100 and P3=101. When the stack length becomes larger than 200 the lower half P1, P2 of the stack (Stack$_1$) is transferred to the backup stack and any further stack elements are added in positions 1 to 100. The stack thus becomes of form Stack$_2$, which has the wraparound feature in that the stack beginning at position P1=101 extends to P2=200 and is then continued at position P3=1. When the top of Stack$_2$ is required to extend beyond the position P4=100 the portion from P1=101 to P2=200 is first transferred to the backup stack so that the in-core stack may extend from P1=1 to P4=200 as shown in Stack$_3$, which has the same form as Stack$_1$. Initially the pointer PS to the top of the stack is to be O, the value of NULL is set to 1 to indicate that the in-core stack is empty, and a counter BACKUP is set to O to indicate that no portions have yet been transferred to the backup stack. Whenever a group of 100 terms is transferred to, or from, the backup stack the value of BACKUP is increased, or decreased, by 1.

5.9 Representation of Queues

Elements are said to be stored in a queue if the order in which the elements are added is also the order in which they may be removed. Such a structure may be used to schedule service to a group of users who share a single resource such as a computer-accessible data base.

Suppose, for example, that a number of users submit search questions through terminals, and that a single central processor is used to access an inverted file. The user names could be identified with elements in a queue, and the inverted file could be accessed for one user at a time in the order in which the questions are input. After submission of a question a user would have to wait until his or her name reached the front of the queue. In

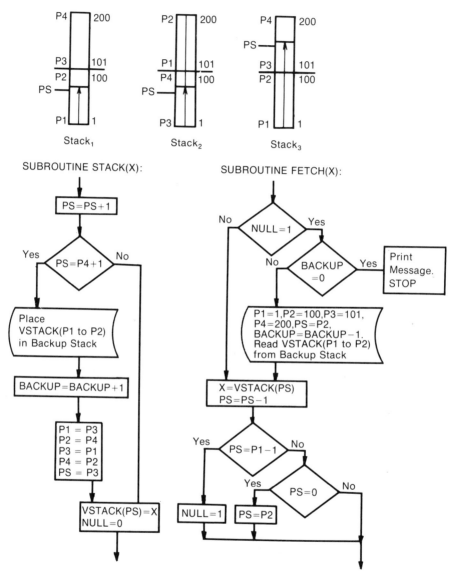

Figure 5.16. Flowcharts of subroutines to process elements of a pushdown stack with a backup stack.

practice, instead of using a queue of elements to record the times at which
questions are input, it is more efficient to have several queues of small
tasks such as a queue that governs the input of single records of a
question, a queue that determines access to a dictionary, a queue that
schedules access to an inverted file, and so forth.

For elements stored in a queue the pair of subroutines listed here could
be used to add a specified element X to the end of the queue or to remove
an element from the front of the queue for storage elsewhere in memory
under the name X. It is supposed that the main program sets N1=N2=0
and NTHRES=50 initially. The queue is created within an array of 100
elements VQUEUE(N) and extends from position N1 to N2. Whenever the
end of the queue reaches the threshold position N1 = NTHRESH the entire
queue is shifted back to occupy a portion of the array beginning at position
N1 = 1. The beginning of the queue is also reset, to position 0, whenever
it becomes empty.

```
SUBROUTINE ADD(X)
COMMON VQUEUE(100),N1,N2,NTHRES
N2=N2+1
IF(N2.GT.100) Print message and stop.
VQUEUE(N2)=X
RETURN
END

SUBROUTINE FETCH(X)
COMMON VQUEUE(100),N1,N2,NTHRES
IF(N2.EQ.0) Print message and stop.
X=VQUEUE(N1)
IF(N1.EQ.N2) Set N1=N2=0 and RETURN
IF(N1.NE.NTHRESH) Set N1=N1+1 and RETURN
Shift VQUEUE(N1+1 to N2) to VQUEUE(1 to N2-N1)
N2=N2-N1
N1=1
RETURN
END
```

Instead of shifting the queue elements back to the beginning of the array
whenever N1 exceeds a threshold value, the queue may be structured
with a wraparound feature as shown in Figure 5.17. In the main program
the values of N1 and N2 are set to 0 initially.

5.10 List Storage Structure

A list storage scheme is one in which the ordering, or sequence of
access, of stored elements is specified by pointers that are stored with the

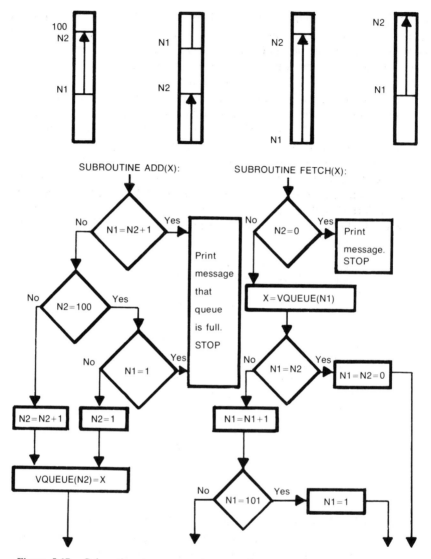

Figure 5.17. Subroutines to process elements of a queue with wraparound feature.

elements. Such a scheme is particularly useful for storage of several stacks and queues in a manner to reduce the total amount of space allocation. The several sets of connected elements are then designated as separate linked lists if there are no pointers between elements of the different sets. A list storage scheme is also useful for storage of elements in which the interconnections through pointers are more complicated than for tree-like structures.

A list storage structure may be represented by pairs of cells consisting of a data cell and a pointer cell. A convenient graphical representation of such a pair of cells is the following

Suppose, for example, that books of a library collection are each given a distinct number and that requests for books of number 1238, 2597, 3804 are received from users of the library in the following sequence

```
JONES(1238),WELLS(2597),SMITH(1238),JONES(3804),CHAN(2597),
DAW(2597),CLARK(1238),SMITH(3804),ADAMS(1238),HALL(2597).
```

The requests may be stored consecutively in memory in the form of three linked lists and a directory, as shown in Figure 5.18.

The linked list structure may also be described by use of the cellular representation, which is also included in Figure 5.18. It may be noted that this cellular representation provides a clear picture of the linking but does not indicate the order in which the terms are stored in memory. Since in many instances the storage order is unimportant, except perhaps that all pointers should be in a single direction if the storage is on magnetic tape, the cellular representation is often to be preferred.

Useful subroutines for processing the terms stored in a list structure include the following:

(i) STORE(X, D): Insert a further term X at the end of the chain of pointers that begins at the directory term D.

(ii) LOOK(X, D): Look at all the terms chained to the directory term D and examine them with respect to some specified condition involving the term X. Such a condition might be equality to X.

(iii) DELETE(X, D): Examine all the terms chained to the directory term D and delete those that satisfy a specified condition involving the term X. Such a condition might be equality to X, or occurrence as the last or first term in the chain.

It may be noted that deletion of all elements chained to D merely involves deletion of the pointer in the pair of cells that contains D. It may also be noted that in Figure 5.18 deletion of the cell that contains DAW involves replacing the pointer at HALL by the value of the pointer at DAW so that the entry DAW becomes inaccessible.

Removal of elements, or chains of elements, from the linked lists causes the appearance of unused cells. After a considerable amount of deletion such unused cells might cause significant waste of storage space, and it might be advisable to determine their locations for future allocation of new cells. Determination of such available space is known as garbage collection.

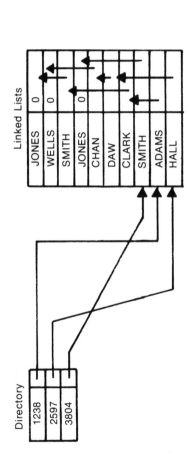

Linked Lists

Directory

1238	
2597	
3804	

JONES	0
WELLS	0
SMITH	
JONES	0
CHAN	
DAW	
CLARK	
SMITH	
ADAMS	
HALL	

Cellular representation:

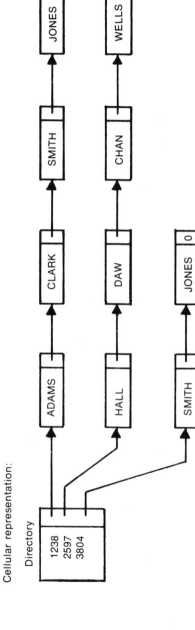

Directory

1238	
2597	
3804	

Figure 5.18. Linked lists and a cellular representation.

An algorithm for garbage collection may be illustrated by reference to Figure 5.19 which represents the structure of Figure 5.18 after deletion of the chains from 1238 and 3804. The steps of the algorithm are as follows:

(*i*) Follow each remaining chain of pointers and tag each remaining entry in each list. The tag need only be of length one bit and is shown as a 1 in Figure 5.19.

(*ii*) Starting at the end (END) of the storage area examine each cell and place a backward pointer in the pointer cell of each untagged pair of cells. The purpose of the pointers is to chain together all the unused pairs of cells. These pointers are shown by numbers in Figure 5.19.

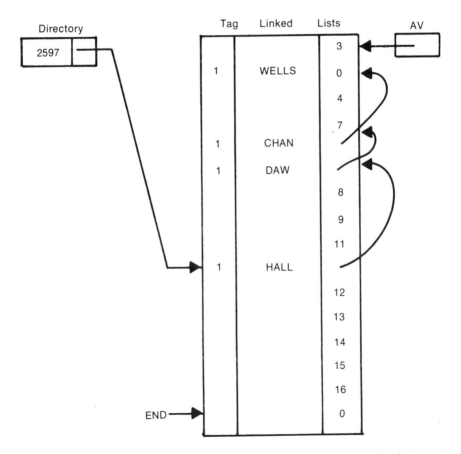

Figure 5.19. Linked list structure with pointers inserted by a garbage collection operation.

(*iii*) Set a pointer AV to point to the beginning of the available storage area.

When new entries are added to the linked lists they are filled into the beginning of the storage area and AV is reset to point to the beginning of the remaining available storage. Pointers to the linked lists are usually arranged to point forward since this simplifies the addition of further entries and preserves the stack-like structure of each linked list.

After a certain number of further deletions a new garbage collection is performed in order to chain together the unused pairs of cells and to reset AV. It is not usually advisable to chain cells together immediately on their deletion since the chaining operation is likely to be quite time consuming, and frequent repetitions will involve a total time that is likely to exceed that used when garbage collection is performed only when space is no longer available.

In some instances it may prove desirable to place all new cells in an overflow area of storage and to periodically recreate the entire list structure in the main storage area. Discussion of the factors to be considered in use of such a scheme has been presented by Scheiderman.[28]

In the list structure just described, the elements are arranged within distinct linked lists, and each element consists of a single pair of cells. Although tags were introduced in the course of the garbage collection, they were not used for other operations on list elements. However, list structures may be used to store elements that are connected in a more complicated manner than through simple linked lists. Also, it may be desirable to generalize the cellular pairs to allow cellular elements of the form

data cells, pointer cells, marker (or tag) cells.

For example the nonbinary tree shown in Figure 5.20 may be represented by the linked structure of cellular elements as shown. Each cellular element consists either of a tag of value 1 followed by a data cell followed by a pointer cell or else of a tag of value 0 followed by two pointer cells. Also, each nonterminal element that contains a data cell is followed by a chain of pointer elements each of which points to a further data element. The tag may be of length one bit. It may be noted that the cellular elements may be stored in any order, and that since every data element is preceded by a pointer element then addition of further data elements requires no change to existing cells except through the placement of new pointers in cells that were previously empty.

[28] B. Schneiderman, "Optimum data base reorganization points," *Communications of the Association for Computing Machinery* 16 (1973):362–365.

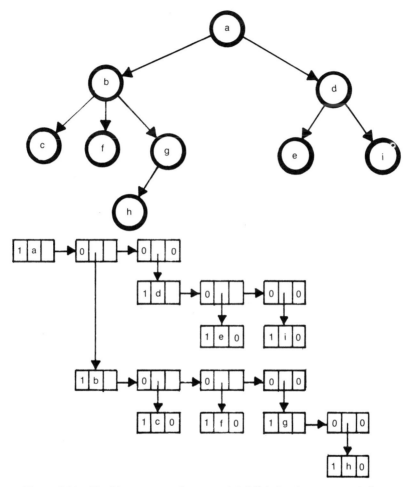

Figure 5.20. Nonbinary tree and an associated list structure representation.

Since any tree of nodes and pointers also may be represented as an equivalent binary tree of downward and horizontal pointers, the tree structure of Figure 5.20 may also be represented by the list structure of Figure 5.21. Each cellular element consists of a data cell, followed by a downward pointer, followed by a horizontal pointer cell.

The list structure of Figure 5.20 contains 34 cells in addition to tag cells. In contrast, the list structure of Figure 5.21 contains 27 cells in which there are only 8 pointers instead of the 16 contained in Figure 5.20. Thus chaining through pointers is faster when the structure of Figure 5.21 is

154

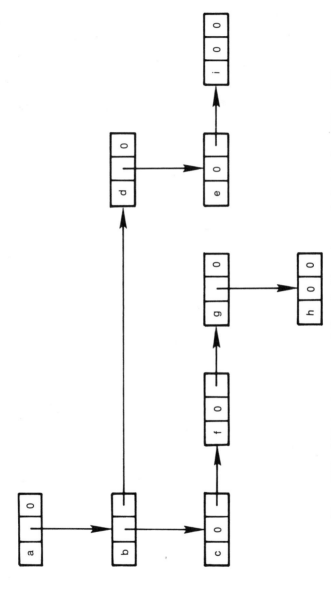

Figure 5.21. List structure representation of a binary tree equivalent to that of Figure 5.20.

adopted. Also, fewer comparisons are required since the structure contains no tag cells.

In Figures 5.20 and 5.21 the terminal nodes are indicated by the presence of zero pointers. It is sometimes convenient to use this space for backward pointers and to indicate the terminal nodes by addition of one-bit tags. The structure is then called a threaded or circular list. A list structure in which there are cycles of connected pointers is said to be a re-entrant list structure.

5.11 Dynamic Storage

It sometimes happens that the size of a list is not known before the start of execution of a program, and so the amount of storage required cannot be allocated until program execution time. Alternatively, there might be several lists whose storage areas may be released for storage of other lists that are generated as execution of the program proceeds. Storage that may be allocated or released during execution of a program is said to constitute dynamic storage.

An illustration of the use of dynamic storage may be made by consideration of processing by use of an inverted file in response to the following question that involves five terms t_1 to t_5.

$$t_2 \quad \text{OR} \quad t_4 \quad \text{OR} \quad (t_1 \text{ AND } t_5) \quad \text{OR} \quad t_3$$

Suppose that in the inverted file the lists of document numbers that correspond to the terms t_1 to t_5 are, respectively

$$
\begin{array}{ll}
L1: & 14, 17, 26 \\
L2: & 12, 28 \\
L3: & 26, 41 \\
L4: & 17, 19, 28 \\
L5: & 13, 17, 26, 41.
\end{array}
$$

They could be read from the file and stored as shown in the first column of Table 5.6. The question could then be regarded as equivalent to

$$(4,5) \quad \text{OR} \quad (8,10) \quad \text{OR} \quad [(1,3) \text{ AND } (11,14)] \quad \text{OR} \quad (6,7)$$

in which each pair of form (n_1, n_2) denotes the list of numbers that occupy positions n_1 to n_2 in Table 5.6.

If the OR operation is applied to lists (4,5) and (8,10) there results the list 12,17,19,28, which is a list of the documents that contain terms t_2 or t_4. The lists (4,5) and (8,10) may be deleted, but neither block of released space is sufficient for storage of the new list, which is therefore placed at

Table 5.6
Successive Combinations of Inverted File Lists with a Dynamic Storage Allocation.

1:	14	14	17		12
2:	17	17	26		17
3:	26	26			19
4:	12				26
5:	28				28
6:	26	26	26	26	41
7:	41	41	41	41	
8:	17			12	
9	19			17	
10:	28			19	
11:	13	13		26	
12:	17	17		28	
13:	26	26			
14:	41	41			
15:		12	12		
16:		17	17		
17:		19	19		
18.		28	28		

the end of the storage area to form (15,18) as shown in the second column of Table 5.6.

Application of the AND logic to lists (1,3) and (11,14) produces the list 17,26, while deletion of (1,3) and (11,14) allows the new list to be stored to form (1,2) as in the third column of Table 5.6. The question has now been reduced to the form

$$(15,18) \quad \text{OR} \quad (1,2) \quad \text{OR} \quad (6,7).$$

The lists (15,18) and (1,2) may be replaced by the list 12,17,19,26,28, which, although too large to be stored at tbe beginning of the table, may be stored in the next block of free space as (8,12) in the fourth column of the table. Finally, combination of (8,12) and (6,7) according to the OR operation leads to the final list (1,6) in Table 5.6.

In the preceding example of a dynamic storage allocation each new list is allocated space within the first block of free storage that is sufficiently large to contain it without subdivision. As old lists are removed, and new lists added, their positions in the table must be recorded in the form (n_1, n_2), the set of all such pairs forming a directory to the stored list.

A dynamic storage table contained in main memory should also have a backup store on a file in order to accomodate any exceptionally long lists that might be formed during the processing. This may be arranged very simply. For example, if only 1000 locations are available for the table in main memory, then magnetic tape or disk storage could be used for storage locations that exceed 1000, the extra condition being imposed that no single list is stored to overlap the 1000th location.

5.12 Problems

1. Describe a storage structure suitable for storage of the terms and structural relations in the *Thesaurus of Engineering and Scientific Terms* described in Section 2.10.
2. Describe the structure of the files, sort steps, and other steps in a program to input textual records and print a KWIC index as described in Section 2.8. Allow the input data to include a stop list. Assume that input records contain up to 200 characters, and that output records are truncated in 110 characters. Assume that the output is too large for storage in main computer memory.
3. Draw the flow chart of a program to read records of the CAIN data base described in Section 3.9, and form two sets of four files of the type shown in Figure 5.13. In the first set let the terms be title words with all punctuation (including asterisks) removed. In the second set let the terms be author names.
4. Draw the flow chart of a program to merge the two document directory files of Problem 3, and also merge the two coded sequential files.
5. The first 32 terms listed in Table 10.1 are to be stored in a table of N locations by use of a hash storage scheme with $h(\text{TERM})$ chosen as

$$h(\text{TERM}) = \text{Remainder}[(\text{Sum of codes of all} \\ \text{characters in TERM})/N]$$

and with collisions resolved through use of the address sequence

$$h(\text{TERM}) + 1, h(\text{TERM}) + 2, \ldots, h(\text{TERM}) - 1.$$

Plot the number of collisions against N as N ranges from 32 to 128. Determine the value of the load factor for which a search of the table requires as many average comparisons as a binary search.
6. Repeat Problem 5 with collisions resolved through use of a sequence of successive locations beginning at position $h_1(\text{TERM})$ equal to the binary number represented by the first letter of the TERM. Can you suggest a better choice of the function $h_1(\text{TERM})$?
7. Show the successive storage of document lists in a dynamic store during processing of the question

$$(t_2 \text{ OR } t_4) \quad \text{AND} \quad (t_1 \text{ OR } t_3)$$

in which the document lists L1 to L4 are as in Section 5.11. Also, show the successive storage of the document lists for the equivalent question

$$(t_2 \text{ AND } t_1) \text{ OR } (t_2 \text{ AND } t_3) \text{ OR } (t_4 \text{ AND } t_1) \text{ OR } (t_4 \text{ AND } t_3).$$

Which form of question is the best with regard to use of storage space, and which is the best with regard to use of computer processing time?

6

Structure of Search Programs

6.1 Sequential Search with Batched Questions

In a sequential search the document items in the data base are examined in sequence, and each searchable term within an appropriate field is compared with the corresponding question terms. If there are several questions it is clearly desirable to batch them so that only one sequential read of the data base is required.

A further reason for batching questions is that if terms of the data base are binary searched against a list of question terms, then each doubling in size of the table leads to only one additional comparison. Hence, to process a batch of questions requires significantly fewer comparisons than are needed to process all questions one at a time. Moreover, if a sequential search compares the text of each document item with a set of question terms structured as described in Section 5.4, the processing time is independent of the number of question terms; thus question batching is clearly desirable.

If questions are processed in a batch, then an error in the statement of any question should not be allowed to affect other questions. Also, at completion of the search each question statement should be printed in association with only those document items, and/or error messages, relevant to that question.

In order to allow for the possible occurrence of a large number of relevant document items, it is usually necessary to store such items on a tape or disk file rather than in internal memory. As items are placed on file they must be tagged to indicate the questions to which they correspond. The question statements, and all other data such as error messages required in the final printout, should also be placed on file and tagged appropriately.

A sequential search program that uses batch questions may therefore consist of three phases. The first is the question input phase in which the question statements are read and placed in a HITS file. Tables are created to contain the logic expressions and question terms. In the second, or search, phase of the program the data base is read, document terms are compared with the question terms, and relevant items of the data base are written on the HITS file. The final phase of the program is the output phase in which the records stored on the HITS file are rearranged in suitable form for output.

As each question card is read it should be examined to determine whether it constitutes a valid component of a question statement. For example, the logic operators must be spelled correctly, the attribute specifications must include only valid attributes, and certain sequences of cards may be invalid. For each error a message should be written on the HITS file and properly associated with the corresponding question card.

The logic operators and terms that appear on valid question cards are placed in appropriate tables for use in the search phase. Also, if a question statement is found to be invalid, then an indicator should be stored and used in the search phase to prevent any further processing of that particular question.

A card deck of batched questions may be read and placed in a file HITS whose records have the form shown in Figure 6.1.

Each record contains a field that consists of either a card image of a question card or of an error message. In the HITS records created during the search phase this field will be used for relevant document details. It is preceded by the number of the question in which it occurs, a record number to indicate the card sequence number within the particular question, and a field number that describes the logical position of any error message associated with the associated term or logic. If a question state-

QUE NUM	REC NUM	FLD NUM	Card Image, or MSG, or Relevant Doc. Details

Figure 6.1.   Structure of records in the HITS file.

ment is found to be invalid an appropriate entry is also made in a question validity table.

Suppose, for example, that the input question deck has the following form, which consists of three questions arranged within two profiles.

```
PRO
QUE
    OR 02
            CON   COMPUT* (TIT)
            CON   CALCUL* (TIT)
            CON   ESTIMAT* (TIT)
            CON   JONES T (AUT)
    END

QUE
    AND
        OR
            CON   RULE$(TIT)
            CON   REGULATION$(TIT)
        CON   GREEN
        CON   TRAFFIC (TIT)
        CON   SAFETY (TIT)
    END

PRO
QUE
    AND
        CON   LIBRARY (ABS)
        OR
            CON   MECHANIZATION (ABS)
            CON   AUTOMATION (ABS)
    END
```

It may be noted that the statement of the second question contains an error due to omission of the attribute descriptor for the term GREEN. The records placed on the HITS file could therefore be as follows:

```
1   1   1   PRO
1   2   1   QUE
1   3   1      OR 02
1   4   1            CON   COMPUT* (TIT)
1   5   1            CON   CALCUL* (TIT)
1   6   1            CON   ESTIMAT* (TIT)
1   7   1            CON   JONES T (AUT)
1   8   1   END
2   1   1   QUE
2   2   1      AND
2   3   1         OR
2   4   1            CON   RULE$ (TIT)
2   5   1            CON   REGULATION$ (TIT)
2   6   0   ***FOLLOWING TERM HAS INCORRECT ATTRIBUTE***
```

```
2   6  1              CON  GREEN
2   7  1              CON  TRAFFIC (TIT)
2   8  1              CON  SAFETY (TIT)
2   9  1     END
2  10  1     PRO
3   1  1     QUE
3   2  1        AND
3   3  1           CON  LIBRARY (ABS)
3   4  1        OR
3   5  1           CON  MECHANIZATION (ABS)
3   6  1           CON  AUTOMATION (ABS)
3   7  1     END
```

During creation of the preceding HITS file the question validity table could be set as

$$0$$
$$1$$
$$0$$

in which the second entry is flagged to indicate that the second question is invalid and that its terms should be ignored during the search phase.

During the search phase each relevant item of the data base is stored in the HITS file and is preceded by the relevant question number. The record number may be set to indicate the order in which the relevant items of each question are to be printed. The order might be, for example, according to the date of publication or to the sum of weights of relevant terms. In any event it should be set to be larger than any record number set during the question input phase. If several records of the HITS file are required to store a single document then the appropriate field sequence numbers are placed as field numbers in the HITS records.

For example, suppose the search phase locates a document x relevant to the first question with weight 5, a document y relevant to the third question with weight 2, a document z relevant to both the first question with weight 2 and the third question with weight 1, and a document t relevant to the third question with weight 7. The records added to the HITS file might be as shown in Figure 6.2 in which each record number is equal to the weight plus 1000.

One of the steps of the question input phase is creation of certain tables required for the search phase. The form of these tables is described in the following, and subsequent, sections.

Following the search phase, the records of the HITS file may be sorted with respect to increasing question number, record number, and field number, so that they may be printed subsequently in the form of question statements followed by relevant document items. For the questions and retrieval documents just described, the sorted HITS file would be as

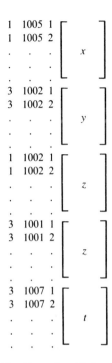

Figure 6.2. Records added to HITS file.

shown in Figure 6.3. Such a HITS file is in suitable form for processing since the question statements, error messages, and retrieved document items, are in proper sequence.

6.2 Single Nested OR Logic within AND Parameters

The tables created during the question input phase may be arranged in a particularly simple form if the question logic described in Chapter 4 is restricted to include only the special form described here.

Suppose the only allowable logic operations are AND, OR, and NOT. A single CON term, or a single NOCON term, or a set of CON terms connected by an OR operator, or a set of NOCON terms connected by an OR operator, may be said to form a parameter. It will be supposed that questions are restricted to consist of either one parameter or several parameters connected by the AND operator. It will be assumed that weights may be attached to single terms but not to entire parameters, and that the weights of all terms are accumulated for comparison to a single threshold value

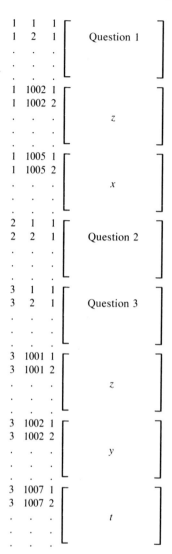

Figure 6.3. Sorted HITS file.

placed after the AND operator. If a weight is omitted its value will be assumed to be unity.

Each question statement will be headed by QUE and terminated by END. A card that contains blanks in all of columns 1–13 will be regarded as a comment card that is not part of the question logic.

An example of an allowable question statement is thus

```
QUE
    AND07
          CON   SMITH A (AUT)
          OR
             03CON   CMEMICAL (TIT)
             02CON   PHYSICAL (TIT)
          OR
             04CON   STRUCTURE$ (TIT)
               CON   COMPOSITION$ (TIT)
               CON   NATURE (TIT)
          NOCON   WATER (TIT)
            CON   LIQUID$ (TIT)
    END
```

which has the form of five parameters connected by AND logic.

When question statements are restricted to have the preceding form of single nesting of OR logic within AND parameters, the tables required for the search phase of the program may be organized around the tables shown in Figure 6.4.

During the question input phase the question terms (QTERM) are read successively into a term stack, and each term is associated with a pointer P to a position stack that records the associated question number, parameter number, and term weight. After all question terms are read the term stack is sorted, and duplicate entries are eliminated and replaced by appropriate links (NEXT) in the position stack. Also, the question validity table is examined so that entries that correspond to invalid questions may be deleted from the tables.

After all questions have been read, and the term stack and position table arranged as in Figure 6.4, a question parameter table is created with as many entries as there are questions. Each entry consists of four portions. The first portion forms a parameter descriptor that contains a bit string of 0s and 1s that is set as the question deck is read; for each question the ith bit is set to be 1 if the question contains an ith parameter of CON terms and to 0 if the question contains either an ith parameter of NOCON terms or if the question has fewer than i parameters. Thus for the five-parameter question listed at the beginning of the present section the portion PARDES would be set to be

$$11101000 \ . \ . \ . \ 0$$

The second portion THRWT of each question parameter table entry is set equal to the threshold weight of the question. The portion PARSET is a bit string of the same length as PARDES and is initialized to be zero. Similarly, each portion SUMWT is initialized to be zero. Both PARSET and SUMWT are set during the search phase of the program.

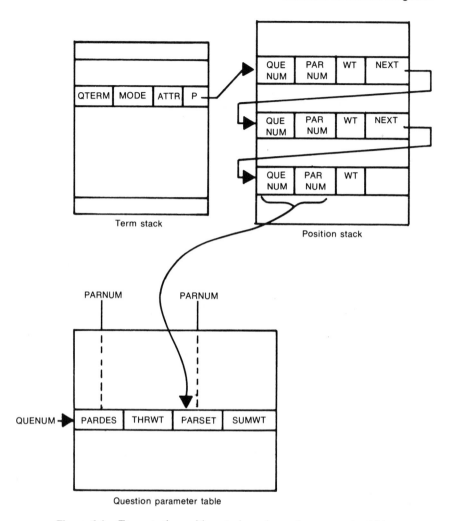

Figure 6.4. Term stack, position stack, and question parameter table.

During the search phase of the program as each term of a searchable field of the data base is read it is searched for in the term stack. If found, then each pair QUENUM, PARNUM in the corresponding chain of the position table is selected and a 1 is placed in the corresponding bit of PARSET in the question parameter table. The term weight is added to SUMWT.

To allow meaningful comparisons between document terms and the question terms, it is necessary either to store an attribute and mode descriptor with each question term in the term stack or else to have a different term stack for each attribute and mode. In either event each chain in the position stack should correspond to a set of repetitions of the same term, attribute, and mode descriptor.

For each document item, after all its terms have been read, each bit string PARSET is compared with the corresponding PARDES. If the two bit strings are identical, and if SUMWT $\geq$ THRWT, then the document fields are transferred from the data base to form appropriate records on the HITS file. All the portions PARSET and SUMWT in the question parameter table are reset to 0, and the terms of the next document item are read.

The flow chart shown in Figure 6.5 summarizes the question input phase of the program without inclusion of any tests for correct question format and output of corresponding error messages. When all question cards have been read the term stack will contain all question terms including repetitions. Each pointer P shown in Figure 6.4 will indicate the position of an entry in the position stack, but the entries will not have been connected by chains of pointers NEXT. The rows of the term stack may then be sorted in alphabetic order with respect to question terms, and term repetitions may be replaced by links (NEXT) that chain together the corresponding rows of the position table.

The search phase of the program is shown in Figure 6.6. It is followed by the output phase in which the HITS file is sorted to arrange the records in ascending order of question number, in ascending order to term number for each question number, and in ascending order of sequence number for each term number.

It may be noted that during the search phase of the program each document term must be searched for in the term stack. The position stack and question parameter table are accessed only when a term is found to be present, with the appropriate mode and attribute, in the term stack. If a document is found to contain no terms stored in the term stack, it is not necessary to examine the question parameter table. The time required to search the sequential data base is thus very dependent on the time required to search the term stack, which also may be replaced by the character tree structure described in Section 5.4.

6.3 Question Processing through Logic Stack

For questions expressed in terms of general logic of the form described in Chapter 4 the question parameter table of Figure 6.4 is not of suitable form to represent the question logic. The table may then be replaced by a logic stack as shown in Figure 6.7.

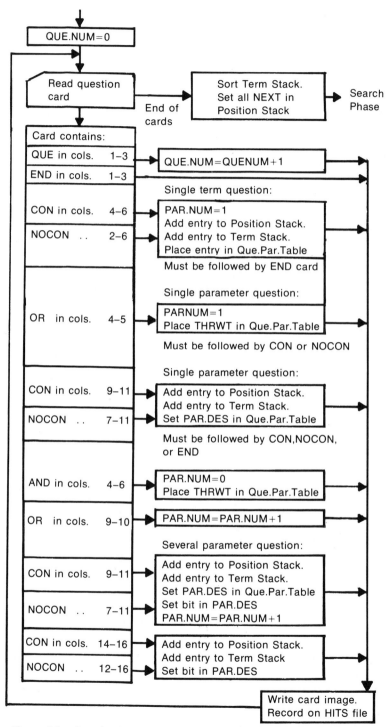

Figure 6.5. Question input phase of program to create tables of Figure 6.4.

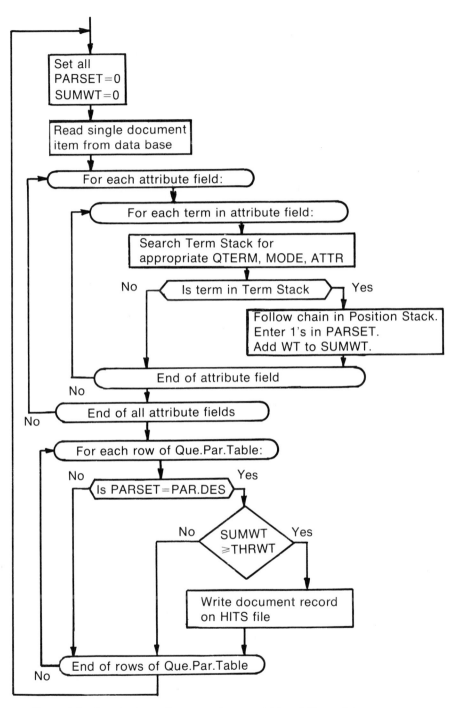

Figure 6.6. Search phase of program that uses tables of Figure 6.4.

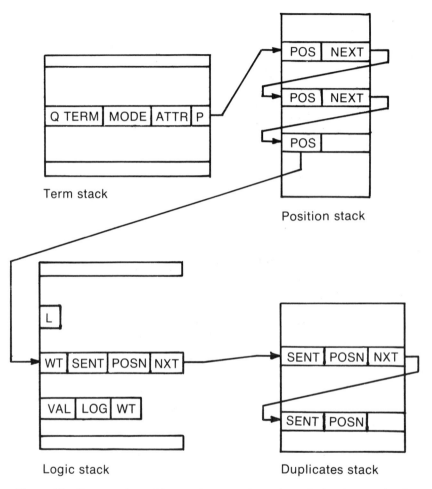

Term stack

Position stack

Logic stack

Duplicates stack

Figure 6.7. Term stack, position stack, and logic stack set during the question input phase of the program. The duplicate stack is set during the search phase.

In Figure 6.7 each entry of the term stack contains a question term, a mode indicator, an attribute descriptor, and a pointer to an entry in the position stack. Each entry in the position stack contains a single pointer POS to the logic stack, and also a pointer NEXT to other entries of the same attribute and mode as in Figure 6.4.

As the questions are input, and the term stack and position stack are created, entries are added successively to the top of the logic stack. Each occurrence of

⟨value⟩ ⟨operator⟩ ⟨weight⟩

within a question statement causes an entry of the form

VAL, LOG, WT,

where LOG denotes a logic operator. Similarly, each occurrence of

⟨weight⟩ CON ⟨term⟩

within a question statement causes the value WT to be placed in the first of the four fields

WT, SENT, POSN, NEXT

and the value of POS in the position stack is set to point to the beginning of the set of four fields. Values of SENT, POSN, and NXT will be entered later.

Each end of a logic level that is followed by a return to a higher level of logic in the question statement causes a flag L to be placed in the logic stack.

Thus for a question statement of the form

```
QUE
    OR 02
        CON  INSURANCE (TIT)
        CON  MARINE (SUB)
        OR 02
            CON  BOAT (ABS)
            AND
                CON  SAILING (ABS)
                CON  SHIP (ABS)
            CON  VESSEL (ABS)
        CON  POLICY (TIT)
        CON  HAZARD (TIT)
    END
```

that appears as the seventh question in a batch, the form of the logic stack is as shown here in which each x_i denotes a set of four fields WT, SENT, POSN, NXT.

$$07QUE,01OR\ 02,x_1,x_2,01OR\ 02,x_3,01AND01,x_4,x_5,L,x_6,L,$$
$$x_7,x_8,L,L,END$$

In the search phase of the program the document records of the searchable data base are examined sequentially. For each single document record the terms in each searchable field are searched for among the question terms in the term stack. Whenever a term is found to be present in the term stack, values are placed in the appropriate SENT fields of the logic stack to indicate the number of the sentence in which the term occurs. A value is also placed in the appropriate POSN field to indicate the word position within the sentence. Since a term may appear several times in an attribute field a duplicate stack is included and its entries are chained to those of the logic stack by means of pointers placed in the NXT fields.

After any document record has been read and the appropriate entries added to the stacks, the logic stack may be processed as described here in order to determine the question numbers, if any, for which the logic is satisfied by the particular document record.

Each sequence of the form

$$m \text{ LOG } n, x_1, x_2, \ldots, x_r, L$$

within the logic stack may be processed by a subprogram that examines $x_1, x_2, \ldots, x_r$ with respect to the operation LOG, the value m, and the weight n. The function of the subprogram is to replace the sequence by a single entry x_i whose first field indicates the resulting weight to be passed to the higher logic level. If the logic LOG is not satisfied, then WT is set to 0. If the logic is satisfied the values of SENT, POSN that may be needed by higher logic levels are appropriately chained through resetting of the pointers NXT.

The method of processing the stack may be illustrated as follows. Consider the stack

$$07\text{QUE}, 01\text{OR } 02, x_1, x_2, 01\text{OR } 02, x_3, 01\text{AND}01, x_4, x_5, L, x_6, L,$$
$$x_7, x_8, L, L, \text{END}$$

Let elements be read from the top of the stack and placed in a temporary stack TSTACK until a logic element is reached. Then TSTACK contains the elements

$$\text{END}, L, L, x_8, x_7, L, x_6, L, x_5, x_4, 01\text{AND}01$$

in which the sequence $L, x_5, x_4, 01\text{AND}01$ may be replaced by an element x_9 so that TSTACK becomes

$$\text{END}, L, L, x_8, x_7, L, x_6, x_9.$$

Further elements of the stack are added to TSTACK until a further logic element is reached. TSTACK then contains

$$\text{END}, L, L, x_8, x_7, L, x_6, x_9, x_3, 01\text{OR } 02$$

which, by an appropriate subprogram, may be reduced to the form

$$END,L,L,x_8,x_7,x_{10}.$$

Transfer of further elements extends TSTACK to contain

$$END,L,L,x_8,x_7,x_{10},x_2,x_1,01OR\ 02$$

which reduces to the form

$$END,L,x_{11}$$

which is then extended to

$$END,L,x_{11},07QUE.$$

The sequence $L,x_{11},07QUE$ is processed by a subprogram that removes the remaining stack element END and examines the value of the WT field of x_{11}. If WT is not 0, the relevant item of the data base is stored in the HITS file since it satisfies the logic of Question 7.

If the stack processing does not collapse a question to the form

$$END,L,x_i,nQUE$$

then the question syntax is in error.

It may be noted that the structure of the search program just described is very modular in the sense that it may be made dependent on a number of relatively simple subprograms. Initially there might be developed only sufficient subprograms to treat simple AND, OR, and NOT logic, the subprograms for more sophisticated logic operations being developed subsequently as users gain experience in use of the search service.

6.4 Question Processing through Logic Tree

An alternative to representation of questions by means of a logic stack is to make use of a tree representation of the question logic. This is discussed below.

Consider the following question statement in which each *tn* denotes a question term and its associated mode and attribute specification

```
QUE
    OR 03
        ADJ02
                CON    t4
                CON    t5
        02CON    t6
          OR 04
                CON    t8
```

```
            02 AND
                      CON   t10
                      CON   t11
              CON     t12
              03 CON  t13
  END
```

It may be represented by the tree structure shown in Figure 6.8 in which the x_i represent logic operations. Each arrow in the tree links a term t_j to the logic operator that acts on it.

The logic elements, term elements, and pointers of the tree may be stored in computer memory in a tree table as shown in Figure 6.9. As the questions are input, and the term stack and position stack are created, each occurrence of

⟨value⟩ ⟨operator⟩ ⟨weight⟩

within a question statement causes an entry of the form

VAL,LOG,WT,x_i

where x_i denotes a set of six fields of form

WT,SENT,POSN,PLOG,SLEV,LLEV

whose content will be explained later.

Similarly, each occurrence of

⟨weight⟩ CON ⟨term⟩

within a question statement causes the value of WT to be placed in the first of five fields

WT,SENT,POSN,PLOG,SLEV.

Any set of five such fields will be denoted by y_i.

As the sets of fields x_i and y_i are placed in the tree table, the value of PLOG is set to point to the position in the table that contains the logic operator that acts on the associated entry. Similarly, the appropriate values of SLEV, and LLEV, are set to point to the elements of the same, and lower, logic levels, respectively. Thus the SLEV and LLEV columns of Figure 6.9 describe the binary tree shown in Figure 6.10.

The pointers POS in a position stack similar to that of Figure 6.7 are set to point to the corresponding y_is of the tree table. Each entry in the tree table should also contain a field NXT that may be used to point to entries in a duplicate stack similar to that of Figure 6.7. The NXT field is not shown in Figure 6.9.

In the search phase of the program, whenever a term t_i is found to be present in the term stack the tree table is processed as follows (see Figures 6.9 and 6.10):

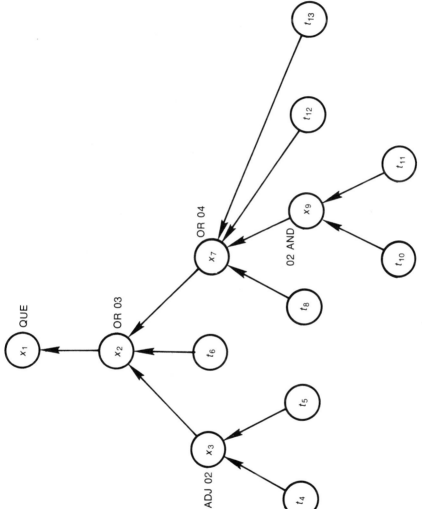

Figure 6.8. Tree representation of question logic. Arrows link a term to the logic operation that acts on it.

175

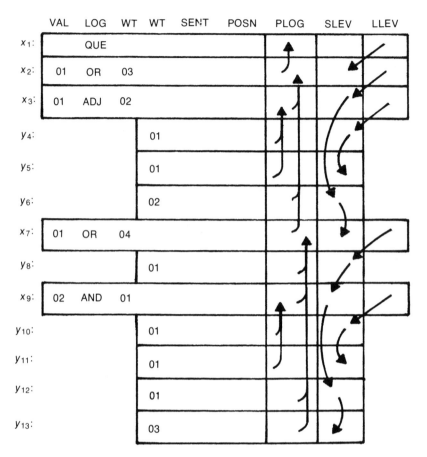

Figure 6.9. Tree table to represent the tree of Figure 6.6.

Step 1. The value of PLOG in the corresponding y_i is used to locate the position of a logic entry x_j.

Step 2. If the logic condition contained in x_j is already satisfied then proceed to Step 6. Otherwise enter the values of SENT, POSN in y_i and proceed to Step 3.

Step 3. Use a subprogram to examine the logic condition in x_j with respect to the appropriate entries x_k and y_k as indicated by LLEV in x_j and the set of pointers SLEV that it leads to. For example, in Figure 6.10 the logic condition x_7 is examined with respect to t_8, x_9, t_{12}, t_{13}.

Step 4. If the logic at x_j is not satisfied then proceed to Step 6. Otherwise place appropriate values in WT, SENT, POSN of x_j, and proceed

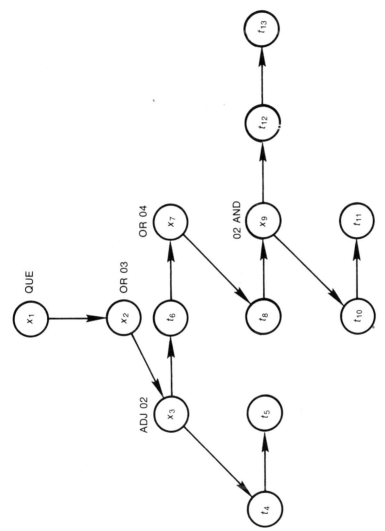

Figure 6.10. Binary tree representation of question logic. Downward arrows point from a logic operation to a term. Horizontal arrows point to an element at the same logic level.

to Step 5 unless x_j contains the logic QUE. Whenever x_j is a QUE element that has its logic satisfied, the entire set of logic elements of this question may be set as if their logic is satisfied in order to indicate that no further testing of the logic is needed for any other terms of the document record under examination.

Step 5. The value of PLOG in x_j is used to locate the position of a higher logic level x_m. If the logic condition in x_m is already satisfied then proceed to Step 5 with x_j replaced by x_m. Otherwise proceed to Step 3 with x_j replaced by x_m.

Step 6. Continue with program by selecting the next term in the data base and searching for it in the term stack, etc.

An important feature of the search procedure described in Steps 1–6 is that as soon as a document record is found to satisfy a particular question logic then that question logic is not examined with respect to subsequent terms. This may allow significant reduction in processing times if one of the searchable fields contains an abstract or other textual data in which there may be frequent repetitions of question terms.

6.5 Question Processing through Inverted File

Suppose a dictionary and document directory of the form shown in Figure 5.1 are used to access an inverted file and sequential file whose terms are replaced by the values of the corresponding addresses in the dictionary.

In order to search with respect to a given question the question terms must be searched for in the dictionary, and the corresponding lists of the inverted file must be read into main memory. The question logic must then be performed on these lists in order to determine the list of document numbers relevant to the question. Each such document number may then be used to access the document directory in order to read the appropriate sets of addresses from the sequential file. The addresses are then used to access the corresponding terms of the dictionary in order to output the relevant document records in textual form.

If truncation specifications are allowed in the question then a question term such as ACID* must cause the dictionary to be searched for the presence of all possible terms such as ACID, ACIDIC, ACIDICITY, and ACIDS. The single term ACID* in the question must then be replaced by the logic group

```
        OR
        CON  ACID
        CON  ACIDIC
        CON  ACIDICITY
        CON  ACIDS
```

together with the appropriate repetition of weights. Thus during the search for question terms in the dictionary, the question statement should be expanded by replacement of each truncated term by the complete set of terms connected by OR logic. Any statements that involve IGNORE logic are, of course, taken into account during the question expansion.

It may prove useful to access the dictionary through an index table of the form shown in Figure 5.9. However, if left truncation specifications are allowed it may be preferable to subdivide the dictionary into a set of tables of fixed length terms and to use an index table in which the index is the term length.

In many instances the number of dictionary addresses transferred from the sequential file is much greater than the number of question terms used to access the inverted file. Thus efficient decoding of addresses in the sequential file may be more important than efficient translation of terms into pointers to access the inverted file.

It is likely that relevant documents will contain a number of common terms, and for efficient decoding it is desirable to access the dictionary only once for each term rather than for each occurrence of each term. This may be achieved as described here; it is supposed that the term addresses of three relevant document records read from the sequential file are stored in records as shown in the first table of Figure 6.11. A sequence number SEQ is included in each record. If the records are sorted in increasing order of address they become arranged as in Table 2. The six different addresses contained in Table 2 may be used to access the dictionary, the resulting terms being stored as in Table 3. The records of Table 3 may then be sorted with respect to increasing order of sequence number to create the list of document terms shown in Table 4, for which the sequence numbers have been omitted. This list is in suitable form for printout.

6.6 Problems

1. Write a computer program to perform the question input phase to create the term stack, position stack, and question parameter table of Section 6.2 subject to the assumption that there are no truncation specifications. Allow each question term to have up to 24 characters. Allow the following five attribute specifications:

   AUT   for author name consisting of a surname followed by one blank followed by initials not separated by blanks or other characters.

   IND   for index term that may be either one word or a sequence of words separated by single blanks.

180

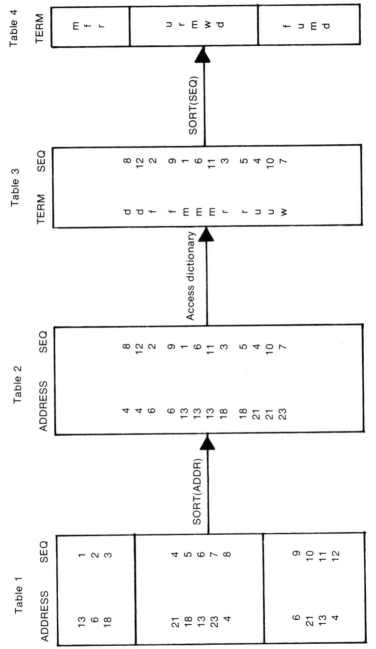

Figure 6.11. Tables used to decode relevant records of the coded sequential file.

JOU   for journal name.
TIT   for title word.
YEA   for year specified by two digits, e.g., 76.

Suppose that no question contains more than 20 cards, including comments. Also, suppose that the entire batch of questions does not contain more than 10 questions or 100 question terms.

Print the term stack, linked position table, and resulting HITS file for some test data.

2. Write a program to perform the search phase of a program as described in Section 6.2. Use it to follow the program of Problem 1, and print the unsorted HITS file for some test data.

3. Write a program to sort and print the HITS file produced by the program of Problem 2 so that printed output consists of each question statement followed by the relevant document items arranged in descending order of weight. Each question statement should begin on a new page, and each document item should begin on a new line and should be preceded by WT=. . . .

4. Modify the programs in Problem 3 to permit question terms to be specified with inclusion of both left and right truncation specifications of form * or of up to four $ characters.

5. Using x_i to denote a set of four fields WT, SENT, POSN, NXT indicate the form of the logic stack for the set of two questions

```
QUE
    ADJ05
        OR
            CON   CORRO* (TIT)
            CON   DETERIORAT* (TIT)
            CON   PITTING (TIT)
        OR
            CON   METAL$$$ (TIT)
            CON   CARBON (TIT)
        CON   ELECTRODE$ (TIT)
END
QUE
    PRE08
        ADJ04
            CON   OIL (ABS)
            CON   POLLUTION (ABS)
        ADJ03
            OR
                CON   RIVER$ (ABS)
                CON   WATERWAY$ (ABS)
            OR
                CON   CANAD* (ABS)
                PRE
                    CON   NORTHWEST (ABS)
                    CON   TERRITOR* (ABS)
END
```

Then indicate the successive forms of TSTACK as elements are added and reduced.

6. Draw the flow chart of a program to process a logic stack through successive additions and reductions of TSTACK. You are not required to include details of the subprograms.

7. Draw the flow chart of a subprogram to process the TSTACK sequence $L,x_1,x_2,...,x_r,m$ORn and reduce it to the form x_i. Include sufficient detail to show the processing of the fields WT, SENT, POSN, NXT.

8. Draw the flow chart of a subprogram to process the TSTACK sequence $L,x_1,x_2,...,x_r,m$PREn and reduce it to the form x_i. Include sufficient detail to show the processing of the fields WT, SENT, POSN, NXT.

9. Draw the flow chart of the search phase of a program to process a logic tree in the manner described in Section 6.4. Your program should include the sequential search through the entire data base and creation of the complete unsorted HITS file. You do not need to include details of question input, creation of the term stack, position stack, and allotment of space for the tree table.

10. By consideration of some simple questions applied to search on a set of titles, compare the effectiveness of the logic stack and logic tree procedures from the point of view of computational requirements.

11. Draw the flow charts of programs to combine lists of an inverted file according to each of the logic operations AND, OR, NOT under the assumption that all lists may be stored in main memory but that dynamic allocation of memory is required.

12. Repeat Problem 11 for the instance in which some, but not necessarily all, lists may be too large for storage in main memory.

7

Vocabulary Characteristics of Document Data Bases

7.1 Dependence of Search Times on Vocabulary Characteristics

In a sequential search of a data base each searchable term in each document record is searched for in a question term table, and so the search time is directly proportional to the number of descriptors in the data base. The length of the descriptors, and the extent to which a descriptor may be repeated in different document records, is not an important consideration.

In contrast, if the data base is represented by an inverted file structure, the amount of processing associated with each question term depends on the number of entries in the corresponding inverted file list. This number is equal to the frequency with which the term occurs in the entire data base. A large amount of space is required for storage of the dictionary required for access to the inverted file lists; the size of this dictionary depends on the number of different descriptors and also on their average length.

If a dictionary is segmented by storage of all descriptors of the same length in common subdictionaries, then in order to allocate the storage required for each dictionary it is necessary to know the distribution of descriptors with respect to their length. Alternatively, if dictionary segmentation is achieved by the grouping of descriptors with the same initial, or initial pair of, characters, the space to be allotted for storage of the subdictionaries depends on the frequencies with which characters, or pairs of characters, occur at the beginning of descriptors.

In Section 5.2 it was noted that the time required to create a dictionary in the form of a sort tree is dependent on both the number of different terms and the total number of occurrences of all terms.

As a data base grows through addition of new document items, both the dictionary and inverted file lists will grow in size. The rate of growth of the dictionary depends on the extent to which the addition of further document items introduces new descriptors not previously present in any document records. The likelihood of occurrence of new descriptors clearly depends on the size of the existing data base as well as on the particular discipline represented. For example, for a large data base that already contains most of the terms that form the vocabulary of the particular discipline, it will be found that most of the descriptors contained in new records will have already been found within existing records. On the other hand if the data base is relevant to a new discipline whose vocabulary is evolving, then new records will have a relatively high probability of containing new terms not present in previous records.

When scatter storage techniques are used to create and access a dictionary, the average time required to determine whether a given descriptor is present in the dictionary does not depend directly on the number of stored terms. It does, however, depend on the average number of collisions, and hence on the amount of unused space allocated for the storage. As the number of stored terms increases, the amount of unused space decreases and the average number of collisions increases.

During question processing by use of an inverted file in which combined lists are handled by a dynamic storage scheme, the amount of space to be allocated for the dynamic storage depends on the size of the various lists. Some knowledge of the statistical distribution of the list lengths is thus useful for determination of the amount of space to be allotted. It also allows a prediction to be made of the probability of requiring a back-up store in the form of a stack stored in a file.

It is clear that in a document retrieval system the search times are dependent on certain characteristics of the vocabulary of the data base. Of particular importance are the number of descriptors, the number of different descriptors and their lengths, and the rate of growth of the number of different descriptors as new records are added to the data base. Such characteristics of data base vocabularies are discussed in the present chapter. An example of the use of such statistics in the design of an information retrieval system is given in Chapter 10.

7.2 Vocabulary Frequencies

In Section 2.11 a document data base was envisaged as a set of document records in which each record contains details that relate to a single document. Each record is divided into fields associated with different attributes, and each field contains a set of terms chosen from the vocabulary associated with the particular attribute.

For each attribute, the occurrence of vocabulary terms in the corresponding field of the documents may be represented by an inverted file in which the number of lists is equal to the number of different descriptors in the vocabulary. In any list of the inverted file the number of entries is equal to the frequency with which the corresponding descriptor occurs in the appropriate field of all document items. Thus a knowledge of term frequencies is useful for prediction of the size of the lists in the inverted file.

Suppose the descriptors of a particular attribute vocabulary are ranked in descending order of their frequencies of occurrence. Suppose there are D different descriptors and a total of N occurrences of these descriptors in the entire data base. Let p_r be defined as the ratio

$$p_r = \frac{\text{Number of occurrences of descriptor of rank } r.}{N} \tag{7.1}$$

Then p_r is the probability that a descriptor chosen randomly from the text of the appropriate fields will be the term of rank r. The frequency of occurrence of the descriptor of rank r is Np_r, and the p_r must satisfy the equation

$$\sum_{r=1}^{D} p_r = 1. \tag{7.2}$$

It is not uncommon to find that the descriptors of an attribute vocabulary occur in such manner that a relation of the form

$$p_r = A/r \tag{7.3}$$

is satisfied approximately, where A denotes the value of an appropriately chosen constant. It is often found that the value of A is approximately equal to .1. The relation (7.3) is equivalent to the relation

$$\text{Rank} \times \text{Frequency} = \text{Constant}, \tag{7.4}$$

which is known as *Zipf's law*.[1]

---

[1] G. K. Zipf, *Human Behaviour and the Principle of Least Effort* (Reading, Mass.: Addison Wesley, 1949).

Relations (7.3) and (7.4) are satisfied approximately by the words that occur in sufficiently large samples of general English text. This is illustrated by the first few columns of Table 7.1 in which values of rp_r are tabulated for words chosen from a large sample of American English text. The text sample is of total length 1 million words and is formed from a number of different texts chosen by Kučera and Francis.[2] It may be observed that the value of rp_r is approximately equal to .1 for many of the listed words.

The remaining columns of Table 7.1 contain values of rp_r for title words in three document data bases. The chemical titles data applies to some of the 1,058,359 title terms of the chemical titles tapes for 1965. The MARC data applies to some of the 317,581 title terms that occur in a set of 58 issues of the MARC library tapes. A data base of 21,607 document items that relate to the specialized topic of gas chromatography has also been examined; the corresponding values of rp_r are shown in the last few columns of Table 7.1. It may be noted that, although the value of rp_r changes from term to term, it tends to fluctuate about an average value of approximately .1 for each of the data bases examined.

It may be remarked that prior to publication of the Kučera and Francis list of word frequencies, one of the most comprehensive set of similar frequencies was that compiled by Dewey.[3] The text examined by Dewey was of length 100,000 words and consisted of samples chosen quite differently from those of Kučera and Francis. Some of the resulting values of rp_r are the following in which the corresponding rank is indicated by a subscript.

$$.073_1, \quad .080_2, \quad .098_3, \quad .117_4, \quad .106_5, \quad .116_{10},$$
$$.124_{50}, \quad .111_{100}, \quad .102_{200}, \quad .100_{400}, \quad .108_{600},$$
$$.104_{800}, \quad .100_{1000}.$$

As in the text examined by Kučera and Francis the values of rp_r are approximately equal to .1.

Values of rp_r for some of the 60,778 subject headings and 53,387 publisher names on the 58 issues of the MARC tapes are shown in Table 7.2. Similar values for three types of descriptors used in the gas chromatography tapes are also listed in Table 7.3. The descriptors included under the heading Keyword 4 are names of chemical compounds, those included under the heading Keyword 5 are substances, while those listed under the heading Keyword 6 are miscellaneous descriptor phrases.

[2] H. Kučera and W. N. Francis, *Computational Analysis of Present-Day American English* (Brown University Press, 1967).

[3] G. Dewey, *Relativ(sic) Frequency of English Speech Sounds* (Cambridge, Mass.: Harvard University Press, 1950).

Table 7.1
Values of rp_r for Title Terms in Four Different Data Bases.

Rank	Kučera and Francis $N = 1,000,000$			Chem. Titles 1965 $N = 1,058,359$			MARC 01-58 $N = 317,581$			Gas Chromatography $N = 220,000$ (approx)		
	Term	Freq	rp_r	Term	Freq	rp_r	Term	Freq	rp_r	Term	Freq	rp_r
1	THE	69,971	.070	OF	107,687	.102	THE	25,647	.081	OF	23,569	.107
2	OF	36,411	.073	AND	37,578	.071	OF	21,471	.135	GAS	11,091	.101
3	AND	28,852	.086	THE	36,318	.103	AND	12,975	.123	THE	9,560	.130
4	TO	26,149	.104	IN	32,868	.124	IN	8,987	.113	AND	8,141	.148
5	A	23,237	.116	ON	10,984	.052	A	5,149	.081	CHROMATOGRAPHY	7,776	.177
6	IN	21,341	.128	BY	10,727	.070	TO	3,741	.071	IN	7,086	.193
7	THAT	10,595	.074	A	10,252	.068	FOR	3,464	.076	BY	4,031	.128
8	IS	10,099	.081	DI	8,419	.064	ON	2,726	.069	CHROMATOGRAPHIC	3,566	.130
9	WAS	9,816	.088	WITH	7,964	.068	HISTORY	1,213	.034	FOR	3,167	.130
10	HE	9,543	.095	FOR	6,509	.062	NEW	1,203	.038	ANALYSIS	3,061	.139
20	I	5,173	.103	METHYL	4,030	.076	LAW	649	.041	FROM	1,223	.111
30	THEY	3,618	.108	ACIDS	2,697	.076	AMERICA	511	.048	COMPOSITION	702	.096
40	THEIR	2,670	.107	5	2,236	.085	INTRODUCTION	439	.055	APPLICATION	576	.105
50	IF	2,199	.110	AN	1,890	.089	HIS	371	.058	OILS	492	.112
100	WELL	897	.090	PER	1,210	.114	BUSINESS	302	.095	MILK	256	.116
200	ALMOST	432	.086	SULFIDE	736	.139	INFORMATION	162	.102	AMINES	136	.124
300	HELP	311	.093	8	503	.143	CONSTRUCTION	118	.111	SPECTROSCOPY	89	.121
400	TURN	233	.093	METALLIC	395	.149	MODEL	93	.117	PEAKS	67	.122
500	STARTED	194	.097	FLUORESCENCE	316	.149	CHARACTERISTICS	78	.123	PRELIMINARY	53	.120
1,000	REACH	106	.106	TOXIN	147	.139	IMPLICATIONS	45	.142	STERIC	24	.109
2,000	SOLDIERS	56	.112	OXYTOCIN	67	.127	DIPLOMACY	20	.126	JUICES	9	.082
3,000	SURVEY	37	.111	DECREASE	36	.102	PSYCHIC	13	.123	DILUENTS	5	.068
4,000	SOUTHERNERS	26	.108	GERMINATING	20	.076	FRICTION	9	.113	ANCHIMERICALLY	3	.055
5,000	ATTRACT	19	.095	RESONATOR	14	.066	PEASANT	7	.110	WORLD	3	.068

Table 7.2
Values of rp_r for Subject Headings and Publisher Names on the MARC O1-58 Tapes.

	Subject headings $N = 60,778$			Publishers names $N = 53,387$		
Rank	Term	Freq	rp_r	Term	Freq	rp_r
1	NEGROES	398	.007	U.S. GOVT. PRINT. OFF	1829	.034
2	GEOLOGY	351	.011	BOOKS FOR LIBRARIES PRESS	1213	.045
3	ENGLISH LANGUAGE	344	.017	GREENWOOD PRESS	795	.045
4	EDUCATION	287	.019	MACMILLAN	569	.043
5	SLAVERY IN THE UNITED STATES	279	.023	DOUBLEDAY	547	.051
6	AGRICULTURE	257	.025	NEGRO UNIVERSITIES PRESS	547	.061
7	ELCTRONIC DATA PROCESSING	288	.026	MCGRAW-HILL	537	.070
8	CITIES AND TOWNS	222	.029	FOR SALE BY THE SUPT. OF DOCS., U.S. . .	524	.079
9	SCIENCE	197	.029	PRENTICE-HALL	495	.073
10	WORLD WAR, 1939–1945	182	.030	KENNIKAT PRESS	438	.082
20	RAILROADS	125	.041	PUTNAM	233	.087
30	WATER	105	.052	NATIONAL AERONAUTICS AND SPACE ADMINISTR	155	.087
40	ANIMALS	96	.063	METHUEN	137	.103
50	ARCHITECTURE	86	.071	F. WATTS	127	.119
100	WOMAN	63	.104	PATTERSON SMITH	76	.142
200	TREES	39	.128	BODLEY HEAD	41	.153
300	COMMUNITY MENTAL HEALTH SERVICES	29	.143	MURRAY	28	.157
400	SOCIAL PROBLEMS	24	.158	IOWA STATE UNIVERSITY PRESS	21	.157
500	TELEVISION BROADCASTING	21	.173	INSTITUTE OF CONTINUING LEGAL EDUCATION	16	.150
1000	ADVENTURE AND ADVENTURES	11	.181	AGRICULTURAL RESEARCH SERVICE, U.S. . . .	6	.112
2000	JUDO	6	.197			
3000	GYMNASTICS FOR WOMEN	4	.197			
4000	MEDICAL STATISTICS	3	.197			
5000	CULVERTS	2	.166			

Table 7.3
Values of rp_r for Keywords on the Gas Chromatography Tapes.

Rank	Keyword 4 $N = 59{,}613$ Term	Freq	rp_r	Keyword 5 $N = 10{,}155$ Term	Freq	rp_r	Keyword 6 $N = 17{,}322$ Term	Freq	rp_r
1	ACIDS	2850	.048	ISOMERS	766	.075	REVIEW	915	.053
2	HYDROCARBONS	1127	.038	ESSENTIAL OILS	658	.130	COLUMN PACKING	769	.089
3	ALCOHOLS	1123	.056	FLAVORS	345	.102	INSTRUMENTATION	721	.125
4	PESTICIDES	678	.045	LIPIDS	305	.120	PYROLYSIS	662	.153
5	NITROGEN COMPOUNDS	651	.054	URINE	291	.144	MASS SPECTROSCOPY	641	.185
6	ALDEHYDES	613	.062	BLOOD	272	.160	DETECTORS	598	.207
7	ESTERS	579	.068	AIR	248	.171	THEORY	554	.224
8	STEROIDS	541	.073	FOODS	217	.171	DERIVATIVES TMS	485	.224
9	KETONES	485	.073	POLYMERS	184	.162	DERIVATIVES	479	.254
10	HALOGENATED COMPOUNDS	427	.072	PETROLEUM	163	.160	PREPARATIVE DETECTORS	393	.227
20	AROMATIC HYDROCARBON	248	.083	CIGARETTE SMOKE	66	.130	IONIZATION	157	.181
30	SUGARS	217	.109	TRIGLYCERIDES	44	.130	GAS SOLID	96	.166
40	ETHYLENE	165	.110	WINE	33	.130	CARRIER GAS	65	.150
50	DIELDRIN	123	.103	COSMETICS	25	.123	ADSORPTION ISOTHERMS	47	.135
100	ISOPROPANOL	60	.100	PHOSPHOLIPIDS	14	.138	MOLECULAR WEIGHT	17	.098
200	BUTENE	31	.104	ALFALFA	7	.138	ARGON IONIZATION	6	.069
300	HYDROCARBONS A E	21	.105	PETROLEUM PRODUCTS	5	.148	DIGITAL CONTROL	4	.069
400	MONOTERPENES	15	.100	AIR SPACECRAFT	3	.118	FLASH EXCHANGE	3	.069
500	PYRUVIC	12	.100	OIL SHALE	3	.148	ATTENUATORS	2	.058
1000	SUGAR ALCOHOLS	6	.100						
2000	ACIDS BRANCHED	2	.067						
3000	PREGNANEDIONE	2	.100						

Relations (7.3) and (7.4), known as Zipf's law, were first stated by Estoup[4] and discussed subsequently in considerable detail by Zipf. It is an empirical law whose value has been criticized severely by Herdan.[5] Nevertheless, it forms a useful formula for prediction of approximate descriptor frequencies in certain attribute fields. An alternative relation between frequency and rank has been proposed and discussed by Mandelbrot.[6,7]

If the probabilities p_r are according to Zipf's law it follows from (7.2) that

$$A = \frac{1}{1 + \frac{1}{2} + \frac{1}{3} + \ldots + 1/D} \tag{7.5}$$

which may be approximated by writing

$$A = \frac{1}{\log_e D + \gamma}, \tag{7.6}$$

where γ denotes Euler's constant whose value is .5772. Thus for values of D equal to 5000, 10,000, 50,000, and 100,000, respectively, the values of A are .11, .10, .09, and .08.

It may be noted that the Zipf law implies that a descriptor that occurs exactly n times has rank $r_n = AN/n$. However, several descriptors may occur the same number of times, and within any group of such descriptors the ordering for the purpose of rank assignment is arbitrary. If it is supposed that the rank given by $r_n = AN/n$ applies to the last of the descriptors that occur at least n times then there are r_n descriptors that occur more than n times, and there are r_{n+1} descriptors that occur more than $n + 1$ times. The number of different descriptors that occur exactly n times is therefore

$$I_n = r_n - r_{n+1} = \frac{AN}{n} - \frac{AN}{n + 1} = \frac{AN}{n(n + 1)}. \tag{7.7}$$

Now the highest ranking term has rank D and so, if there is at least one term that occurs only once, it follows that

$$D = AN/1. \tag{7.8}$$

[4] J. B. Estoup, *Games Stenographies* 4th edition (Paris: Gauthier-Villars, 1916).

[5] G. Herdan, *The Advanced Theory of Language as Choice and Chance* (New York: Springer-Verlag, 1966).

[6] B. Mandelbrot, *Théorie Mathématique de la d'Estoup-Zipf* (Paris: Institute de Statistique de l'Univèrsité, 1957).

[7] B. Mandelbrot, *American Mathematical Society Symposium in Applied Mathematics* (1960): 108–219.

Substitution of AN from (7.8) into (7.7) then leads to

$$I_n/D = [n(n + 1)]^{-1} \qquad (7.9)$$

and hence

$$I_n/I_1 = 2/[n(n + 1)] \qquad (7.10)$$

It may be noted that the last two equations are independent of both text length and the constant A.

Equations (7.9) and (7.10) were first derived by Booth,[8] who verified them by examination of four English texts with regard to the occurrence of the words of low frequency. As n ranges from 2 to 10 the values of I_n/I_1 according to (7.10) are

.33,   .17,   .10,   .071,   .048,   .036,   .028,   .022,   .018.

For one text examined by Booth the corresponding values of I_n/I_1 were found to be

.36,   .17,   .10,   .070,   .051,   .035,   .028,   .029,   .015

which are in remarkably close agreement with the predicted values. The worst agreement was for text that gave I_n/I_1 values of

.32,   .13,   .06,   .05

as n ranged from 2 to 5. It therefore appears that the formula (7.10) for I_n/I_1 is reliable for use in prediction of the frequencies of occurrence of words of low frequency in general English text.

Verification of (7.9) for the vocabularies of titles in some document data bases is provided by Table 7.4. As predicted by the formula it is found that approximately 50% of the different title terms occur in only one title, 16% occur in only two titles, 8.3% occur in only three titles, and 5% occur in only four document titles. Thus 80% of the different title terms each appear in not more than four titles and in an average of only 1.6 titles.

Values of I_n for some nontitle fields are shown in Table 7.5. It may be observed that subject headings on the MARC tapes have values of I_n that are well predicted by the value of $1/n(n + 1)$. In contrast, the keywords on the gas chromatography tapes, publishers on the MARC tapes, and authors on the gas chromatography tapes all have very similar values of I_n but the values are not closely approximated by $1/n(n + 1)$; for each of these fields, between 87 and 94% of the terms appear in not more than four documents.

---

[8]A. D. Booth, "A 'Law' of occurrences for words of low frequency," *Information and Control* 10(1967): 386–393.

Table 7.4
Number I_n of Title Terms of Frequency n in Four Different Data Bases.

n	$1/n(n+1)$	K and F $D = 50,406$		CT-1965 $D = 34,943$		MARC 01-58 $D = 31,004$		Gas Chrom. $D = 14,926$	
		I_n	I_n/D	I_n	I_n/D	I_n	I_n/D	I_n	I_n/D
1	.500	22,543	.447	16,631	.476	16,259	.524	7,693	.510
2	.167	7,233	.143	4,767	.136	4,496	.145	2,211	.148
3	.083	3,947	.078	2,433	.070	2,097	.068	1,077	.072
4	.050	2,465	.049	1,484	.042	1,140	.037	627	.042
5	.033	1,820	.036	1,055	.030	900	.029	452	.030
6	.024	1,279	.025	773	.022	670	.022	320	.021
7	.018	1,121	.022	524	.015	580	.019	265	.018
8	.014	824	.016	516	.015	450	.014	198	.013
9	.011	695	.014	429	.012	350	.011	175	.012
10	.009	559	.011	373	.011	310	.010	132	.009
11	.008	498	.010	274	.008	270	.009	119	.008
12	.006	434	.009	268	.008	220	.007	116	.008
13	.006	390	.008	226	.006	210	.007	66	.004
14	.005	324	.006	213	.006	190	.006	69	.005
15	.004	301	.006	200	.006	160	.005	69	.003
20	.002	207	.004	125	.004	90	.003	39	.003
30	.001	92	.002	58	.002	46	.001	22	.001
40	.001	77	.002	46	.001	32	.001	9	.001
50	.000	46	.001	28	.001	16	.000	9	.001

As an alternative to the Zipf law a rule known as *Lotka's law* has been suggested for prediction of the frequencies of occurrence of author names.[9,10] Lotka's law states that for author names

$$I_n/I_1 = 1/n^2 \qquad (7.11)$$

which is smaller than the value (7.10) as predicted by the Zipf law.

Schorr[11] has concluded that Lotka's law may be used as a valid approximation for prediction of I_n for a data base of 436 articles relating to map librarianship. However, the ratios I_n/I_1 listed in Table 7.6 suggest that the Zipf law provides at least as good an approximation and has the advantage of allowing prediction of I_1. The Table 7.6 includes the author names in four small data bases of articles from single journals; the particular journals are *Communications of the Association for Computing Machinery*

[9] A. J. Lotka, "The frequency distribution of scientific productivity," *Journal of the Washington Academy of Sciences* 16(1926): 317–323.

[10] L. Murphy, "Lotka's law in the humanities," *Journal of the American Society for Information Science* 24(1973): 461–462.

[11] A. E. Schorr, "Lotka's law and map librarianship," *Journal of the American Society for Information Science,* 26(1975): 189–190.

Table 7.5
Number I_n of Descriptors of Frequency n in Subject Heading, Keyword, Publisher, and Author fields.

n	$1/n(n+1)$	MARC Sub. Hds $D = 13,636$		G.C Keyword$_4$ $D = 9815$		G.C Keyword$_5$ $D = 3319$		G.C Keyword$_6$ $D = 2673$		MARC Pub $D = 11,527$		G.C Author $D = 25,563$	
		I_n	I_n/D	I_n	I_n/D	I_n	I_n/D	I_n	I_n/D	I_n	I_n/D	I_n	I_n/D
1	.500	6883	.505	6616	.674	2328	.701	1860	.696	8123	.705	16135	.631
2	.167	2264	.166	1220	.124	443	.133	336	.126	1234	.107	5645	.221
3	.083	1068	.078	491	.050	150	.045	132	.049	538	.046	1429	.056
4	.050	760	.056	266	.027	138	.042	75	.028	302	.026	748	.029
5	.033	489	.036	208	.021	51	.015	43	.016	209	.018	429	.017
6	.024	319	.023	154	.016	33	.010	28	.011	134	.012	284	.011
7	.018	260	.019	110	.011	27	.008	16	.006	100	.009	231	.009
8	.014	186	.014	84	.009	31	.009	18	.007	71	.006	132	.005
9	.011	147	.011	59	.006	23	.007	11	.004	61	.005	104	.004
10	.009	114	.008	54	.006	15	.005	7	.003	62	.005	69	.003
11	.008	105	.008	47	.005	8	.002	10	.004	55	.005	59	.002
12	.006	74	.005	37	.004	6	.002	12	.004	43	.004	42	.002
13	.006	76	.005	45	.005	13	.004	8	.003	32	.003	41	.002
14	.005	66	.005	19	.002	8	.002	7	.003	32	.003	29	.001
15	.004	65	.005	25	.003	7	.002	6	.002	31	.003	37	.001
20	.002	31	.002	9	.001	7	.002	2	.001	14	.001		

Table 7.6
Number I_n of Author Names of Frequency n in Six Different Data Bases.

	$n = 1$	2	3	4	5
Map. Lib.					
$D = 326$					
I_n	245	48	17	8	3
I_n/D	.75	.15	.05	.02	.01
I_n/I_1		.19	.07	.03	.01
Gas Chrom.					
$D = 25{,}563$					
I_n	16,135	5645	1429	748	429
I_n/D	.63	.22	.06	.03	.02
I_n/I_1		.35	.09	.05	.03
CACM					
$D = 599$					
I_n	301	123	33	12	2
I_n/D	.50	.20	.06	.02	.00
I_n/I_1		.41	.11	.04	.01
JACM					
$D = 301$					
I_n	166	85	14	1	0
I_n/D	.55	.28	.05	.00	.00
I_n/I_1		.51	.08	.01	.00
AFIPS					
$D = 1021$					
I_n	520	185	83	18	12
I_n/D	.51	.18	.08	.02	.01
I_n/I_1		.36	.16	.03	.02
IEEE					
$D = 851$					
I_n	366	277	48	7	1
I_n/D	.43	.32	.06	.01	.00
I_n/I_1		.76	.13	.02	.00
Zipf					
$1/n\,(n + 1)$	.50	.17	.08	.05	.03
Lotka					
$1/n^2$		.25	.11	.06	.04

(CACM), *Journal of the Association for Computing Machinery* (JACM), *Proceedings of the American Federation of Information Processing Societies* (AFIPS), and *Proceedings of the Institute of Electrical and Electronic Engineers* (IEEE).

The significance of the vocabulary characteristics described in the present section may be illustrated by consideration of an inverted file for the 31,004 title words that account for 317,581 words of the MARC tape referred to in Tables 7.1 and 7.4. It may be noted that 80% of the different terms occur in not more than 5 titles and in an average of 1.6 titles. However, the average number of titles in which each of the 31,000 different words occur is 317,581/31,004 = 10.2. Therefore, the remaining 20% of the title words must occur in an average of n titles, where

$$.80 \times 1.6 + .20n = 10.2,$$

and hence in an average of $n = 45$ titles. Thus the logic operations that act on lists of the inverted file will treat lists of various lengths, 80% of the lists having an average of 1.6 entries, and 20% having an average of 45 entries.

For the larger chemical titles data base of 1 million title words, it is found that 75% of the different title words occur in not more than five titles and hence require an average of 1.7 inverted file entries, whereas the remaining 25% require an average of 115 entries in the inverted file.

Some further frequency counts of title terms are shown in Tables 7.7 and 7.8 in which the words are grouped according to word length. For the chemical titles and the CAIN tapes the listed 128 words account respectively for 44 and 42% of all title word occurrences. The frequent terms that are underlined account respectively for 26 and 29% of word occurrences. Thus although the individual terms occur with different frequencies in the different data bases, the overall vocabulary statistics are similar. It may be noted that in either instance the 15 most frequent terms are of little importance as question terms, and omission of their entries in the inverted file would allow a space saving of 26 and 29%.

7.3 Distribution of Term Lengths

In general English text, as examined by Kučera and Francis, the average word length is 4.7 characters. This low value results, in part, from the fact that some very short words are repeated many times. On the other hand, when words are stored in a dictionary each word is stored only once and the average word length is then found to be 8.1 characters.

The proportion of title terms of different lengths that occur in dic-

Table 7.7
Most Frequent Title Terms of Lengths 1–8 in 1,058,359 Title Terms on the Chemical Titles Tapes for 1965.

	Length 2	Length 3	Length 4	Length 5	Length 6	Length 7	Length 8	
A/	10252 OF	107687 AND	37578 WITH	7964 OXIDE	3564 EFFECT	6015 EFFECTS	2081 REACTION	2991
2	5779 IN	32868 THE	36318 ACID	6098 AMINO	2919 METHYL	4030 SPECTRA	1827 CHLORIDE	2439
1	4379 ON	10984 FOR	6509 FROM	5564 ACIDS	2697 CARBON	2542 BETWEEN	1782 MAGNETIC	2360
3	4135 BY	10727 TRI	3072 POLY	3294 AMINE	2081 METHOD	2299 STUDIES	1519 ACTIVITY	1973
4	3219 DI	8419 ITS	1527 SOME	2498 CYCLO	1856 PHENYL	2187 HYDROXY	1481 HYDROGEN	1970
N	2465 TO	4544 RAT	1514 IRON	1583 WATER	1619 SYSTEM	1847 NUCLEAR	1410 ELECTRON	1913
5	2236 AT	2236 GAS	1451 HIGH	1571 STUDY	1554 SODIUM	1813 TERMAL	1302 ANALYSIS	1901
B	2085 AN	1890 ION	1369 THIO	1297 ETHYL	1427 DURING	1656 ORGANIC	1213 CHEMICAL	1584
6	1679 AS	1763 OXY	1229 IONS	1136 METAL	1366 CHLORO	1653 CRYSTAL	1125 CRYSTALS	1300
X	1142 II	1165 PER	1210 MONO	1059 ALKYL	1343 OXYGEN	1562 SYSTEMS	1113 KINETICS	1215
D	1108 DE	858 ISO	1190 ANTI	1047 TETRA	1338 LIQUID	1407 PROTEIN	1071 ALUMINUM	1173
P	1060 CO	743 LOW	987 ZINC	910 THEIR	1320 COPPER	1310 SILICON	979 NITROGEN	1171
L	1015 14	656 USE	985 FREE	909 GAMMA	1146 FLUORO	1201 CALCIUM	975 INFRARED	1162
S	948 OR	519 III	917 RATS	885 PHASE	1118 ENERGY	1182 AQUEOUS	935 EXCHANGE	1135
C	830 12	440 RAY	831 SPIN	827 LIVER	1079 NICKEL	1151 INDUCED	928 ETHYLENE	1055
	10	433 RNA	827 THIN	779 PHOTO	988 ACTION	1076 BENZENE	911 SOLUTION	1055
	42332	185932	97514	37421	27415	27415	20652	26397

196

Table 7.8
Most Frequent Title Terms of Lengths 1–8 in 100,000 Title Terms on the CAIN Tapes.

1		2		3		4		5		6		7		8	
A	1331	OF	8680	THE	4965	WITH	562	PLANT	277	EFFECT	437	CONTROL	319	RESEARCH	152
L	250	IN	3914	AND	3693	FROM	506	WHEAT	203	CATTLE	307	STUDIES	299	INDUSTRY	142
I	168	ON	1790	FOR	979	SOME	326	STUDY	182	GROWTH	254	SPECIES	223	NITROGEN	132
S	116	TO	805	NEW	412	SOIL	277	WATER	178	PLANTS	226	EFFECTS	222	ANALYSIS	128
2	105	BY	537	ITS	166	MILK	209	DAIRY	164	DURING	144	QUALITY	142	BREEDING	124
U	66	AS	255	USE	159	ACID	201	SHEEP	159	FOREST	133	BETWEEN	124	DISEASES	119
N	65	AN	234	TWO	124	FOOD	186	SOILS	157	METHOD	126	DISEASE	120	CHEMICAL	108
1	60	AT	166	OIL	79	SEED	136	VIRUS	139	INSECT	109	CONTENT	111	ACTIVITY	106
3	58	II	144	III	70	FARM	123	YIELD	130	ANIMAL	105	METHODS	109	PROBLEMS	98
4	57	IS	59	HOW	48	1969	101	FRUIT	126	REPORT	93	PROTEIN	101	PRODUCTS	96
R	53	OR	58	DOG	47	RICE	98	THEIR	111	COTTON	91	FEEDING	97	TAXONOMY	95
D	50	IV	34	LOW	47	FEED	95	GRAIN	102	BARLEY	79	FACTORS	93	RELATION	89
C	41	BE	29	NON	40	CORN	91	SWINE	99	ANNUAL	70	STORAGE	86	ECONOMIC	84
X	35	SP	25	RED	40	1968	89	UNDER	94	CITRUS	64	CHANGES	83	MOISTURE	61
P	30	IT	21	DRY	32	LEAF	80	FIELD	90	MARKET	63	POULTRY	80	RESPONSE	57
F	29	NO	19	EGG	32	HIGH	77	CROPS	78	LEAVES	61	TOBACCO	78	BEHAVIOR	42

Table 7.9

Proportion of Different Title Terms of Length L in Five Data Bases, and Proportion of Terms with Repetitions in the Kučera and Francis Data Base.

L	K and F $D = 50,406$	CT63-65 $D = 63,316$	MARCOI $D = 31,004$	58 CAIN $D = 15,907$	CANDICT $D = 10,804$	K and F $N = 1,000,000$
1	.001	0.	.001	.002	0.	.032
2	.005	.011	.011	.012	.006	.172
3	.024	.029	.033	.028	.021	.215
4	.060	.044	.084	.067	.060	.159
5	.092	.062	.108	.091	.084	.110
6	.128	.094	.135	.103	.105	.086
7	.145	.105	.142	.128	.118	.078
8	.138	.126	.137	.129	.133	.057
9	.120	.136	.115	.123	.127	.041
10	.096	.119	.089	.102	.111	.028
11	.068	.091	.059	.072	.080	.016
12	.046	.066	.037	.056	.059	.009
13	.029	.048	.023	.037	.038	.005
14	.020	.030	.012	.020	.023	.003
15	.011		.007	.013		.001
16	.007		.003	.006		.001
17	.004		.002	.004		0.
18	.002		.001	.004		0.
19	.002		.001	.001		0.
20	.001		0.	.001		0.
AV_D	8.1	8.2	7.6	8.2	8.4	
AV_N	4.7	5.6	5.6		—	4.7

tionaries for some particular data bases are listed in Table 7.9. The average term lengths Av_D are also shown. The averages for the full texts that include repetitions are listed as Av_N. The data base sample designated as CANDICT was prepared by Treleaven[12] and contains all terms in the right-hand column of odd-numbered pages of the *Dictionary of Canadian English;*[13] it contains some compound terms, such as FILING CABINET and COMMANDER-IN-CHIEF, which tend to increase the average term length.

It is clear that, although the data bases used to obtain Table 7.9 refer to different subject areas, the distributions of term length are similar, par-

[12] R. L. Treleaven, *Abbreviation of English Words to Standard Length for Computer Processing* (Master's Thesis, University of Alberta, 1970).

[13] W. S. Avis, P. D. Drysdale, R. J. Gregg, and M. H. Scargill, eds., *Dictionary of Canadian English. The Senior Dictionary.* (Toronto: W. J. Gage, 1967).

ticularly with regard to average term length. The smaller value of Av_N obtained for general English text reflects the fact that the short words tend to be repeated more frequently in general text than in titles.

Consider the amount of space required for storage of a dictionary for the 15,907 title terms that appear in the CAIN data base, and suppose it is desired to search this dictionary for the presence of untruncated question terms.

If the table is subdivided into a set of 20 tables, each used to store terms of a fixed length, then a total storage area of $15,907 \times 8.2 = 130,000$ characters is required. The table to store words of length 8 characters will have the largest number of entries, approximately 2050, and a binary search for a word may require up to 12 comparisons. In contrast, the tables for words of 2 or 15 characters will each contain about 200 words and hence a binary search will require up to 8 comparisons.

7.4 Frequency Distribution of Characters

The frequency of occurrence of characters in English text chosen from many different sources was determined by Dewey. The text examined consisted of 100,000 words, and the letter frequencies were determined by examination of the 1027 words that occurred more than 10 times. These words comprise 78,633 words of the entire text. The 500 words that occur more than 20 times account for 71% of the entire text. The total number of sentences is 5446, and the average length of the sentences is 19.6 words. This is in agreement with the Kučera and Francis data in which the average sentence length is 19.3 words.

The frequencies of letters in the 100,000 words examined by Dewey are shown in the third column of Table 7.10. The remaining columns show the number of occurrences of letters at the beginning of words; at the end of words; and within, but not the first or last letter, of a word. The number of occurrences of the apostrophe and hyphen are also listed.

For arrangement of dictionaries in computer accessible files it may be useful to know how many entries begin with a given initial letter. This is shown in Table 7.11 in which the second column is for the 1027 most commonly occurring words of Dewey. The third and fourth columns are respectively for the words in the *Concise Oxford Dictionary*[14] and the *Dictionary of Canadian English*. The fifth column applies to the 90,000 proper names, including repetitions, that are listed in the 10th edition of

---

[14] H. W. Fowler and F. G. Fowler, eds., *The Concise Oxford Dictionary of Current English* 5th edition. (Cambridge: Oxford University Press, 1964).

Table 7.10
Frequencies of Letters in the 100,000 Words Examined by Dewey.

Letter	Probability	Occurrences	Initial	Medial	Final
E	.127	55,405	2,123	32,472	20,870
T	.098	42,815	17,182	15,210	10,423
A	.079	34,536	9,477	22,791	148
O	.078	33,993	7,764	21,608	4,617
I	.071	30.955	6,691	23,094	15
N	.071	30,902	2,317	20,521	8,064
S	.063	27,642	6,119	9,508	12,015
R	.059	26,051	2,165	17,734	6,152
H	.057	25,138	4,916	17,772	2,450
L	.039	17,261	2,118	12,155	2,988
D	.039	17,046	2,756	4,227	10,063
U	.028	12,285	1,214	10,278	793
C	.027	11,747	4,327	7,170	250
F	.026	11,199	4,037	2,550	4,612
M	.024	10,678	4,010	5,198	1,470
W	.021	9,367	6,839	1,604	953
Y	.020	8,837	1,454	971	6,412
G	.019	8,191	1,588	3,588	3,015
P	.019	8,162	3,476	4,213	473
B	.016	6,838	4,788	2,006	44
V	.010	4,481	537	3,944	0
K	.010	2,610	436	1,373	801
X	.010	687	0	626	61
J	.010	421	256	165	0
Q	.009	403	171	232	0
Z	.006	284	15	265	4
Totals	1.036	438,023	96,776	241,275	96,693
'		674	17	644	13
–		28		25	3

American Men of Science.[15] The final column is equivalent to the fourth column of Table 7.10 and is included for comparison.

Further information concerning the frequencies of letters in different positions within words is contained in Tables 7.12 and 7.13, which contain results obtained by Bourne and Ford.[16] The values listed in Table 7.12 apply to letters within so-called subject words and do not include noncontent words as prepositions. In the text examined there were 2082 different

[15] J. Cattell, ed., *American Men of Science* 10th edition. (Tempe, Arizona: Jacques Cattell Press,)

[16] C. P. Bourne and D. L. Ford, "A study of the statistics of letters in English words," *Information and Control* 4(1961): 48–67.

Table 7.11
Proportion of Different Words that Have a Given Initial Letter, and Similar Proportion for Full Text.

Letter	Dewey	Oxford Dictionary	Canadian Dictionary	Am. Men Science	Full Text Dewey
A	.070	.053	.064	.030	.098
B	.047	.053	.061	.091	.049
C	.071	.090	.104	.063	.045
D	.037	.051	.058	.040	.028
E	.042	.031	.039	.021	.022
F	.062	.043	.044	.042	.042
G	.030	.035	.031	.053	.016
H	.040	.030	.044	.082	.051
I	.032	.032	.039	.004	.069
J	.004	.008	.010	.023	.003
K	.009	.008	.008	.049	.005
L	.043	.038	.036	.051	.022
M	.056	.044	.051	.088	.042
N	.034	.019	.020	.019	.024
O	.035	.040	.024	.013	.080
P	.068	.085	.078	.044	.036
Q	.005	.007	.006	.001	.002
R	.035	.058	.040	.051	.022
S	.112	.139	.115	.110	.063
T	.075	.062	.047	.033	.178
U	.014	.016	.019	.003	.013
V	.008	.018	.016	.013	.006
W	.060	.033	.029	.063	.071
X	.000	.000	.000	.000	.000
Y	.011	.004	.004	.006	.015
Z	.000	.002	.000	.007	.000

subject words. Interpretation of the tabulated probabilities may be illustrated as follows: If text of length N words contains D_s different subject words which, including repetitions, form N_s words of the text, then $.06N_s$ words of the text are subject words that begin with the letter A. Thus the probabilities refer to occurrences in text and not to occurrences in D_s different words. The results are similar to those obtained by Yerkey[17] in a study of letter occurrences within titles of articles published in engineering periodicals.

Bourne and Ford also measured the frequencies of letters within a set of 8207 proper names that formed the entire student registration at Stanford University. These frequencies are shown in Table 7.13.

[17] A. N. Yerkey, "Occurrence of letters in engineering periodical titles," *Journal of the American Society for Information Science* 22(1971): 290–292.

Table 7.12
Subject Words of Bourne and Ford. Probability that Letter Appears in nth position.

	Any N	N=1	2	3	4	5	6	7	8	9	10
A	.08	.06	.13	.085	.075	.075	.065	.10	.075	.055	.065
B	.015	.05	0	.05	.01	.015	.01	.005	0	.005	0
C	.045	.10	.01	.05	.05	.03	.045	.035	.05	.045	.045
D	.025	.06	.005	.025	.035	.025	.02	.02	.035	.035	.02
E	.11	.05	.15	.06	.125	.11	.10	.12	.12	.145	.15
F	.015	.04	.005	.015	.01	.015	.01	.005	.005	.005	0
G	.02	.025	0	.025	.02	.025	.02	.025	.02	.025	.025
H	.025	.05	.04	.01	.025	.025	.025	.02	.025	.025	.015
I	.09	.05	.11	.05	.08	.10	.095	.01	.095	.105	.08
J	.005	.01	0	.005	0	0	0	0	0	0	0
K	.01	.01	0	.01	.015	.01	0	0	.005	.005	0
L	.05	.025	.06	.08	.055	.05	.055	.05	.06	.04	.04
M	.03	.06	.015	.03	.025	.03	.05	.025	.03	.03	.02
N	.075	.02	.055	.09	.05	.06	.08	.075	.10	.125	.13
O	.08	.02	.14	.06	.075	.11	.075	.11	.075	.065	.12
P	.03	.10	.01	.045	.025	.025	.02	.015	.02	.015	.01
Q	0	0	.005	0	0	.005	0	0	0	.01	0
R	.085	.055	.08	.011	.08	.095	.10	.08	.07	.07	.07
S	.05	.10	.01	.05	.055	.055	.055	.045	.05	.055	.05
T	.08	.075	.02	.08	.09	.09	.085	.095	.105	.09	.10
U	.025	.005	.075	.03	.025	.03	.025	.015	.02	.02	.01
V	.01	.02	.005	.01	.005	.01	.01	.005	.005	.01	.005
W	.01	.025	0	.01	.005	.01	.005	0	0	.005	0
X	.005	0	.01	.005	0	0	.005	0	0	.005	0
Y	.02	0	.02	.015	.01	.01	.015	.02	.02	.03	.025
Z	.03	0	.005	0	0	.005	.005	.005	0	.005	.01

A character string formed from a single pair of adjacent characters within text may be called a bigram. Since certain combinations of letters are more frequent than others it is clear that certain bigrams account for a relatively large proportion of text. The frequencies of the different bigrams L_1L_2, as determined by Bourne and Ford are shown in Tables 7.14 and 7.15. Tables of frequencies of trigrams have been used by Carlson[18] to reconstruct partially mutilated text in which some characters are unrecognizable.

Tables 7.10–7.15 relate to frequencies of alphabetic characters. Most document data bases that refer the scientific or engineering data bases contain other special characters such as + and /. The values tabulated in

[18] G. Carlson, "Techniques for replacing characters that are garbled on input," *Proceedings Spring Joint Computer Conference* (1966): 189–192.

Table 7.13
Proper Names of Bourne and Ford. Probability that Letter Appears in nth Position.

	Any N	$N=1$	2	3	4	5	6	7	8	9	10
A	.10	.05	.210	.08	.04	.075	.085	.10	.115	.115	.125
B	.025	.10	.005	.02	.025	.02	.015	.015	.02	.025	.02
C	.03	.07	.035	.04	.025	.02	.025	.025	.025	.03	.03
D	.04	.045	.005	.025	.06	.025	.025	.05	.04	.035	.035
E	.115	.025	.145	.08	.105	.195	.11	.08	.09	.10	.11
F	.015	.04	0	.01	.015	.01	.01	.01	.01	.01	.01
G	.025	.05	.005	.02	.035	.025	.015	.03	.025	.025	.02
H	.04	.075	.04	.03	.035	.045	.03	.035	.045	.055	.045
I	.06	.005	.11	.07	.05	.07	.04	.045	.055	.07	.07
J	.02	.025	0	0	.005	.015	.025	.04	.03	.025	.015
K	.015	.04	.005	.015	.045	.025	.01	.015	.015	.01	.01
L	.075	.05	.04	.105	.095	.045	.055	.055	.06	.075	.08
M	.035	.085	.015	.025	.04	.03	.025	.03	.025	.025	.025
N	.08	.02	.015	.095	.09	.075	.11	.085	.085	.09	.085
O	.06	.02	.165	.06	.03	.07	.065	.08	.08	.07	.065
P	.015	.05	.01	.015	.025	.015	.01	.015	.01	.01	.01
Q	.005	.005	0	0	0	0	0	0	0	0	0
R	.10	.055	.08	.125	.075	.07	.14	.10	.095	.11	.11
S	.045	.10	.005	.04	.06	.085	.07	.055	.045	.03	.03
T	.045	.035	.02	.045	.08	.04	.05	.045	.035	.03	.035
U	.02	.005	.07	.025	.015	.01	.02	.025	.02	.025	.02
V	.01	.01	.005	.015	.01	.005	.005	.01	.01	.015	.01
W	.02	.065	.01	.025	.02	.015	.02	.025	.02	.02	.015
X	.005	0	0	.01	0	0	0	0	0	0	0
Y	.02	.01	.01	.025	.01	.02	.025	.025	.02	.02	.025
Z	.005	.005	0	.005	.01	.01	.01	.01	.01	.005	0

Table 7.16 are from the results of Clare *et al.*[19] obtained from a sample of 2000 titles of the chemical titles tapes. The 47 different characters include numbers, punctuation, and other special characters. The frequencies of bigrams, and sets of n characters designated as n-grams, were also computed.

The frequencies of letters that occupy given positions in words, and the frequencies of bigrams, have been computed by Treleaven for data bases consisting of 53,316 different terms of the chemical titles tapes, 6354 different words of the MARC tapes, and 10,804 terms in the Canadian dictionary.

[19] A. C. Clare, E. M. Cook, and M. F. Lynch, "The identification of variable-length equifrequent character strings in a natural language data base," *The Computer Journal* 15(1972): 259–262.

Table 7.14

Frequencies of Bigrams L_1L_2 within Subject Words of Bourne and Ford. The Listed Numbers Divided by 10,000 Are the Probabilities of Occurrence of Letter Pairs.

L_1 \ L_2	A	B	C	D	E	F	G	H	I	J	K	L	M	N	O	P	Q	R	S	T	U	V	W	X	Y	Z	ḅ
A	23	13	46	30	3	8	24	1	25	1	10	105	35	119		29		101	44	137	7	13	5	4	9	7	23
B	57	2	5		20			44	25		15	13			20			14	5		17				8	1	5
C	17		5		52				21			14			83			24	7	56	18				8		57
D	35	1	1		78	12	4		54		1	2	2	1	18			17	6	1	15	9	1		5		58
E	12	5	56	33	15	10	14	2	6		1	68	22	104	12	19	5	223	84	89	5	9	4	20	3	1	213
F	17				17	10			27			19			17	17		14	4	5	7						2
G	33				34			11	10			11	2	10	7	7		27		1	7						55
H	35				53				24			3	1	2	47			13	4	8	5				8		24
I	1	13	111	36	23	18	22				2	43	24	174	121	13		27	54	85	18	17		1	26	11	2
J									1											5							
K	2				5							1			2				2		5						
L	81	1	2	8	89	3	1	9	76		4	42	3	2	55	2			2	24	23	2	2		4		18
M	50	7			76				50				9		45	18					20				17		85
N	51	13	39	40	88	7	66		53	1	7		1	6	37	1		2	40	91	10	7	2		5	1	162
O	10		24	25	5	10	26	3	17	1	2	69	68	213		11		111	43	41	28	7	14	7	5	1	12
P	29	13			60		54		24		2	28			49	4		28	5	12	9				7		14
Q																					13						
R	128	12	14	15	109	5	13	5	86		5	4	32	15	128	13		18	26	21	18	7	2		23		142
S	11	24	24		47	2	25	25	65		6	9	7	3	36	27	1	27		86	26		2		8		122
T	69	3			143		46	178	178		4	4	2	31	69			108	7	17	23	1	1		26		92
U	18	11	12	8	8	2		8	8			41	33	31	5	17		39	28	24	1			1			72
V	1				40				17			1			7												1
W	3				9		3		8		1	1		2	8	2			1								7
X	6	2	2		3											2				5							8
Y	3	2	6	10								16	2	12						5						3	8
Z	6		2						4					2				9	13	1						1	72

204

Table 7.15

Frequencies of Bigrams L_1L_2 within Proper Names of Bourne and Ford. The Listed Numbers Divided by 10,000 Are the Probabilities of Occurrence of Letter Pairs.

L_1	$L_2=$ A	B	C	D	E	F	G	H	I	J	K	L	M	N	O	P	Q	R	S	T	U	V	W	X	Y	Z	ƀ
A	8	15	25	17	18	5	10	11	19	8	9	107	91	216		5		248	39	30	27	30	12	2	29	2	17
B	34	3			91			99	8	1	34	6			13			28	3	2	11				4		3
C	35	5	5	2	33		2	5	14			12		5	29			10	15	5	5	1	27		7		6
D	57	5	6	10	59		9	9	21	13	2	12	9	5	40	4		20	15	4	7	1	27	2	5		49
E	42	10	14	51	40	8	12		21	16	4	119	22	132	22	21		255	90	59	8	13	24	2	40	1	89
F	5				8	12	4	13	9	1		3	1		13			35	3	1	3				3		3
G	27	1	1	2	62			13	13	3		14	2	2	14			19	5	2	6		2				7
H	121	2	3	1	64		1	2	28	6	1	8	7	44	49	1		12	4	5	21	5	3				25
I	58	3	73	28	37	5	12		9	1	4	89	10	105	7	9		19	61	33		5		1		9	8
J	49				17				2						68			27			10						2
K	20	1	1	1	42	1		2	14	5		8	3	2	6			6	7		3	6	3		1		12
L	85	11	5	45	139	9	4	4	97	8	5	126	12	2	41	7		4	18	17	6	6	4		22		35
M	105	6	16	1	58		1	2	40	4	1	2	7	2	28	7		3	7		10		2	2	2		16
N	56	13	42	65	118	8	44	11	27	30	19	19	17	65	21	9		32	43	31	2	2	14		6	3	108
O	8	43	8	16	9	6	7	44	2	2	4	48	27	146	18	7		81	28	17	30	5	26	2	12		7
P	28	1			27			31	5	1	1	3	1		5	4		7	5		1						3
Q																					3						
R	86	16	12	87	95	4	33	5	102	16	16	43	17	23	112	6		45	28	87	20	7	8		40	1	60
S	34	7	24	8	54	4	7	32	12	16	8	13	17	4	52	10		12	23	61	12	1	14		2		47
T	26	3	9	4	71	3	3	93	22	9	2	10	6	2	39	2		22	11	36	7		5		3	6	28
U	5	3	11	11	11	2	20	1	12		1	22	6	18		2		35	28	10				1	1		2
V	12				22				41						3												1
W	54			1	22	1		5	60	1		2	4	5	9			8	4	1	3				1		5
X	2																			1							1
Y	13	3	6	11	11	2	3	3	1	12	2	15	9	21	4	3		11	6	4	1	1	4				36
Z	12				4				3	1		1	1		1												

Table 7.16
Character Probabilities Computed from a Sample of 2000 Titles of the Chemical Titles Tapes.

Character	Probability	Character	Probability
A	.065	7ɓ	.146
B	.011	0	.000
C	.038	1	.001
D	.030	2	.001
E	.084	3	.001
F	.025	4	.001
G	.012	5	.001
H	.024	6	.000
I	.077	7	.000
J	.000	8	.000
K	.002	9	.000
L	.038	=	.000
M	.026	(	.002
N	.065	)	.002
O	.075	*	.000
P	.022	+	.000
Q	.001	,	.003
R	.052	−	.006
S	.050	.	.014
T	.066	/	.000
U	.023	$	.000
V	.006		
W	.003		
X	.004		
Y	.018		
Z	.003		

7.5 Vocabulary Growth

As new document items are added to a data base the vocabulary of the attributes may grow in size but, because of repetitions of terms, the rate of growth is likely to be less than that of the total text length. It might be thought that as a data base grows its fields will eventually include all possible terms and the vocabulary will then cease to increase. In practice, however, such does not usually happen and many of the vacabularies appear to grow indefinitely, although their rate of growth decreases with increase in size of the data base.

For general English text of up to at least 20,000 words it is found that as the text length increases the number D of different words is related to the total number N of words by an equation of the form

$$D = kN^\beta \qquad (7.12)$$

where k and β are constants that depend on the particular text. Hence

$$\log D = \beta \log N + \log k \qquad (7.13)$$

and so $\log D$ is a linear function of $\log N$.

The observed dependence of $\log D$ on $\log N$ is shown in Figure 7.1 for title words of the chemical titles tape, title words of the MARC tapes, and subject headings of the MARC tapes. It is clear that the dependence of $\log D$ on $\log N$ is closely approximated by a linear relation and it may easily be verified that appropriate values of k and β in (7.12) are as follows:

Chem. Titles:	$k = 35$	$\beta = .5$
MARC Titles:	$k = 15.5$	$\beta = .6$
MARC Sub. Heads:	$k = 9$	$\beta = .66$

If a retrieval program uses a dictionary to access an inverted file then as the number of document items increases the number of document numbers in the inverted file increases linearly. According to the Zipf law the

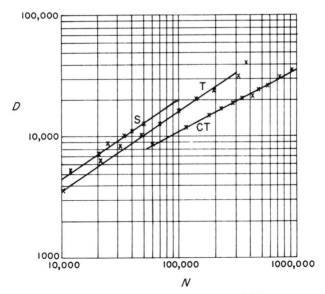

Figure 7.1. Logarithmic relation between the number D of different terms and the total number N of terms for Chemical Titles (CT), and for MARC titles (T) and subject headings (S).

length of each list of document numbers will also increase linearly, but the number of infrequent descriptors of frequencies 1, 2, etc. will increase as a linear function of D and hence more slowly than the growth of N.

All document data bases that contain fields of textual words will contain some terms created as a result of spelling mistakes or keypunch errors. It is virtually impossible to correct all such errors; the resulting infrequent terms will appear in dictionaries and will have corresponding lists, hopefully of length one, in the inverted file. Their presence is not likely to be noticed until they appear in an output document item.

There are other descriptors that occur in a single document title or abstract and might never be used by any other author. Such a term might not be regarded as a spelling error even although it might never be found in a dictionary. Examples of such terms are mathematizational, microstatistical, and booleanization. If they appear in only a single document item they must be included in the relevant dictionaries since in fact it is never certain that they will not be used in the future by other authors.

7.6 Problems

1. A KWIC index is to be created for 5000 document titles whose average length is 18 words. If words are distributed according to the Zipf law then how many stop words should be used in order to reduce the number of lines by 25%? Also, how many stop words should be used if it is desired to reduce the number of lines by 33%?

2. For a data base organized as an inverted file structure as shown in Figure 5.13 it is found that the dictionary contains 3000 different terms. It is supposed that they are distributed in the data base according to the Zipf law. Estimate the number of different questions of the form

$$\text{term}_1 \quad \text{OR} \quad \text{term}_2$$

that would each locate exactly 10 document items, where both term_1 and term_2 are stored in the dictionary.

8

Information Theory Considerations

8.1 Information Content of Textual Data

In information retrieval the output received from the computer is usually in the form of a sequence of printed, or otherwise displayed, characters. The information content of the output may be defined in terms of the extent to which it removes some of the receiver's uncertainty about the answer to some question. The information content of a message is thus dependent on the receiver's prior knowledge as well as on the message itself.

For example, suppose a person knows that the mathematical constant π is equal to 3.1415 . . . , but does not know the decimal digits in the fifth to seventh decimal places. In answer to a request for the value of π, a computer printout of

$$3.1415$$

does not provide the person with any information content, since it does not remove any of the uncertainty about the value of π. In contrast, a printout

$$3.1415927$$

removes the uncertainty about the fifth to seventh decimal digits, and hence it contains information content. If the computer printout is treated as a time sequence of successive characters then the first five characters, 3.1415, contain no information content, whereas the successive printed characters each serve to remove some uncertainty and hence contain some information content.

It may be remarked that the receiver of a message is seldom completely uncertain about the message prior to its reception. For example, in the above instance the person who knew the four-decimal representation of π to be 3.1415 would also know that the five-decimal representation is one of the 10 numbers.

| 3.14150, | 3.14151, | 3.14152, | 3.14153, | 3.14154, | 3.14155, |
| 3.14156, | 3.14157, | 3.14158, | 3.14159. | | |

Before printout of 3.14159 the person could only predict the five-decimal representation to be 1 of 10 equally probable values. However, after printout of 3.14159 the person knows the five-decimal representation to be 3.14159.

The extent of the receiver's lack of prior knowledge may be measured in terms of the probability with which he is able to predict the correct result. In the preceding instance this probability is $\frac{1}{10}$. For prediction of the seven-decimal representation the corresponding probability is $1/1000$. The information content of a printout

$$3.1415927$$

should, of course, be regarded as greater than that contained in a printout

$$3.14159.$$

Because of the similar, and independent, information contained in the printout of each of the fifth to seventh decimal digits, it appears reasonable for the receiver to regard the information content of the 3.1415927 to be three times that of the 3.14159.

The preceding discussion suggests that information content H of computer output be defined as a decreasing function $H(P)$ of the a priori probability p with which the output could be predicted by the receiver. If the person is able to predict the received output with certainty, that is with probability one, then its information content is zero. The reduction of the receiver's a priori uncertainty is greatest if the prediction is that the output will occur with probability zero. In such an instance his a priori ignorance may be regarded as infinitely large and the output provides the receiver with the greatest possible, that is infinite, information content.

It is desirable to define information content to be additive in the sense that the total information content provided by two mutually independent output messages should be the sum of the information content of the two separate messages. Thus the information content H of a received message should be defined to be a decreasing function of its a priori probability of occurrence p and it should satisfy the equations

$$H(p_1 p_2) = H(p_1) + H(p_2) \tag{8.1}$$

$$H(1) = 0. \tag{8.2}$$

It may easily be shown that the only continuous decreasing function $H(p)$ that satisfies the conditions (8.1) and (8.2) is the logarithmic function

$$H(p) = -\log p. \tag{8.3}$$

Throughout the present chapter a message with a priori probability p will be said to have information content equal to $H(p) = -\log p$ and will be said to reduce the receiver's uncertainty, or entropy, by $-\log p$. For reasons that will become apparent later it proves convenient to take logarithms to the base 2 and to regard the unit of information content and entropy as one bit. Unless otherwise indicated it will be assumed that all logarithms are taken to the base 2, and hence

$$H(p) = -\log_2 p = -3.322 \log_{10} p = -1.443 \log_e p.$$

It may be noted that a message that is a priori predictable with probability .5 contains information content of $-\log_2 .5 = 1$ bit. Thus if an output may be only one of two separate messages, each of which is predicted to occur with equal probability, then receipt of either message provides an information content of $-\log_2(\frac{1}{2}) = 1$ bit. The messages may also be coded as 0 or 1 for representation in one bit of computer memory.

Suppose that each of a number of n possible alternate messages are predictable with probability p_r respectively where r ranges from 1 to n. If the rth message occurs it provides information content of amount $-\log p_r$. The average, or expected, information content to be gained through receipt of one of the n possible messages is therefore

$$\bar{H} = -\sum_{r=1}^{n} p_r \log p_r. \tag{8.4}$$

The question arises as to what probability of message occurrence will allow the messages to convey the maximum average information content per message. The question may be answered as follows. The probabilities p_r of the n possible messages must satisfy the equation

$$\sum_{r=1}^{n} p_r = 1 \tag{8.5}$$

Hence the average information content of the messages is

$$\bar{H} = -\sum_{r=1}^{n-1} p_r \log p_r \times p_n \log p_n \tag{8.6}$$

where

$$p_n = 1 - \sum_{r=1}^{n-1} p_r. \tag{8.7}$$

If $\bar{H}$ is regarded as a function of the $n-1$ independent probabilities p_r, its stationary value occurs when the p_r are chosen to satisfy the equations $\partial \bar{H} / \partial p_r = 0$ for $r=1$ to $n-1$. Hence

$$0 = \partial \bar{H} / \partial p_r = -1.443 (\partial / \partial p_r) \sum_{r=1}^{n-1} p_r \log_e p_r + p_n \log_e p_n)$$

$$= -1.443[1 + \log_e p_r + (1 + \log_e p_n) \, \partial p_n / \partial p_r]$$

$$= -1.443[1 + \log_e p_r - (1 + \log_e p_n)] \tag{8.8}$$

and therefore

$$\log_e p_r = \log_e p_n. \tag{8.9}$$

Since this equation is to be satisfied for each r it follows that $\bar{H}$ is a maximum when the p_r are equal and hence of value $1/n$.

Thus a set of n messages will convey the maximum average information content when each message has the same a priori probability of occurrence. If follows that if the receiver known only that there are n possible messages, the person should assume them to occur with equal probability since any other assumption implies that the person has further information, or less uncertainty, about their occurrence.

Suppose a message formed from a sequence of alphabetic characters is transmitted to a receiver whose only a priori information is that the alphabet contains 26 characters. For purposes of illustration we neglect the occurrence of nonalphabetic characters, although their inclusion presents no special problem. Before each character is received its occurrence could be predicted with probability 1/26, and hence its occurrence provides an information content of $H_0 = -\log(1/26) = 4.70$ bits.

Suppose the receiver has access to a table that lists the a priori probabilities p_r of the occurrences of alphabetic characters within the received message. The average information content of each received character is then

$$H_1 = -\sum_{r=1}^{26} p_r \log p_r \tag{8.10}$$

which is necessarily less than for the assumed uniform distribution.

If the received alphabetic message is known to have letter frequencies predicted by the 26 entries in the second column of Table 7.10 the value of (7.10) may be computed to show that H_1 is equal to 4.29 bits. Thus if the receiver has access to this table the average information content of each received letter is reduced by $4.70 - 4.29 = .41$ bits. It may thus be said that the information content of the column of the table is worth .41 bits for each received character.

In the preceding discussion it was assumed that the second column of Table 7.10 forms the only available statistics regarding the occurrence of characters with the received sequence. If also bigram statistics similar to those of Table 7.14 are used then the occurrence of each letter may be predicted with greater accuracy provided the previous letter is known. Let p_r denote the probability of occurrence of the rth character according to the second column of Table 7.10 and let p_{rs} denote the probability of occurrence of a character pair as given by the rth row and sth column of Table 7.14. Following an occurrence of the rth letter expression (8.11) gives the uncertainty involved in prediction that it will be followed by the sth character

—log(Probability of sth character when given that it is preceded by the rth character)

$$= -\log(p_{rs}/p_r)$$
$$= -\log p_{rs} + \log p_r, \tag{8.11}$$

and the average entropy involved in a single prediction is therefore

$$- \sum_{r,s} p_{rs} \log p_{rs} + \sum_r p_r \log p_r. \tag{8.12}$$

If this quantity is computed it will be found to have a smaller value than the average entropy based only on the probabilities p_r since the additional bigram statistics of Table 7.14 reduce the uncertainty of each prediction.

Shannon[1] has investigated the information content of letters in English text subject to inclusion of additional information regarding the occurrences of letter strings of various lengths. If the given information includes only the p_r for single letters, then Shannon lists the average entropy of each letter as 4.14 bits. Inclusion of probabilities p_{rs} reduces the value to 3.56, and inclusion of probabilities p_{rst} for triads of letters causes a further reduction to 3.3 bits. Shannon concludes that a knowledge of the statistical behavior of long strings of text is likely to reduce the average information content to less than 1 bit per character.

The extent to which the individual letters of a word provide information content for word identification may be illustrated further as follows.

[1] C. E. Shannon, "Prediction and entropy of printed English," *Bell System Technical Journal* 30(1951): 50–65.

Suppose the first two letters of a word have been received as TA, and suppose the word is assumed to be in the Concise Oxford Dictionary, fifth edition. On the basis of this information only, the word may be any one of approximately 300 words that begin with TA and hence the entropy involved in identification of the word is approximately

$$-\log(1/300) = 8.2 \text{ bits.}$$

If the third letter is read, and found to be B, then the word is one of the following 24

```
tab,    tabard,    tabaret,    tabasheer,    tabby,    tabefaction,
taberdar,    tabernacle,    tabes,    tabetic,    tabinet,    tablature,
table,    tableau,    tablet,    tablier,    tabloid,    taboo,    tabor,
tabouret,    tabu,    tabula,    tabular,    tabulate
```

and its identification now involves entropy of amount

$$-\log(1/24) = 4.6 \text{ bits.}$$

If the fourth letter is read as L then the word may be any of the six, and the entropy involved in its identification is therefore reduced to

$$-\log(1/6) = 2.6 \text{ bits.}$$

If the fifth letter is read as E the word may be any one of three, and the entropy is reduced to

$$-\log(1/3) = 1.6.$$

Reading the sixth letter as A identifies the word completely and the remaining letter U provides no further information content.

The information contents contained in the successive letters BLEAU of the word TABLEAU while it is received as just described are therefore

$$H_B = -\log(24/300) = 3.6,$$
$$H_L = -\log(6/24) = 2.0,$$
$$H_E = -\log(3/6) = 1.0,$$
$$H_A = -\log(1/3) = 1.6,$$
$$H_U = -\log 1 = 0,$$

and the average information content of each of the above five letters is 1.64 bits.

Shannon estimated the average entropy in words of English text to be 11.82 bits per word, but further calculation by Grignetti[2] led to a value of 9.82 bits per word. It may be noted that if the words are distributed according to the Zipf law their average information content is

[2] M. C. Grignetti, "A note on the entropy of words in printed English," *Information and Control* 7(1964): 304–306.

$$\bar{H} = - \sum_{r=1}^{D} p_r \log p_r$$

$$= - \sum_{r=1}^{D} (A/r) \log (A/r). \tag{8.13}$$

The sum may be approximated by an integral to give

$$\overline{H} = (A/2) (\log_2 e) [\log_e(D + 1/2)]^2$$

$$-(A \log_2 A) \log_e(2D+1). \tag{8.14}$$

and likewise the value of A from (7.5) of Section 7.1 may be approximated by an integral to give

$$A = [\log_e(2D+1)]^{-1} \tag{8.15}$$

The for $D = 10,000$, $50,000$ and $100,000$ respectively, the value of $\bar{H}$ is 9.5, 10.9, and 11.4 bits. In contrast, if the words were distributed with equal probability the average entropy of each word would be $-\log(1/D)$, which for $D = 10,000$, $50,000$, and $100,000$ is equal to 13.3, 15.6 and 16.6 bits, respectively. The reduction in information content caused by words being distributed according to the Zipf law rather than uniformly is therefore of average value 4 to 5 bits.

It may be remarked that for a data base for which $D = 50,000$, and in which the average term length is 5.6 characters as for the chemical titles or MARC data bases described in Table 7.9, the average information content of each stored character is 10.9/5.6, which is less than two bits. Since characters are usually stored in six or eight bits of computer memory it is clear that the natural representation of words in terms of alphabetic characters is very inefficient with respect to utilization of computer storage. More efficient means of representing words in computer memory will be discussed in Chapter 9.

The preceding discussion of information content has been concerned with information regarding the form of printed output and has not taken into account the significance or meaning of the output. Suppose, however, that whenever a certain word of probability p_r occurs it may have two possible meanings that are predictable with probabilities p_{r1} and p_{r2} respectively. Prediction of the meaning of the next word to be read then involves an average entropy of amount.

$$
\begin{aligned}
\bar{H} &= - \sum_r [p_r p_{r1} \log(p_r p_{r1}) + p_r p_{r2} \log(p_r p_{r2})] \\
&= - \sum_r [p_r (p_{r1} + p_{r2}) \log p_r - p_r (p_{r1} \log p_{r1} + p_{r2} \log p_{r2})] \\
&= - \sum_r p_r \log p_r - \sum_r p_r (p_{r1} \log p_{r1} + p_{r2} \log p_{r2}) \\
&= \bar{H}_{\text{ID}} + \sum_r p_r H_r, \tag{8.16}
\end{aligned}
$$

where $\bar{H}_{\text{ID}}$ is the average entropy involved in identification of a word, and H_r is the entropy involved in prediction of the meaning of the rth word after it has been identified. The term $\sum p_r H_r$ may be regarded as that portion of $\bar{H}$ that may be reduced by considerations based on human experience, intuition, or knowledge of the subject matter as a whole, whereas $\bar{H}_{\text{ID}}$ is the entropy that may be reduced by purely mechanistic means of word identification without regard to the context. Information retrieval by computers is usually concerned with providing the information content $\bar{H}_{\text{ID}}$, whereas the portion $\sum p_r H_r$ is added by the human receiver on the basis of experience or by examination of further data, such as an entire printed article rather than only the portion in the computer accessible file.

A comprehensive list of word frequencies in a sample of text formed from many sources, and totalling 5 million words, has been compiled by M. West.[3] This listing also includes the frequencies of occurrence of the different usages of each word. For example the word ARRANGE is found to occur with a frequency of 280 in 5 million, and is listed in the form

```
ARRANGE 280(1)   (set in order)   43%
        (2)   (plan)            28%
        (3)   (agree)           17%
```

Consider the following pair of book titles

```
Title 1:  THE GATHERING STORM
Title 2:  PRACTICAL ELECTRICITY.
```

According to West the transitive use of GATHER occurs with probability .33 and the intransitive use occurs with probability .33; other unspecified uses therefore occur with probability .34. Three uses of STORM occur with probabilities .60, .21, and .19. The uncertainty involved in prediction of the meaning of Title 1 is thus

$$-.33 \log .33 - .33 \log .33 - .34 \log .34$$
$$-.60 \log .60 - .21 \log .21 - .19 \log .19$$
$$= .89.$$

Similarly, the uncertainty involved in prediction of the meaning of Title 2 is

$$-.61 \log .61 - .25 \log .25 - .08 \log .08$$
$$-.06 \log .06 - 1.0 \log 1.0$$
$$= .44.$$

---

[3] M. West, *A General Service List of English Words* (New York: Longmans, Green, and Co., Inc., 1953).

The preceding remarks serve to emphasize that the result of a computer search of a data base is to provide a list of documents whose relevance to the user is predicted to be higher than that of other documents in the data base. However, there is still some uncertainty about the relevance of the retrieved documents, and it may be removed only by examination of the documents by the user.

The discussion in the present section has been concerned with the concept of information content as it relates to identification of textual data. More general formulation of information theory is readily available in the literature.[4,5,6]

8.2 Information Content of Message Constraints

Suppose it is known that a message will specify nine integers each of which may have a value between 0 and 15. Since each number may be specified in 4 bits the total information content of the message will be 36 bits.

Suppose it is known, however, that all numbers will be different. The first number may thus take any of 16 values, the second may take any of 15 values, and so forth. The number of different possible messages is therefore $16 \times 15 \times 14 \times \cdots \times 8 = 4{,}151{,}347{,}200$ and the information content of the received message is $\log_2(4{,}151{,}347{,}200) = 31.9$ bits. Hence each of the possible forms of transmitted message may be coded to occupy 32 bits. On the other hand if the message is transmitted in the form of nine numbers each of 4 bits, then each number transmits an average of only $32/9 = 3.56$ bits of information despite the fact that it uses four bits of storage.

Alternatively, if it is known in advance that the message will specify the nine numbers in ascending order, then the number of different possible messages is reduced by a factor of $9 \times 8 \times 7 \times \cdots \times 1 = 362{,}880$. The number of different possible messages is $4{,}151{,}347{,}200/362{,}880 = 11{,}440$, the information content of the received message is $\log_2(11{,}440) = 13.5$ bits, and hence 1.5 bits per transmitted number.

If a further constraint on the message is that the nine transmitted numbers shall be in ascending order and that each differ only by unity from its predecessor, then only eight different messages (such as

[4] N. Abramson, *Information Theory and Coding* (New York: McGraw-Hill, 1963).

[5] A. I. Khinchin, *Mathematical Foundations of Information Theory* (New York: Dover, 1957).

[6] A. N. Kolmogorov, "Three approaches to the quantitative definition of information," *International Journal of Computer Mathematics* 2(1968): 157–168.

3,4,5,6,7,8,9,10,11) may be transmitted and the information content of each message is $\log_2(8) = 3$ bits. In fact it is only necessary to transmit the first number of each message since the remaining eight are then known.

The preceding discussion illustrates that any a priori information about the message, or any constraints placed on the form of the message, has the effect of reducing the information content of the message and hence of allowing the message to be coded so as to occupy fewer bits. Any statistical information about the occurrence of characters or words within a textual message also reduces the information content of the possible messages. This is further illustrated by the following discussion of the information content of frequency tables.

If an alphabet has n characters and no information is available regarding the probabilities of the occurrences of letters in text, then all that may be assumed is that each letter of text is any one of n. The uncertainty, or entropy, involved in prediction of any character of the text is therefore

$$H'_1 = \log n \qquad (8.17)$$

and so each character within a message conveys an information content of $\log n$.

Now suppose that the probabilities of occurrence of each of the n characters x_i are known to have values p_i where $i = 1$ to n. The information content of each character is now

$$H_1 = -\sum p_i \log p_i, \qquad (8.18)$$

and so the additional information acquired by a knowledge of the probabilities p_i is equal to

$$H'_1 - H_1 = \log n + \sum_i p_i \log p_i \qquad (8.19)$$

for each received character.

In the absence of further knowledge of second-order probabilities p_{ij} regarding the probabilities of occurrence of pairs of characters $x_i x_j$, one can assume only the maximum unpredictability consistent with the known values of the first-order probabilities p_i. Such maximum unpredictability results when it is supposed that each pair of characters $x_i x_j$ occurs with probability $p_i p_j$. The average information content of each bigram $x_i x_j$ is then

$$H'_2 = -\sum_i \sum_j p_i p_j \log(p_i p_j) \qquad (8.20)$$

with summation over all pairs i, j. However, if the second-order probabilities p_{ij} are known then the average information content is

$$H_2 = -\sum \sum p_{ij} \log p_{ij}, \qquad (8.21)$$

and hence the additional average information content acquired by knowledge of all the p_{ij} is

$$
\begin{aligned}
H_2' - H_2 &= \sum_i \sum_j p_{ij} \log p_{ij} - \sum_i \sum_j p_i p_j \log(p_i p_j) \\
&= \sum_i \sum_j p_{ij} \log p_{ij} - (\sum_j p_j) \sum_i p_i \log p_i - (\sum_i p_i) \sum_j p_j \log p_j \\
&= \sum_i \sum_j p_{ij} \log p_{ij} - \sum_i p_i \log p_i - \sum_j p_j \log p_j \qquad (8.22) \\
&= 2H_1 - H_2. \qquad (8.23)
\end{aligned}
$$

Also, since $\sum_j p_{ij} = p_i$ and $\sum_i p_{ij} = p_j$, equation (8.22) may be rewritten in the form

$$
\begin{aligned}
H_2' - H_2 &= \sum_i \sum_j p_{ij} \log p_{ij} - \sum_i \sum_j p_{ij} \log p_i - \sum_i \sum_j p_{ij} \log p_j \\
&= \sum_i \sum_j p_{ij} \log(p_{ij}/p_i p_j). \qquad (8.24)
\end{aligned}
$$

The quantity $H_2' - H_2$ given by (8.23) or (8.24) describes the information content per received character provided by a knowledge of the probabilities p_{ij} of occurrences of bigrams of character $x_i x_j$. It has also been termed the *logarithmic correlation index*. Further discussion of its significance is given by Linfoot.[7]

If the first-order probabilities p_i had not been given, the information content contained in the p_{ij} would be

$$
\sum p_{ij} \log(p_{ij}) + \log(n^2). \qquad (8.25)
$$

The difference between this value and $H_2' - H_2$ is $2(H_1' - H_1)$, which is consistent with the fact that use of the p_i to predict $x_i x_j$ involves the assumption of information $H_1' - H_1$ for prediction of the first letter x_i together with information $H_1' - H_1$ for prediction of the second letter x_j.

If the second-order probabilities are known, but the third-order probabilities are not, then the maximum unpredictability of triplets of letters $x_i x_j x_k$ consistent with the given values of p_{ij} results when the probability of $x_i x_j x_k$ is assumed to be

$$
p(x_i x_j x_k) = p_{ij} \text{ (Probability of } x_j x_k \text{ for given } x_j)
$$

$$
= p_{ij} p_{jk}/p_j. \qquad (8.26)
$$

The additional information provided by a table of values of p_{ijk} of 3-grams is therefore

$$
\begin{aligned}
H_3' - H_3 &= \sum p_{ijk} \log p_{ijk} - \sum \frac{p_{ij} p_{jk}}{p_j} \log\left(\frac{p_{ij} p_{jk}}{p_j}\right) \\
&= \sum p_{ijk} \log p_{ijk} - \sum p_{ij} \log p_{ij} - \sum p_{jk} \log p_{jk} \\
&\quad + \sum p_j \log p_j \\
&= 2H_2 - H_3 - H_1, \qquad (8.27)
\end{aligned}
$$

[7] E. H. Linfoot, "An informational measure of correlation. Information and Control, 1(1957): 85–89.

which may also be expressed in the form

$$H_3' - H_3 = \sum_i \sum_j \sum_k p_{ijk} \log\left(\frac{p_{ijk}p_j}{p_{ij}p_{jk}}\right). \tag{8.28}$$

The quantities $H_2' - H_2$ of (8.23) and $H_3' - H_3$ of (8.27) apply to second- and third-order probabilities respectively. For nth-order probabilities of occurrences of n-grams for which $n \geqslant 3$ a similar analysis leads to the result

$$H_n' - H_n = 2H_{n-1} - H_n - H_{n-2} \tag{8.29}$$

It thus follows from (8.23) and (8.29) that

$$H_2 - H_1 = H_1 - (H_2' - H_2) \tag{8.30}$$

$$H_n - H_{n-1} = H_{n-1} - H_{n-2} - (H_n' - H_n) \qquad \text{for } n \geqslant 3 \tag{8.31}$$

and, since the terms in parentheses represent nonnegative amounts of information content, then

$$H_2 - H_1 \geqslant H_1 \tag{8.32}$$

$$H_n - H_{n-1} \geqslant H_{n-1} - H_{n-2} \qquad \text{for } n \geqslant 3. \tag{8.33}$$

A consequence of the relations (8.32) and (8.33) is that if the table of nth-order probabilities provides an additional information content of amount $\Delta H_n = H_n - H_{n-1}$ for each received character, then no table of higher order probabilities may provide more than ΔH_n of additional information content for each received character. Thus although the amount of computation required to compute n-gram frequencies increases with n, the additional information content gained through the computations tends to decrease with successive increases in n. If it is found that for some n a knowledge of n-gram probabilities provides no information content then no further information content may be gained by computation of higher order probabilities.

Relations (8.32) and (8.33) were derived by use of equations similar to (8.20) for H_2', H_3', etc. The validity of (8.30) is subject to the assumption that the probabilities of occurrence of the characters x_i in a single position of the text may also be used to predict the occurrences of the single character x_j in any other position within the text. Such an assumption is not correct if x_i and x_j are known to be respectively the first and second letters of a word since Table 7.10 for example, shows that the probabilities p_i and p_j are different. However, if x_i is not specified with regard to position in a word, then the second column of Table 7.10 may be used correctly to predict either of the single letters x_i and x_j.

When the statistics used for prediction of the occurrence of characters or strings of characters are independent of the position in the text at which the character or string occurs the statistics are said to be stationary. Statistics that depend on position of the items predicted are said to be nonstationary. Thus Tables 7.14 and 7.15 present stationary statistics. When applied to letters in text without specification of letter position within words, only the second columns of Tables 7.12 and 7.13 represent stationary statistics.

The bounds on successive information contents described by (8.32) and (8.33) arise from the condition that the p_1 and higher order probabilities are stationary. If in fact there is a value of n for which (8.33) is satisfied in the form

$$H_n - H_{n-1} = H_{n-1} - H_{n-2}, \tag{8.34}$$

then the occurrences of $n+1$ successive characters of text depend only on any restrictions concerning the occurrence of sequences of smaller length. In such an instance the set of $(n+1)$th-order probabilities is said to be a free extension of the set of nth-order probabilities.[8] If equality (8.34) is not satisfied, the quantity

$$\Delta H_{n-1} - \Delta H_n = H'_n - H_n \tag{8.35}$$

represents a measure of the extent to which the character structure of the n-grams is not a consequence of the character structure of the n-grams of smaller length.

8.3 Information Gain of a Retrieval System

In the previous sections the concept of information content was introduced as a measure of the amount of information required for identification of characters or words represented within a received message. Apart from the brief discussion that led to the derivation of (8.16), no mention was made of the semantic meaning or semantic information conveyed by the words of the text. The use of the term information content was consistent with its use in statistical communication theory, which is concerned with the correct transmission of information rather than with its interpretation or its value to a human receiver.

Some semanticists and psychologists have strongly criticized the adoption of the communication theory of information for application to information retrieval. Their criticism is that identification, or retrieval, of a string of textual characters is quite different from retrieval of worthwhile facts in response to a given request.

[8] J. Hartmanis, "The application of some basic inequalities for entropy," *Information and Control* 2(1959): 199–213.

This criticism may be answered, in part, by stating that most document retrieval systems do not provide information in the form of details about a particular discipline but, instead, provide information that indicates which documents should be consulted by a user who wishes to obtain further information about some branch of a discipline. Thus if the data base represents N documents that are numbered in sequence, the function of a search program is equivalent to providing a sequence of N values of a quantity $r(n)$ whose value is equal to 1, or 0, according as the nth document is, or is not, predicted as relevant to the user's interest. For example, in response to a given request the output might have the form

$$000101100 \ldots \tag{8.36}$$

to indicate that only the fourth, sixth, and seventh documents are predicted to be relevant. The prediction may or may not be wholly correct, as it depends on whether the search query correctly represents the user's interests and whether the data stored in the computer-accessible files forms a valid representation of the contents of each document.

The form of output of an information retrieval program is seldom in the form (8.36). More usually each printout of $r(n) = 1$ is replaced by a print of some details of the nth document such as its title and so forth. This provides the receiver with further information, which the person may use, correctly or incorrectly, to modify the computer prediction of relevance.

If the output (8.36) is wholly correct the information transferred to the user may be computed as follows. Suppose that prior to formulation of the search question the user estimates that a proportion p of the documents in the data base will be found to be relevant to the user's interest. An estimate of p might be based on past experience, such as finding that certain journals contain articles of which a proportion p are relevant. In the absence of any knowledge regarding the proportion of relevant items it would be consistent to assume that each item is equally likely to be relevant or nonrelevant and hence that $p = \frac{1}{2}$. Each relevant item output from the computer search provides the receiver with information content of $-\log_2 p$ bits, whereas each omission of any printed output provides an information content of $-\log_2(1-p)$ bits. If the output (8.36) contains rN values of 1, and hence $(1-r)N$ values of 0, the information content supplied by the search is thus

$$-rN \log p - 1-r)N \log(1-p). \tag{8.37}$$

It may be remarked that for a fixed value of r the quantity (8.37) is least when $p = r;$ this is consistent with the fact that the user had correctly estimated the proportion of relevant documents. With such a correct estimate the search provides information content equal to

$$-rN \log r - (1-r)N \log(1-r). \tag{8.38}$$

The value of (8.38) is thus the information content of the list of relevant documents, and the difference between the values of (8.37) and (8.38) is the amount of information content involved in correcting a user's false estimate of the expected number of relevant documents.

To analyze the information content transmitted to the user when the output (8.36) is not wholly correct, consider the instance in which the user wishes to determine the R most relevant items from a data base of N document items. Suppose the computer search produces a list of n_1 documents, which the user examines and decides that n_{11} are sufficiently relevant and that the remaining n_{10} ($= n_1 - n_{11}$) are not relevant. The result of the computer search, followed by the user examination of output items, is to supply the user with information content about each document item as follows:

(i) For an output item that the user classifies as relevant, the person has received information content of amount $\log(R/N)$. There are n_{11} such items.

(ii) For an output item that the user classes as nonrelevant the person has received information content of amount $\log(1 - R/N)$. There are n_{10} such items.

(iii) Of the $N - n_{11} - n_{10}$ items that have not been output, there are $R - n_{11}$ relevant items and $N - R - n_{10}$ nonrelevant items. Each such relevant item may be predicted with a probability of $(R - n_{11})/(N - n_{11} - n_{10})$. Similarly, each such nonrelevant item may be predicted with a probability of $(N - R - n_{10})/(N - n_{11} - n_{10})$. However, before the computer search these relevant and nonrelevant items could only be predicted with probabilities R/N and $1 - R/N$, respectively.

The total information content received by the user is thus

$$I = -n_{11} \log(R/N) - n_{10} \log(1 - R/N)$$

$$-(R - n_{11}) \left[\log\left(\frac{R}{N}\right) - \log\left(\frac{R - n_{11}}{N - n_{11} - n_{10}}\right) \right]$$

$$-(N - R - n_{10}) \left[\log\left(1 - \frac{R}{N}\right) - \log\left(\frac{N - R - n_{10}}{N - n_{11} - n_{10}}\right) \right]$$

$$= -n_{11} \log(R/N) - n_{10} \log(1 - R/N) - (R - n_{11}) \log\left[\frac{R(N - n_{11} - n_{10})}{N(R - n_{11})}\right]$$

$$- (N - R - n_{10}) \log\left[\frac{(1 - R/N)(N - n_{11} - n_{10})}{N - R - n_{10}}\right].$$

$$(8.39)$$

Table 8.1
Information Content Gained by a User After Examination of the Output of a Search for the
20 Most Relevant Documents in Data Bases of 10,000 and 100,000 Documents.

		I (bits)	
n_{11}	n_{10}	$N = 10,000$	$N = 100,000$
0	0	0	0
0	10	.029	.0029
0	20	.058	.0058
5	—	46	62
10	—	94	127
15	—	146	196
20	—	208	275

Some values of the expression (8.39) are listed in Table 8.1 for data
bases of 10,000 and 100,000 document items in which the user wishes to
search for the 20 most relevant. Values of n_{10} over a range from zero to
several hundreds have negligible effect on the value of I.

The expression (8.39) describes the information content gained by the
user after the person has classed the output items, and is subject to the
assumption that the user is prepared to classify an item as among the 20
most relevant without examining the entire data base. An alternative
analysis, based on the assumption that the user is prepared to examine the
entire data base, may proceed in a manner as described by Meetham.[9] The
use of information content to formulate a measure of retrieval efficiency,
and its relation to the alternative approach based on precision and recall,
has been described by Cawkell.[10]

8.4 Huffman Codes for Compact Information Storage

Suppose that some stored data, or a printed output, may be regarded as
a sequence formed from D different items $x_1, x_2, \ldots, x_D$ combined in
suitable order, possibly with repetitions, to form a sequence of N items.
Suppose the frequency f_i of occurrence of each x_i is known.

Before the output is received, or the stored data examined, the occur-

[9] A. R. Meetham, "Communication theory and the evaluation of information retrieval
systems," *Information Storage and Retrieval* 5(1969): 129–134.

[10] A. E. Cawkell, "A measure of "efficiency factor"—communication theory applied to
document selection systems," *Information Processing and Management* 11(1975): 243–248.

rence of each x_I may be predicted with probability $p_i = f_i/N$. The average information content of each item is then

$$-\sum_{i=1}^{D} p_i \log p_i, \tag{8.41}$$

and this also represents the average number of bits that could be occupied by each x_i within the sequence.

Suppose, for example, that there are eight items $x_1, x_2, \ldots, x_8$ that occur with respective probabilities .338, .203, .135, .088, .081, .061, .054, and .040. The different values of x_i could all be represented by a binary code of 3 bits, but the value of (8.41) is 2.65 bits, which represents the average information content conveyed by each x_i. The question arises as to whether x_i may be represented in binary code so as to require an average of 2.65 bits of storage.

It has been shown by Huffman[11] that a certain code, known as the *Huffman code*, provides the most compact representation of the x_i, and in many instances leads to an average code length only slightly in excess of the value (8.41). The method of selection of Huffman codes may be illustrated as described here for eight items x_i with probabilities as shown previously.

The second column of List 1 in Table 8.2 contains the given probabilities in descending order of magnitude. The last two numbers may be removed from the list and their sum .094 placed in the list, which is rearranged if necessary to place the numbers in descending order. The resulting list is shown in the third column of the Table. The last two values in this list are similarly combined to create a further list as shown in the

Table 8.2
Successive Lists for Determination of the Huffman Codes for $x_1, x_2, \ldots, x_8$.

	List 1	List 2	List 3	List 4	List 5	List 6	List 7
x_1	.338	.338	.338	.338	.338	.385	.615
x_2	.203	.203	.203	.203	.277	.338	.385
x_3	.135	.135	.142	.182	.203	.277	
x_4	.088	.094	.135	.142	.182		
x_5	.081	.088	.094	.135			
x_6	.061	.081	.088				
x_5	.054	.061					
x_8	.040						

[11] D. A. Huffman, "A method for the construction of minimum redundancy codes," *Proceedings of the Institute of Radio Engineers* 40(1952): 1098–1101.

fourth column of Table 8.2. The process is continued until there results only one pair of numbers as in List 7.

The pointers of Table 8.2 are shown in reverse form in Table 8.3. The binary codes in Table 8.3 are chosen as follows. A 0 and 1 are placed in the right-hand list. List 6 is created by transferring the 0 from List 7 as shown by the arrows and following it by a 0 or 1 to form the last two codes in List 6. The remaining element of List 7 is transferred to the top of List 6.

An element of List 6 is transferred to the last two positions in List 5 where it is followed by a 0 or 1. The remaining elements of list 6 are placed in the same order at the top of List 5.

An element of List 5 is transferred to the last two positions of List 4 where it is followed by a 0 or 1. The remaining elements of List 5 are placed in the same order at the top of List 4. The process is continued to create List 1, which contains the Huffman codes for $x_1, x_2, \ldots, x_8$.

If the N occurrences of the x_i are replaced by the Huffman codes of List 1 the average code length is

$$.338(2) + .203(2) + .135(3) + \ldots + .040(4) = 2.70 \text{ bits},$$

which exceeds the average information content of 2.65 but is less than the 3 bits required if the constant length binary code is used.

It may be noted that the Huffman codes are separable in the sense that any sequence of such codes is uniquely decodable since no code forms the left-hand portion of any other code. For example, the sequence

$$011111111011000011011100$$

of Huffman codes is uniquely decodable as representing

$$x_3 x_4 x_4 x_3 x_1 x_1 x_8 x_7.$$

Although the Huffman codes are useful in providing a realization of the

Table 8.3
Lists of Binary Codes Used to Derive the Huffman Codes of List 1.

	List 1	List 2	List 3	List 4	List 5	List 6	List 7
x_1	00	00	00	00	00	1	0
x_2	10	10	10	10	01	00←	1
x_3	011	011	010	11	10←	01←	
x_4	111	110	011	010←	11←		
x_5	0100	111	110←	011←			
x_6	0101	0100←	111←				
x_7	1100←	0101←					
x_8	1101←						

most compact binary codes, they have few practical applications to information retrieval because they require relatively complicated procedures for the operations of coding and decoding. Also, they are of variable length. However, the fact that there exists a method of coding that produces codes whose average length closely approximates their average information content clearly offers an encouragement to seek other more convenient codes whose average length does not greatly exceed their average information content. The Huffman codes thus provide a standard by which to judge the effectiveness and convenience of other schemes of binary coding such as those to be discussed in Chapter 9.

8.5 Problems

1. By reference to the K and F (D = 50,406) column of Table 7.9, determine the average amount of information content that is conveyed by specification of the length of a word in general English text.
2. Determine the Huffman codes for representation of the 16 most frequent characters of text under the assumption that their probabilities are as listed in the second column of Table 7.10. Find the average code length, and describe an efficient method of decoding.
3. Textual data may be stored in the form of words separated by either

   (*i*)   a special delimiting tag, or
   (*ii*) a directory number that specifies the number of characters in the word that follows.

   In case (*i*) all characters, and the delimiting tag, may be represented by Huffman codes. In case (*ii*) the directory numbers may be represented by one set of Huffman codes, and the textual words by another set of Huffman codes. Determine whether method (*i*) or (*ii*) allows the more compact storage. Also determine which method is the more convenient for purposes of decoding.

9
Coding and Compression of Data Bases

9.1 Restricted Variable Length Term Codes

In Section 5.6 the files associated with an inverted file structure were described, and it was indicated how space could be saved if terms in the sequential file are replaced by the corresponding addresses of their locations in a dictionary. A greater saving in space would result if terms in the sequential file were replaced by their Huffman codes determined as described in Section 8.4.

However, since Huffman codes are of variable lengths, in order to decode any record in the sequential file it would be necessary to examine the record bit by bit, a procedure that would be very time consuming. It is therefore desirable to consider alternative coding schemes with a view to achieving a data compression ratio close to that of the Huffman codes while allowing more rapid decoding of the stored data. A purely fixed length code would be more convenient to decode, but would have the disadvantage of requiring as much space for storage of frequent terms as for infrequent ones.

A scheme designed to combine some of the advantages of the Huffman codes with some of the advantages of a fixed length code has been described by Thiel and Heaps.[1,2] It constitutes a restricted variable length code, and may be described as follows.

Suppose the most frequent 2^7 (= 128) terms in the dictionary are assigned different codes, each of 8 bits, of which the first bit is always set equal to 1. The next most frequent 2^{14} (= 16,384) terms in the dictionary are assigned different codes of length 16 bits in which the first bit is always 0 and the ninth bit is always 1. The remaining dictionary terms are assigned 24 bit codes in which the first and ninth bits are always 0 and the seventeenth bit is always 1; there may therefore be up to 2,097,152 such dictionary terms.

All terms in the sequential data base may be replaced by their codes assigned as just shown. If the frequencies with which terms occur in the sequential data base are according to the Zipf law, and if the dictionary contains D different terms, then the average number of bits required for storage of each coded term in the sequential data base is given by the expression

$$y = 8 \sum_{r=1}^{128} (A/r) + 16 \sum_{r=129}^{16,512} (A/r) + 24 \sum_{r=16,513}^{D} (A/r). \qquad (9.1)$$

The value of A is given by Eq. (7.6) of Section 7-1, and since any sum of the form

$$\sum_{r=1}^{R} (1/r)$$

may be approximated by $\log_e R + \gamma$ where γ is Euler's constant, then y may be expressed in the form

$$y = \frac{8(\log_e 28 + \gamma) + 16(\log_e 16,512 - \log_e 128) + 24(\log_e D - \log_e 16,512)}{\log_e D + \gamma}$$

$$= \frac{24 \log_e D - 112}{\log_e D + .5772}. \qquad (9.2)$$

For values of D in the range from 20,000 to 50,000 the value of y lies between 12 and 13 bits. In contrast, adoption of the Huffman code would lead to an average code length close to the average information content given by $\overline{H}$ of Eq. (8.14) of Section 8.1 and in the range of 10 to 11 bits. Thus the restricted variable length codes just described allow the sequen-

---

[1] H. S. Heaps and L. H. Thiel, "Optimum procedures for economic information retrieval," *Information Storage and Retrieval* 6(1970): 137–153.

[2] L. H. Thiel and H. S. Heaps, "Program design for retrospective searches on large data bases," *Information Storage and Retrieval* 8(1972): 1–20.

Table 9.1
Average Code Length of Restricted Variable Length Codes in the Sequential Data Base.

	$D/1000$					
$n_1, n_2, n_3, ...$	15	25	50	100	150	1,000
3,6,12,18,...	11.1	11.5	12.4	13.1	13.4	14.8
3,6,9,12,...	10.9	11.4	12.1	12.8	13.2	15.3
4,8,12,16,...	10.7	11.1	11.7	12.4	12.8	14.6
5,10,15,20,...	10.8	11.3	11.8	12.3	12.8	14.4
6,12,18,24,...	11.1	11.4	11.8	12.7	13.1	14.5
8,16,24,32,...	11.7	11.9	12.9	13.5	13.9	15.2
4,8,16,24,...	11.0	12.1	12.8	13.4	13.8	15.1
$\bar{H}$	9.8	10.3	10.9	11.4	11.8	13.4

tial file to be compressed to within 20% of the size to which it could be reduced by use of the Huffman codes. If the average length of uncoded terms in the sequential data base is 5.6 8-bit characters together with a delimiting 8-bit blank then the compression ratios that result from use of the restricted variable length codes and the Huffman codes are respectively .24 and .20.

Adoption of codes of lengths 8, 16, and 24 bits is particularly convenient for use with a computer that is oriented toward storage of 8 bit characters. For a computer with a 6 bit representation of characters it is more convenient to use codes of length 6, 12, 18, and 24 bits. More generally, codes of length $n_1, n_2, n_3, ...$ bits may be used; then all codes of length n_1 have the first bit set to 1, all codes of length n_2 have the first bit set to 0 and the $(n_1 + 1)$th bit set to 1, etc. For a number of such codes the average length has been computed and is shown in Table 9.1 for values of D between 15,000 and 1 million.[3] The corresponding values of $\bar{H}$ are also given. It may be observed that the different choices of discrete code lengths lead to very similar average code lengths, and so the choice of code may be made for convenience of programming and speed of the required computations with the particular computer used.

An advantage of the use of the restricted variable length codes instead of Huffman codes is that they may be used to address storage positions in the term dictionary. Thus the last 7 bits of the 8-bit codes may be chosen as the dictionary locations of the most frequent 128 terms. Likewise, the the 16-bit codes the bits 2 to 8 and 10 to 16 may be chosen as the dictionary locations of the $2^{14} = 16,384$ next most frequent terms, and so

[3] H. S. Heaps, "Storage analysis of a compression coding for document data bases," *INFOR* 10(1972): 47–61.

forth. In contrast, use of Huffman codes as dictionary addresses is not convenient since they do not range through all possible values.

In order to make the dictionary conveniently searchable for the presence of question terms it may be sorted so that its first 128, next 16,384, and similar subsequent sets of terms, are in alphabetic order. Creation of the dictionary, inverted file, directory, and sequential file may proceed in a similar manner to that described in Section 5.6 except that File 2 of Figure 5.16 is scanned to determine the most frequent 128 terms, which are placed in one dictionary DICT1; the next most frequent 16,384 terms, which are placed in a second dictionary DICT2; the remaining terms being placed in a third dictionary DICT3. The appropriate dictionary addresses may be added to the records of File 2 to replace the numbers CODE in Figure 5.15.

With the dictionary segmented as just described, each question term must first be searched for in DICT1, if not present it must then be searched for in DICT2, and if still not found it must be searched for in DICT3. Thus efficient compression of the sequential file is gained at the expense of additional time required for search of the dictionary for the presence of question terms. Since it is likely that DICT1 may be stored in computer memory, and since only very infrequent terms are stored in DICT3, the additional time required because of dictionary segmentation is not a serious disadvantage of the coding scheme.

The terms stored in the dictionary are of various lengths, and if each dictionary location is allotted sufficient space to store the longest terms then considerable wastage of storage space will result. It is therefore desirable to further segment each dictionary so that it contains terms of length 1 arranged in alphabetic order, then terms of length 2 arranged in alphabetic order, and so forth. Such additional segmentation also allows a reduction in the time required to search the dictionary for any untruncated question term. The dictionary storage, and the codes for representation of terms in the sequential file, may then be allotted as follows.

Each dictionary may be partitioned into variable length term strings, each of which is used to store terms of a given length. Each term string may store up to m terms and the associated pointers to the inverted file, where m is a fixed number that is a power of 2 and is the same for all term strings. For example, m might be chosen equal to 16. A sufficient number of term strings are allotted for storage of the terms of length 1 arranged in alphabetic order, then a sufficient number of storage of the terms of length 2 arranged in alphabetic order, and so forth.

If the number of terms of a given length in DICT1 is not a multiple of m, then either further terms of the same length are stored in DICT1 so that the term string is filled or else some of the least frequent terms are removed for storage in DICT2. Similarly, some terms may be moved from

DICT2 and DICT3 to ensure that all term strings of DICT2 are filled. For example, for the data base of Table 7.8 the 128 listed terms could be stored in DICT1 in 8-term strings each of length 16 terms, or in 16-term strings each of length 8 terms, or in 32-term strings each of length 4 terms.

A term of DICT1 that is stored as the m_2th term in the m_1th term string is assigned the code

$$1, m_1, m_2$$

where m_1 is expressed in 7-m bits and m_2 is expressed in m bits for suitable choice of m. Similarly, if a term of DICT2 is stored as the m_2th term in the m_1th term string it is assigned a code of form

$$0xxxxxxx1xxxxxxx$$

where the 14 bits xxxxxxxxxxxxxx represent the pair of numbers m_1, m_2. The terms of DICT3 are coded in a similar manner.

With each dictionary partitioned into variable length regions as just described, it is necessary to create an index table that lists the dictionary locations of the beginning of the storage areas for the terms of each length. This table is used to determine the region to be searched for a given question term, and is also used in the decoding operation to indicate the length of the stored term.

The preceding storage scheme allows the sequential file to be stored in a manner that is close to the most compact that would be achievable by use of Huffman codes, and also allows the dictionary to be stored without inclusion of any delimiting characters between terms. The index table requires little storage space. Of course, any alphabetically ordered dictionary does not allow fast search for question terms that are specified with left truncation.

Use of restricted variable length codes with a dictionary arranged for access by a virtual hash storage scheme has been described by Dimsdale and Heaps.[4] Application was outlined for a library catalogue of 1 million volumes. Different arrangements of storage on disk and core were considered so that a trade-off could be made between fast-access and minimum-core storage requirements.

9.2 Hash Storage Based on Partial Keys

Instead of the codes being chosen to correspond to the addresses at which terms are stored in an alphabetically ordered dictionary as de-

---

[4] J. J. Dimsdale and H. S. Heaps, "File structure for an on-line catalog of one million titles," *Journal of Library Automation* 6(1973): 37–55.

scribed in the previous section, they may be chosen as addresses determined by means of a hashing function as described in Section 5.7. Such a choice has the advantage that, not only does the code in the sequential file point directly to the location of the term in the dictionary, but the question term itself may be operated on by the hashing function in order to locate its position, if present, in the dictionary and hence to determine the corresponding pointer to the list in the inverted file.

However, a serious disadvantage of hash storage is that the hash address of a truncated question term bears no relation to the hash address at which the untruncated term is stored. In order to allow specification of truncated question terms a form of two-dimensional hash storage may be used as described here.

Let h_1 and h_2 be two hashing functions each of whose values range over all the integers from 1 to 16 and 1 to 8 respectively. Let the value of h_1 depend only on the first n characters of the term, and let the value of h_2 depend only on the last n characters of the term. The value of n is chosen according to the total number of characters in the term, and is as follows

Term Length	n
1 character	1
2 characters	1
3 characters	2
4 characters	3
≥5 characters	4

Thus for the word COMPUTATION the letters COMP and TION are used to determine h_1 and h_2, respectively. For the word COLUMN the letters COLU and LUMN are used.

Let the dictionary DICT1 consist of 16 variable length term strings as shown in Figure 9.1 in which each term string is preceded by a number that indicates the length of the stored terms. The memory location of the beginning of each term string is stored in an index table. There is also a two-dimensional hash address table HASH1 of 128 elements each of which contains a collision bit c preceded by a four-bit pointer to a position in the index table.

The most frequent term, TERM$_1$, of the data base is stored as the h_2th term of the first term string in DICT1, the first element of the index table is set, and the location at location h_1 (TERM$_1$), h_2 (TERM$_1$) in the hash address table is set to point to the first element of the index table. The next

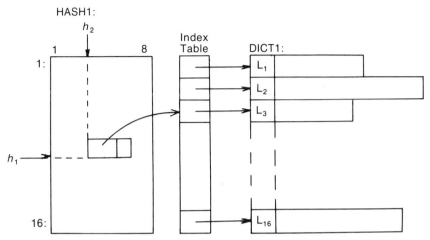

Figure 9.1. Dictionary of variable length term strings accessed through hash address table and index table.

most frequent term, $TERM_2$, is stored in the h_2th position, either in the first term string or in a new one according to whether or not it has the same length as $TERM_1$; and the element in the hash address table at position h_1 ($TERM_2$), h_2 ($TERM_2$) is set to point to the appropriate location in the index table.

The process of storing the next most frequent terms is continued until there is found a term, $TERM_c$, for which either the element at position h_1 ($TERM_c$), h_2($TERM_c$) has been set previously or else there is no available space in the dictionary for a term of the given length at a position h_2. The collision bit is then set and $TERM_c$ is stored in another dictionary. Each term stored in DICT1 is represented in the sequential data base by an eight-bit code whose last seven bits specify the term string and location within it at which the term is stored in DICT1.

Terms that cause collisions in HASH1 are stored in a similar dictionary DICT2 by reference to a hash address table HASH2, and terms that cause collisions in HASH2 are stored either in an overflow dictionary or at the first free position within a hierarchy of similar dictionaries. If HASH2 is allocated space for 128 rows and 128 columns then 16,384 terms may be stored in DICT2.

If terms are distributed in the sequential data base according to the Zipf law then the proportion of terms that are stored in DICT1 and DICT2 are as follows, apart from a small correction caused by term collisions,

$$D_1 = \frac{1}{\log_e D + y} \sum_{r=1}^{128} (1/r)$$

$$= \frac{\log_e 128 + \gamma}{\log_e D + \gamma}. \tag{9.3}$$

$$D_2 = \frac{1}{\log_e D + \gamma} \sum_{r=129}^{16512} (1/r)$$

$$= \frac{\log_e 16{,}512 - \log_e 128}{\log_e D + \gamma}. \tag{9.4}$$

As D ranges from 20,000 to 50,000 the values of D_1 and D_2 range from .518 to .476 and .464 to .426, respectively. Thus only relatively rare terms are not stored in either DICT1 or DICT2.

A question term that is specified without truncation may be searched for in the dictionary by first computing h_1 and h_2 to locate the corresponding term of DICT1. If not equal to the question term and the collision bit indicates that no collision has occurred, then the question term is not in the dictionary. However, if the dictionary term is not equal to the question term and the collision bit indicates that a collision has occurred, then DICT2, and possibly other dictionaries, must be examined.

For a question term that is specified in the form of at least four characters with right truncation, the pointers from an entire row of HASH1 must be used to locate possible matching terms in DICT1. The collision bits indicate when the pointers of HASH2 must be followed. For question terms specified in the form of at least four characters preceded by left truncation, it is necessary to follow similarly the pointers from entire columns of HASH1.

The optimum sizes to choose for the dictionaries DICT1, DICT2, and so forth, depend on the size of the data base, the type of computer and its ability to manipulate six- or eight-bit characters, and also on the available storage devices. It is clearly advantageous to store the most frequently used dictionaries in main memory, but the advantage of rapid access must be weighed against the storage costs. A discussion of storage allocation and access times for a retrieval system that uses a form of hash addressing and restricted variable length codes is contained in the 1973 paper of Dimsdale and Heaps.

9.3 Coded Text Fragments

As indicated in Section 7.4, as a document data base increases in size the number of different words continues to grow. Thus the dictionary file for an inverted file structure may become very large, although approximately half of the words it contains appear in only one document. Also, many dictionary words have character strings in common, and it may appear wasteful of space to store in their entirety each of a set of terms that contain a common stem. For example, the three terms ORDER, ORDERED, and ORDERING might be stored in the form ORDER, +ED, and +ING in which the presence of the + character indicates that the term consists of a previous stem together with some following characters.

An alternative approach is to regard certain fragments of text, not necessarily words, as the basic elements. The fragments may be stored in a dictionary with pointers to an inverted file that indicates the documents that contain such fragments. In the sequential data base the text fragments may be replaced by codes. A question formed from complete terms must then be automatically transformed into a question that involves the dictionary fragments.

Compression of text through coding of common phrases has been described by Wagner.[5,6] Schwartz and Kleiboemer[7] also have discussed the use of compression coding of text elements that are larger than single words.

The use of text fragments as the basic language elements of a data base for information retrieval was proposed by Columbo and Rush.[8] The representation of names by concatenation of variable length character strings called X-grams was suggested by Walker.[9] Lynch and others[10,11,12] have

---

[5] R. A. Wagner, "Common phrases and minimum text storage," *Communications of the Association for Computing Machinery* 16(1973): 148–153.

[6] R. A. Wagner, "An algorithm for extracting phrases in a space-optimal fashion," *Communications of the Association for Computing Machinery* 76(1973): 183–185.

[7] E. S. Schwartz and A. J. Kleiboemer, "A language element for compression coding," *Information and Control* 10(1967): 315–333.

[8] D. S. Columbo and J. E. Rush, "Use of word fragments in computer based retrieval systems," *Journal of Chemical Documentation* 9(1969): 47–50.

[9] V. R. Walker, "Compaction of names by X-grams," *Proceedings of the American Society for Information Science* 6(1969): 129–135.

[10] A. C. Clare, E. M. Cook, and M. F. Lynch, "The identification of variable length equifrequent character strings in a natural language data base," *The Computer Journal* 15(1972): 259–262.

[11] I. J. Barton, S. E. Creasey, M. F. Lynch, and M. J. Snell, "An information-theoretic approach to text searching in direct access systems," *Communications of the Association for Computing Machinery* 17(1974): 345–350.

[12] M. F. Lynch, J. H. Petrie, and M. J. Snell, "Analysis of the microstructure of titles in the INSPEC data-base," *Information Storage and Retrieval* 9(1973): 331–337.

proposed that text in document retrieval systems be represented in terms of equifrequent text fragments in which the fragments may overlap word boundaries rather than be fragments from within single words.

The advantage of using equifrequent text fragments is that each fragment then contains the same amount of information content. Thus the fragments may be coded in the most compact manner by use of fixed length codes that range through all possible addresses within the appropriate range. Furthermore, the equifrequency property implies that each list in the fragment-oriented inverted file has the same number of document numbers; this facilitates organization of the inverted file as a collection of fixed length records. Barton et al.[11] and Lynch et al.[12] have discussed the use of equifrequent text fragments for title searches on the INSPEC tape issued by the Institution of Electrical Engineers. Factors affecting the design of a document retrieval system based on use of equifrequent fragments as the basic codeable elements have been examined by Schuegraf and Heaps.[13-16]

Suppose a data base may be formed by concatenation of T_F fragments of which D_F fragments are different. If all the different fragments occurred with the same frequency they would each contain an information content of $\log_2 D_F$ bits, and could each be represented by codes of length ceil($\log_2 D_F$) bits. If they are not of equal frequency their average information content H_F may be computed in terms of their frequencies, and the ratio

$$\eta = H_F/\log_2 D_F \qquad (9.5)$$

may be regarded as a measure of the extent to which the fragments approximate an equifrequent distribution. The ratio never exceeds 1 and is equal to 1 for a perfectly equifrequent set.

Selection of an approximately equifrequent set of fragments from a given data base may proceed as follows. All word fragments of length up to, say, eight characters that occur in the data base are listed, together with their frequencies. A threshold value t is chosen, and all fragments whose frequencies are less than t are discarded. From the fragments of

---

[13] E. J. Schuegraf, *The Use of Equifrequent Fragments in Retrospective Retrieval Systems* (Ph.D thesis, University of Alberta, Edmonton, Canada, 1974).

[14] E. J. Schuegraf and H. S. Heaps, "Selection of equifrequent fragments for information retrieval," *Information Storage and Retrieval* 9(1973): 697–711.

[15] E. J. Schuegraf and H. S. Heaps, "A comparison of algorithms for data base compression by use of fragments as language elements," *Information Storage and Retrieval* 10(1974): 309–319.

[16] E. J. Schuegraf and H. S. Heaps, "Query processing in a retrospective document retrieval system that uses word fragments as language elements," *Information Processing and Management* 12(1976): 283–292.

greatest length there is selected the one whose frequency is closest to t. All occurrences of this fragment are deleted from the data base and a new list of fragments with frequencies greater than t is then examined. The process of selecting a fragment, removing it from the data base, and examining the new list of fragments, is continued until the list contains no fragments of frequency greater than t. The chosen fragments all have frequencies greater than t, but have been chosen in such a manner as to encourage the selection of fragments with frequencies close to t.

Application of the preceding selection procedure to a set of 495 records, each containing author names, titles, and subject headings, from the MARC tapes, leads to the results shown in Table 9.2. Four different threshold values were chosen. Table 9.2 also contains the results of application of the selection procedure to fragments chosen without regard to word boundaries, the resulting fragments being termed text fragments instead of word fragments. It may be noted that with increase in threshold value the number of different word, or text, fragments decreases. In each instance the values of η are close to 1.00, and hence the selection leads to an approximately equifrequent set of fragments. The extent to which the approximation applies is illustrated in Table 9.3, which contains a list of the selected five-character fragments and their frequencies.

To illustrate the difference between word coding and fragment coding it may be remarked that for the preceding sample of the MARC data base the uncoded sequential file of 7418 words and delimiters requires storage for approximately 50,000 characters. If words are coded the sequential file may be reduced to occupy the equivalent of 8300 characters of 8 bits. The inverted file requires 68,000 bits, and the word dictionary of 2891 words requires storage for 16,500 characters.

In contrast, if word fragments are coded then for thresholds of $t = 5, 10, 15,$ and 20 the coded sequential data base is increased by factors of 1.69, 1.80, 1.81, and 1.85, respectively. Likewise, the inverted file is increased

Table 9.2

Statistics of Sets of Approximately Equifrequent Fragments Selected from Records of the MARC Tapes.

Threshold t	Word fragments			Text fragments		
	D_F	Average length	n	D_F	Average length	n
5	1387	4.01	.97	1600	5.04	.95
10	824	3.50	.97	933	4.12	.95
15	601	3.23	.97	692	3.61	.95
20	490	3.07	.97	556	3.37	.95

Table 9.3

Selected Five-character Word Fragments and Their Frequencies, for a Threshold of 10.

ACHIN	11	ANDER	12	ARING	12	ATIVE	15
BIBLI	14	CATIO	10	CHANG	10	CHILD	10
CIVIL	18	COLLE	16	COMME	10	COUNT	14
DAVID	12	EADER	11	ELECT	10	GRAMME	12
GUIDE	14	HOLOG	12	IENCE	15	INTER	26
IONAL	11	ITIES	17	ITION	12	IVERS	10
JAMES	11	LABOR	10	MATHE	10	MATIC	10
MENTA	14	NAMES	11	NNING	10	NOLOG	11
ONALD	11	POLIC	11	PROCE	12	PROGR	11
RENCE	14	RONIC	10	SCIEN	11	SHING	10
SIONS	12	SPECT	14	STATE	17	STORI	11
STORY	11	STRAT	11	STUDY	23	TEACH	15
THEOR	12	THERN	10	TICAL	19	TIONS	12
TRAIN	10	UTHER	10	UTION	11	WORLD	20

by factors of 1.43, 1.63, 1.77, and 1.86, respectively. However the fragment dictionary contains only 1,387, 824, 601, and 490 fragments whose total storage requirement is for only 5500, 2900, 1900, and 1500 characters, respectively.

Thus coding of fragments instead of full words allows a spectacular reduction in the size of the dictionary, and for a large data base the reduction might permit the dictionary to be stored in main memory instead of on disc. Since each question term must be located in the dictionary in order to access the inverted file there could result significant reduction in search times. However, the reduction in dictionary space is gained at the expense of an increase in the size of the inverted file and the coded sequential file.

In order to ensure that all terms in the data base may be represented by concatenation of fragments present in the dictionary, it is desirable to include all possible single letter fragments, although it is to be hoped that they will be used relatively infrequently. As the data base grows it will then not be necessary to increase the size of the fragment dictionary; this offers a significant advantage over the use of a dictionary of complete words. Moreover, if the equifrequency property continues to be satisfied then as the data base grows all lists in the inverted file will grow at the same rate.

For the fragment dictionaries corresponding to the small data base used to compile Table 9.2 it is found that a significant number of single letter fragments occur, although there are very few words that must be built entirely from such fragments. It therefore appears desirable to omit the corresponding lists from the inverted file, under the assumption that each question term is sufficiently characterized by its fragments of length more than two characters. This would seem to be justified in view of the low information content of single letters, and the fact that less space is required for storage of the inverted file, and since it results in fewer inverted file lists to be processed for each question.

Apart from the initial selection of fragments, there are two problems that arise in information retrieval from a fragment oriented data base. The first is the representation of the sequential file in terms of the selected fragments. There will be many words whose representation in terms of dictionary fragments is not unique, and the different representations will have different effects on the preservation of the equifrequency property. For example, the term ILLUSTRATED has a number of possible representations in terms of the dictionary fragments

        ATED, RAT, RATE, STR, STRA, STRAT, TED, UST

together with single letter fragments.

One method of representation is through use of the "longest fragment first" (LFF) algorithm, which proceeds as follows. The largest fragment STRAT is removed to leave ILLU and ED whose longest fragments are single letters. The representation is thus in terms of the seven fragments

I/L/L/U/STRAT/E/D.

A further method is through the "longest match" (LM) algorithm in which the longest possible fragments are removed successively from the beginning of the term. This results in representation through the six fragments

I/L/L/UST/RATE/D.

A third method is through use of the "minimum space" (MS) algorithm in which the representation is chosen to minimize the number of fragments used. This is achieved by any of the following three representations in terms of fragments

I/L/L/UST/RATE/D
I/L/L/U/STRA/TED
I/L/L/U/STR/ATED

The MS algorithm clearly leads to the most compact representation of the sequential data base, but the LM algorithm is the fastest to execute. Some experimantal results regarding the equifrequency of fragments in the fragmented data base, and the space required for storage of the sequential data base in coded form, are given by Schuegraf and Heaps (1974). It is found that the resulting distributions of fragments in the sequential file are not as equifrequent as predicted by Table 9.2, and the space required for storage of the sequential file is considerably greater than as predicted from Table 9.2. Thus if compaction of the fragmented data base, rather than the creation of a small dictionary, is the prime concern then more efficient algorithms should be developed for fragmentation of the data base.

A further problem concerns the representation of question terms as concatenations of fragments. Clearly the same algorithm should be used as for representation of terms in the data base. Suppose, however, that the terms RACER and TERRACE are fragmented respectively into RAC/ER and T/ER/RAC/E. If single letter fragments have no lists in the inverted file then a search for either term becomes a fragment oriented search for

RAC and ER.

The unwanted term may be eliminated by performing a sequential search on the output that results from the fragment-oriented search. This adds to the time required to process each question but is not prohibitive provided the output from the fragment-oriented search may be stored either in main memory or in a relatively small file.

Truncation specifications in question terms are more easily treated when fragments are used instead of words because the smaller dictionary may be structured to indicate all the fragments that contain given combinations of characters. This allows a question term such as *PACTION to be expanded to represent all of the following

(i) The fragments that end with P, followed by the fragmented representation of ACTION.

(ii) The fragments that end with PA, followed by the fragmented representation of CTION.
etc.

9.4 Partial Coding of Text

When text is compressed by representation of words or character strings by codes of shorter length it is the most frequent terms that contribute the most to the effectiveness of the compression. With this in view it has been suggested by Notley[17] and by Mayne and James[18] that only the most frequent character strings be coded. While this implies

---

[17] M. G. Notley, "The cumulative recurrence library," *The Computer Journal* 13(1970): 14–19.

[18] A. Mayne and E. B. James, "Information compression by factorising common strings," *The Computer Journal* 18(1975): 157–160.

some increase in code length, since the codes must be tagged in some manner to distinguish them from uncoded character strings, it has the advantage of allowing relatively small tables to be used for the coding operations.

Partial coding of text has proved useful for compaction of compiler error messages. The messages form a very small vocabulary in comparison to that of most document data bases, but it is found that the terms are distributed in close agreement with the Zipf law. Further details and references to published work are contained in a paper by Heaps and Radhakrishnan.[19]

9.5 Term Compression by Abbreviation

The methods of compression described in the previous sections are based on the representation of terms by codes chosen after determination of term, or fragment, frequencies. Other methods of compression depend on more direct term abbreviations or truncations.

Bourne and Ford[20,21] have discussed 13 techniques for the representation of words by abbreviations of standard length. Illustration was made by application to two small data bases of 2082 and 8184 terms. It was regarded as desirable that each coded word should be represented as a string of characters with some mnemonic similarity to the uncoded word so that decoding could proceed manually.

Ruecking[22] has described the use of an abbreviation procedure for title words. It is based on delection of all suffixes and inflections that terminate a word, followed by deletion of vowels, followed by further reduction if necessary in order to produce a code of four consonants. The method was applied to a small data base, and it has been remarked by Lipetz, et al.[23] that it is likely to reduce seriously the efficiency of document retrieval if used for a data base of considerably more than 48,000 documents. This is

[19] H. S. Heaps and T. Radhakrishnan, "Compaction of diagnostic error messages for compilers," *Software: Practice and Experience* 7(1977): 139–144.

[20] C. P. Bourne, *Methods of Information Handling* (New York: Wiley, 1963).

[21] C. P. Bourne and D. F. Ford, "A study of methods for systematically abbreviating English words and names," *Journal of the Association for Computing Machinery* 8(1961): 538–552.

[22] F. H. Ruecking, "Bibliographic retrieval from bibliographic input: the hypothesis and construction of a test," *Journal of Library Automation* 1(1968): 227–238.

[23] B-A. Libetz, P. Sangl, and K. F. Taylor, "Performance of Ruecking's word-compression method when applied to machine retrieval from a library catalog," *Journal of Library Automation* 2(1969): 266–271.

because as the data base increases in size there is an increasing tendency for more than one word to have the same abbreviation code.

Four compressions techniques have been discussed by Nugent.[24] Also, Dolby[25] has described a method of variable length name compaction and a method based on truncation. He found it desirable to retain at least five characters in the truncated code.

Treleaven[26] has examined several methods of word abbreviation based on selective deletion of characters according to character frequency, character position within the word, and frequency of association of each character with the adjacent characters. He considered the advantage of including check digits and word length indicators within each code. The code length was fixed and equal to 40 bits.

Codes formed from a combination of author names and title words have been used by Kilgour[27] and by Burgis and Buchinski.[28] The codes are formed by deleting certain characters as in word abbreviation codes, and are primarily for use as addresses for stored records rather than for coding of data.

The advantage of the codes described in the previous sections is that they are more compact than codes based on abbreviation or truncation. Moreover, since the codes are assigned in ascending numerical order then all possible codes of a given length are used before introducing any codes of greater length. Furthermore, the codes are unique, no collisions arise, and the uncoded words may be reconstructed by purely automatic means. The user who receives the decoded output, or who inputs uncoded question terms, need not be aware of the coding process.

However, a useful feature of coding based on truncation is that words with the same stem may be assigned the same code, and this may be useful for retrieval purposes if it avoids the need for truncation specifications within questions. Some coding schemes based on deletion of certain characters are unaffected by certain spelling errors, whereas the

[24] W. R. Nugent, "Compression word coding techniques for information retrieval," *Journal of Library Automation* 1(1968): 250–260.

[25] J. L. Dolby, "An algorithm for variable-length proper name compression," *Journal of Library Automation* 3(1970): 257–275.

[26] R. L. Treleaven, *Abbreviation of English Words to Standard Length of Computer Processing* (M.Sc. thesis, University of Alberta, Edmonton, Canada, 1970).

[27] F. G. Kilgour, "Retrieval of single entries from a computerised library catalog file," *Proceedings of the American Society for Information Science* 5(1968): 133–136.

[28] G. C. Burgis and E. Buchinski, MARC at the University of Saskatchewan. Proceedings 2nd Annual Meeting of the Western Canada Chapter of the American Society for Information Science, September, 1970. Information Systems, University of Calgary, Canada.

coding schemes described in the previous sections will assign different codes to the misspelt words.

Use of letter deletion codes for correction of commonly misspelt words has been described by Blair.[29] However, commonly occurring spelling errors tend to be different from common keypunch errors, and it has not been established to what extent abbreviation codes may be designed to be unaffected by the most commonly occurring errors in keypunching.

9.6 Problems

1. One method of reducing the size of a dictionary and sequential file is to store only the first five letters of each title term. Estimate the amount of file space to be saved by use of such a technique. How serious is the loss of information to the user if all titles are printed with words reduced to not more than five letters?

2. Would your answer to Problem 1 be different if the words were reduced to either four or six letters?

3. Suggest a method of coding names and initials in order to reduce the space required for storage of a computer accessible telephone directory. State the total amount of space saved.

4. Consider the method of partial coding of text as outlined in Section 9.4. Assume the Zipf law, and estimate the amount of saving that could be achieved by the coding of various sets of relatively frequent words. Consider the amount of space required for any dictionaries needed for coding or decoding. Also, consider the amount of computer processing time that is needed. How does the space saving depend on the size of the data base?

[29] C. R. Blair, ``A program for correcting spelling errors,`` *Information and Control* 3(1960): 60–67.

10

Example of Design of a Document Retrieval System

10.1 Functional Description

The aim of the present chapter is to illustrate the concepts introduced in the previous chapters by consideration of the factors involved in the design of an on-line document retrieval system to fulfill a given function. The first step in the design is a description of the general requirements of the retrieval service.

For purposes of illustration it will be supposed that a searchable data base is to be created by merging document descriptions that are obtained from three different sources and in the form of records on magnetic tape files. The records supplied by the first source are divided into fields that contain author names; titles; journal codens; and journal details such as volume, date (year), and page numbers. The records of the second source are divided into fields that contain author names; titles; a reference to either a journal name, conference proceedings, or issuing body; details of volume numbers, dates, page numbers, and place of publication; and a set of keywords. The records supplied by the third source contain fields of author names; titles; abstracts; name of a journal or conference proceedings or other issuing body; place of publication; volume numbers, dates, and page numbers.

It will be supposed that approximately 10,000 document records are received each month, 6000 being on tapes supplied by the first source, and 2000 on each of the tapes supplied by the second and third sources. It is known that some document items may be contained on two, or more, tapes.

It is desired to search for question terms that may be author names, title words or phrases, dates, codens, or keywords and terms in abstracts when such are present in the records. The logic is to include the Boolean operators AND, OR, NOT. Right, but not left, truncation of question terms, keywords, and abstract terms is to be allowed. Author searching may be performed with respect to surname only or surname followed by initials. The conditions $\leq$, $\geq$, or $\neq$ may be applied to dates, and the condition $\neq$ may be applied to codens.

Searches are to be made on-line. An inverted file will be used but, because of space limitations, it will contain no information about position of terms. During execution of the search program each question phrase will be treated as a sequence of terms connected by AND logic; the retrieved document items will then be scanned sequentially in order to eliminate those that do not contain the required phrases.

In order to economize on storage space and search time the abstracts will not be stored in full. Instead, the first sentence of the abstract will be pruned of all words present in a given stop list, and the remaining sequence of words will be placed in parentheses within the keyword field. Thus a search for a keyword will also find the specified word within the first sentence of an abstract.

Question statements will be allowed in the form of sequences of input lines that are numbered sequentially as 1,2,3, etc. For each set of questions the first line must have the form

1. QUE

and each search is requested by a statement of the form

N. SEARCH n xxxx

where n is a line number of a previous line and the meaning of xxxx is explained subsequently in (iv). Intermediate lines must consist of the line number followed by one of the following:

(i) One search term or phrase.

(ii) A sequence of search terms and/or phrases and/or line numbers, each followed by a comma, followed by one of the logic operators AND, OR.

Each search term may be chosen as explained in (i)–(iv) that follows:

(i) An alphabetic character string, or sequence of such strings each separated by one space, may be used to indicate a term or phrase to be searched for within a title field. Right truncation may be signified by * or by a sequence of $ symbols.

(*ii*) The symbols A/ followed by an author surname, or by a surname followed by a single space, and one, or more, initials not separated by spaces or punctuation, may be used to indicate a term to be searched for within an author field.

(*iii*) The symbols K/ followed by an alphabetic character string with, or without, right truncation may be used to indicate a term to be searched for within a keyword field.

(*iv*) The xxxx may denote either a space or a sequence of one or more of the following:

(*a*) Line number of one or two digits preceded by $\neq$ to indicate NOT logic.

(*b*) Four-digit dates which may, or may not, be preceded by $\leqslant$, $\geqslant$, or $=$.

(*c*) Five-character codens which may, or may not, be preceded by $\leqslant$, $\geqslant$, or $=$.

An example of a set of two questions is thus

```
1. QUE
2. IMPLEMENTAT*, DESIGN, CONSTRUCTION, OR
3. DIGITAL SYSTEM$
4. A/WITHERS GA, A/SMITH, OR
5. 2, 3, AND
6. SEARCH 5, ≠4
7. K/DIGITAL, K/SYSTEM$, AND
8. 2,7,4, NUMERICAL, AND
9. SEARCH 8, ≥75, ≠CDEAG, ≠BWXCA
```

The reason that dates, codens, and NOT logic are allowed to appear only in the SEARCH line is that the corresponding inverted file lists are likely to be very large. In fact, for the reasons described in Section 10.4 it is believed desirable to create no inverted file lists for dates or codens. By placing all reference to NOT logic, dates, and codens in the final line of the search request the required processing may be performed by a sequential scan at the same time that retrieved documents are examined for phrases.

10.2 Creation of Reformatted Tapes

Before creation of a dictionary and inverted file structure it is desirable to reformat the tapes from the three sources so that they have a common format suitable as input to a program that creates the inverted, and associated, files.

Records from the first source may be rewritten on a tape file formatted as described in Figure 3.1. The date and the coden may be placed in a fixed length field. The author names may be placed in a variable length field with a comma acting as a delimiter to separate the different author names. Each title may be placed in a variable length field, as may details concerning volume and page numbers, etc. Each directory to the variable length fields will show that a null field is used to indicate the absence of keywords or an abstract.

Records from the second source may be rewritten in the same manner with each reference to a journal name being replaced by the appropriate coden. If the journal or conference proceedings, etc., does not have an assigned coden, then the coden field is filled with an exceptional data code and the journal or proceedings details are included in the variable field that is used for the volume, page numbers, and so forth. The keywords may be placed in a variable field, separated by commas. Records from the third source are rewritten in a similar manner except that each keyword field is filled with the words selected from the first sentence of the abstract and placed within parentheses.

The records of the three new tapes created as just described each contain two fixed length fields, and four variable length fields of which only three are searchable. The fourth variable length field contains journal details that are not searched on, but which are printed along with the other five fields when relevant items are output.

It is supposed that the reformatted tapes may be created automatically from the source tapes. However, the reformatted author names, codens deduced from journal names, dates, and keywords extracted from the abstract should be displayed for manual examination. Appropriate corrections may be made to correct errors that might arise because of errors on the source tapes or because of the presence of data in a form not envisaged during the design of the reformatting programs.

Suppose that in selection of keywords from the abstracts a stop list containing the following words is used.

```
THE,   OF,   AND,   TO,   A,   IN,   THAT,   IS,
WAS,   FOR,   IT,   WITH,   AS,   ON,   BE,   AT,
BY,   THIS,   HAD,   NOT,   ARE,   BUT,   FROM,   OR,
HAVE,   AN,   WHICH,   ONE,   WERE,   ALL,   THERE,   SOME
```

This list includes the fifteen underlined words in Tables 7.7 and 7.8, which account for 26 and 29% of the words in the corresponding data bases. Frequencies of the most frequent words in general English text are given in Table 11.1 from which it may be seen that the preceding 32 words account for about 35% of the words in general text. Thus if the first sentence of an abstract contains an average of 12 words then the average number of selected keywords will be 4.2.

10.3 Estimation of Data Base Statistics

A knowledge of the discipline and examination of a number of issues of the reformatted tapes will allow some prediction of the statistics and expected growth rate of the vocabularies of the various fields. The predictions might be made as follows:

(*i*) Because of some duplication of items from the different sources it might be estimated that the data base will grow at the rate of 9000, instead of 10,000, document records each month.

(*ii*) From consideration of a number of sample document records it might be predicted that the records contain an average of 1.6 authors, 10 title words, and two keywords.

(*iii*) It might be found that there are approximately 1,000 different codens and that 90% of the document items contain codens. For the remaining 10% the coden fields contain an exceptional data code. Suppose it is found that the most frequent coden appears in 5% of the document items.

(*iv*) According to (*iii*), in 90% of the document items the nonsearchable field of journal details contains only volume and page numbers. For the remaining 10% of the document items the nonsearchable field also contains the journal name or a reference to a conference, or etc. If the corresponding average lengths of the two types of non-searchable fields are 15 and 165 characters respectively their average length is 30 characters.

(*v*) The total number of author names will increase at the rate of 14,400 per month. If the frequencies of author repetitions are according to Table 7.5, then approximately 90% (= .631 + .221 + .056)100% of the authors publish one, two, or three papers, and hence (.631 + .221 × 2 + .056 × 3 + . . .) D = Total No. Authors from which it follows that

$$D \leq (\text{Total No. Authors}) /1.24$$

It therefore appears that, when the data base has reached a sufficient size, the increase in the number of different authors should not exceed 14,400/1.24 ≤ 12,000 per month.

(*vi*) If it is assumed that the number of different title words, and the number of different keywords, continue to grow according to the CT graph in Figure 7.1 then the number of different terms will increase as shown in Table 10.1.

10.4 Possible File Structure

A possible file structure is in the form of a separate dictionary and inverted file for each of the five searchable fields. However, the inverted file list for each date would contain over 100,000 document numbers. Also if, as supposed in Section 10.3, the most frequent coden appears in 5% of the document items then after a period of 4 years the corresponding inverted file list will contain over 20,000 document numbers.

In order to avoid the occurrence of such large lists no inverted file will be created for codens or dates. Searches that involve only dates and codens will not be allowed, but questions that contain dates or codens in addition to other terms will be allowed. The procedure for processing such questions is described later.

In order to economize on storage for the inverted file it will be supposed that no inverted file entries are created for the 32 words in the stop list of Section 10.2. According to the frequency list of Table 11.1, all other words should have a probability of occurrence of less than .003. After 4 years the largest inverted file list for title words will therefore contain about 13,000 document numbers. The inverted file lists for author names, title words, and keywords will have lengths as shown in Table 10.2. In

Table 10.1
Variation of Size of Data Base as a Function of Age in Years.

Age of Data Base (Years):	1	2	3	4
No. Documents:	110,000	220,000	330,000	440,000
Total No. Title Words:	1,100,000	2,200,000	3,300,000	4,400,000
No. Different Title Words:	40,000	55,000	70,000	80,000
Total No. Keywords:	220,000	440,000	660,000	880,000
No. Different Keywords:	18,000	25,000	30,000	33,000
No. Authors:	180,000	360,000	540,000	720,000
No. Different Authors:	140,000	280,000	420,000	560,000
Total No. Codens:	100,000	200,000	300,000	400,000
No. Different Codens:	1,000	1,000	1,000	1,000
Total No. Dates:	110,000	220,000	330,000	440,000
No. Different Dates:	1	2	3	4
Total No. Nonsearch Fields:	110,000	220,000	330,000	440,000

Table 10.2
Length of the Inverted File Lists of Document Numbers.

Age of Data Base (Years):	1	2	3	4
Lists for Title Words:				
Maximum Length:	3300	6600	9900	13000
L(100):	1100	2200	3300	4300
Average Length:	27	40	47	50
Lists for Keywords:				
Maximum Length:	700	1300	2000	2600
L(100):	230	430	660	860
Average Length:	12	18	22	27
Lists for Authors:				
Average Length:	1.6	1.6	1.6	1.6

Table 10.2 the expression $L(100)$ is used to signify the length of the inverted file list for the 100th most frequent term. According to the Zipf law

$$L(100) = \frac{\text{Maximum length } [=L(33)]}{(100/33)}$$

Since the document numbers may range from 1 to 440,000 a storage of at least 19 bits is required for each. If 20 bits are used then the data base could continue to grow for 9 years. The inverted files for title words, keywords, and author names will then increase at the rates of approximately 22, 4, and 3.6 million bits per year.

It may be noted that if a stop list of the most frequent 100 words were used the maximum length of the inverted file lists would be reduced by a factor of ⅓. Such an advantage must be weighed against the disadvantage of not being able to search for certain terms by use of the inverted file.

Dictionary pointers of 24 bits may be used to address an inverted file for a data base of up to 16 million title words or keywords. Pointers of 20 bits may be used to address an inverted file for a data base of 1 million authors.

It could be assumed that title words and keywords have an average length of 8.2 characters, in agreement with Table 7.9. Suppose it is found that author names have an average of 10 characters. If a 6-bit character representation is used the dictionary of different title words and associated pointers to the inverted file will require a total space of 40,000 (6 × 8.2 + 24)=3 million bits in the first year and 6 million bits by the end of 4 years. The similar space requirements for the dictionary of keywords and associated pointers are 1.3 and 2.4 million bits, respectively. The space requirements for the dictionary of author names and pointers are 11 and 45 million bits. The variation of space requirements with age of the data base is shown in Table 10.3.

Table 10.3
Space Requirements, in Millions of Bits, for Dictionaries, Inverted Files, and Sequential
Data Base.

Age of Data Base (Years)	1	2	3	4
Inverted File (Titles)	22	44	66	88
Inverted File (Keywords)	4.4	8.8	13	18
Inverted File (Authors)	3.6	7.2	11	14
Dictionary (Titles)	2.9	4.0	5.1	5.9
Dictionary (Keywords)	1.3	1.8	2.2	2.4
Dictionary (Authors)	11	22	34	45
Sequential File:	100	200	300	400
Coded:	50	100	150	200
Compressed:	43	87	131	175
(Uncoded journal details):	(20)	(40)	(60)	(80)

In addition to the dictionaries and inverted files it is necessary to have a sequential file of document records. If stored in uncoded form it will contain author names of average length 10 characters = 60 bits, title words and keywords of average length 8.2 characters = 49 bits, codens of length 5 characters, dates of length 2 characters such as 77 or 78, and nonsearchable fields of average length 30 characters. The sequential file will therefore grow at a yearly rate of

$$180{,}000 \times 10 + 1{,}320{,}000 \times 8.2 + 100{,}000 \times 5 + 110{,}000 \times 2$$
$$+ 110{,}000 \times 30$$
$$= 16.6 \text{ million characters}$$
$$= 100 \text{ million bits.}$$

This amount of storage is less than that available on a single 2400 foot magnetic tape of density 800 bytes per inch. It is slightly more than half of the storage available on an IBM2314 disk drive.

If the author names, title words, and keywords in the sequential file are replaced by codes that consist of their dictionary addresses as described in Section 5.6, then the corresponding code lengths may be 20, 18, and 16 bits, respectively. The sequential file will then grow at a yearly rate of

$$180{,}000 \times 20 + 1{,}100{,}000 \times 18 + 220{,}000 \times 16 + 100{,}000$$
$$\times 30 + 110 \times 12 + 110{,}000 \times 180$$
$$= 51 \text{ million bits.}$$

An alternative representation of title words and keywords in the sequential file is by the restricted variable length codes of type 6, 12, 18, 24, . . . as described in Section 9.1. It follows from Tables 9.1 and 10.1 that over a 4-year period the average length of codes for title words will increase from 11.8 to 12.3 bits. Similarly, the average code length for keywords will increase from 11.2 to 11.6 bits.

The space requirements of a compressed sequential file, in which title words and keywords are represented by restricted variable length codes, are included in Table 10.3. It may be noted that the uncoded journal details occupy about 50% of the compressed sequential file. The storage requirements might be reduced significantly by coding words such as PROCEEDINGS and CONFERENCE, or by eliminating any information that might be regarded as not strictly necessary to the user of the search service. Further space could also be saved by a more compact representation of codens and dates. For example the 1000 codens could each be replaced by a 10-bit code, and dates could each be replaced by a 4-bit code.

It should be noted that the dictionary sizes shown in Table 10.3 are estimated on the basis of average term lengths, and are meaningful estimates only if the terms are stored without the use of blanks to maintain a constant field length. The assumed average term length could be obtained if the dictionaries are segmented so that each component dictionary stores only terms of the same length. The variation in the size of the component dictionaries may be estimated by use of a frequency table similar to Table 7.9. According to the CANDICT column of Table 7.9 no such component dictionary should be larger than 14% of the entire dictionary. A search for an untruncated question term would be made in one of the component dictionaries and would involve fewer disk accesses than when an unsegmented dictionary is used. On the other hand, a right-truncated search term may have to be searched for in several component dictionaries.

The discussion of space requirements has not referred to any particular type of computer, and storage estimates have been based on characteristics of the data rather than on consideration of the computer word length or instruction set. In practice such considerations are likely to lead to an increase in the use of storage space, but the estimates of Table 10.3 are nevertheless useful in providing an indication of storage requirements.

10.5 File Update Procedure

During creation of each reformatted file from the original source tape the first author name of each document item may be searched for in the dictionary of author names. If found, then any further author names and the title words may be searched for in order to determine whether the item is a duplicate of one already present in the data base. It is probably advisable to have a printout of each such item, together with the one in the data base, so that a manual examination may be made in order to verify that the documents are in fact the same. It could happen, for example, that two different papers have the same author and title but are published in different years or in different journals.

Update of the dictionary, inverted files, and coded sequential file, in order to include document items of a new reformatted file may proceed as follows. Following the procedure indicated in Figure 5.14 the File 1 may be created for the new data, the document numbers being assigned to follow those of document numbers already present in the data base. A sort operation may be used to create a File 2, which may then be merged with the previous File 2 that was obtained during creation of the previous dictionary and inverted files. The updated File 2 may then be processed as in Figure 5.14 in order to create an updated dictionary, inverted file and coded sequential file. The newly created File 2 is retained until the next time it is required to add document items.

It may be noted that since 90,000 title terms are added to the data base each month the corresponding File 2 will require a storage space of

$$90,000(20 + 8.2 \times 6 + 5) = 7 \text{ million bits}$$

provided that each title contains not more than 32 words. The merged File 2 will, of course, continue to increase in size at the rate of approximately 7 million bits each month.

It may be remarked that creation of a nonalphabetically ordered dictionary, such as one designed for access through hash addressing, does not affect the creation of the inverted file and coded sequential file except that the codes in the sequential file must be chosen to be the appropriate dictionary addresses. The file creation procedure of Figure 5.14 may be modified accordingly, with updates still proceeding by a merge of files similar to File 2.

If terms in the sequential file are represented by codes that are addresses to where the uncoded terms are stored in an alphabetically ordered dictionary then addition of further document items will change the position of terms stored in the dictionary, and the entire sequential file will have to be recoded. However, if the dictionary terms are accessed by hash addressing the insertion of further terms does not change the addresses of terms already in the dictionary, and it is not necessary to change the document records previously stored in the sequential file.

10.6 Structure of Dictionary

It is expected that the dictionary will be stored on a disc file. As mentioned in Section 3.1, in order to examine any data stored on disc a complete physical record is transferred from disk to core, and the time required for the operation is dependent on the access time and transfer rate of the disk drive. The most convenient size to choose for the stored records depends on the particular computer configuration; for the IBM 2314 disk pack referred to in Section 3.1 the track capacity has 7294 characters, and so a record length of 7200 characters might prove convenient.

If the dictionary of Table 10.1 is stored with terms arranged in alphabetic order then after 4 years there are some 80,000 different title terms in the dictionary. A binary search for a term may then require up to 17 comparisons with dictionary terms. According to Table 10.3 the dictionary will occupy about 6 million bits, and hence 1 million characters. If the comparisons are performed after transferring records of length 7200 characters into core then after 8 comparisons, and therefore 8 disk accesses, the search may be performed on a contiguous 4000 characters in the dictionary and hence on a single record. Thus up to 9 disk accesses may be required in order to determine whether a given title term is present in the dictionary. Similarly, since there will be 560,000 different authors in a dictionary of 45 million bits, or 7.5 million characters, the required 20 comparisons will involve up to 12 disk accesses.

It is apparent that the times required to search for a term in the dictionary may be reduced significantly if the dictionary is segmented into component dictionaries of size equal to the physical records, and if the component dictionaries are arranged so that a search for any term requires access to only one dictionary. One approach to such segmentation is by use of a set of dictionaries each of which is used to store terms whose first two characters have specified values. Thus one component dictionary could be used to store all terms that begin with the letters AA.

In order to allow for the inclusion of single letter words, and all combinations of initial pairs of letters, it would be necessary to have 702 component dictionaries. However, certain combinations of initial letters will not occur, and it may be estimated from Table 7.14 that the number of component dictionaries might be of the order of 350. After 4 years the average size of each component dictionary for title words would thus be 1,000,000/350 = 2860 characters. Unfortunately, it is clear from Table 7.14 that some dictionary sizes will be much larger than the average, and the larger ones will occupy 1,000,000 × .025 = 25,000 characters. Thus although a search for some title terms will require only one disk access, there will be some terms for which a binary search will require three disk accesses.

Similar segmentation of the keyword dictionary will result in smaller component dictionaries. Segmentation of the author dictionary will create some component dictionaries of 7,500,000 × .025 = 188,000 characters which, if divided into records of length 7000 characters, may require five disk accesses for a binary search. This may not be a serious disadvantage if it is found that few questions specify a search for author names.

With dictionary segmentation as just described it is necessary to create an index table in which is stored the file address of each component dictionary. The space required is relatively small, but it should be kept in core while all dictionary addressing is being performed. Since each component dictionary contains words of the same pair of initial letters it is not necessary to store the first two initial letters, and this allows the dictionary space to be reduced accordingly.

The use of component dictionaries addressed by the initial two letters of the words provides a feasible solution to the problem of dictionary segmentation, but it has two main disadvantages. Firstly, if each term in the sequential file is represented by its dictionary address then addition of new document items requires reassignment of codes and consequent modification of document items in the sequential file. Secondly, the component dictionaries may exhibit considerable variations in size, and hence in their required numbers of disk accesses. The variation in size also makes it less convenient to store terms of various lengths. A method of storage that does not require words to be padded with right-hand blanks is described here for use with a hash storage scheme. It may also be used with component dictionaries of variable length but it is not quite as convenient as when all dictionaries have the same length.

An alternative scheme of dictionary segmentation is through use of hash functions as follows. Let each component dictionary be designed for storage of up to 512 terms. It follows from Section 10.4 that for title words, keywords, and author names the size of each dictionary will be approximately 6250, 6250, and 6830 characters, respectively. Then only one disk access is required in order to transfer any dictionary from disk to core. The number of such dictionaries required for storage of up to 100,000 title words, 50,000 keywords, and 1 million author names is 196, 98, and 1954 respectively. Suppose the number of dictionaries is, in fact, chosen to be 200, 100, and 2000 respectively.

Let a hash function $h_{200}(\text{TERM})$ be defined to act on the first four letters of any title word to give a value that is an integer in the range of 1 to 200. Let a further hash function $h_4(\text{TERM})$ be defined to act on the first four letters of each title word to give an integer value in the range of 1 to 16. For any word of less than four letters the hash functions may operate on the entire word. Each title term will be stored in the component dictionary of number $h_{200}(\text{TERM})$. The position in this dictionary is determined as described in the following.

Each component dictionary comprises of up to 32 term strings each of which has space for storage of 16 terms of the same length. It also has an index table of up to 32 pointers to the beginning of each term string. A single index table and its associated term strings are depicted in part of Figure 9.1. Each term string is created only when it is required for storage of a new term.

A term of length L which is to be stored in the $h_{200}(\text{TERM})$th component dictionary is placed in the $h_4(\text{TERM})$th position in the first term string of appropriate length that has a vacancy at that position. If all such positions are filled then a collision function is used to allocate an appropriate storage position and a collision bit is tagged appropriately. Since the entire component dictionary has been transferred to core no further disk accesses are needed in order to locate the storage position for the term.

A similar procedure may be used for storage of keywords and author names. If terms in the sequential file are to be compressed by storage as codes that represent addresses, the codes may be chosen as follows:

(*i*) *Title Terms:* Use an 18-bit code in which the first 9 bits indicate the dictionary number, the next 5 bits represent the term string number, and the next 4 bits represent the position within the term string at which the term is stored.

(*ii*) *Keywords:* Use a 16-bit code in which the first 7 bits indicate a dictionary number, and the last 9 bits are chosen as in (*i*).

(*iii*) *Author names:* Use a 20-bit code in which the first 11 bits indicate a dictionary number, and the last 9 bits are chosen as in (*i*).

Each coded term in the sequential file may be decoded by a single disk access followed by retrieval of the term stored at the appropriate address. No dictionary search is required. When new document items are added to the data base it is not necessary to change the codes of any terms already in the data base.

It may be noted that collisions resulting from use of the functions $h_{200}(\text{TERM})$ and $h_4(\text{TERM})$ do not cause serious problems, although it is desirable that the values of both functions be distributed in a reasonably uniform manner over their respective ranges. Since the hashing is on only the first four characters of each term then each right-truncated question term that contains at least four characters will be hashed into the dictionary that contains all the terms to which it could correspond. It would therefore be appropriate to require that at least four characters be included in any question term that is specified with right truncation.

Further details of implementation of the retrieval system described in the present chapter will, of course, be dependent on the particular computer configuration and any additional constraints regarding efficient use of storage resources. It is believed that sufficient detail has been given to illustrate the steps in the design process.

More detailed consideration of the efficiency of dictionary searching has been presented by Lowe and Roberts,[1] and by Grimson and Stacey.[2] Discussion of the organization of the inverted file in order to facilitate access and fast processing has been given by Cardenas,[3] who also has discussed the overall organization of files for information retrieval.[4] A general discussion of the considerations that affect the organization of files stored on sequential or direct access devices has been given by Buchholz.[5] An application of scatter storage techniques to a bibliographic file of 250,000 titles has been described by Long et al.[6] A description of the sequential record format, the file structure, and the methods used to access the files in the CAN/OLE retrieval system has been given by Heilik.[7] In 1976 the files for the CAN/OLE system contained over 3 million bibliographic records.

10.7 Problems

1. Describe the structure and method of processing a stack that represents the question syntax introduced in Section 10.1.

2. Describe a dictionary structure that would allow question terms to be specified with either left or right truncation (but not both). *Hint:* Would it be feasible to use the structure described in Section 10.6, together with a table that is accessed by hashing on right-most characters of a question term, and which contains pointers to where the terms are stored in the dictionary. State how much additional storage space, if any, would be required to support the use of left truncation.

[1] T. C. Lowe, and D. C. Roberts, "Analysis of directory searching," *Journal of the American Society for Information Science,* 23 (1972):143–149.

[2] J. B. Grimson, and G. M. Stacey, "A performance study of some directory structures for large files," *Information Storage and Retrieval* 10 (1974):357–364.

[3] A. F. Cardenas, "Analysis and performance of inverted data base structures," *Communications of the Association for Computing Machinery* 18 (1975):235–263.

[4] A. F. Cardenas, "Evaluation and selection of file organization—a model and system," *Communications of the Association for Computing Machinery* 16 (1973):540–548.

[5] W. Buchholz, "File organization and addressing," *IBM Systems Journal* 2 (1963):86–111.

[6] P. L. Long, K. B. L. Rastogi, J. E. Rush, and J. A. Wyckoff, "Large on-line files of bibliographic data: An efficient design and a mathematical predictor of retrieval behavior," *Information Processing* 71 (1972):473–478.

[7] J. Heilik, "Can/Ole: A technical description," Fourth Canadian Conference on Information Science in Canada. London, Ontario, May 11–14, 1976. pp. 47–55.

3. Discuss the extent to which the use of a computer of a particular word length, such as 4 or 10 characters, affects the design of the dictionary and the inverted file. Pay particular attention to the resulting storage requirements.

4. In Section 10.1 it was suggested that the question formulation be such as to separate the question into two portions. The first portion is processed by means of an inverted file, and the second portion is processed by a sequential search of the retrieved records. Describe how such a question structure might be used to search records that also contain numerical, or other, fields of a form not discussed in the present text. Suggest the content of such fields, and further logic operators that might be allowed for processing during the sequential search phase.

11

Document Indexing and Term Associations

11.1 Document Representation through Index Terms

In the previous chapters each document was envisaged as possessing a number of attributes whose values are stored in fields of the document data base. A search on the data base was specified through logic operations that link descriptors contained in various attribute fields. In the present chapter the emphasis is on representation of a document solely by means of a set of descriptors, rather than by descriptors associated with attributes. Such a set of descriptors will be said to constitute a set of index terms.

The difference in the two forms of document representation is that attributes often represent features physically present in the document; such features might include the title, the abstract, and author names. In contrast, index terms are often chosen in reference to an external scheme of indexing such as might be described by a thesaurus. The two approaches to document representation are not mutually exclusive since one attribute might be a set of index terms, and likewise the title words of a document might be chosen to form the index terms.

The distinction between the two methods of document representation is perhaps most apparent through its effect on the form of the search question allowed in each case. The present chapter is concerned with search procedures when the searchable data is organized with emphasis on a set of distinct indexing terms rather than as textual material.

11.2 Assignment of Index Terms

The efficiency of any document retrieval system that uses a set of index terms to represent each document is clearly dependent on the choice of index terms. Also, the response to any search request is dependent on having a satisfactory formulation of the request in terms of the index terms.

If index terms are assigned manually by a reader who has a good understanding of the document subject then it is reasonable to suppose that the chosen index terms will be meaningful to others who are also familiar with the subject. However, the more specialized the subject matter, the more difficult it is to find a person with the knowledge and time to read the document with a view to assignment of index terms. The problem is particularly acute within a research establishment that employs specialists who require rapid information about available documents, but that is not sufficiently large to employ legions of document abstractors.

Most specialists who keep their own keyworded lists of relevant documents tend to index the documents with respect to their own current interests rather than with respect to all subjects to which the document may relate. Thus such lists tend to be inadequate after any change in the direction of development of the particular specialization. In this respect an automatic allocation of index terms, either by a relatively unskilled person or by a machine, may be superior to that of a specialist in the field. On the other hand, any automatic assignment of index terms based only on extraction of elements of the text of documents will at best describe only what the author has emphasized as the subject matter, and it may overlook important applications not stressed by him.

A very rapid procedure for choice of index terms is to use words that appear in the title of a document, with possible addition of the names of the authors. Such addition is useful because it provides a link to other documents by the same author. Nonessential words, such as articles and prepositions, may be omitted. Although title words do not always provide an accurate indication of the subject matter, most authors and editors of scientific material tend to choose titles with some care. For a given cost, and with expenditure of relatively unskilled help, the use of title words has much to recommend it as a choice of index terms. An obvious extension is to include also the words that appear in section or chapter headings, but this clearly produces a significant increase in the number of index terms associated with any document.

For many documents of a nonscientific nature the title words afford a very poor indication of the subject matter. Examples of titles whose separate words provide no indication of subject matter, and yet are suitable titles for interpretation by a reader who has appropriate experience and intuition, are those of the books *The Gathering Storm* by Sir Winston Churchill and *Animal Farm* by George Orwell.

A purely automatic assignment of index terms may be made by noting the frequency of occurrence of all words in a document. Words of common stem may be combined, and reference may be made to a stop list in order to eliminate certain common words such as prepositions or words that occur so frequently as to have little indexing value. From the resulting list of words the ones of highest frequency may be chosen as the index terms for the document. Such a procedure for choice of index terms is discussed by Luhn,[1,2] who also discusses automatic grouping of words and machine preparation of abstracts. It is clear that, apart from the computer time required to calculate word frequencies and eliminate words contained in a stop list, to place an entire document text on punched cards, paper tape, or magnetic tape for computer input is very time consuming and hence expensive if performed by manual means. However, with the development of optical readers as computer input devices, and with the increased use of data on paper tape for purposes of typesetting the procedure is becoming more economical.

Index terms may also be deduced from examination, either manually or by machine, of the abstract of a document. In many instances, however, automatic analysis of an abstract leads to surprisingly poor results even if the abstract gives a clear indication of the document content. This is due, in part, to the fact that the traditional purpose of an abstract is to summarize the approach and conclusions of the author, whereas the purpose of a set of index terms is to summarize what the document is about. However, when index terms are derived by some other procedure it may prove useful to augment them by addition of the words that occur most frequently in the abstract.

Consider the following document title and abstract.[3]

Title: A Bibliographic Search by Computer.

Abstract: Updating plasma–physics data was a chance to experiment with informa-

---

[1] H. P. Luhn, "A statistical approach to mechanized encoding and searching of literary information," *IBM Journal of Research and Development* 1 (1957).

[2] H. P. Luhn, "Auto-encoding of documents for information retrieval systems," in *Modern Trends in Documentation,* M. Boaz, ed. (New York: Pergamon, 1959), pp. 45–58.

[3] S. C. Brown, "A bibliographic search by computer," *Physics Today* (1966):59–64.

tion and programs of the Technical Information Project at MIT. The computer searched for indicative words in titles, papers that shared bibliographical references and those that referred to papers that have become classics in plasma physics.

The title suggests the three index terms

BIBLIOGRAPHIC, SEARCH, COMPUTER

which give a good indication of the subject matter of the document. The three most frequently occurring words in the abstract are

PLASMA-PHYSICS, INFORMATION, PAPERS.

When examined alone these last three words give a misleading impression of the subject matter, although the entire abstract provides a clear indication of the subject discussed in the document. If these three words are added to the three suggested by the title the resulting six index terms appear to form a satisfactory set.

Now consider the following document title and abstract.[4]

Title: The Association Factor in Information Retrieval.

Abstract: This paper describes an all computer document retrieval system that can find documents related to a request even though they may not be indexed by the exact terms of the request, and can present these documents in the order of their relevance to the request. The key to this ability lies in the application of a statistical formula by which the computer calculates the degree of association between pairs of index terms. With proper manipulation of these associations (entirely within the machine) a vocabulary of synonyms, near synonyms and other words closely related to any given term or group of terms is derived. Such a vocabulary related to a group of request terms is believed to be a much more powerful tool for selecting documents from a collection than has been available heretofore. By noting the number of matching terms between this extended list of request terms and the terms used to index a document, and with due regard for their degree of association, documents are selected by the computer and arranged in the order of their relevance to the request.

The title suggests the following four index terms

ASSOCIATION, FACTOR, INFORMATION, RETRIEVAL

The three most commonly occurring words in the abstract are

DOCUMENT, TERMS, REQUEST

and these occur significantly more frequently than any other word. After examination of the entire document it is believed that a satisfactory short list of index terms might be chosen as

TERM, ASSOCIATION, COMPUTER, INFORMATION, RETRIEVAL.

[4] H. E. Stiles, "The association factor in information retrieval," *Journal of the Association for Computing Machinery* 8 (1961):271–279.

Thus if index terms are to be chosen without reading the entire document, the four title words are more satisfactory than the three words that occur most frequently in the abstract. On the other hand, if the three words from the abstract are added to the four title words there result seven index terms that may be more useful than only the four from the title.

It may be noted that a computer analysis of the entire text of the preceding document has been reported by Booth.[5] The frequencies of words in the text were compared with their frequencies in general English text as listed by Dewey.[6] Retaining only those words whose frequencies in the document are at least 10 times greater than their frequencies in the same length of general English text led to the following set of index terms.

```
TERMS,  REQUEST,  DOCUMENTS,  TERM,  DOCUMENT,  ASSOCIATION,
GENERALIZATION,  LIST,  INDEXED,  USED,  PROFILES,  NUMBER,
SECOND,  RELATED,  INFORMATION,  INDEX,  COLLECTION,  SYSTEM,
PROFILE,  RELEVANCE,  EXPANDED,  THIN,  STEP,  STATISTICAL,
FRICTION,  FILM,  FACTORS,  EXPOSURE,  APPEAR,  SYNONYMS,
RETRIEVAL,  LANGUAGE.
```

Of these words, the first three occurred more than 100 times more frequently in the text than in general English text of the same length. These three words are also the ones, apart from differences between singular and plural, that occur most frequently in the abstract.

It may be noted that although the index terms of Booth do suggest, to some extent, the content of the article they are far from being the most compact, or efficient, set of index terms.

Although for the two documents just considered the index terms may be chosen from the title, with possible addition of words from the abstract, the extent to which such a choice is satisfactory varies considerably with the field to which the document relates. In general it appears that papers in specialized scientific journals tend to have titles whose subject words may be used as index terms. This is less true of articles that appear in trade journals. Titles of articles in the field of history or English tend to describe article content in terms of emotional or intuitive associations and hence may be useless as a source of index terms.

A general discussion of the problems that arise in connection with choice of keywords to index documents is given by Bourne[7] and by Vickery.[8]

---

[5] A. D. Booth, "Characterizing documents—A trial of an automatic method," *Computers and Automation* 14 (1965):32–33.

[6] G. Dewey, *Relativ(sic) Frequency of English Speech Sounds* (Cambridge, Mass.: Harvard University Press, 1950).

[7] C. P. Bourne, *Methods of Information Handling* (New York: Wiley, 1963), Chapter 2.

[8] B. C. Vickery, *On Retrieval System Theory* 2nd. edition (London: Butterworths, 1965).

Problems of classification and indexing in the social sciences are discussed by Foskett.[9]

It has been suggested by Maloney et al.[10] that the internal index of a document be used as the source of index terms. An alternative would be to use a table of contents or chapter headings, possibly with section headings as a lower hierarchy of terms. However, many journal articles and short reports have neither an internal index nor a table of contents, although many such documents do contain internal section headings. As illustrated by these authors, even a very carefully compiled internal index may fail to point to some of the most important concepts in the document, since at the time of writing the author may have been unaware of certain implications of his work.

For choice of index terms for documents in the social sciences de Grazia[11] has suggested that they should be chosen to answer the questions "Who says? Who does what with whom, where and when, by what means, why, and how does he know so?" With this in mind he subdivided index words of a "Universal Reference System" under the following headings:

1. Topics (action pattern described in the work). Subdivided into time–space–culture, institutional, manipulative, etc., each of which is further subdivided.
2. Methodology (used or dealt with by author). Subdivided into ethical standards, concepts, interviews, etc., with each heading further subdivided.
3. Unique descriptions such as colonial, Nazi, UNESCO.

Dyson[12] has suggested that the languages of scientific disciplines form a system of interlocking vocabularies, each with some definite structure. His suggested division of vocabulary in use by chemists and biochemists is as follows:

A) Animal names and related words.
B) Biochemical and physiological chemical terms.
C) General scientific (chemical) terms.
D) Drug and related names from CBAC.
E) Chemical element roots.

[9] D. J. Foskett, *Classification and Indexing in the Social Sciences* (London: Butterworths, 1963).

[10] C. J. Maloney, J. Duke, and S. Green, Indexing reports by computer. Proceedings of Colloquium on Technical Preconditions for Retrieval Centre Operations. Sparton, Washington, D.C., 1965.

[11] A. de Grazia, "The Universal Reference System," *American Behavioral Scientist* 8 (1965):3–14.

[12] G. M. Dyson, "Computer input and the semantic organization of scientific terms—I," *Information Storage and Retrieval* 3 (1967):35–115.

F1) Prefixes.
F2) Suffixes.
G) Geological.
H) Chemical engineering terms.
J) Management, business and legal terms.
K) Greek letters.
L) Analytical chemical terms.
M) Micro-organisms.
N) Counting series (numbers).
O) Preparative and chemical apparatus.
P) Physics terms.
Q)
R) Registry numbers—trivial names.
S) Registry numbers—systematic names.
T) Some common chemicals.
V) Vegetable words and related names.
X) Proper names (persons, countries).
Z) Semantic indicators.

Of the words listed by Dyson there are approximately 2500 in vocabulary C alone. He believes that a complete listing of all categories might involve up to 200,000 words. As a result of the analysis Dyson concludes that there is a basic vocabulary common to the majority of experimental disciplines, that for each subdiscipline there is a special vocabulary of words that are essentially the names of forms and systems of matter, and that for each subdiscipline there is also a specific vocabulary of specialized terms that form the so-called jargon of the subdisciplines.

It appears that a simple search for words of the various vocabularies should allow document classification into subdisciplines of the form just described. Further subdivision may require a finer analysis of vocabulary, or may be better undertaken by other methods. The vocabularies peculiar to various disciplines may be estimated from examination of thesauri and technical dictionaries. Unfortunately there are relatively few disciplines for which word frequency, or structure, statistics are available.

11.3 Relative Frequencies of Terms in Text of Documents

If the full text of a document is in computer readable form, a list may be made of all terms in descending order of their frequencies. Suppose a particular term occurs significantly more frequently in the document than would be predicted from a knowledge of its frequency of occurrence in general English text. It might then be concluded that its increased frequency of occurrence either provides some indication of the special subject matter of the document or else provides some information about the author's style of writing. The present section is concerned with the extent to which increased frequencies of word occurrences indicate the subject matter of documents.

As mentioned in Section 7.2, a list of the frequencies of words in various types of English text is given by Kučera and Francis, who examined a total of 1 million words in which there occurred 50,406 different terms.[13] The text samples covered a wide range of subject categories, and hence the listed frequencies may be used to predict the frequencies of terms in general text. The most frequent 200 words of the Kučera and Francis list are shown in Table 11.1.

Suppose the full text of a document is examined, and the 50 most frequent words are listed in descending order of frequency. Let N denote the total number of words in the text, and let D denote the number of different words. For the ith term (term$_i$) let p_i, q_i, and r_i be defined as follows:

$$p_i = \frac{(\text{Frequency of term}_i \text{ in the document text}) \times 1000}{N},$$

$$q_i = \frac{\text{Frequency of term}_i \text{ as listed by Kučera and Francis}}{1000},$$

$$r_i = \frac{p_i}{q_i}.$$

Then r_i is the relative frequency of term$_i$ in the particular document text measured in relation to its frequency of occurrence in general text.

For a particular set of seven documents the values of p_i and q_i for up to 50 words of most frequent occurrence are listed in Table 11.2. The words underlined are those for which r_i exceeds 10. A description of each document is given here.

Doc 1:   H. E. Stiles, "The association factor in information retrieval," *Journal of ACM* 8 (1961):271–279.

   For this document $N = 3188$ and $D = 777$. The abstract is listed in the previous section.

Doc 2:   G. D. Lowenstein and V. C. Anderson, "Quick characterisation of the directional response of point array," *Journal of the Acoustical Society of America* 43 (1968):32–46.

---

[13] H. Kučera, and W. N. Francis, *Computational Analysis of Present-Day American English* (Brown University Press, 1967).

Table 11.1

Most Frequent Words and Their Frequencies in the General English Text Examined by Kačera and Francis.

THE	69971	OUT	2096	DOWN	895	TAKE	611
OF	36411	SO	1984	SHOULD	888	THREE	610
AND	28852	SAID	1961	BECAUSE	883	STATES	605
TO	26149	WHAT	1908	EACH	877	HIMSELF	603
A	23237	UP	1895	JUST	872	FEW	601
IN	21341	ITS	1858	THOSE	850	HOUSE	591
THAT	10595	ABOUT	1815	PEOPLE	847	USE	589
IS	10099	INTO	1791	MR	839	DURING	585
WAS	9816	THAN	1789	HOW	834	WITHOUT	583
HE	9543	THEM	1789	TOO	832	AGAIN	578
FOR	9489	CAN	1772	LITTLE	831	PLACE	571
IT	8756	ONLY	1747	STATE	808	AMERICAN	569
WITH	7289	OTHER	1702	GOOD	807	AROUND	561
AS	7250	NEW	1635	VERY	796	HOWEVER	552
HIS	6997	SOME	1617	MAKE	794	HOME	547
ON	6742	COULD	1599	WORLD	787	SMALL	542
BE	6377	TIME	1599	STILL	782	FOUND	536
AT	5378	THESE	1573	OWN	772	MRS	534
BY	5305	TWO	1412	SEE	772	THOUGHT	515
I	5173	MAY	1400	MEN	763	WENT	507
THIS	5146	THEN	1377	WORK	760	SAY	504
HAD	5133	DO	1363	LONG	755	PART	500
NOT	4609	FIRST	1360	GET	750	ONCE	499
ARE	4393	ANY	1345	HERE	750	GENERAL	497
BUT	4381	MY	1319	BETWEEN	730	HIGH	497
FROM	4369	NOW	1314	BOTH	730	1	496
OR	4207	SUCH	1303	. . .	721	UPON	495
HAVE	3941	LIKE	1290	LIFE	715	SCHOOL	492
AN	3747	OUR	1252	BEING	712	EVERY	491
THEY	3618	OVER	1236	UNDER	707	DON'T	489
WHICH	3562	MAN	1207	NEVER	698	DOES	485
ONE	3292	ME	1181	DAY	686	GOT	482
YOU	3286	EVEN	1171	SAME	686	UNITED	482
WERE	3284	MOST	1160	ANOTHER	683	LEFT	480
HER	3037	MADE	1125	KNOW	683	NUMBER	472
ALL	3001	AFTER	1070	WHILE	680	COURSE	465
SHE	2859	ALSO	1096	LAST	676	WAR	464
THERE	2724	DID	1044	MIGHT	672	UNTIL	461
WOULD	2714	MANY	1030	US	672	ALWAYS	458
THEIR	2670	BEFORE	1016	GREAT	665	AWAY	456
WE	2653	MUST	1013	OLD	660	SOMETHING	450
HIM	2619	Ø	1010	YEAR	660	2	450
BEEN	2472	THROUGH	969	OFF	639	FACT	447
HAS	2439	BACK	967	COME	630	THOUGH	442
WHEN	2331	YEARS	949	SINCE	628	WATER	442
WHO	2252	WHERE	938	AGAINST	626	LESS	438
WILL	2244	MUCH	937	GO	626	PUBLIC	438
MORE	2216	YOUR	923	CAME	622	PUT	437
NO	2201	WAY	909	RIGHT	613	THINK	433
IF	2199	WELL	897	USED	612	ALMOST	432

Table 11.2

Frequencies p_i of Terms in Text of Certain Documents. The q_i Are According to Kučera and Francis.

STILES:	p_i	q_i	LOWENSTEIN:	p_i	q_i	HOLTSLANDER:	p_i	q_i
THE	77	70	THE	96	70	THE	94	69
OF	44	36	OF	62	36	OF	42	36
TERMS	31	.163	A	33	23	TO	31	26
TO	25	26	ARRAY	25	.011	AND	25	29
AND	21	29	AND	24	29	N	23	.041
A	21	23	FOR	21	9.4	IN	22	21
IN	18	21	TO	21	26	DI	19	
WE	16	2.6	IS	18	10	O	16	.022
REQUEST	15	.049	FIG	16	.072	MCH	15	.055
DOCUMENTS	13	.019	IN	14	21	SF	14	
BY	13	5.3	AS	13	7.2	WAS	13	9.8
IS	13	10	LOBE	13	.003	A	13	23
TERM	11	.079	DIRECTION	11	.134	THAT	12	10
BE	10	6.4	ARE	9.3	4.4	WITH	12	7.2
FOR	10	9.5	THAT	9.3	10	H	11	.074
THAT	10	11	ALPHA	8.5	.006	REACTION	10	.124
ARE	10	4.4	SIDE	8.5	.380	MIXTURE	9.4	.030
DOCUMENT	10	.013	BETA	7.8	.002	BE	8.6	6.3
WITH	8.8	7.3	BY	7.8	5.3	SCAVENGERS	7.8	
WHICH	8.2	3.6	ELEMENT	7.8	.052	ARE	7.1	4.3
ASSOCIATION	7.8	.132	ON	7.8	6.7	AT	7.1	5.4
OUR	7.2	1.3	THIS	7.1	5.1	BY	7.1	5.3
AS	6.9	7.3	ARRIVAL	6.4	.023	C	7.1	.130
HAVE	6.9	3.9	BE	6.4	6.3	ELECTRON	7.1	.030
NOT	6.9	4.6	CAN	6.4	1.7	FROM	7.1	4.4
ON	6.9	6.7	DIRECTIONS	6.4	.030	HD	7.1	
GENERATION	6.6	.055	FUNCTION	6.4	.113	MIXTURES	7.1	.004
THIS	6.6	5.1	LEVEL	6.4	.213	WERE	7.1	3.3
FIRST	6.3	1.4	PI	6.4	.003	YIELDS	7.1	.007

	p_i	q_i
WOULD	6.3	2.7
BEEN	6.0	2.5
NUMBER	6.0	.472
LIST	5.6	.133
INDEXED	5.3	
PROFILES	5.3	.003
USED	5.3	.612
EACH	5.0	.877
ALL	4.7	3.0
WILL	4.7	2.2
OR	4.4	4.2
THESE	4.4	1.6
WERE	4.4	3.3
AN	4.1	3.7
HAD	4.1	5.1
ONLY	4.1	1.7
INDEX	3.8	.081
RELATED	3.8	.102
SECOND	3.8	.373
THIN	3.8	.092
INFORMATION	3.5	.269

	p_i	q_i
DB	5.7	.007
DISTORTION	5.7	.002
LATTICE	5.7	.008
PARAMETERS	5.7	.004
STEERED	5.7	1.6
THESE	5.7	.005
TRIANGULAR	5.7	7.2
WITH	5.7	

	p_i	q_i
EFFECT	6.3	.21
G	6.3	.044
IS	6.3	10
MOLE	6.3	.004
NOT	6.3	4.6
PRESENT	6.3	.377
SCAVENGER	6.3	.001
THAN	5.4	1.8
ADDITION	5.4	.142
D	5.4	.090
FOR	5.4	9.5
HAS	5.4	2.4
THIS	5.4	5.1
YIELD	5.4	.035
ADDED	5.4	.172
AS	5.4	7.3
BINARY	5.4	.076
FORMED	5.4	8.7
IT	5.4	.149
RESULTS	5.4	.135
S	5.4	

NEEDHAM:	p_i	q_i		p_i	q_i
THE	73	70	A	46	23
OF	38	36	THE	46	70
TO	26	26	OF	35	36
IN	24	21	AND	25	29
A	21	23	IN	20	21
CIRCUIT	20	.023	TO	17	26
THIS	16	5.1	IS	14	10
AND	14	29	ARE	12	4.4
INTEGRATED	13	.011	BE	9	6.4

ORWELL:	p_i	q_i
THE	44	70
I	42	5.1
OF	33	36
TO	31	26
A	30	23
AND	30	29
IN	21	21
THAT	14	11
IS	13	10

Table 11.2 (*Continued*)

Word			Word			Word		
BE	13	6.4	OR	9	4.2	IT	12	8.7
CIRCUITS	13	.004	FOR	8	9.5	MY	11	1.3
THAT	13	11	WILL	8	2.2	WAS	10	9.8
WE	13	2.6	CHIPS	7	.003	ONE	8.7	3.3
FOR	12	9.5	CIRCUIT	7	.023	FOR	8.3	9.5
PACKAGE	12	.020	IT	7	8.7	BUT	8.0	4.4
WHICH	11	3.6	SIZE	7	.138	HAVE	7.6	3.9
IT	10	8.7	THAT	7	13	WITH	7.6	7.3
IS	9.2	10	AN	6	6.6	THIS	6.9	5.1
WITH	8.6	7.3	AT	6	5.4	WHICH	6.9	3.5
AS	7.3	7.3	CAN	6	4.6	OR	6.5	4.2
CHIP	7.3	.017	OTHER	6	1.7	NOT	6.2	4.6
HAS	7.3	2.4	RADIO	6	.120	ABOUT	5.8	1.8
AN	6.6	3.7	THAN	6	1.8	AT	5.1	5.4
INDIVIDUAL	6.6	.293	THEY	6	3.6	BE	5.1	6.4
ON	6.6	6.7	ALREADY	6	.273	BOOK	5.1	.193
WILL	6.6	2.2	BY	5	5.3	ON	5.1	6.7
ARE	5.9	4.4	CIRCUITS	5	.004	ALL	4.7	3.0
BEEN	5.9	2.5	ELECTRONIC	5	.068	ARE	4.7	4.4
WOULD	5.9	2.7	MAY	5	1.4	FROM	4.7	4.4
BY	5.3	5.3	NOT	5	4.6	HE	4.7	9.5
OR	5.3	4.2	ON	5	6.7	TIME	4.7	1.6
THREE	5.3	.610	SO	5		AS	4.3	7.3
CAN	4.6	4.6				WERE	4.3	3.3
DIMENSIONAL	4.6	.011				WRITE	4.3	.106
FORM	4.6	.370				POLITICAL	4.0	.258
COST	4.0	.229				AN	3.6	3.7
FIGURE	4.0	.209				WHAT	3.6	1.9
LEADS	4.0	.033				YEARS	3.6	.949

MIGHT 4.0 .672

HAD	3.3	5.1
ME	3.3	1.2
WILL	3.3	2.2
WOULD	3.3	2.7
WRITING	3.3	.117
YOU	3.3	3.3
AGE	2.9	.227
DO	2.9	1.4
HIS	2.9	6.9
KIND	2.9	.313
LIKE	2.9	1.3
MORE	2.9	2.2

ZANELLI:	p_i	q_i
THE	77	70
OF	42	36
A	38	23
AND	29	29
IN	22	21
TO	20	26
IS	20	10
IT	13	8.7
AT	11	5.4
THAT	9.8	13
WAS	9.8	9.8
THERE	8.3	2.7
AN	6.8	3.7
BY	6.0	5.3
FOR	6.0	9.5
S	6.0	.135
WHICH	6.0	3.5
WITH	6.0	7.3

275

Table 11.2 (*Continued*)

AREA	5.3	.324
AS	5.3	7.3
DEPTH	5.3	.053
LAKES	5.3	.008
LAKE	5.3	.054
LLYDAW	5.3	
LLYN	5.3	
ON	5.3	6.7
WATER	5.3	.442
FEET	4.5	.283
THESE	4.5	1.6
WE	4.5	2.6
AGO	3.8	.246
BOAT	3.8	.072
BOTTOM	3.8	.088
BUT	3.8	4.4
GLASLYN	3.8	
HAVE	3.8	3.9

For this document $N = 1404$ and $D = 383$. The abstract is as follows:

The directional response of a two- or three-dimensional point array is a function of two independent directions and also a function of frequency. A suitable mapping of these three parameters into a pseudodirection and a pseudofrequency allows the examination of the major and minor lobe structure of the array response with only a two-parameter computation. This method has been applied during the design of a 32-element planar array, to permit adjustment of the element positions for a minimum and uniform minor-lobe structure.

Doc 3: W. J. Holtslander and G. R. Freeman, "Competition between scavengers in the vapor-phase radiolysis of hydrocarbons," *Journal of Physical Chemistry* 71 (1967):2562–2564.

For this document $N = 1275$ and $D = 368$. The abstract is as follows:

When two electron scavengers S_1 and S_2 are present in a radiolysis system, the reaction $S_1^- + S_2 \rightarrow S_1 + S_2^-$ can occur if S_2 has a greater electron affinity than does S_1 and if S_1^- has a long enough lifetime to enable it to encounter an S_2 and react with it. In 380 Torr of methylcyclohexane vapor at $110°$, the half-lives of N_2O^- and SF_6^-, with respect to decomposition, are $\geq 10^{-4}$ sec and $\geq 10^{-7}$ sec, respectively. The electron affinities of the three electron scavengers used apparently decrease in the order $DI > SF_6 > N_2O$.

Doc 4: G. A. Needham, "Advanced integrated circuit packaging," *SCP and Solid State Technology* (June 1965):22–29.

For this document $N = 1515$ and $D = 500$. The abstract is as follows:

Current research and development in the field of integrated circuit packaging is treated in this article. It is pointed out that the package as we know it today may be completely obsolete in the next three of four years if present research bears fruit. The discussion includes a survey of past, present, and possible future methods of lead attachment; the "flip-chip," or upsidedown mounting technique; elimination of the individual chip package which has the potential of a twenty to one saving in space; and the inclusion of many circuit functions within a single chip. Finally three-dimensional packaging as opposed to the planar package is discussed.

Doc 5:   The Chip

This is the title of an anonymous article published in a popular magazine and related in subject matter to Doc 4. $N = 1018$.

Doc 6:   G. Orwell, "Why I Write."

This is contained in *A Collection of Essays by George Orwell* (New York: Doubleday, 1954), pp. 313–320. $N = 2758$ and $D = 947$.

Doc 7:   L. Zanelli, "The Land of King Arthur," *Yachts and Yachting* (February 2, 1968): 292–293.

This article is about diving in the Welsh Lakes. $N = 1324$ and $D = 567$. There is no abstract. It may be noted that the title of the article is a poorer indication of the subject matter than are the underlined words in Table 10.2.

The terms listed in Table 11.3 are those for which r_i has a value of at least 10. It may be noted that many of these terms do provide an indication of the subject matter of the document. In fact, it might be concluded that in several instances the sets of listed terms are superior to titles in describing what the document is about. On the other hand the title often provides more indication of what the author was attempting to do.

A more difficult problem than automatic selection of index terms is the problem of computer abstracting of documents. Since frequently occurring phrases often provide information about document content, it is tempting to consider the possibility of using a computer to reduce full text of many sentences to a short abstract of only a few important sentences. Such sentences may or may not occur as sentences in the full text. Use of a computer for automatic abstracting was suggested by Luhn[14] and has been discussed by many authors. The problems that arise are as outlined by Edmundson.[15,16]

[14] H. P. Luhn, "The automatic creation of literature abstracts," *IBM Journal of Research and Development* 2 (1958):159–165.

[15] H. P. Edmundson, and R. E. Wyllys, "Automatic abstracting and indexing—survey and recommendations," *Communications of the Association for Computing Machinery* 4 (1961):226–234.

[16] H. P. Edmundson, "Problems in automatic abstracting," *Communications of the Association for Computing Machinery* 7 (1964):259–263.

Table 11.3 (*Continued*)
Relative Frequencies r_i of Terms in Text of Certain Documents.

STILES:	r_i	LOWENSTEIN:	r_i	HOLTSLANDER:	r_i
INDEXED	>5300	DB	>5000	MCH	15000
PROFILES	1800	LOBE	4300	SF	14000
DOCUMENT	770	BETA	3900	SCAVENGERS	>7800
DOCUMENTS	680	LATTICE	2800	HD	>7100
REQUESTS	300	ARRAY	2300	SCAVENGER	6300
TERMS	190	PI	2100	BINARY	>5400
TERM	140	ALPHA	1400	MIXTURES	1800
GENERATION	120	STEERED	1400	MOLE	1600
ASSOCIATION	59	TRIANGULAR	1100	YIELDS	1000
INDEX	47	DISTORTION	810	DI	860
THIN	41	PARAMETERS	710	N	560
LIST	38	ARRIVAL	280	MIXTURE	310
RELATED	37	FIG	220	O	290
INFORMATION	13	DIRECTIONS	210	ELECTRON	240
NUMBER	13	ELEMENT	150	H	150
SECOND	10	DIRECTION	82	YIELD	150
		FUNCTION	57	G	143
		LEVEL	30	REACTION	81
		SIDE	22	FORMED	71
				D	60
				C	55
				S	40
				ADDITION	38
				RESULTS	36
				ADDED	31
				EFFECT	30
				PRESENT	17

NEEDHAM:	r_i	The Chip:	r_i	ORWELL:	r_i
CIRCUITS	3000	CHIPS	2300	WRITE	41
INTEGRATED	1100	CIRCUITS	1200	WRITING	28
CIRCUIT	870	CIRCUIT	300	BOOK	26
PACKAGE	600	ELECTRONIC	74	AGE	13
CHIP	430	SIZE	51		
DIMENSIONAL	420	RADIO	50		
LEADS	120	ALREADY	22		
INDIVIDUAL	22				
FIGURE	19				
COST	17				
FORM	12				

Table 11.3 *(Continued)*

ZANELLI:	r_i
LLYN	5300
LLYDAW	5300
GLASYLN	3800
LAKES	670
DEPTH	100
LAKE	98
BOAT	53
S	44
BOTTOM	43
AREA	16
FEET	16
AGO	15
WATER	12

11.4 Document Term and Term Connection Matrices

Consider a data base in which each document is described by a set of assigned relevance values, or weights, that indicate the degree to which each of a given set of index terms is relevant to the subject matter of the document. An index term that affords no useful indication of the document content may be given a relevance value of 0, whereas a term that is highly relevant may be given a weight of 1. In general, all relevance values will be supposed to lie between 0 and 1, although in some instances it may be convenient to allow values in the range -1 to 1.

The relevance of the ith term to the nth document may be denoted by $d_i(n)$, and the set of all $d_i(n)$ may be arranged to form a document term matrix as introduced in Section 2.8. Thus if there are N documents and M index terms, the document term matrix is

$$\mathbf{D} = \begin{bmatrix} d_1(1) & d_2(1) & \cdots & d_M(1) \\ d_1(2) & d_2(2) & \cdots & d_M(2) \\ \cdot & \cdot & & \cdot \\ \cdot & \cdot & & \cdot \\ \cdot & \cdot & & \cdot \\ d_1(N) & d_2(N) & \cdots & d_M(N) \end{bmatrix}$$

of N rows and M columns.

With an efficient choice of index terms it is to be expected that in any row of the document term matrix most of the elements are zero. The nonzero elements indicate the particular index terms that are relevant to the corresponding document.

The M relevance values $d_1(n)$, $d_2(n)$, ..., $d_M(n)$ for the nth document may be regarded as components of a vector in space of M dimensions. Likewise, for the ith index terms the set of N relevance values $d_i(1)$, $d_i(2)$, ..., $d_i(N)$ may be regarded as a vector in space of N dimensions.

It is often convenient to assign only values of 0 or 1 to the relevance values $d_i(n)$ so that each index term and each document are regarded as either totally relevant or totally irrelevant. Clearly, such a classification may introduce a distortion of fact. However, the distortion is only similar to that produced by use of a title or abstract to describe the content of a document. One important difference between a set of index terms and a document title or abstract is that the set of index terms contains no grammatical structure and therefore does not describe functional relations. On the other hand, titles and abstracts usually contain some words that do not add to an understanding of the content.

If the values of the $d_i(n)$ are not restricted to values of 0 and 1 they may be said to form a weighted coordinate index of each document. It is sometimes convenient to restrict the relevance values to particular quantized values such as 0, .5, 1 or such as 0, .25, .5, .75, 1. This is usually sufficiently accurate since assignment of relevance often depends on subjective human judgment or on some empirical measure of relevance.

It may be noted that if the elements of the document–term matrix are restricted to have values of 0 or 1 then

$$\sum_i d_i(n) = \text{Number of keywords associated with the } n\text{th document.}$$

$$\sum_n d_i(n) = \text{Number of documents relevant to the } i\text{th keyword.}$$

Furthermore, if a matrix $\mathbf{K}$ of elements k_{ij} is defined by the equation

$$k_{ij} = d_i(1)d_j(1) + d_i(2)d_j(2) + \cdots + d_i(N)d_j(N).$$

then $\mathbf{K}$ is a square matrix of M rows and M columns. It may be written in the form

$$\mathbf{K} = \mathbf{D}^\mathrm{T}\mathbf{D}$$

in which $\mathbf{D}^\mathrm{T}$ denotes the transpose of the matrix $\mathbf{D}$.

In the equation that defines k_{ij} the term $d_i(1)d_j(1)$ is equal to 1 or 0, according as the first document is, or is not, relevant to both the ith and jth terms. A similar observation regarding the subsequent terms leads to the conclusion that:

k_{ij} = Number of documents relevant to both the ith and jth index terms.

The matrix $\mathbf{K}$ may be called the term connection matrix since its elements indicate the number of documents that are relevant to pairs of index terms. Each diagonal element k_{ii} of $\mathbf{K}$ indicates the number of documents that relate to the ith term.

The matrix $\mathbf{K}^2$ has elements $k_{ij}^{(2)}$ whose values are given by

$$k_{ij}^2 = \sum_p k_{ip} k_{pj} = \sum_p \sum_r \sum_s d_i\,(r)d_p\,(r)d_p\,(s)d_j\,(s)$$

Now $d_i\,(r)d_p\,(r)d_p\,(s)d_j\,(s) = 1$ only if the pth term is relevant to an rth document that is relevant to the ith term, and the pth term is also relevant to an sth document that is relevant to jth term. It may therefore be said that the ith and jth terms are linked by $k_{ij}^{(2)}$ pairs of documents, the definition of a linked pair of documents being that both documents have at least one index term in common.

If the ith and jth index terms are contained respectively in documents y_{i_1} and y_{i_n}, and there is a sequence of n documents

$$y_{i_1},\, y_{i_2},\, \ldots,\, y_{i_n}$$

such that adjacent documents of the sequence have at least one index term in common, then the ith and jth terms may be said to be linked by a link of length n documents. It may readily be shown that if $k_{ij}^{(n)}$ denotes an element of the matrix $\mathbf{K}^n$ then

$$k_{ij}^{(n)} = \text{Number of links of length } n \text{ documents}$$
$$\text{between the } i\text{th and } j\text{th index terms.}$$

If a subset of the entire set of index terms contains a large number of links of small length, then the various terms of the subset are closely related to each other in the sense that they tend to be relevant to the same documents.

If $k_{ij} = 0$, but $k_{ij}^{(2)}$ is significantly different from zero, it might be supposed that many documents relevant to one of the ith and jth terms also have some relevance to each other. Thus the set of index terms initially assigned to each document might be enlarged by addition of further terms found by examination of the elements of $\mathbf{K}^2$, then $\mathbf{K}^3$, and so forth.

In the instance that the elements of the document term matrix are not restricted to have values only of 0 and 1 the matrix elements $k_{ij}^{(n)}$ represent sums of weighted links, but the concept of enlargement of relevance remains valid.

An important property of the matrix $\mathbf{K}$, and also of each matrix $\mathbf{K}^{(2)}$, is that regardless of the number of documents the matrix $\mathbf{K}$ is a square matrix of M rows and M columns. Computations involving the matrix $\mathbf{K}$ are generally less cumbersome than those that involve the matrix $\mathbf{D}$.

In order to illustrate some of the preceding remarks consider a set of three documents whose titles are:

Doc$_1$: EFFECT OF TEMPERATURE ON VELOCITY OF SOUND
Doc$_2$: TEMPERATURE IN THE OCEAN
Doc$_3$: SOUND PROPAGATION

If four terms VELOCITY, SOUND, OCEAN, and TEMPERATURE are chosen to index the documents the matrices $\mathbf{D}$ and $\mathbf{D}^{\mathrm{T}}$ are

$$\mathbf{D} = \begin{bmatrix} 1 & 1 & 0 & 1 \\ 0 & 0 & 1 & 1 \\ 0 & 1 & 0 & 0 \end{bmatrix}, \qquad \mathbf{D}^{\mathrm{T}} = \begin{bmatrix} 1 & 0 & 0 \\ 1 & 0 & 1 \\ 0 & 1 & 0 \\ 1 & 1 & 0 \end{bmatrix}$$

The matrices $\mathbf{K} = \mathbf{D}^{\mathrm{T}}\mathbf{D}$ and $\mathbf{K}^2$ are

$$\mathbf{K} = \begin{bmatrix} 1 & 1 & 0 & 1 \\ 1 & 2 & 0 & 1 \\ 0 & 0 & 1 & 1 \\ 1 & 1 & 1 & 2 \end{bmatrix}, \qquad \mathbf{K}^2 = \begin{bmatrix} 3 & 4 & 1 & 4 \\ 4 & 6 & 1 & 5 \\ 1 & 1 & 2 & 3 \\ 4 & 5 & 3 & 7 \end{bmatrix}$$

A person interested in both SOUND and OCEAN would note that since $k_{23} = 0$ the subject is not covered by any single document of the collection. However, the fact that $k^{(2)}_{23} = 1$ suggests that the subject be studied by reference to a single pair of documents. In fact, since $k^{(2)}_{23} = k_{24}k_{43}$ the common index term is the fourth one TEMPERATURE, which is common to the pair of documents Doc_1 and Doc_2.

In the matrix $\mathbf{K}$ and its powers, the diagonal elements k_{ii} etc. are often significantly larger in value than the nondiagonal elements. The question arises as to what value of a nondiagonal element k_{ij} is to be regarded as being significantly different from zero. One method of answering this question is discussed here.

If N is the total number of documents the fraction of them that are relevant to the ith index term is k_{ii}/N. Similarly, the fraction relevant to the jth term is k_{jj}/N. If the ith and jth terms occur quite independently, with no tendency either to mutually associate or mutually exclude each other's association with documents, then the fraction of documents relevant to both terms is equal to $(k_{ii}/N)(k_{jj}/N)$. Hence for mutually independent index terms

$$k_{ij}/N = (k_{ii}/N)(k_{jj}/N)$$

and so

$$Nk_{ij}/k_{ii}k_{jj} = 1.$$

The preceding remarks suggest that the matrix $\mathbf{K}$ might be normalized by multiplication of each element k_{ij} by $N/(k_{ii}k_{jj})$. There then results a new matrix $\mathbf{F}$, which may be regarded as a normalized version of $\mathbf{K}$. Any nondiagonal elements of $\mathbf{F}$ that are significantly greater than 1 indicate a pair of index terms that tend to be mutually associated with certain documents more frequently than if they occurred independently. Similarly, any nondiagonal elements of $\mathbf{F}$ that are significantly less than 1 indicate a pair of keywords whose relevance to documents tends to be mutually exclusive.

For the matrix **K** just displayed the normalized matrix **F** is as follows

$$\begin{bmatrix} 3 & 1.5 & 0 & 1.5 \\ 1.5 & 1.5 & 0 & .75 \\ 0 & 0 & 3 & 1.5 \\ 1.5 & .75 & 1.5 & 1.5 \end{bmatrix}$$

Another possible choice of the matrix **F** is to define its elements f_{ij} by means of the equation

$$f_{ij} = \frac{k_{ij}}{(k_{ii}k_{jj})^{1/2}} \tag{11.1}$$

as has been done by Salton.[17] Alternatively Doyle[18] has defined it by the equation

$$f_{ij} = \frac{k_{ij}}{k_{ii} + k_{jj} - k_{ij}} \tag{11.2}$$

in which the denominator represents the number of documents that contain either, but not both, of the ith and jth terms. A further form of the matrix **F** has been used by Dennis[19] in the form

$$f_{ij} = \frac{Nk_{ij} - k_{ii}k_{jj}}{(Nk_{ii}k_{jj})^{1/2}} \tag{11.3}$$

The choice of index terms and their weights is discussed by Stiles (1961) in terms of association factors f_{ij} that are defined by the relation[20]

$$f_{ij} = \begin{cases} \log_{10}\left[\dfrac{(Nk_{ij} - k_{ii}k_{ij} - N/2)^2 N}{k_{ii}k_{jj}(N - k_{ii})(N - k_{jj})}\right] & \text{if } Nk_{ij} \geq k_{ii}k_{jj}. \\ 0 & \text{if } Nk_{ij} < k_{ii}k_{jj} \end{cases} \tag{11.4}$$

With such a definition of **F** the diagonal elements are

$$f_{ii} = \log_{10}\left\{\frac{[(N - k_{ii})k_{ii} - N/2]^2 N}{k_{ii}^2(N - k_{ii})^2}\right\}$$

It may be noted that if N is sufficiently large, and the ith index term is sufficiently significant that k_{ii} is not negligible, then $N/2$ may be neglected

[17] G. Salton, "Some hierarchical models for document retrieval," *American Documentation* 14 (1963):213–222.

[18] L. B. Doyle, "Indexing and abstracting by association," *American Documentation* 13 (1962):378–390.

[19] S. F. Dennis, "The construction of a thesaurus automatically from a sample of text," Symposium on Statistical Association Techniques for Mechanized Documentation, Washington, D.C., 1964.

[20] F. Yates, "Contingency tables involving small numbers and the chi square test," *Supplement to Journal of the Royal Statistical Society* 1 (1934):217–235.

in comparison with $(N - k_{ii})k_{ii}$ and so the diagonal elements have the approximate values

$$f_{ii} = \log_{10}N.$$

If a collection of 100 documents with four index terms gives rise to the term connection matrix

$$\mathbf{K} = \begin{bmatrix} 20 & 0 & 10 & 0 & 0 \\ 0 & 12 & 2 & 8 & 1 \\ 10 & 2 & 30 & 0 & 0 \\ 0 & 8 & 0 & 10 & 4 \\ 0 & 1 & 0 & 4 & 12 \end{bmatrix}$$

then computation of elements of $\mathbf{F}$ by use of (11.4) gives

$$\mathbf{F} = \begin{bmatrix} 1.98 & 0 & 0.56 & 0 & 0 \\ 0 & 2.00 & 0 & 1.62 & 0 \\ 0.56 & 0 & 1.98 & 0 & 0 \\ 0 & 1.62 & 0 & 1.95 & 0.75 \\ 0 & 0 & 0 & 0.75 & 2.00 \end{bmatrix}$$

It may be observed that, although the first and third keywords are common to 10 documents, and the second and fourth keywords are common to only 8 documents, yet the association factor $f_{24} = 1.62$ significantly exceeds the association factor $f_{13} = 0.56$. This is because k_{24} is larger in comparison to k_{22} and k_{44} than k_{13} is in comparison to k_{11} and k_{33}.

11.5 Term and Document Association Matrices

The term connection matrix may be used to determine pairs of index terms that tend to associate with the same documents, but such terms are not necessarily related in meaning. In fact, terms of similar meaning often tend to be excluded from association with the same documents since any such association represents some indexing redundancy.

A person who formulates a search question may use a term that is different from, although of similar meaning to, an index term used to index a relevant document. To allow for this it may prove convenient to introduce a term association matrix $\mathbf{T}$ whose element t_{ij} indicates the extent to which a document relevant to the ith index term may also be supposed relevant to the jth index term.

Consider, for example, a set of six documents indexed by five terms

WAVE, VELOCITY, SEA, OCEAN, WIND

according to the following document term matrix

$$\mathbf{D} = \begin{bmatrix} 1 & 1 & 0 & 0 & 0 \\ 1 & 0 & 1 & 0 & 0 \\ 1 & 0 & 0 & 1 & 0 \\ 0 & 1 & 0 & 0 & 1 \\ 0 & 0 & 1 & 0 & 1 \\ 0 & 0 & 0 & 1 & 1 \end{bmatrix}$$

A term association matrix equal to

$$\mathbf{T} = \begin{bmatrix} 1 & 0 & 0 & 0 & 0 \\ 0 & 1 & 0 & 0 & 0 \\ 0 & 0 & 1 & 1 & 0 \\ 0 & 0 & 1 & 1 & 0 \\ \frac{1}{2} & 0 & 0 & 0 & 1 \end{bmatrix}$$

might be used to indicate an assumed equivalence of meaning of the third and fourth indexing terms SEA and OCEAN. The fact that t is different from zero indicates that all documents indexed by the fifth term WIND are assumed to have some, but not total, relevance to the first term WAVE. However, since $t = 0$ it is not assumed that all documents indexed by WAVE are also relevant to the index term WIND.

The extended relevance of documents to terms may then be expressed by the new document term matrix

$$\mathbf{DT} = \begin{bmatrix} 1 & 1 & 0 & 0 & 0 \\ 1 & 0 & 1 & 1 & 0 \\ 1 & 0 & 1 & 1 & 0 \\ \frac{1}{2} & 1 & 0 & 0 & 1 \\ \frac{1}{2} & 0 & 1 & 1 & 1 \\ \frac{1}{2} & 0 & 1 & 1 & 1 \end{bmatrix}$$

which indicates, for example, that the fifth document is relevant to SEA, OCEAN, WIND, and (to a lesser extent) to WAVE.

It may be noted that, although the term connection matrix is symmetric since $k_{ij} = k_{ji}$, the same is not necessarily true of the term association matrix. Thus in the preceding example t_{15} is different from t_{51}.

Just as the term association matrix $\mathbf{T}$ may be used to indicate similarities in the meanings of descriptors, a document connection matrix $\mathbf{C}$ may be used to indicate document connections not expressed through the presence of mutual keywords. It may be formed from elements $c(m, n)$ chosen so that the value of $c(m, n)$ indicates the extent to which the nth document is regarded as associated in some manner with the mth document.

A special form of document connection matrix $\mathbf{C}$ is the citation matrix in which the presence of a nonzero element $c(m, n)$ indicates that the nth document is associated with the mth document in the sense that it is cited by the mth document. In order to ensure that each document is connected to itself each diagonal element is set equal to 1. In the subsequent discussion each document is therefore regarded as included in its own list of citations.

Consider a set of six documents. If the third document contains a citation to both the first and second document then $c(3, 1) = c(3, 2) = 1$. If also the sixth document contains a citation to the third then $c(6, 3) = 1$. The corresponding citation matrix is therefore

$$\mathbf{C} = \begin{bmatrix} 1 & 0 & 0 & 0 & 0 & 0 \\ 0 & 1 & 0 & 0 & 0 & 0 \\ 1 & 1 & 1 & 0 & 0 & 0 \\ 0 & 0 & 0 & 1 & 0 & 0 \\ 0 & 0 & 0 & 0 & 1 & 0 \\ 0 & 0 & 1 & 0 & 0 & 1 \end{bmatrix}$$

The elements $x_i (m)$ of the matrix $\mathbf{CD}$ are given by

$$x_i (m) = \sum_n c(m, n)d_i (n).$$

Thus if the elements of $\mathbf{C}$ and $\mathbf{D}$ are restricted to have only values of 1 and 0, the value of $x_i (m)$ is equal to the number of documents that contain the ith index term and are also cited by the mth document. The value of $x_i (m)$ is zero only if the ith term does not index the mth document or any of the documents cited by the mth document.

It may be noted that if $\mathbf{C}$ is a citation matrix the matrix $\mathbf{CC}^\mathrm{T}$ is a square symmetric matrix of N rows and N columns whose m, nth element indicates the number of documents cited by both the mth and nth documents. Likewise, $\mathbf{C}^\mathrm{T}\mathbf{C}$ is a square symmetric matrix of N rows and N columns whose m, nth element indicates the number of documents that cite both the mth and nth documents.

Documents are sometimes grouped by subject classes, which are further subdivided with respect to more specific subject specification. Thus each class may belong to a more general class, and may itself be subdivided into several more specific classes. Illustration of a hypothetical such classification for documents relating to history is shown in Figure 11.1.

Figure 11.1 illustrates a hierarchy of 20 index terms. Thus SOCIAL is used as a broader term than CHURCH, and ESTABLISHED is used as a narrower term than CHURCH. The figure indicates how a request for information may be made either more specific or more general. Thus a request for information on:

Influence of the CHURCH on POLITICAL EVENTS

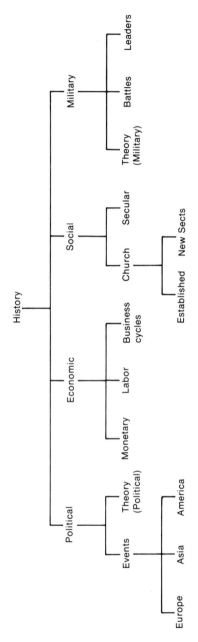

Figure 11.1. A hierarchy of broader and narrower terms in document classification.

may be specialized to:

`Influence of NEW SECTS in AMERICA`

and may be broadened to:

`Influence of SOCIAL on POLITICAL.`

The terms included in Figure 11.1 may be arranged as components x_i of a vector of dimension 20, and the hierarchy relations between the terms may be expressed by a hierarchy matrix $\mathbf{H}$ of 20 rows and 20 columns in which each element h_{ij} is defined by the relation

$$h_{ij} = \begin{cases} 1 & \text{if term } x_j \text{ is a narrower subdivision of term } x_i \\ 0 & \text{otherwise.} \end{cases}$$

It may be noted that multiplication of the vector [x] by the matrix $\mathbf{H}$ defines a vector $\mathbf{H}[x]$ as follows

$$\mathbf{H}[x] = \mathbf{H} \begin{bmatrix} \text{HISTORY} \\ \text{POLITICAL} \\ \text{ECONOMIC} \\ \text{SOCIAL} \\ \text{MILITARY} \\ \text{EVENTS} \\ \text{THEORY (POL)} \\ \text{MONETARY} \\ \text{LABOUR} \\ \text{BUS.CYCLES} \\ \text{CHURCH} \\ \text{SECULAR} \\ \text{THEORY (MIL)} \\ \text{BATTLES} \\ \text{LEADERS} \\ \text{EUROPE} \\ \text{ASIA} \\ \text{AMERICA} \\ \text{ESTABLISHED} \\ \text{NEW SECTS} \end{bmatrix} = \begin{bmatrix} \text{POLITICAL + ECONOMIC + SOCIAL + MILITARY} \\ \text{EVENTS + THEORY (POL)} \\ \text{MONETARY + LABOUR + BUS.CYCLES} \\ \text{CHURCH + SECULAR} \\ \text{THEORY (MIL) + BATTLES + LEADERS} \\ \text{EUROPE + ASIA + AMERICA} \\ 0 \\ 0 \\ 0 \\ 0 \\ \text{ESTABLISHED + NEW SECTS} \\ 0 \\ 0 \\ 0 \\ 0 \\ 0 \\ 0 \\ 0 \\ 0 \\ 0 \end{bmatrix}$$

and it indicates the division of each component of [x] into narrower terms. Alternatively, multiplication of the vector [x] by the transposed matrix $\mathbf{H}^{\text{T}}$ defines a vector $\mathbf{H}^{\text{T}}[x]$ as follows

$$\mathbf{H}^T\,[\mathbf{x}] = \begin{bmatrix} 0 \\ \text{HISTORY} \\ \text{HISTORY} \\ \text{HISTORY} \\ \text{HISTORY} \\ \text{POLITICAL} \\ \text{POLITICAL} \\ \text{ECONOMIC} \\ \text{ECONOMIC} \\ \text{SOCIAL} \\ \text{SOCIAL} \\ \text{MILITARY} \\ \text{MILITARY} \\ \text{MILITARY} \\ \text{EVENTS} \\ \text{EVENTS} \\ \text{EVENTS} \\ \text{CHURCH} \\ \text{CHURCH} \end{bmatrix}$$

in which each term of [x] has been replaced by the corresponding broader term.

11.6 Information Retrieval through Stored Associations, Citation Indexing

The information contained in the matrices discussed in the previous sections may be stored in computer memory to be available to the user of a document retrieval system. Just as parts of a thesaurus may be displayed to indicate broader, narrower, and related terms, the term and document association matrices may be made available for examination by the user prior to formulation of the user's request.

Alternatively, the appropriate matrices may be used to add automatically further terms to a question or to add additional document items to the listed output. For a given data base of stored document texts such as titles, abstracts, or complete documents, the document term and term connection matrices may be computed automatically, whereas matrices that describe terms of equivalent or related meanings must be compiled manually.

Information retrieval through citation indexing links is provided by the Institute for Scientific Information (ISI) and has been studied extensively by Garfield.[21] Studies of the extent to which published articles are cited by

---

[21] E. Garfield, and I. H. Sher, "New factors in the evaluation of scientific literature through citation indexing," *American Documentation* 14 (1963):195–201.

subsequent publications have been made by Ghosh,[22,23] who found that of 222 test articles in the *Journal of the American Chemical Society* there were 15% that were not cited within 1 year. Of 327 test articles published in the more general scientific journal *Nature,* there were 49% not cited within 1 year, and there were 7% not cited within 8 years. Different results have been noted by other authors[24-26] in their examinations of different journals, and it appears that the effectiveness of document links through citations is dependent on the particular disciplines considered.

As indicated by Abbot *et al.*[27] the use of citation indexing is likely to retrieve some articles that cannot be retrieved by search on titles or abstracts only. On the other hand, the occurrence of an article that deals with a very broad topic and that has an extensive bibliography may lead to retrieval of many nonrelevant items if citation links are used.

The MEDLARS data base is also designed to allow retrieval through citation indexing. Its coverage of journals, query language, and two available search programs have been described in detail.[28-30]

11.7 Problems

1. The abstracts of papers published in the Communications of the Association for Computing Machinery are followed by sets of keywords or key phrases. Examine a number of such articles and comment on the effectiveness of the keywords or phrases as index terms when presented to someone who has a specialized knowledge of the subject matter. Also, comment on their effectiveness when

[22] J. S. Ghosh, and M. L. Neufeld, "Uncitedness of articles in the American Chemical Society," *Information Storage and Retrieval* 10 (1974):365–369.

[23] J. S. Ghosh, "Uncitedness of articles in Nature, a multidisciplinary scientific journal," *Information Processing and Management* 11 (1975):165–169.

[24] D. J. De Solla Price, "Network of scientific papers," *Science* 149 (1965):510–515.

[25] A. E. Cawkell, "Citation practices," *Journal of Documentation* 24 (1968):299–302.

[26] S. Cole, "Professional standing and the reception of scientific discoveries," *American Journal of Sociology* 76 (1970):286–306.

[27] M. T. J. Abbot, P. S. Hunter, and M. A. Simkins, "Current awareness searches on CT, CBAC and ASCA," *Aslib Proceedings* 20 (1968):129–143.

[28] S. M. Humphrey, "Searching the MEDLARS citation file on-line using ELHILL 2 and STAIRS: A comparison," *Information Storage and Retrieval* 10 (1974):321–329.

[29] J. Egeland, *System User Manual.* State University of New York (SUNY), Biomedical Communication Network, Albany, New York, March 1973.

[30] MEDLARS Management Section, Bibliographic Services Division, National Library of Medicine, MEDLINE Reference Manual, PB-222 991. National Technical Information Service, Springfield, Virginia. September 1973.

presented to someone with a more general, rather than detailed, knowledge of the topics covered.

2. Discuss the relative advantages of storing:

(*i*) A thesaurus of broader, narrower, and related terms.
(*ii*) A term association matrix.
(*iii*) A document association matrix.
(*iv*) A matrix to represent a hierarchical classification of documents.

Estimate the relative amounts of computer storage required in the four cases. Also estimate the amount of time required to prepare the data for storage.

3. Examine a number of issues of a particular journal and determine the extent to which the authors tend to cite previous articles in the same journal. State whether your observations provide any information regarding the desirability of citation indexing.

12

Automatic Question Modification

12.1 Weight and Response Vectors Related by Association Matrices

The form of question logic described in Chapter 4 allows the user to specify his request in a precise manner, but in order to take full advantage of the different features of the query language he should have some familiarity with the vocabulary used in specification of the descriptors. In many instances, however, the user may not have sufficient familiarity with the data base to know which synonyms to use or which terms should be included as IGNORE concepts. The present chapter is concerned with automatic procedures that may be used to broaden or improve the form of a question.

To simplify the discussion it will be supposed that each question is in the form of a single parameter of weighted descriptors connected by OR logic. Thus each request may be specified in the form of a set of weights

$$q_1, q_2, \ldots, q_K \qquad (12.1)$$

to be attached to the first, second, . . . , Kth terms. A weight of 0 signifies that the corresponding index term is not relevant to the interest of the user. The values of $q_1, q_2, \ldots, q_K$ may be regarded as components of a request vector $\mathbf{q}$ in space of K dimensions.

Suppose that in the data base each document is described by a set of relevance values as discussed in Section 10.4, so that $d_i(n)$ specifies the relevance of the nth document to the ith index term. For any request that is specified in the form (12.1) the value, or response, of the nth document may be computed as

$$r(n) = \sum_{i=1}^{K} d_i(n)q_i \qquad (12.2)$$

and the set of values $r(n)$, where n ranges through all document numbers, may be regarded as the set of components of a response vector $\mathbf{r}$. Then in matrix notation the response vector is related to the request vector through the equation

$$\mathbf{r} = \mathbf{Dq}. \qquad (12.3)$$

Nonzero components in the response vector indicate the documents that are indexed by one or more of the descriptors that correspond to nonzero weights in the request vector.

It may be noted that if $\mathbf{C}$ is a citation matrix then the response vector

$$\mathbf{r} = \mathbf{CD}q \qquad (12.4)$$

has components

$$r(m) = \sum_n \sum_i c(m, n)d_i(n)q_i. \qquad (12.5)$$

Now the term $c(m, n)d_i(n)q_i$ is equal to 0 unless the ith index term is a descriptor of the nth document and this document is also cited by the mth document. Thus the response vector $\mathbf{r}$ given by (12.4) has nonzero components for documents that either contain one of the descriptors specified in the request vector or else cite such documents.

If a term association matrix $\mathbf{T}$ is used to indicate associations between index terms the document term matrix $\mathbf{D}$ should be replaced by $\mathbf{DT}$ so that (12.3) becomes of the form

$$\mathbf{r} = \mathbf{DTq}. \qquad (12.6)$$

The nonzero components of $\mathbf{r}$ indicate the documents that are indexed by descriptors whose presence implies relevance to some of the terms, or associated terms, of the request vector.

For a given query vector $\mathbf{q}$ and matrix $\mathbf{T}$ the nonzero components of $\mathbf{Tq}$ indicate the index terms that the matrix $\mathbf{T}$ associates with those specified by $\mathbf{q}$. Suppose that M is used to denote the masking operation of reducing to 0 all vector components of less than a given threshold value, and replacing all other components by 1. Then $\mathbf{MTq}$ is a vector $q^{(1)}$ in which the components of value 1 indicate the index terms that are regarded as significantly associated with those of the question vector $\mathbf{q}$. Such index terms may be called first generation terms.

Suppose, for example, that $\mathbf{q}$ is the vector

$$\begin{bmatrix} 1 \\ 0 \\ 0 \\ 1 \\ 0 \end{bmatrix},$$

which specifies a request in terms of weights to be given to five descriptors. Suppose $\mathbf{T}$ is the matrix $\mathbf{F}$ shown at the end of Section 12.4, and $\mathbf{M}$ is defined with a masking level equal to 1. Then

$$\mathbf{q}^{(1)} = \mathbf{Tq} = \begin{bmatrix} 1.98 \\ 1.62 \\ .56 \\ 1.95 \\ .75 \end{bmatrix} \quad , \quad \mathbf{Mq}^{(1)} = \begin{bmatrix} 1 \\ 1 \\ 0 \\ 1 \\ 0 \end{bmatrix} \qquad (12.7)$$

and so the first generation terms are term_1, term_2, and term_4.

In the same manner that the first generation terms are derived from the vector $\mathbf{q}$, a set of second generation terms may be derived from the vector $\mathbf{q}^{(1)}$. Thus for the preceding example

$$\mathbf{q}^{(2)} = \mathbf{Tq}^{(1)} = \begin{bmatrix} 1.98 \\ 3.62 \\ .56 \\ 3.57 \\ .75 \end{bmatrix} \quad , \quad \mathbf{Mq}^{(2)} = \begin{bmatrix} 1 \\ 1 \\ 0 \\ 1 \\ 0 \end{bmatrix} \qquad (12.8)$$

and the second generation terms are term_1, term_2, and term_4. Although in this instance the first and second generation terms coincide, such a coincidence does not always occur.

The totality of the question terms, first generation terms, second generation terms, and further generation terms, correspond to the nonzero components of the vector

$$\mathbf{q} + \mathbf{MTq} + (\mathbf{MT})^2\,\mathbf{q} + \cdots, \qquad (12.9)$$

which may be written symbolically in the form

$$(\mathbf{I} - \mathbf{MT})^{-1}\,\mathbf{q} \qquad (12.10)$$

where $\mathbf{I}$ denotes the unit matrix. If it is desired to give decreasing weights to terms of successive generations the preceding series may be modified to the form

$$\mathbf{q} + \lambda\mathbf{MTq} + (\lambda\mathbf{MT})^2\mathbf{q} + \cdots, \qquad (12.11)$$

where λ is a constant multiplier of value between 0 and 1. It may be noted that (12.11) may also be written in an abbreviated form as

$$(\mathbf{I} - \lambda\mathbf{MT})^{-1}\mathbf{q} \tag{12.12}$$

although the form (12.11) is likely to be the more convenient for computer processing.

Use of the term association matrix as just described extends the association between indexing terms and documents by causing the document term matrix $\mathbf{D}$ to be replaced by $\mathbf{D}(\mathbf{I} - \lambda\mathbf{MT})^{-1}$, and hence the relation (12.3) to be replaced by

$$\mathbf{r} = \mathbf{D}(\mathbf{I} - \lambda\mathbf{MT})^{-1}\mathbf{q}. \tag{12.13}$$

For purposes of computation, however, it is more convenient to regard the relation (12.13) as indicating a modification of the request vector $\mathbf{q}$ to become a new request vector

$$(\mathbf{I} - \mathbf{MT})^{-1}\mathbf{q} \tag{12.14}$$

that specifies a search on the original data base in which the relevance of indexing terms to documents is described by the matrix $\mathbf{D}$.

A very brief experimental test of the effectiveness of document retrieval using keyword association and connection has been made by Tague.[1] The documents consisted of 210 that were cited by 10 papers in the journal *Diabetes*. The title words were chosen as descriptors. The title words of 10 of the papers were then used to form request vectors, and just two terms were included in the series expansion (12.11). Only the five largest nonzero components were retained in the vector of each term. It was concluded that for the documents considered, the inclusion of keyword association and connection through various definitions of the matrix $\mathbf{T}$ did not increase the effectiveness of the document retrieval. It may be noted, however, that the documents were chosen from a very narrow field, and it might be expected that the request vectors were sufficiently well specified in terms of subject matter that further keyword association and connection was not required.

Document retrieval by use of term associations as expressed by a term association matrix has been severely criticized by Bar-Hillel.[2] His criticism is that if the index terms term_i and term_j are believed to be relevant there is little merit in retrieving a document that contains the index terms

---

[1] J. M. Tague, "An evaluation of statistical association measures," Proceedings of the American Documentation Institute, Santa Monica, October 3–7, 1966, pp. 391–397.

[2] Y. Bar-Hillel, *Language and Information*. (Reading Mass.: Addison-Wesley, 1964), Chapter 18.

term$_i$ and term$_k$ but not term$_j$ merely because another document contains term$_k$ and term$_j$ but not term$_i$. While there is some justification for this criticism, it is valid only in the instance that it is known with certainty that term$_i$ and term$_j$ are the best pair of descriptors to use in the request.

In many instances the requestor might be in doubt regarding the proper choice of descriptors to use in a request. By means of the term connection matrix the person may be informed, for example, that term$_i$ and term$_j$ appear together less frequently than do either term$_i$ and term$_k$ or term$_j$ and term$_k$. The requestor may then decide to modify the request in some appropriate manner.

The preceding remarks suggest a search procedure as represented in Figure 12.1. The requestor R formulates a request vector $\mathbf{q}$ and notes the response $\mathbf{r}^{(1)} = \mathbf{DTq}$. There is then a time delay while the requestor examines the response $\mathbf{r}^{(1)}$ to decide which of its components might be meaningful for modification of the request. In Figure 12.1 the examination process is represented by E, and it results in formulation of a new request vector $\mathbf{q}^{(2)}$. During the next delay the requestor notes how the modification has changed $\mathbf{r}^{(1)}$ to $\mathbf{r}^{(2)}$, and then formulates a new request vector $\mathbf{q}^{(3)}$. The process is repeated until the requestor believes the request to be properly formulated as indicated by a satisfactory response vector. If citation indexing is desired then **DT** should be replaced by **CDT**. In any practical implementation of such a retrieval system the user should also have the option of specifying that certain question terms are not to be expanded.

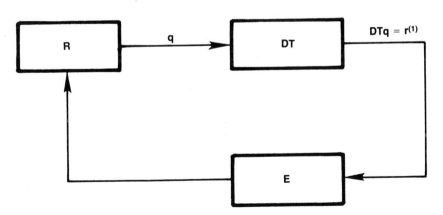

Figure 12.1. A search procedure with provision for feedback and request modification by the user.

12.2 Automatic Question Modification through Association Feedback

The remarks in the previous section suggest a search procedure with feedback interaction between the searcher and the computer. An initial request is modified by use of association matrices, and the resulting output is examined manually to provide information that will allow the user to formulate a more suitable request.

In Figure 12.1 the process of manual examination of the output was represented by E. The process may be examined in more detail as follows.

The response vector has components $r(n)$ that weight the output document items with respect to their predicted relevance to the request. For each descriptor the sum of the values of $r(n)$, where n corresponds to an output document item, may be regarded as a measure of the relevance weight of that descriptor to the entire set of output document items. For the ith index term such a sum is given by

$$\sum_n r(n)d_i(n) \tag{12.15}$$

and the set of all such sums for all K index terms form the K components of the vector

$$\mathbf{D}^T\mathbf{r}. \tag{12.16}$$

If the weights that form the components of the vector (12.16) are added to the corresponding initial request weights $q_i(n)$, there results a modified request vector $\mathbf{q} + \mathbf{D}^T\mathbf{r}$ that is based not only on the original request but also on the resulting output. The degree to which the modified request is dependent on the output may be controlled by introducing a parameter λ and a modified request vector $\mathbf{q} + \lambda\mathbf{D}^T\mathbf{r}$.

The processing of each request vector $\mathbf{q}$ according to the above form of feedback is represented in Figure 12.2. The response vector $\mathbf{r}$ is that which would result if the data base were searched with respect to the modified request vector $\mathbf{q} + \lambda\mathbf{D}^T\mathbf{r}$. Thus the relation (12.6) is replaced by

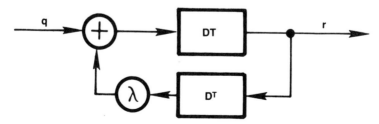

Figure 12.2. Document processing system in which the user's request is modified automatically by feedback from the output.

$$r = DT(q + \lambda D^T r) \tag{12.17}$$

from which it follows that

$$r = (I - \lambda DTD^T)^{-1}DTq$$
$$= [I + \lambda DTD^T + (\lambda DTD^T)^2 + (\lambda DTD^T)^3 + \cdots]DTq. \tag{12.18}$$

The modified request vector is $q + \lambda D^T r$ which, by substitution of r from (12.18), becomes

$$q + \lambda D^T DTq + \lambda^2 D^T DTD^T DTq + \cdots$$
$$= [I + \lambda D^T DT + (\lambda D^T DT)^2 + \cdots]q$$
$$= (I - \lambda D^T DT)^{-1}q$$
$$= (I - \lambda KT)^{-1}q, \tag{12.19}$$

where K is the term connection matrix introduced in Section 12.4.

It may be noted that if T is the unit matrix then the series (12.18) reduces to a series of increasing powers of λK, and the successive terms of the series represent the inclusion of longer document links in the sense defined in Section 12.4. Specifically, according to (12.19) each q_i in the initial request is replaced by the weight of value

$$q_i + \lambda \Sigma_j [k_{ij} + \lambda k_{ij}^{(2)} + \lambda 2_{k_{ij}}^{(3)} + \cdots]. \tag{12.20}$$

Suppose that, starting from a request vector q, a searcher requests a list of 100 relevant documents. Starting with $\lambda = 0$ each component $r(n)$ of r may be computed in order to output a list of all documents for which $r(n) \neq 0$. If the number of listed documents is less than 100, the components $r(n)$ may be computed for a small nonzero value of λ and a new output list of documents obtained. If this list still contains less than 100 documents the computations may be repeated with increasing values of λ. The successive lists contain increasing numbers of documents related by broader concepts of relevance that arise as increasing values of λ allow successive terms to be significant in the expansion of r.

The retrieval scheme represented by Figure 12.2 provides an automatic procedure for making a request more general by increasing the value of the parameter λ. However, the direction in which any request is broadened is governed by the internal associations of descriptors and not by the interest of the user. It may be preferable for the user to have some control over the manner in which the request is broadened. Thus subsequent to each change in the value of the feedback parameter λ, it may be desirable to have a printout of all the descriptors in the output items together with the corresponding weights computed by (12.15) so that the user is aware of the expansion of his original choice of q. The user should then be given the opportunity to have some of the new descriptors suppressed if it is believed that their inclusion would expand the request into irrelevant areas.

A retrieval system with feedback as described in the present section was first described by Guiliano and Jones,[3] who used an analog electrical network to represent the equation for **r**. The analog system was designated ACORN-I and was wired to search 42 sentences, or documents, coded with respect to 42 keywords. A digital computer is clearly more suitable for use with a large data base.

The effectiveness of automatic question modification as just described is dependent on the extent to which the term connection matrix is a good indicator of significant associations of relevant terms. Experimental tests of the method may be made by determination of precision and recall values for varying amounts of feedback. However, the method of question modification is not based directly on an attempt to optimize precision and recall, and it might therefore be regarded as influenced more by data base characteristics than by user requirements. In the following two sections consideration is given to automatic question modification that is more closely directed to improvement of precision and recall.

12.3 Optimization of Retrieval Effectiveness

In the previous section the term connection matrix was used to modify a question by broadening it to include further terms not originally present in the question. An alternative approach to question formulation is to use a rather general query on a representative subset of the data base and then modify the question after examination of the resulting output. This is the approach that forms the basis of the analysis of the present section.

When the user of a retrieval service specifies a request in the form of a set of weights

$$q_1, q_2, \cdots, q_K \qquad (12.21)$$

the user is indicating an estimate of the relative importance (to personal interests) of the terms used to index the documents represented in the data base. Computation of the responses

$$r(m) = \sum_i q_i d_i (m) \qquad (12.22)$$

for each data base item, or for each item of a subset of the data base, followed by comparison with a threshold value t, allows output of details

---

[3] V. E. Guiliano, and P. E. Jones, "Linear Associative Information Retrieval," Chapter 2 of *Vistas in Information Handling* Vol. I, P. W. Howerton and D. C. Weeks eds., (Washington, D.C.: Spartan, 1963).

of documents whose indexing is consistent with the user's question. The output documents are not necessarily relevant to the user's interest since the person may have used a poorly formulated question or searched an inappropriate data base.

When the user assesses the relevance of each output item, the person does so with regard to his or her own special interest rather than with regard to the question vector. It is therefore appropriate to regard the manually chosen set of weights as the initial input to a retrieval system whose effectiveness may be measured in terms of its ability to produce output that the user will classify as relevant.

In a method of question modification proposed by Yu and Salton[4] each term$_i$ of the query is assigned a precision weight p_i according to the formula

$$p_i = \frac{r_i}{R - r_i} \frac{I - h_i}{h_i} \qquad (12.23)$$

in which R and I are, respectively, the total number of relevant and nonrelevant documents, r_i denotes the number of relevant documents indexed by term$_i$, and h_i denotes the number of nonrelevant documents indexed by term$_i$. It is, of course, assumed that there is some way of estimating the values of the r_i and h_i. Yu and Salton use the precision weights to determine a set of new question weights q_i, and give examples of questions for which modification through precision weighting leads to an improvement in the variation of precision with recall.

It may be noted that the ratios $r_i/(R - r_i)$ and $h_i/(I - h_i)$ have been discussed by Rothenberg[5]. They are respectively the proportion of relevant documents that are retrieved and the proportion of nonrelevant documents that are not retrieved. For ideal retrieval the ratios should equal 1 and 0, respectively.

The effectiveness of the method of Yu and Salton is dependent on the assumption that the relevance of a document to a user's interest is dependent on the number of question terms that are contained as index terms of the document. While this may well be true for well-chosen questions it may not be true for a poorly formulated question or for a question that contains some index terms that tend to occur together.

Suppose, for example, that a sample of a data base is searched for all items that contain any of six index terms, term$_i$ where $i = 1$ to 6, with the response function chosen as

[4] C. T. Yu, and G. Salton, "Precision weighting—an effective automatic indexing method," *Journal of the Association for Computing Machinery* 23 (1976): 78–88.

[5] D. H. Rothenberg, "An efficiency model and a performance function for an information retrieval system," *Information Storage and Retrieval* 5 (1969): 109–122.

$$r(m) = \sum_i d_i(m)$$

and suppose the output items are as represented in Table 12.1. The 20 output documents are examined by the user who classifies 10 as relevant and 10 (shown in parentheses) as nonrelevant. The variation of precision with recall is shown in Figure 12.3. If the method of Yu and Salton is used to modify the question so that the weights q_i are

$$1.20, \qquad 1.35, \qquad 1.05, \qquad 1.00, \qquad 1.10, \qquad 1.65$$

then the variation of precision with recall is as shown by the graph of broken lines.

As indicated in Section 2.9, for a perfectly chosen set of question weights as the threshold decreases a plot of precision versus recall should trace a step function of unit height over the range $0 <$ Recall < 1, with points of the form $(1, y)$ corresponding to threshold values so small that output of some nonrelevant items is inevitable.

Table 12.1

· Values of $d_i(m)$ Corresponding to Output of 20 Document Items. Nonrelevant Values Are Included in Parentheses.

m			$d_i(m)$				$r(m)$
	$i = 1$	2	3	4	5	6	
1	1	1	0	0	1	1	4
(2)	(1	1	1	1	0	0)	(4)
(3)	(1	1	1	0	1	0)	(4)
(4)	(1	1	0	1	1	0)	(4)
(5)	(1	0	1	0	1	1)	(4)
(6)	0	1	0	0	1	1	3
7	1	1	0	1	0	0	3
8	0	1	1	0	0	1	3
9	1	0	1	0	0	1	3
(10)	(1	0	1	1	0	0)	(3)
(11)	(0	1	1	1	0	0)	(3)
(12)	(0	0	1	1	1	0)	(3)
(13)	(0	0	1	1	1	0)	(3)
(14)	(0	0	1	1	0	1)	(3)
(15)	(0	0	1	0	1	1)	(3)
16	0	1	0	0	1	0	2
17	0	0	1	0	0	1	2
18	0	0	0	0	1	1	2
19	0	0	0	0	1	0	1
20	0	0	0	0	1	1	1

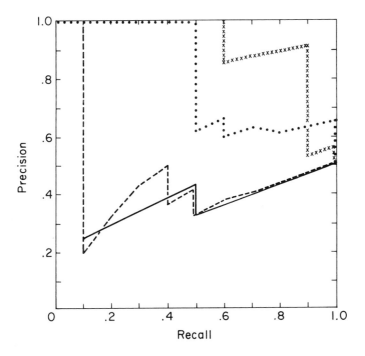

Figure 12.3. Variations of precision with recall. Initial question corresponds to continuous graph. Precision weighted modification of Yu and Salton corresponds to graph of broken lines. Graph of dotted lines corresponds to rms question, and graph of crosses corresponds to question formulated at end of Section 12.3.

If the question vector could be chosen so that, after appropriate reordering of the output documents the response function has the form

$$r(m) = f(m), \qquad (12.24)$$

where $f(m)$ is a nonincreasing function of m such that $f(m_1) > f(m_2)$ for every relevant document $doc(m_1)$ and every nonrelevant document $doc(m_2)$, then the variation of precision with recall would have the form of the desired step function. In general, such a choice of question vector is not possible, but the equality (12.24) will be best approximated in the least mean square sense when the q_i are chosen to minimize the mean square error

$$E = (1/M) \sum_m [\sum_i q_i d_i(m) - f(m)]^2. \qquad (12.25)$$

Expansion of the squared term in (12.25) allows E to be expressed in the form

$$E = \sum_i \sum_j u_{ij}q_iq_j - 2 \sum_i v_iq_i + (1/M) \sum_m f(m)^2, \qquad (12.26)$$

where

$$u_{ij} = u_{ji} = (1/M) \sum_m d_i(m)d_j(m) \qquad (12.27)$$

and

$$v_i = (1/M) \sum_m f(m)d_i (m). \qquad (12.28)$$

The expression (26) assumes its minimum value when the q_i are chosen so that $\partial E/\partial q_i = 0$ for all q_i, and this condition is satisfied when

$$2 \sum_j u_{ij}q_i - 2v_i = 0 \qquad \text{for each } i \qquad (12.29)$$

and hence when the q_i are chosen to satisfy the K equations

$$\sum_j u_{ij}q_j = v_i \qquad (12.30)$$

The resulting minimum value of E is

$$E_{min} = (1/M) \sum_m f(m)^2 - \sum_i \sum_j (\mathbf{U}^{-1})_{ij}v_iv_j \qquad (12.31)$$

where $(\mathbf{U}^{-1})_{ij}$ denotes an element of the inverse of the matrix $\mathbf{U}$ of elements u_{ij}.

A particular choice of the function $f(m)$ results when $f(m)$ is chosen equal to 1 for all relevant documents and equal to 0 for all nonrelevant documents. For the output documents represented by Table 11.1 the values of U, v_i, q_i, and E_{min} are as follows:

$$
\mathbf{U} =
\begin{bmatrix}
.40 & .25 & .25 & .20 & .20 & .15 \\
.25 & .45 & .20 & .20 & .25 & .15 \\
.25 & .20 & .60 & .30 & .25 & .30 \\
.20 & .20 & .30 & .40 & .15 & .05 \\
.20 & .25 & .25 & .15 & .60 & .25 \\
.15 & .15 & .30 & .05 & .25 & .45
\end{bmatrix}
\qquad (12.32)
$$

$$v_i = .15, \qquad .25, \qquad .15, \qquad .05, \qquad .30, \qquad .30 \qquad (12.33)$$

$$q_i = -.02, \qquad .37, \qquad -.24, \qquad -.02, \qquad .21, \qquad .59 \quad (12.34)$$

$$E_{min} = .206. \qquad (12.35)$$

For a question with component weights chosen according to (12.34) the variation of precision with recall is as shown by the dotted graph in Figure 12.3. It is clear that such a modification of the initial question vector gives rise to considerable improvement in the variation of precision with recall.

A question whose component weights are chosen to satisfy Eq. (12.30) may be called a root-mean-square (rms) question, since its derivation is based on minimization of the mean square error (12.26) and is analogous to derivation of the rms filter used for signal processing in electrical communication theory.[6] No other choice of question vector could lead to a smaller of (12.25). The result of using such question modification to search a data base of 26,000 titles has been described briefly in a previous paper.[7]

Specification of a question by means of a set of term weights for computation of a response function of the form (12.22) may be extended to specification of weights of specified logic combinations of terms. For example, six weights q_i may be chosen to weight respectively the occurrence of $term_3$, $term_4$, $term_5$, both $term_3$ and $term_4$, both $term_3$ and $term_5$, and both $term_4$ and $term_5$. For the documents of Table 1.1 the corresponding matrix U and the v_i are

$$U = \begin{bmatrix} .60 & .30 & .25 & .30 & .25 & .10 \\ .30 & .40 & .15 & .30 & .10 & .15 \\ .25 & .15 & .60 & .10 & .25 & .15 \\ .30 & .30 & .10 & .30 & .10 & .10 \\ .25 & .10 & .25 & .10 & .25 & .10 \\ .10 & .15 & .15 & .10 & .10 & .15 \end{bmatrix} \qquad (12.33)$$

$$v_i = .15, \quad .05, \quad .30, \quad 0, \quad 0, \quad 0. \qquad (12.34)$$

Solution of Eq. (12.30) gives

$$q_i = .72, \quad .16, \quad .86, \quad -.67, \quad -1.30, \quad -.19 \quad (12.35)$$
$$E_{min} = .126 \qquad (12.36)$$

and the variation of precision with recall is as shown by the graph of crosses in Figure 12.3, It is clear that the variation is a better approximation to the desired step function than are any of the other graphs of Figure 12.3.

Choosing the weighted combinations of terms as described above is equivalent to weighting single terms while replacing the response function (12.22) by one of the form

$$r(m) = q_3 d_3(m) + q_4 d_4(m) + q_5 d_5(m)$$
$$+ q_{34} d_3(m) d_4(m) + q_{35} d_3(m) d_5(m) + d_{45} q_4(m) q_5(m). \qquad (12.37)$$

A still more general response function could be chosen in the form

---

[6] N. Wiener, *Extrapolation, Interpolation, and Smoothing of Stationary Time Series* (New York: Wiley, 1949).

[7] H. S. Heaps, "Criteria for optimum effectiveness of information retrieval systems," *Information and Control* 18 (1971): 156–167.

$$r(m) = \sum_i q_i d_i(m) + \sum_i \sum_j q_{ij} d_i(m) d_j(m)$$
$$+ \sum_i \sum_j \sum_k q_{ijk} d_i(m) d_j(m) d_k(m) + \cdots$$

$$(12.38)$$

which, since it is a generalization of both (12.22) and (12.37), will lead to an rms question for which E_{min} is further reduced. In fact, for the documents of Table 12.1 the value of E_{min} may be reduced to zero by use of the response function

$$r(m) = d_3(m) + d_4(m) + d_5(m) - 2d_3(m)d_4(m) - 2d_3(m)d_5(m)$$
$$- 2d_4(m)d_5(m) + 3d_3(m)d_4(m)d_5(m),$$

$$(12.39)$$

which corresponds to a question that specifies a search for all documents that are indexed by any one, but not more than one, of $term_3$, $term_4$, or $term_5$.

12.4 Further Discussion of the rms Search

In the previous section the rms question was chosen to best approximate a response function equal to 1 for each of a set of relevant documents and to 0 for each of the set of nonrelevant documents. It might be regarded as equally desirable to maximize the values of the response function for relevant documents in comparison to its average value for all documents. One might therefore consider choice of the question weights q_i in order to maximize the expression

$$Q = \frac{(1/M) \sum_m [f(m) \sum_i q_i d_i(m)]}{\{(1/M) \sum_m [\sum_i q_i d_i (m)]^2\}^{1/2}},$$

$$(12.40)$$

which represents the weighted mean of the response function divided by its root-mean-square value. In the special instance that the $f(m)$ are chosen equal to 1 for relevant documents and to 0 for nonrelevant documents the value of (12.40) represents the average response to relevant output documents divided by the root-mean-square response to all output documents.

By consideration of $\partial Q / \partial q_i$ it may readily be verified that the maximum value of (12.40) is

$$Q_{max} = [\sum_i \sum_j (U^{-1})_{ij} v_i v_j]^{1/2},$$

$$(12.41)$$

which occurs when the q_i are chosen to satisfy Eq. (12.30). Thus the question vector that makes the response function best approximate $f(m)$ is also the question vector that maximizes the expression (12.40). This provides further justification for regarding the optimization procedure as justified.

It may be noted that for a query that corresponds to a single nonzero weight q_i the value of E_{min} is

$$E_1 = \frac{R}{M} - \frac{v_i^2}{u_{ii}}. \tag{12.42}$$

Similarly, for a query that corresponds to only two nonzero weights q_i and q_j the value of E_{min} is

$$E_2 = \frac{R}{M} - \frac{u_{ii}v_j^2 - 2u_{ij}v_iv_j + u_{jj}v_i^2}{u_{ii}u_{jj} - u_{ij}^2}. \tag{12.43}$$

Thus after examination of output items a first query term may be selected as that which corresponds to the greatest value of v_i^2/u_{ii}. A second query term may then be selected as that for which the difference between (12.43) and (12.42) is the greatest. Similarly, a third query term may be selected to give the greatest value to $E_3 - E_2$, and so forth until successive differences are negligible. Such a procedure for selection of query terms will lead to a compact form of question that does not include query terms of negligible value. Choice of such a compact set of query terms also avoids the need for inversion of a matrix U of large order.

After selection of a set of r question terms, and inversion of the matrix U to determine the q_i and E_r, the effect of adding a further question term may be estimated in the following manner, which does not require a further matrix inversion. The matrix U_r of r^2 elements u_{ij} may be written in the form $U_r = D_r + N_r$, where D_r is the diagonal matrix of elements u_{ii} and N_r is the matrix of elements n_{ij}, where $n_{ij} = 0$ if $i = j$ and $n_{ij} = u_{ij}$ if $i \neq j$. Then

$$U_r^{-1} = (I_r + D_r^{-1} N_r)^{-1} D_r^{-1} \tag{12.44}$$

and expansion as a series leads to

$$U^{-1} = D_r^{-1} - D_r^{-1}N_rD_r^{-1} + (D_r^{-1} N_r)^2 D_r^{-1} - \dots . \tag{12.45}$$

Substitution into (12.31), with neglect of $(D_r^{-1} N_r)^2$ and terms of higher order, shows that

$$E_{min} = \frac{R}{M} - \sum_{i \leq r} \frac{v_i^2}{u_{ii}} + \sum_{i \leq r} \sum_{j \neq i} \frac{u_{ij}v_iv_j}{u_{ii}u_{jj}}. \tag{12.46}$$

The approximation (12.45) is, of course, only valid if the series is convergent. A sufficient condition for convergence is that

$$u_{ij}/u_{ii} < 1/r \tag{12.47}$$

for all $i, j \leq r$.

Thus if $r - 1$ index terms have been chosen, and labelled as term$_1$, term$_2$, ... , term$_{r-1}$, then addition of a further rth term will reduce E_{min} by

$$\frac{v_r}{u_{rr}} \left(v_r - 2 \sum_{i=1}^{r-1} \frac{u_{ir}v_i}{u_{ii}} \right) \tag{12.48}$$

provided $u_{ij}/u_{ii} \ll 1/r$ for each $i \neq j \leqslant r$. The weights q_i may be computed by the approximation

$$q_i = \frac{v_i}{u_{ii}} - \sum_{j \neq i} \frac{u_{ij}v_j}{u_{ii}u_{jj}}. \tag{12.49}$$

The form of (12.49) serves to emphasize that the weight q_i to be assigned to any query term depends on the ratio v_i/u_{ii} and on a combination of values of u_{ij}. The ration v_i/u_{ii} represents the number of occurrences of the term in relevant output documents divided by the number of occurrences of the term in all the output documents. The weight is reduced by subtraction of terms that contain u_{ij}, which measures the extent to which the ith term tends to be associated with terms already selected as query terms. Frequent associations, as indicated by nonzero values of u_{ij}, tend to make the ith term redundant as a further indexing term.

12.5 Problems

1. In Section 12.1 the question formulation was in terms of a single parameter of weighted descriptors. A different form of question statement was used in Chapter 4. Discuss the two forms with respect to use of computer processing time and expected values of precision and recall.

2. Write a set of rules to be used as a guide for manual improvement of a question statement in order to improve the precision ratio. Write a similar set of rules to be used to improve the recall ratio. State whether the initial form of question is to be as in Chapter 4 or Section 12.1.

3. Discuss the advantages and disadvantages and the costs of automatic question reformulation in comparison to manual modification of question statements.

4. Examine a set of papers in a scientific journal, and state whether the methods of question modification described in the chapter would tend to locate the articles cited by each paper.

13
Automatic Document Classification

13.1 Document Classification by Categories

An efficient scheme of document classification may greatly facilitate the task of document retrieval. For example, if all documents within a collection relate to either automobiles or fish then it appears reasonable to divide the documents into two separate groups. For information related to automobiles, only the first group would be examined. Most documents could easily be assigned to the appropriate group, but there might be some difficulty in placing documents that relate to such topics as "Game Laws Relating to the Use of Automobiles in Fishing on Frozen Lakes" or "The Use of Fish Oils in the Automobile Industry."

For most collections of documents the choice of subclasses of related documents is much more difficult than in the preceding instance. The general problem of classification is to make the most efficient choice of K subclasses so that within each class the documents are closely related but documents in different classes are not closely related. A summary and discussion of the principles involved, with appropriate references, has been presented by van Rijsbergen.[1]

---

[1] C. J. van Rijsbergen, *Information Retrieval* (London: Butterworths, 1975), Chapter 3.

13.2 Attribute Analysis

One of the earliest proposals for a scheme of automatic document classification was made by Maron[2] who applied a method based on use of attribute numbers to index 260 documents within 32 categories. The documents, each consisting of a title and abstract, were those listed in the March and June 1959 issues of the *IRE Transactions Professional Group on Electronic Computers* (*PGEC*). The 10 major subject categories listed by PGEC were further subdivided to yield the 32 categories listed in Table 13.1.

Each word from the title or abstract of each of the 260 documents was punched on cards, which were then analyzed to determine the word frequencies. The average number of words per document was 79. In the entire 20,515 words there were 3263 different words, and the number of occurrences of each word varied from 1 to several hundred.

From among the 3263 different words a set of approximately 1000 was chosen by eliminating words of the following types:

(*i*) The 55 most frequently occurring words of the form THE, OF, A, etc., which produced 8402 of the total 20,515 occurrences. Thus less than 2% of the different words accounted for over 40% of the total occurrences.

(*ii*) The most frequently occurring descriptive words such as COMPUTER, SYSTEM, etc., which were considered to be too general for use in specification of categories.

(*iii*) The 2120 words that appeared only once or twice in the 20,515 occurrences. These were considered to be inefficient because of their rare occurrence.

Each of the 1000 words was examined to determine whether it tended to occur predominantly in documents that belonged to a single category. Ninety such words were found. They are listed in Table 13.2 and were chosen to form the set of descriptors to be used to categorize the 260 documents.

The automatic classification procedure used by Maron was based on considerations equivalent to the following, which may be applied when given two matrices **C** and **D** regardless of the particular method of choice of the descriptors. A more rigorous discussion of the theoretical basis is given by Maron and Kuhns.[3]

[2] M. E. Maron, "Automatic indexing: An experimental Inquiry," *Journal of the Association for Computing Machinery* 8 (1961): 404–417.

[3] M. E. Maron and J. L. Kuhns, "On relevance, probabilistic indexing and information retrieval," *Journal of the Association for Computing Machinery* 7 (1960): 216–244.

Table 13.1
Subject Categories Chosen by Maron.

1. Logical design and organization of digital computers
2. Digital data transmission systems
3. Information theory
4. Intelligent machines and programs
5. Number theory
6. Cybernetics
7. Pattern recognition techniques
8. Digital computer storage devices
9. Language translation and information retrieval
10. Digital counters and registers
11. Error control techniques
12. Number systems and arithmetic algorithms
13. Arithmetic units
14. Digital logical circuitry
15. Analog circuits and subsystems
16. Digital switching components
17. Physical characteristics of switching and memory materials
18. Automatic control and servomechanisms
19. Input–output devices
20. Analog-to-digital conversion devices
21. Analog system descriptions
22. Business applications of digital computers
23. Scientific and mathematical applications of digital computers
24. Real-time control system applications of digital computers
25. Digital computer programming
26. Applications and theory of analog computers
27. Simulation applications of computers
28. Glossaries, terminology, history and surveys
29. Numerical analysis
30. Boolean algebra
31. Switching theory
32. Combined analog–digital systems and digital–differential analyzers

Let M denote the number of documents to be indexed, N the number of different descriptors, and K the number of different categories. The classification of the M documents within the K categories may be described by a document category matrix $\mathbf{C}$, of M rows and K columns, with elements $c_k(m)$ chosen so that

$$c_k(m) = \begin{cases} 1 & \text{if the } m\text{th document is in the } k\text{th category.} \\ 0 & \text{otherwise.} \end{cases}$$

(13.1)

Likewise, the occurrence of the N descriptors in the M documents may be described by a document term matrix $\mathbf{D}$, of M rows and N columns, with elements $d_i(m)$ chosen so that

Table 13.2
Document Descriptors Chosen by Maron.

1. Abacus	31. Equation	61. Program
2. Adder	32. Equations	62. Programming
3. Analog	33. Error	63. Programs
4. Arithmetic	34. Expressions	64. Pseudorandom
5. Average	35. Fields	65. Pulse
6. Barium	36. File	66. Randomness
7. Boolean	37. Films	67. Recording
8. Bound	38. Function	68. Register
9. Carry	39. Functions	69. Scientific
10. Character	40. Generator	70. Section
11. Characters	41. Information	71. Shift
12. Chess	42. Language	72. Shuttle
13. Circuit	43. Library	73. Side
14. Circuits	44. Logic	74. Simulation
15. Code	45. Magnetic	75. Solution
16. Coding	46. Matrix	76. Speech
17. Communications	47. Mechanical	77. Square
18. Complexity	48. Mechanisms	78. Stage
19. Compression	49. Memory	79. Storage
20. Control	50. Monte (Carlo)	80. Switching
21. Conversion	51. Multiplication	81. Synthesis
22. Counter	52. Network	82. Tape
23. Decoder	53. Networks	83. Traffic
24. Definition	54. Numbers	84. Transistor
25. Delays	55. Office	85. Transistors
26. Differential	56. Parity	86. Translation
27. Diffusion	57. Plane	87. Transmission
28. Division	58. Printed	88. Uncol
29. Element	59. Process	89. Unit
30. Elements	60. Processing	90. Wire

$$d_i(m) = \begin{cases} 1 & \text{if the } m\text{th document contains the } i\text{th descriptor.} \\ 0 & \text{otherwise.} \end{cases} \tag{13.2}$$

The matrix **C** represents the manual indexing into categories of documents whose relation to the chosen descriptors is expressed by the matrix **D**. The task of an automatic classification scheme is to determine the matrix **C** when given only the matrix **D**.

If a document is selected at random from the entire collection the probability of it being in the kth category is

$$p(k) = \frac{\sum_m c_k(m)}{M}. \tag{13.3}$$

Similarly, the probability that it is indexed by the ith descriptor is

$$p(i) = \frac{\sum_m d_i(m)}{M}.$$ (13.4)

Let $p_k(i)$ denote the probability that a document of the kth category is indexed by the ith descriptor, and let $q_i(k)$ denote the probability that a document indexed by the ith descriptor is in the kth category. Then the probability that a document selected from the entire collection is both in the kth category and contains the ith descriptor may be expressed in either of the forms

$$p(k)p_k(i)$$ (13.5)

and

$$p(i)q_i(k).$$ (13.6)

In view of the equality of (13.5) and (13.6) it follows that

$$q_i(k) = \frac{p(k)p_k(i)}{p(i)}.$$ (13.7)

The number of documents in the kth category that are also indexed by the ith descriptor may be expressed in terms of elements of the matrices $\mathbf{C}$ and $\mathbf{D}$ in the form

$$\sum_m d_i(m)c_k(m).$$ (13.8)

Since the number of documents in the kth category is equal to

$$\sum_m c_k(m)$$ (13.9)

it follows that

$$p_k(i) = \frac{\sum_m d_i(m)c_k(m)}{\sum_m c_k(m)}$$ (13.10)

Substitution of (13.3), (13.4), and (13.10) into (13.7) then leads to

$$q_i(k) = \frac{\sum_m d_i(m)c_k(m)}{\sum_m d_i(m)}$$

$$= \frac{\text{Number of documents in } k\text{th category indexed by } i\text{th descriptor.}}{\text{Total number of documents indexed by } i\text{th descriptor.}}$$ (13.11)

In a similar manner the following expression may be derived for the probability $q_{\text{set}}(k)$ that a document indexed by a given set of descriptors is contained in the kth category

$$q_{set}(k) = \frac{\text{Number of documents in } k\text{th category indexed by all descriptors of the set.}}{\text{Total number of documents indexed by all descriptors of the set.}} \quad (13.12)$$

In order to index a new document that contains a given set of descriptors the quantities $q_{set}(k)$ may be computed for each value of $k = 1$ to K. They may be termed the attribute numbers for the new document. In order to be most consistent with the classification of the previous documents the new document should be assigned to the category k for which $q_{set}(k)$ assumes its maximum value.

In the application of the procedure by Maron the attributes were not computed according to (13.12) but were approximated through the assumption that in any category the probability of a document being indexed by any set of descriptors is equal to the product of the probabilities of it being indexed by any of the single descriptors. This neglects the fact that some descriptors may tend to associate within the same documents while other descriptors may tend to exclude each other. Of the 260 documents treated by Maron there were 247 that contained one or more descriptors, and 190 of these documents were placed in the correct category by use of the procedure based on maximum attribute number. There were 210 documents that contained at least two descriptors, and 190 of these documents were classified correctly. Correct classification was also obtained for 117 of the 123 documents that each contained at least four descriptors.

After using the 260 documents to determine the attribute numbers, Maron then considered 145 new abstracts that appeared in the September 1959 issue of *PGEC*. After automatic classification using attribute numbers the documents also were indexed manually and the results were two descriptors, and in 44 instances the automatic classification agreed with the manual one.

In a similar experiment performed by Hoyle,[4] in which 124 documents were assigned to nine categories, it was found that in 97 instances the categorization was in agreement with that of professional indexers. Hoyle noted that human indexers may be expected to be consistent for 87% of the indexed documents and that this should be borne in mind when evaluating the agreement of $97/124 = 71\%$ between the computer and the manual indexers.

Attribute numbers have also been used for automatic medical diagnosis

---

[4] W. G. Hoyle, "Automatic indexing and generation of classification systems by algorithm, "*Information Storage and Retrieval* 9 (1973): 233–242.

of patients who exhibit particular combinations of symptoms.[5-8] The problem is analogous to document classification, the diseases corresponding to the categories and the symptoms to the presence of descriptors. The results obtained for automatic diagnosis are very similar to those for document classification in that there is agreement with manual diagnosis in about 80% of the cases examined. In both the experiment of Maron and the applications to medical diagnosis the documents, or patients, were selected from a small and specialized group. Thus it is dangerous to assume that the agreement between the automatic and manual classifications would be as good if applied to more general situations. However, the agreement is sufficiently good to suggest that automatic methods may be useful as an aid to classification of documents.

13.3 Automatic Choice of Categories

Any scheme of document classification is clearly dependent on the particular choice of categories. The choice usually is made by workers familiar with the field and on the basis of their experience. Such a method of choosing categories is clearly subjective and there arises the question as to whether the choice may be made automatically according to clearly defined rules.

With this in mind Borko and Bernick[9] applied factor analysis to the set of documents and descriptors considered by Maron. Using 21 factors they deduced subject categories as listed in Table 13.3. The listed names were chosen to describe generally the most commonly occurring descriptors within the particular subject category. For example, the name ARITHME-TIC COMPUTATIONS was chosen to designate the category that involved the keywords AVERAGE, MULTIPLICATION, PROCESS, DIVI-SION, and EQUATIONS. Similarly, the name MAGNETIC FILM MEMORY DEVICES was chosen to designate a category with the keywords MAG-

[5] R. S. Ledley and L. B. Lusted, "Reasoning foundations of medical diagnosis," *Science* 130 (1959): 9–21.

[6] R. S. Ledley and L. B. Lusted, "The use of electronic computers in medical data processing: Aids in diagnosis, current information retrieval, and medical record keeping," *EIE Transactions on Medical Electronics* 7 (1960): 31–47.

[7] F. T. De Dombal, D. J. Leaper, J. R. Staniland, A. P. McCann and J. C. Horrocks, "Computer-aided diagnosis of acute abdominal pain," *British Medical Journal* 2 (1972): 9–13.

[8] P. A. Scheinok and J. A. Rinaldo, "Symptom diagnosis: Optimum subsets for upper abdominal pain," *Computers and Biomedical Research* (1967): 221–236.

[9] H. Borko and M. Bernick, "Automatic document classification," *Journal of the Association for Computing Machinery* 12 (1965): 151–162.

Table 13.3
Subject Categories of Borko and Bernick Derived by Factor Analysis.

Arithmetic computations
Differential and integral equations, systems of equations
Random number generation and random samples
Code compression and conversion
Boolean algebra and matrices
Parity checking, problems of logical complexity
Logical circuitry and design
Pulse counters, arithmetic units, components and circuits
Shift registers and decoders
Memory and storage devices
Character readers and techniques
Digital and analog control systems, analog computers, function generators
Data transmission
Switching networks
Industrial material movement simulation studies
Programming languages and auto codes, linear programming
File and data processing systems, magnetic and paper tape, input, output, and data conversion
Cybernetics, intelligent mechanisms
Speech and system simulation studies
Information processing storage and retrieval
Computers and programs applied to scientific and engineering problems, mechanical translation

NETIC, MEMORY, FILMS, STORAGE, RECORDING, ELEMENT, and ELE-MENTS.

Examination of the subject categories deduced by Borko and Bernick leads to the conclusion that factor analysis leads to a reasonable grouping of descriptors into subject categories, but the results are inconclusive with regard to whether the categories are better than ones chosen by people generally familiar with the fields covered by the documents.

13.4 Indexing Worth of Descriptors

Since the work of Maron and Borko and Bernick there have been a number of papers that have discussed document classification as a special instance of the general problem of pattern recognition and determination of clusters of related items. Other papers have discussed measures of the importance of the various descriptors in contributing information of use in classification. Further details may be found in the footnotes.[10-16]

In the present section the indexing worth of descriptors is examined by application of the procedure used to derive the matched search for optimization of retrieval effectiveness in Chapter 12. The method provides a quantitative indication of how the choice of descriptors affects the efficiency of automatic document classification.

Following the procedure presented in a previous paper,[17] the problem of document classification by categories may be regarded as equivalent to determination of a set of relevance ratings $r_k(m)$ whose values indicate the degree of relevance of the mth document to the kth category. Automatic document classification then requires the computation of values of $r_k(m)$ that are close to the values obtained after a manual examination of the mth document.

The task of determining the relevance ratings $r_k(m)$ may be represented in the form

$$r_k(m) = F_k \text{ (text of } m\text{th document)} \tag{13.13}$$

where text is used to signify the full text of the document, which may include author names, title, section headings, bibliography, and so forth. The function F_k represents the process used by the classifier to assess the relevance of the text to the kth category. In manual classification the function F_k is extremely complex and depends on the experience and memory of the classifier. It is neither possible, nor necessary, to describe the function precisely.

[10] R. T. Dattola, "A fast algorithm for automatic classification," *Journal of Library Automation* 2 (1969): 31–48.

[11] N. Jardine and C. J. van Rijsbergen, "The use of hierarchic clustering in information retrieval," *Information Storage and Retrieval* 7 (1971): 217–240.

[12] S. Schiminovich, "Automatic classification and retrieval of documents by means of a bibliographic pattern discovery algorithm," *Information Storage and Retrieval* 6 (1971): 417–435.

[13] K. L. Kwok, "The use of title and cited titles as document representation for automatic classification," *Information Processing and Management* 11 (1975): 201–206.

[14] G. Salton, A. Wong, and C. S. Yang, "A vector space model for automatic indexing," *Communications of the Association for Computing Machinery* 18 (1975): 613–620.

[15] G. Salton, C. S. Yang, and C. T. Yu, "A theory of term importance in automatic text analysis," *Journal of the American Society for Information Science* 26 (1975): 33–44.

[16] C. J. van Rijsbergen and K. Sparck Jones, "A text for the separation of relevant and non-relevant documents in experimental retrieval collections," *Journal of Documentation* 29 (1973): 251–257.

[17] H. S. Heaps, "A theory of relevance for automatic document classification," *Information and Control* 22 (1973): 268–278.

If a computer is used to classify the documents then the function F_k must be specified precisely. It is clear that computation time will be reduced significantly if the relation (13.13) is replaced by one of the form

$$y_k(m) = f_k \text{ (set of descriptors of the } m\text{th document)} \qquad (13.14)$$

where the set of descriptors is significantly smaller than the set of words in the entire text. The numbers $y_k(m)$ may be regarded as computer predictions of the relevance ratings $r_k(m)$.

The set of descriptors associated with the mth document may be described by means of the document term matrix **D** of Section 12.2, and hence $y_k(m)$ may be expressed in the form

$$y_k(m) = f_k[d_1(m), d_2(m), \dots, w_N(m)]. \qquad (13.15)$$

The form of the function f_k is unknown, but various forms may be tried and tested with respect to their ability to approximate the known values of $r_k(m)$. A particularly simple form to assume for the f_k is a linear function of the $d_i(m)$ so that

$$y_k(m) = \sum_i a_{ki} d_i(m) \qquad (13.16)$$

in which the a_{ki} are parameters to be determined in order to allow the best approximation to the $r_k(m)$.

A measure of the exactness of the approximation of the computed $y_k(m)$ to the given $r_k(m)$ is given by the following measure of the mean square error averaged over all possible values of k and m

$$
\begin{aligned}
E &= (1/KM) \sum_m \sum_k [\sum_i a_{ki} d_i(m) - r_k(m)]^2 \\
&= (1/K) \sum_k [\sum_i \sum_j a_{ki} a_{kj} u_{ij} - 2 \sum_i a_{ki} v_{ki} + (1/M) \sum_m r_k(m)^2] \qquad (13.17)
\end{aligned}
$$

where

$$
\begin{aligned}
Mu_{ij} = Mu_{ji} &= \sum_m d_i(m) d_j(m) \qquad (13.18) \\
&= \text{Number of documents indexed by both the} \\
&\quad\ i\text{th and } j\text{th descriptors}
\end{aligned}
$$

and

$$
\begin{aligned}
Mv_{ki} &= \sum_m r_k(m) d_i(m) \qquad (13.19) \\
&= \text{Number of documents that contain the } i\text{th} \\
&\quad\ \text{descriptor and are in the } k\text{th category.}
\end{aligned}
$$

The mean square error E in the computer predictions of the relevance ratings may be minimized by choosing the parameters a_{ki} so that for each value of k and i the relation $\partial E/\partial a_{ki} = 0$ is satisfied. By virtue of (13.17) this relation takes the form

$$2 \sum_j a_{kj} u_{ij} - 2v_{ki} = 0 \qquad (13.20)$$

and hence for each value of k the N parameters a_{kj} must be chosen to satisfy the N equations

$$\sum_j a_{kj} u_{ji} = v_{ki} \qquad i = 1 \text{ to } N. \qquad (13.21)$$

With such a choice of the a_{kj} the resulting value of E is

$$E_{min} = (1/KM) \sum_k \sum_m r_k(m)^2 - (1/K) \sum_i \sum_k a_{ki} v_{ki}. \qquad (13.22)$$

For any given set of document descriptors the value of E_{min} according to (13.22) provides a measure of the closeness to which the given relevance ratings $r_k(m)$ may be approximated by a linear relation of the form (13.16). It also may be regarded as a measure of the consistency of the given relevance ratings or the suitability of the vocabulary from which the descriptors were chosen, since any inconsistencies will clearly be at variance with the assumption of the prediction formula (13.16). Similarly, if an insufficient number of descriptors is chosen, then the number of terms $a_{ki} v_{ki}$ present in (13.22) will be insufficient to decrease E_{min} to an acceptable level. If E_{min} is found to be zero then the choice of descriptors is such as to allow perfect automatic classification, and there is no advantage in adding further descriptors.

If r descriptors are used to index the documents assigned to the kth category, and if the resulting matrix U_r of elements u_{ij} is expanded as described in Section 12.4, then E_{min} may be approximated in the form

$$E_{min} = (1/KM) \sum_k \sum_m r_k(m)^2 - (1/K) \sum_k \sum_i \frac{v_k^2}{u_{ii}}$$

$$+ (1/K) \sum_k \sum_i \sum_{j \neq i} \frac{u_{ij} v_{ki} v_{kj}}{u_{ii} u_{jj}}. \qquad (13.23)$$

The contribution to E_{min} caused by errors in the automatic prediction of relevance of documents to the kth category is given by E_k where

$$KE_k = (1/M) \sum_m r_k(m)^2 - \sum_i \frac{v_{ki}^2}{u_{ii}} + \sum_i \sum_{j \neq i} \frac{u_{ij} v_{ki} v_{kj}}{u_{ii} u_{jj}}. \qquad (13.24)$$

If only a single descriptor, say the qth, is used to determine the relevance of documents to the rth category the value of KE_k is reduced from the value of $(1/M) \sum_m r_k(m)^2$ by an amount

$$v_{kq}/u_{qq}. \qquad (13.25)$$

Thus the most effective single descriptor for documents of the kth category is the one that corresponds to the largest value of (13.25). Since computation of (13.25) may be performed very rapidly for all possible descriptors, it is simple to select the most effective descriptor and to regard it as descriptor No. 1.

After the first descriptor has been chosen, a further one, say the qth, will further reduce KE_k by an amount

$$\frac{v_{kq}^2}{u_{qq}} - \frac{2u_{1q}v_{k1}v_{kq}}{u_{11}u_{qq}}. \tag{13.26}$$

Hence, the second descriptor should be chosen as the one for which the value of (13.26) is greatest.

The selection process may be continued so that, after choice of $q - 1$ descriptors for the kth category, the qth descriptor is chosen to correspond to the largest value of

$$\Delta_k(q) = \frac{v_{kq}^2}{u_{qq}} - \frac{2v_{kq}}{u_{qq}} \sum_{i=1}^{q-1} \frac{u_{iq}v_{ki}}{u_{ii}}. \tag{13.27}$$

If it is found that (13.27) is zero for all values of q then the remaining descriptors have no value for classification of documents in the kth category. In practice it may, in fact, be found that there are descriptors for which $\Delta_k(q) < 0$; this is usually due to nonconvergence of the expansion used to derive (13.23), and a closer examination of the derivation indicates that such descriptors are not sufficiently independent of the ones chosen previously and hence are poor choices as index terms for the kth category.

Automatic classification based on computation of the expressions (13.25), (13.26), and (13.27) may be illustrated by application to articles published in the *Journal, and the Communications, of the American Society for Computing Machinery*.[18] For each printed article the abstract is followed by a set of manually assigned category numbers that are chosen with respect to the classification scheme shown in Table 13.4. For a set of 746 articles published between 1968 and 1972, the numbers of articles associated with each category are indicated in parentheses after the category names. The average number of categories assigned to each article is 2.1.

For each of the 746 articles the title words may be regarded as descriptors, and they provide an average of 7.9 descriptors per title. Suppose there is no preediting of titles, so that noncontent words such as OF and FROM are included, and also plurals and singulars of the same word are treated as different descriptors.

---

[18] H. S. Heaps and K. V. Leung, "Automatic document classification based on a theory of relevance," Proceedings of the Third International Study Conference on Classification Research, Bombay, 1975.

If descriptors are chosen successively to maximize the expressions (13.25), (13.26), and (13.27) the resulting sequences of descriptors and corresponding values of MKE_k are as listed in Table 13.5 for three particular categories. It may be noted that the descriptors at the top of each list are obviously very relevant to the particular category and that descriptors at the bottom of each list are generally less relevant. However, the method of selection tends to reduce the selection of redundant terms so that, for example, in Category 3.7, Information Retrieval, the early selection of RETRIEVAL prevents the selection of INFORMATION as a descriptor since it usually occurs in conjunction with RETRIEVAL and is therefore redundant for purposes of document classification.

The computed value of $y_k(m)$ is a prediction of the value of $r_k(m)$, which was chosen to be either 1 or 0, according as the mth document is, or is not, manually classed as relevant to the kth category. If a value of $y_k(m)$ less than a threshold value of .5 is regarded as a prediction of nonrelevance, and a value greater than .5 is regarded as a prediction of relevance, then the results of the automatic classification are as shown in the fifth and sixth columns of Table 13.6. The fifth column indicates the number of documents that are automatically classified in the correct kth category. The sixth column indicates the number of documents that are incorrectly automatically classified in the kth category. It may be noted that 1366, and hence 87%, of the 1560 relevant categories are assigned correctly. A total of 217 category assignments are in disagreement with the manual assignment.

If a threshold value of .05 is chosen as the boundary for prediction of relevance and nonrelevance the results are as shown in the seventh and eigth columns of Table 13.6. Few relevant categories are missed, but the number of false predictions of relevance is increased.

Some associations of descriptors with categories, and the corresponding weights a_{ki}, are shown in Table 13.7. It may be noted that some descriptors are associated with several categories, and that different descriptors with a common stem may be associated with different categories. Thus although the descriptors DOCUMENT and DOCUMENTA-TION are both associated with the category Information Retrieval, the descriptor DOCUMENT alone is associated with the category Artificial Intelligence, while DOCUMENTATION alone is associated with the category Management Data Processing. A reduction of the descriptors to common word stems would therefore destroy some information that is of use for document classification.

Document classification based on consideration of the indexing worth of descriptors as measured by Eq. (13.27) may involve more complex computations than are needed for application of attribute analysis. On the other hand, the procedure allows very compact selection of descriptors

Table 13.4
Classification Scheme Used by the Association for Computing Machinery. Number of Articles in Each Category Are Shown in Parentheses.

1. GENERAL TOPICS AND EDUCATION (60)

1.0 General (4)
1.1 Texts; Handbooks (2)
1.2 History; Bibliographies (10)
1.3 Introductory and Survey Articles (16)
1.4 Glossaries (1)
1.5 Education (36)
1.9 Miscellaneous (0)

2. COMPUTING MILIEU (43)

2.0 General (5)
2.1 Philosophical and Social Implications (13)
2.2 Professional Aspects (3)
2.3 Legislation; Regulations (1)
2.4 Administration of Computing Centers (24)
2.9 Miscellaneous (1)

3. APPLICATIONS (290)

3.0 General (1)
3.1 Natural Sciences (46)
3.2 Engineering (35)
3.3 Social and Behavioural Sciences (22)
3.4 Humanities (30)
3.5 Management Data Processing (33)
3.6 Artificial Intelligence (85)
3.8 Real-Time Systems (39)
3.9 Miscellaneous (3)

5. MATHEMATICS OF COMPUTATION (419)

5.0 General (8)
5.1 Numerical Analysis (147)
5.2 Metatheory (146)
5.3 Combinatorial and Discrete Mathematics (102)
5.4 Mathematical Programming (43)
5.5 Mathematical Statistics, Probability (44)
5.6 Information Theory (12)
5.7 Symbolic Algebraic Computation (0)
5.9 Miscellaneous (9)

6. DESIGN AND CONSTRUCTION (89)

6.0 General (6)
6.1 Logical Design; Switching Theory (15)
6.2 Computer Systems (47)
6.3 Components and Circuits (30)
6.4 Patents, Hardware (0)
6.9 Miscellaneous (6)

7. ANALOG COMPUTERS (1)

7.0 General (0)
7.1 Applications (0)
7.2 Design; Construction (0)
7.3 Hybrid Systems (1)
7.4 Programming; Techniques (0)
7.9 Miscellaneous (0)

4. PROGRAMMING (296)

4.0 General (18)
4.1 Processors (101)
4.2 Programming Languages (99)
4.3 Supervisory Systems (110)
4.4 Utility Programs (72)
4.5 Patents, Software (0)
4.6 Software Evaluation, Tests, and
   Measurements (0)
4.9 Miscellaneous (29)

8. FUNCTIONS (7)

8.0 General (0)
8.1 Simulation and Modeling (2)
8.2 Graphics (0)
8.3 Operations Research/Decision Tables (5)
8.9 Miscellaneous (0)

Table 13.5
Sequences of Optimally Chosen Descriptors and Corresponding Values of MKB_k.

Category 1.5 Education	Category 5.5 Math. Stat, and Prob.	Category 3.7 Information Retrieval
MKE_k	MKE_k	MKE_k
36.0	44.0	98.0
28.3 SCIENCE	38.2 RANDOM	88.0 RETRIEVAL
24.3 EDUCATION	34.6 QUEUING	82.0 HASH
22.3 BUSINESS	31.4 STATISTICAL	77.0 DISK
20.3 INSTRUCTIONAL	29.2 PROBABILITY	72.9 SEARCH
18.3 UNIVERSITIES	26.9 SAMPLING	68.9 HASHING
17.3 APPRECIATION	24.8 SHARING	65.4 TECHNIQUES
16.3 AUTHORED	23.5 PSEUDORANDOM	62.4 DEADLOCKS
15.3 COMMUNITY	22.2 CUSTOMERS	60.1 INDEX
14.3 CONTROLLER	21.0 SERVICE	58.1 ANSWERING
13.3 CONVERTING	20.0 APPROXIMATELY	56.1 CODES
12.3 COURSE	19.0 ASSEMBLY	54.1 TEXT
11.3 EXERCISES	18.0 CARLO	52.8 OPTIMIZING
10.3 IITRAN	17.0 CENTERS	51.5 SCIENTIFIC
9.3 MERIT	16.0 EFROYMSON	50.3 DATA
8.3 NEATER2	15.0 ERGODIC	49.2 TREE
7.3 PROFESSIONAL	14.0 PROBABILISTIC	48.2 ACCESSING
6.3 REFINEMENT	13.0 SOLVE	47.2 ALPHANUMERIC
5.3 TEACH	12.4 BUSY	46.2 BIERSTONE
4.3 TRAINING	11.9 MULTIVARIATE	45.2 CARD
3.3 TUTORIAL	11.6 DESIGNED	44.2 CENTERS
2.8 SPECIAL	11.3 PRIORITIES	43.2 COMPREHENDER
	11.14 PRIORITY	42.2 CONSTRUCT
	11.10 MATHEMATICAL	41.2 CORRECTION
		40.2 CRT
		39.2 DEADLOCK
		38.2 DETERMINISTIC
		37.2 DOCUMENT
		36.2 DOCUMENTATION
		35.2 EXPECTED
		34.2 EXTRACTING
		33.2 HIERARCHICAL
		32.2 INCREASING
		31.2 MEANING
		30.2 MEASURES
		29.2 MERCURY
		28.2 MULTIHEAD
		27.2 MUSE
		26.2 MUX
		25.2 RELEVANCE
		24.2 RESIDUE
		23.2 STRUCTURES

Table 13.5

Category 1.5 Education	Category 5.5 Math. Stat, and Prob.	Category 3.7 Information Retrieval
MKE_k	MKE_k	MKE_k
		22.2 TRANSITIVE
		21.2 URBAN
		20.2 2048
		19.7 CANONICAL
		19.2 CLASS
		18.7 TABLE
		18.4 MULTICS
		18.2 ACCESSED
		etc.

and, through use of Eq. (13.22) or (13.23), provides a measure of classification effectiveness.

13.5 A Measure of Classification or Retrieval Consistency

Retrieval of documents relevant to a user's interest may, of course, be regarded as classification of documents into two classes of which one contains only relevant documents and the other contains only nonrelevant documents. Thus formulation of the classification criterion in terms of Eq. (13.17) for each value of k is equivalent to minimization of Eq. (12.25) of Chapter 12 for a corresponding question. In either instance it was supposed that there was available a given set of relevant documents.

It was also supposed that the extent of the relevance of a relevant document could be specified quantitatively by a response function $r(m)$ or $f(m)$. In fact such a quantitative measure introduces an unnecessary artificiality since in practice it may be preferable to describe documents in terms of relevance and nonrelevance rather than in terms of degrees of relevance, and similarly to accept any positive value of $r(m)$ as signifying relevance.

The purpose of the present section is to consider in more detail the formulation of the expression to be minimized and to allow a nonquantitative specification of relevance.

Suppose relevance is described only in the form of a listing of relevant documents, and hence through specification of the values of m for which $f(m) \neq 0$. Suppose the values of $f(m)$ are to be determined only to allow the most effective minimization of (12.25) of Chapter 12. In order to

Table 13.6
Automatic Classification of the 746 Documents.

| | | | | Predicted relevancies | | | |
| | | | | Threshold = .5 | | Threshold = .05 | |
Category	Number of descriptors	MKE_k	Number of documents	Category k	Other	Category k	Other
1.0	4	0	4	4	0	4	0
1.1	2	0	2	2	0	2	0
1.2	9	1.4	10	9	1	9	1
1.3	15	2.0	16	16	1	16	13
1.4	1	0	1	1	0	1	0
1.5	21	2.8	36	36	3	36	3
2.0	4	.7	5	4	0	5	3
2.1	13	1.0	13	13	2	13	2
2.2	3	0	3	3	0	3	0
2.3	1	0	1	1	0	1	0
2.4	21	4.1	24	22	5	24	26
2.9	1	0	1	1	0	1	0
3.0	1	0	1	1	0	1	0
3.1	35	7.8	46	46	11	46	11
3.2	30	4.4	35	34	7	35	9
3.3	21	2.5	22	22	2	22	2
3.4	22	4.8	30	28	3	30	10
3.5	25	4.7	33	33	8	33	8
3.6	52	11.5	85	79	7	84	50
3.7	52[a]	17.5	98	85	12	95	22
3.8	30	10.2	39	31	4	39	42
3.9	6	1.3	3	2	1	3	14
4.0	16	2.5	18	17	3	18	10
4.1	56	23.8	101	77	11	100	63
4.2	57	25.7	99	91	25	98	76
4.3	48	21.8	110	94	7	110	44
4.4	54	15.5	72	61	13	71	39
4.9	27	4.4	29	26	4	29	30
5.0	9	1.1	8	7	1	8	11
5.1	40[a]	37.5	147	128	18	134	21
5.2	40[a]	46.1	146	115	10	120	20
5.3	52[a]	18.5	102	92	16	96	23
5.4	34	14.1	43	30	9	43	84
5.5	23	11.1	44	42	10	44	34
5.6	12	3.5	12	11	5	12	27
5.9	10	2.2	9	9	3	9	15
6.0	6	1.0	6	6	2	6	2
6.1	15	3.0	15	14	3	15	8
6.2	38	11.6	47	35	2	47	75
6.3	27	5.9	30	26	5	30	30
6.9	6	.5	6	6	1	6	1
7.3	1	0	1	1	0	1	0
8.1	3	1.1	2	1	1	2	7
8.3	8	1.1	5	4	1	5	9

[a] Indicates a partial set of descriptors.

326

Table 13.7
Some Associations of Descriptors with Categories.

Descriptor	a_{ki}	Category
ARCHITECTURE	1.0	6.2 Computer Systems
	.5	1.2 History; Bibliographies
	.5	2.1 Philosophical and Social Implications
	.5	6.0 General Design and Construction
ALGORITHMIC	.5	5.4 Mathematical Programming
ALGORITHMS	.04	4.0 Programming, general
DOCUMENT	1.0	3.6 Artificial Intelligence
	1.0	3.7 Information Retrieval
DOCUMENTATION	1.0	3.5 Management Data Processing
	1.0	3.7 Information Retrieval
OPERATORS	1.0	5.1 Numerical Analysis
OPERATING	.7	4.3 Supervisory Systems
	.4	6.2 Computer Systems
PARSER	1.0	3.4 Humanities
PARSERS	.7	4.1 Processors
PARSING	.6	4.1 Processors
SEARCH	.5	3.7 Information Retrieval
SEARCHING	.3	5.4 Mathematical Programming

obtain a minimization criterion that is independent of the scale of the $f(m)$ the quantity (12.25) of Chapter 12 may be replaced by

$$E' = \frac{(1/M) \sum_m [\sum_i q_i d_i(m) - f(m)]^2}{(1/R) \sum_m f(m)^2} \tag{13.28}$$

in which the denominator is the mean square value of the R nonzero, but unspecified, values of $f(m)$.

The analysis of the previous section shows that for fixed values of $f(m)$ the minimum value of E' occurs when the q_i are chosen to satisfy an equation analogous to (13.21), and the resulting minimum value of E' is

$$E'_{min} = \frac{(1/M) \sum_m f(m)^2 - \sum_i \sum_j (U^{-1})_{ij} v_i v_j}{(1/R) \sum_m f(m)^2}, \tag{13.29}$$

where $(U^{-1})_{ij}$ denotes an element of the inverse of the matrix of elements u_{ij}, and

$$v_i = (1/M) \sum_m f(m) d_i(m). \tag{13.30}$$

It proves convenient to rewrite (13.29) in the form

$$E'_{min} = \frac{R}{M}\left(1 - \frac{F}{M}\right) \tag{13.31}$$

where

$$F = M^2 \frac{\sum_i \sum_j (\mathbf{U}^{-1})_{ij} v_i v_j}{\sum_m f(m)^2}. \tag{13.32}$$

The expressions (13.29) and (13.31) contain R unspecified values $f(s)$ of $f(m)$ and have a minimum value when these values are chosen to maximize F. This occurs when

$$\partial F / \partial f(s) = 0 \qquad \text{for the } R \text{ values of } s \tag{13.33}$$

and hence

$$[\sum_m f(m)^2] \, 2M \sum_i \sum_j (\mathbf{U}^{-1})_{ij} v_j d_i(s)$$
$$- M^2 [\sum_i \sum_j (\mathbf{U}^{-1})_{ij} v_i v_j] 2 f(s) = 0. \tag{13.34}$$

Substitution for v_j from (13.30), and division by $\sum f(m)^2$, allows the condition to be expressed in the form

$$\sum_m f(m) \sum_i \sum_j (\mathbf{U}^{-1})_{ij} d_j(m) d_i(s) - F f(s) = 0 \tag{13.35}$$

and hence

$$\sum_m c(s, m) f(m) - F f(s) = 0 \tag{13.36}$$

where

$$c(s, m) = \sum_i \sum_j (\mathbf{U}^{-1})_{ij} d_i(s) d_j(m). \tag{13.27}$$

The form of (13.36) shows that the maximum value of F is equal to the largest eigenvalue of the symmetric matrix of R^2 elements $c(s, m)$, where s and m correspond to relevant documents. It is not appropriate to allow m to range through nonrelevant documents since the factor $f(m)$ in (13.36) reduces each corresponding term to zero. The minimum value of $E'_{\min}$ is given by (13.31) with the F chosen as the largest eigenvalue of equations (13.36) and with the $f(s)$ chosen as the components of the corresponding eigenvector. The corresponding v_i are given by (13.30), and the q_i are the solutions of the following equations, which are analogous to (13.21)

$$\sum_j u_{ij} q_j = v_i. \tag{13.38}$$

Although the condition $f(m) > 0$ was not used in the preceding derivation of (13.36) it may be noted from Section 13.4 that the solution of (13.36) also maximizes the mean of the responses to relevant documents, and this tends to ensure that the $f(m)$ have positive values.

This analysis may be illustrated by consideration of a greatly simplified situation in which there are only three descriptors and a data base of only four documents represented by the vectors $\mathbf{d}(s)$ of components $d_1(s)$,

$d_2(s)$, $d_3(s)$, where the relevant documents are $d(1) = (1, 1, 1)$, $d(2) = (1, 1, 0)$, and the nonrelevant documents are $d(3) = (1, 0, 1)$, $d(4) = (0, 1, 1)$. Then

$$U = (1/4) \begin{bmatrix} 3 & 2 & 2 \\ 2 & 3 & 2 \\ 2 & 2 & 3 \end{bmatrix} \tag{13.39}$$

and

$$U^{-1} = (4/7) \begin{bmatrix} 5 & -2 & -2 \\ -2 & 5 & -2 \\ -2 & -2 & 5 \end{bmatrix}. \tag{13.40}$$

According to (13.37) the matrix **C** of elements $c(s, m)$ is given by

$$C = D^T U^{-1} D$$
$$= (4/7) \begin{bmatrix} 1 & 1 & 1 \\ 1 & 1 & 0 \end{bmatrix} \begin{bmatrix} 5 & -2 & -2 \\ -2 & 5 & -2 \\ -2 & -2 & 5 \end{bmatrix} \begin{bmatrix} 1 & 1 \\ 1 & 1 \\ 1 & 0 \end{bmatrix}$$
$$= (4/7) \begin{bmatrix} 3 & 2 \\ 2 & 6 \end{bmatrix}. \tag{13.41}$$

Equation (13.36) may then be expressed in the matrix form

$$[C - FI] \begin{bmatrix} f(1) \\ f(2) \end{bmatrix} = 0 \tag{13.42}$$

where **I** denotes the unit matrix. This equation implies that

$$\begin{bmatrix} 12/7 - F & 8/7 \\ 8/7 & 24/7 - F \end{bmatrix} = 0 \tag{13.43}$$

and hence $F = -8/7$ or 4. The maximum value of F is thus 4.

With $F = 4$ the value of E'_{min} according to (13.31) is $(2/4)(1 - 4/4) = 0$, and so the response function indicates the relevant and nonrelevant documents without any ambiguity. With $F = 4$ the expression (13.42) reduces to the equations

$$(12/7 - 4)f(1) + (8/7)f(2) = 0,$$
$$(8/7)f(1) - (24/7 - 4)f(2) = 0, \tag{13.44}$$

equal to 1 and 2, respectively.

The values of v_1, v_2, v_3 from (13.30) are, respectively, $\frac{3}{4}, \frac{3}{4}, \frac{1}{4}$, and it follows from (13.38) that

$$\begin{bmatrix} q_1 \\ q_2 \\ q_3 \end{bmatrix} = (\frac{1}{4})\mathbf{U}^{-1} \begin{bmatrix} 3 \\ 3 \\ 1 \end{bmatrix} = \begin{bmatrix} 1 \\ 1 \\ -1 \end{bmatrix}. \qquad (13.41)$$

the response function is thus

$$\begin{aligned} f(m) &= \Sigma_i\, q_i d_i(m) \\ &= d_1(m) + d_2(m) - d_3(m). \end{aligned} \qquad (13.42)$$

It may readily be verified that this response function gives a value of 0 for the two nonrelevant documents.

It may be noted that if the two relevant documents had been specified as requiring $f(1) = f(2) = 1$, and hence as being equally relevant, then the procedure of Section 11.3 may be applied. The values of v_1, v_2, v_3 are then $\frac{1}{2}, \frac{1}{2}, \frac{1}{4}$, and solution of Eq. (12.30) of Chapter 12 leads to q_1, q_2, q_3 values of $\frac{4}{7}, \frac{4}{7}, -\frac{3}{7}$ and hence a response function of

$$f(m) = (4/7)d_1(m) + (4/7)d_2(m) - (3/7)d_3(m). \qquad (13.43)$$

The response to the documents as $s = 1$ to 4 is then $\frac{5}{7}, \frac{8}{7}, \frac{1}{7}, \frac{1}{7}$ and the value of E' is $\frac{1}{28}$.

In conclusion it may be remarked that for any given subset of documents doc(m) the value of E' according to (13.29) with $f(m) = 1$, or of E'_{min} according to (13.31) with F chosen to satisfy (13.36), provides a measure of the extent to which the documents may be classed as different from the remaining documents. Use of E' with $f(m) = 1$ emphasizes the mutual relevance of documents within the subset, whereas use of E'_{min} with F chosen to satsify (13.36) emphasizes the total nonrelevance of the documents not in the subset.

13.6 Problems

1. Examine a particular classification scheme, such as is shown in Table 13.4, and state whether you believe that the author of a paper would be likely to assign the same categories as a reader.
2. Examine a particular classification scheme, such as is shown in Table 13.4, and state whether you believe that it would serve as a satisfactory basis for segmenting a data base so that each question could be searched on only one, or several, distinct segments.
3. After examination of articles published in a journal that has a classification scheme, describe the extent to which cited articles tend to be in the same categories.

4. Compare the advantages and disadvantages of segmenting a data base by content classification rather than by a simpler criterion such as date or journal.

5. How useful do you feel it would be to allow the user of an information retrieval system to use category number as a search term? Would you then change the file structure in any way? How would it affect the inverted file?

14
Concluding Remarks

14.1 Limitations of Present Approach

In the previous chapters an attempt has been made to outline the computational techniques that are required in the application of computers to information retrieval from document data bases. Some of the problems of information retrieval have been discussed with emphasis on their solution by use of computers. Although some generality has been attempted, there also has been an imposition of certain constraints in order to simplify some of the discussion, and in order to emphasize the connection between the goals of information science and the utilization of particular principles of computer science.

For example, in Chapter 4 it was supposed that questions would be stated in a form closely related to matching of terms or character strings. This was reflected in the emphasis on either sequential search or search by use of an inverted file. The approach has been justified by the definition of a document data base as one whose records are divided into fields of textual data. However, it was suggested in the illustrative example in Chapter 10 that dependence on an inverted file would be undesirable for questions that involve dates, codens, or NOT logic. In the illustrative example the difficulty was resolved by adoption of a question structure that would allow the processing to use an inverted file followed by a sequential search of the output.

The convenience of processing by means of an inverted file is found when all document lists are relatively small. This occurs when the structuring of the data base as reflected in the inverted file is similar to what appears to the user as a natural structure in terms of his question formulation. From the point of view of economic storage or computation such structural relations as $\leqslant$, or $\neq$, or "within a given range" are not conveniently represented by an inverted file. The processing of questions strongly oriented to specification of algebraic relations to be satisfied, rather than terms to be matched, has been omitted from the present discussion because efficient processing is likely to require particular techniques that are very dependent on the particular form of the relations. However, it should be mentioned that much attention has been given to the relational concept of data organization as proposed by Codd[1,2] and applied, for example, by Boyce et al.[3] and by McLeod.[4]

It might be contended that most work relating to information retrieval has, in fact, been restricted to data retrieval in the sense that queries are formulated to specify the particular pieces of data that are to be searched for. The retrieved output thus answers a question of the form "who has done work relating to TERM, etc." rather than "what is the answer to my question about. . . ." In order to allow a search for the answer to this second form of question a data base would have to contain far more information, and far more structure, than the data bases of the type described in Chapter 3. Such a highly structured data base might more properly be described as a "knowledge data base." The cost of its preparation would, of course, be very high, and the proper method of structuring such a data base is not yet known. It might be questioned whether development of such a data base is worthwhile, or whether it is more efficient to train human beings to deduce the answers after intelligent use of document data bases and examination of the retrieved documents.

[1] E. F. Codd, "A relational model of data for large shared data banks," *Communications of the Association for Computing Machinery* 13 (1970):377–387.

[2] E. F. Codd, "Recent investigations in relational data base systems," IFIP Congress, August 5–10, 1974, Stockholm, pp. 1017–1021.

[3] R. F. Boyce, D. D. Chamberlin, W. F. King, and M. H. Hammer, "Specifying queries as relational expressions: The SQUARE data sublanguage," *Communications of the Association for Computing Machinery* 18 (1975):621–628.

[4] I. A. McLeod, "Towards an information retrieval language based on a relational view of data," *Information Processing and Management* 13 (1977):167–175.

14.2 Hardware Aspects

In the description of different search procedures and record processing it has been supposed only that a computer is available to perform the required tasks such as sorting, matching character strings, retrieval and placing of records on computer-accessible files, or manipulations of various matrices, and so forth. The computer may, of course, be a general purpose one that is being time-shared with other computational tasks, or it may be a special purpose computer dedicated to the single task of information retrieval.[5,6]

With the increasing availability of microprocessors, which are designed to perform very specific computational tasks at very low cost and at high speed, an important aspect of the design of many future information retrieval systems will be the allocation of particular retrieval functions to special purpose hardware. Also, it may prove desirable to have a number of different data bases linked within a network so that users at different locations may access any data base within the network. In addition to having the files distributed throughout the network, it may be desirable to distribute some of the processing units in a similar manner. A request for information might then be processed by several computers at different locations, the particular allocation of the different processors being determined on the basis of their suitability for the task and their availability at the particular time of the request.

The cost of high-capacity, rapid-access file storage is continuing to decrease. At the same time there is a steady increase in the amount of material that is being prepared for storage on computer-accessible files. The addition of information in the form of a thesaurus, various document–term and document–document matrices, or records of the groupings of relevant documents for previous queries, may greatly increase the amount of storage required. Storage of the full text of a document, rather than only the titles and abstracts, will clearly increase the demand for storage capacity. It remains to be seen whether the demand for more storage capacity may be met in an economic manner by the continuing reduction of storage costs or whether it will require that more attention be given to the development of more compact ways of representing textual data.

[5] B. J. Hurley, "Analysis of computer architectures for information retrieval," Department of Computer Science, University of Illinois, Report U1UCDCS-R-76-806, May, 1976.

[6] L. A. Hollaar and W. H. Stellhorn, "A specialized architecture for textual information retrieval," *National Computer Conference* (1977):765–770.

14.3 Theoretical Foundations

Present-day technology has become highly dependent on the use of computers, and as new computer hardware is developed it finds immediate application. The theoretical aspects of computer science are being studied by many researchers, and the application of theory to the solution of practical problems often occurs after a relatively short period of time. However, more knowledge is required regarding the efficient organization of large computer systems and networks, particularly with regard to problems of file privacy, correctness of data, and recovery from serious system or hardware failures.

The present text has been concerned with the application of computers to information retrieval, and the emphasis has been on the step that involves the retrieval of specified information from the file of document records. This is only part of the retrieval service and, as recognized in the measurement of retrieval performance by use of precision and recall, it is relevance to the user's interest that is of prime concern.

The use of a query language to represent the user's interest was discussed in Chapter 4. The efficiency of the representation was not discussed although it would be of considerable value to have a measure, or a theoretical prediction, of the extent to which a user's desire for information may be expressed by a description suitable for input to a computer search. The measure is clearly dependent on the user's knowledge of the particular area and the existing literature.

If the document records of a document data base are regarded as pointers to the entire documents then it is desirable that each record contain the most economic representation of the document consistent with the ability to allow efficient searching. Whether the representation is best achieved through use of title terms, abstract terms, keywords, or category numbers, and so forth, may depend on the particular data base and on the type of user. It would be useful to have some sound theoretical basis, rather than only empirical evidence, on which to base decisions regarding the information to be stored in the searchable fields.

The information science, in contrast to the computer science, aspects of information retrieval have been studied so far mainly be experimental procedures. Because of the many parameters that affect the effectiveness of information retrieval and document classification, it is often difficult to generalize experimental results. Data bases vary considerably with regard to both content and size. Also, the collection of a sufficiently large number of experimental results may be very costly with regard to both computer and manpower costs. It is therefore of interest to formulate mathematical models of information retrieval systems.[7-9]

It is hoped that, as information science receives further study, there will be developed a broader base of knowledge on which to build a sound theory that will be useful for the design of future information retrieval systems. In such an event the principles described in the present text will require the appropriate refinements in order to take advantage of the additional knowledge.

[7] D. Soergel, "Mathematical analysis of documentation systems," *Information Storage and Retrieval* 3 (1967):129–173.

[8] T. Takahama, "A model for a document retrieval system," *Information Storage and Retrieval* 9 (1973):143–169.

[9] M. D. Cooper, "A simulation model of an information retrieval system," *Information Storage and Retrieval* 9 (1973):1–12.

Subject Index